ADVANCE PRAISE FOR
The Resilient Gardener:

"*The Resilient Gardener* is so essential, timely and important, and I will recommend it to everyone I know. It doesn't matter if you garden or if you don't—this is practical wisdom good for humans to know, passed on by a careful student who has deeply studied her life. Carol Deppe's lens is the garden—which is great for gardeners, but really, she speaks clearly to all of us. If you try to think like Deppe, you will find you have a new view of your life no matter who you are. This is a wise and intelligent book. Hats off to Carol Deppe!"

—DEBORAH MADISON, author of *Local Flavors*
and *Vegetarian Cooking for Everyone*

"*The Resilient Gardener* is the most comprehensive and detailed book about gardening that I have read to date, and I could not find one sentence that I would quibble with. Not only does Deppe discuss all the immediate, nose-to-the-grindstone kind of information about producing and using home-grown food, but also all the surrounding environmental and cultural aspects of gardening that are so vital to success. A must-read for beginning gardeners, and full of details even the most experienced will find invaluable."

—GENE LOGSDON, author of *Small-Scale Grain Raising*
and *Holy Shit: Managing Manure to Save Mankind*

"In the years since Carol Deppe wrote the classic *Breed Your Own Vegetable Varieties*, she has continued to grow in deep wisdom and experience. *The Resilient Gardener* is brilliantly timely, and shows us how to create gardens that can survive our increasingly erratic weather, while supplying key nutrition lacking in most vegetable gardens. This book fills a critical niche, and I recommend it unreservedly."

—TOBY HEMENWAY, author of *Gaia's Garden:
A Guide to Home-Scale Permaculture*

"Carol Deppe's celiac-friendly approach to gardening and nutrition provides a wealth of information on how to overcome food intolerances many are confronted with each day. If you struggle with food allergies or sensitivities—or want to use natural resources to create a healthy world for you and your family—this book is for you."

—PETER H. R. GREEN, MD, Director,
Celiac Disease Center at Columbia University

"Growing food is among the most positive changes anyone can make in the face of uncertainty about the future. *The Resilient Gardener* is an information-packed resource for people starting or expanding a garden practice. This book empowers readers with skills and understanding, as did Deppe's previous book, *Breed Your Own Vegetable Varieties.*"

—SANDOR ELLIX KATZ, author, *Wild Fermentation* and
The Revolution Will Not Be Microwaved

"*The Resilient Gardener* gives concrete examples of how to deal with diet, climate, and economic changes before the need arises. Deppe challenges us to experiment with and practice all aspects of gardening, seed saving, and food storage, and advises on the growing need to meet special food and climate requirements in the face of our food system's fragility. This book is an invaluable tool for gardeners and farmers as we experience more and more volatility in our food systems."

—SUZANNE ASHWORTH, author of *Seed to Seed*

"Carol Deppe is informative, funny, and intriguing as she guides us through every phase of gardening—dispelling myths while also orienting us to the technical, emotional, and spiritual aspects of growing food. *The Resilient Gardener* is the quintessential guide to gardening from an authority who also knows how to enjoy herself."

—DIDI EMMONS, author of *Vegetarian Planet*

THE RESILIENT GARDENER

Food Production and Self-Reliance
in Uncertain Times

CAROL DEPPE

Chelsea Green Publishing
White River Junction, Vermont

Project Manager: Patricia Stone
Developmental Editor: Benjamin Watson
Copy Editor: Cannon Labrie
Proofreader: Eileen M. Clawson
Indexer: Peggy Holloway
Designer: Peter Holm, Sterling Hill Productions

All photographs by Carol Deppe, unless otherwise credited.
Illustrations by Abrah Griggs, Sterling Hill Productions

Printed in the United States of America
First printing September, 2010
10 9 8 7 6 5 4 3 2 1   10 11 12 13

Chelsea Green Publishing is committed to preserving ancient forests and natural resources. We elected to print this title on 30-percent postconsumer recycled paper, processed chlorine-free. As a result, for this printing, we have saved:

33 Trees (40' tall and 6-8" diameter)
10 Million BTUs of Total Energy
3,094 Pounds of Greenhouse Gases
14,899 Gallons of Wastewater
905 Pounds of Solid Waste

Chelsea Green Publishing made this paper choice because we and our printer, Thomson-Shore, Inc., are members of the Green Press Initiative, a nonprofit program dedicated to supporting authors, publishers, and suppliers in their efforts to reduce their use of fiber obtained from endangered forests. For more information, visit: www.greenpressinitiative.org.

Environmental impact estimates were made using the Environmental Defense Paper Calculator. For more information visit: www.papercalculator.org.

Our Commitment to Green Publishing

Chelsea Green sees publishing as a tool for cultural change and ecological stewardship. We strive to align our book manufacturing practices with our editorial mission and to reduce the impact of our business enterprise on the environment. We print our books and catalogs on chlorine-free recycled paper, using vegetable-based inks whenever possible. This book may cost slightly more because we use recycled paper, and we hope you'll agree that it's worth it. Chelsea Green is a member of the Green Press Initiative (www.greenpressinitiative .org), a nonprofit coalition of publishers, manufacturers, and authors working to protect the world's endangered forests and conserve natural resources.

The Resilient Gardener was printed on Natures Book Natural, a 30-percent postconsumer recycled paper supplied by Thomson-Shore.

Library of Congress Cataloging-in-Publication Data
Deppe, Carol.
 The resilient gardener : food production and self-reliance in uncertain
times / Carol Deppe.
   p. cm.
 Includes bibliographical references and index.
 ISBN 978-1-60358-031-1
 1. Vegetable gardening. 2. Organic gardening. 3. Natural foods. 4.
Self-reliant living. I. Title.

 SB324.3.D475 2010
 635--dc22

                    2010023535

Chelsea Green Publishing Company
Post Office Box 428
White River Junction, VT 05001
(802) 295-6300
www.chelseagreen.com

to
Merry Youle

CONTENTS

ACKNOWLEDGMENTS

For information, encouragement, company, and camaraderie, I thank Merry Youle, Nate France, Alan and Linda Kapuler, Rose Marie Nichols McGee, Mike Hessel, Harry MacCormack, Paul Harcombe, Dave Holderread, and Tom Wagner.

For their belief in me and support of this book project I thank Mark Deppe, Nick Routledge, Charlotte Anthonisen, Julia Mallalieu, Janet and Jerry Russell, Dawn McGee, Mary Saunders, Andrew Still, Sarah Kleeger, Kathy Ging, Denise-Christine, James Rodell, Janice Wilson, Beverly Scholz, Bev Koch, Kathy Saranpa, Jacqueline and Joseph Freeman, Elaine Zablocki, and Tree Bressen.

Anything I accomplish in this world is in its turn part of the accomplishments of my special mentors, whom I pause to remember and acknowledge now: my scientific mentors, geneticist Henry Wallbrunn, biochemist Arthur L. Koch, and fungal geneticist John R. Raper; my writing mentors, Roger Swain and Christina Ward.

I thank my literary agent Christina Ward for encouragement and guidance at every stage as well as occasional hand-holding beyond the call of duty.

Finally, I thank Ben Watson for his expert, gentle editing and Cannon Labrie for his tough, thorough copyediting.

CHAPTER ONE

Gardening and Resilience

Hard Times Great and Small. Special Dietary Needs as Hard Times—and an Invitation to Gardening Adventures. A Funny Thing Happened on the Way to Y2K. Practicing Balance. Appropriate Self-Sufficiency. How Much Land Do You Need? Gardening—an Essential Survival Skill.

For ten years, I cared for my ill and elderly mother while she was bedridden and slipping into oblivion. Ultimately, she died at home—peacefully—holding my hand. It was worth it. But it was the hardest thing I ever did. At times my garden and my gardening was an immense comfort and satisfaction. It grounded me. It soothed and restored me. It reminded me of the basics. It regularly ushered me into a contemplative time and space that allowed me to see the bigger picture. It also gave me something to show and tell to my mother that she could still understand and take pleasure in. She loved to look at and touch the bright delicious fruits and vegetables and hear the stories about what they were and exactly how I grew them. She couldn't remember the stories, but she liked hearing them. And she still enjoyed good food. Really superb food of the most flavorful varieties, picked at its prime and prepared optimally—it is a special pleasure. My mother enjoyed that great food until the end. The garden helped sustain us both, physically and emotionally.

However, there were plenty of times my gardening fell apart or overwhelmed me instead of sustaining me. There were medical emergencies that took my full time and attention for weeks. The garden wouldn't get tended until they were over. Many times I lost entire crops and much of the season's labor because of my inability to tend the garden at critical times. I myself sometimes suffered from health problems and injuries that interfered with gardening. When I most needed help, my garden often created pressures and contributed to my problems instead of relieving them.

These days, we tend to design our gardens and our gardening for good times, times when everything is going well. That isn't what we need. Reality is, there is almost always something going wrong. Hard times are normal. My experience of gardening while caring for my mother helped me realize that I needed to garden differently. My garden needed to be designed around the reality that life has its ups and downs. It has good times and bad. How to garden in the best of times was not the issue. I didn't need a "good-time garden." I needed to understand more about how to garden in hard times. I needed a more resilient garden. And I needed a garden that better enhanced my own resilience, in all kinds of times, good and bad.

Hard Times Great and Small

Hard times happen. They happen in the lives of every individual creature, the histories of every country and culture, the evolution of every species. They come in all sizes and shapes. They may affect just you, or they may affect your entire neighborhood, country, or planet. They may be temporary, requiring only survival until things get better. Or they may be permanent, and require transition to a dramatically new and different way of life.

Hard times are often individual, personal, and private. They can be primarily physical, emotional, spiritual, or some combination of all three. Or they may be primarily financial. Hard times in the garden sometimes simply represent a time of change in which the garden suffers because people have other priorities. This book is about all these situations.

In a classic Taoist story, Confucius and his disciples are sightseeing below the falls in Lu Liang, where the river races and boils with whirlpools and cataracts. Suddenly, the figure of a man appears on the opposite side of the river and jumps into the torrent. Confucius thinks the man must be committing suicide, and he positions his disciples along the bank to recover the body. The man soon emerges unscathed before them, however, and saunters along the bank, dripping water, singing a cheerful song. Confucius immediately asks the man how he managed to swim in such wild waters. The man explains that he goes in where the whirlpools go in and comes out where they come out. He moves with and uses the currents around him instead of fighting them and drowning. The Taoist tries to live in the world thus. Doing so requires attention to positioning with respect to the various currents around us. That swimmer knew a good bit about water and currents, however, before he ever jumped into the river. And long before he needed to jump into any rivers, *he had learned to swim*. This book is about

positioning ourselves and working with nature, and with the natural and social forces and currents around us. It is also about learning to swim.

The first half of this book is a synthesis of practical gardening with newly emerging information in many fields—resilience science, climatology, climate change, ecology, anthropology, paleontology, sustainable agriculture, nutrition, health, and medicine. The second half of the book illustrates and extends the ideas and principles with detailed hands-on information about growing and using five kinds of yard and garden crops—potatoes, corn, beans, squash, and eggs. This is a supremely optimistic as well as realistic book about resilient gardeners and resilient gardens surviving and thriving and helping their communities to survive and thrive through everything that comes their way—from tomorrow through the next thousand years.

The first focus of this book is on contemporary personal survival. It's about achieving greater control over our food supply. It's about having gourmet-quality, optimally healthful food in spite of agribusiness patterns that drive out much of the best and best-tasting food, and that virtually eliminate some critical nutrients from the commercial food supply. This book is about yards and gardens that best promote our health and happiness in good times and bad.

The second focus of this book is on surviving the kinds of individual ordinary traumas and minor disasters that happen in the lives of most people and gardens. A drought can mean that you aren't allowed to water your garden. Or there might be no electricity or water because you couldn't pay the bill. A well might run low or dry. Or the well pump might fail, and your garden might have to do without water for a week or two while the pump is pulled and repaired. A financial setback could mean that you can afford only the vegetables in your garden or the fruit from the trees and bushes in the landscape.

A family emergency or an injury can mean that there is no one to work the garden for a while. You might be injured yourself. Or you might be unable to garden because of the injury or illness or problems of others, whose needs become your first priority. What happens when no one waters, weeds, or tends your yard or garden for a week? A month? All season? Many modern gardens can be destroyed by a mere week or two of neglect—just when their owner most needs their benefits. Many landscape plantings, orchards, and vegetable gardens are completely dependent upon regular watering, which is itself dependent upon electricity. This book is about creating more resilient yards and gardens—yards and gardens that can thrive with minimal care or even total neglect for substantial periods of time, and that create an oasis of restorative peace, normality, and security.

When you or someone in your family has special dietary needs, it constitutes a kind of ongoing hard times. In chapter 4 we will consider how to customize our gardens in ways that help us deal with such problems as gluten intolerance, asthma and allergies, food allergies, diabetes and sugar-control problems, obesity and weight control, and other individual health issues.

Climate change is happening. Even ordinary weather regularly creates bad times in the garden. The last hundred years was an unusually stable weather period. We are likely in for wilder and weirder weather in future years. Chapter 3 focuses on gardening in times of wild weather and climate change.

A third focus of this book is upon gardening in mega-hard times. Mega-hard times do happen. They may not happen in any individual lifetime. But over the generations, they do occur. I like to think in terms of the next thousand years. Can I do the exploring and adventuring, gain the knowledge, help create the patterns, and pass on the knowledge and patterns that will help my own or future generations to survive and thrive? A gardener who knows how to garden in both good times and bad can be a reservoir of knowledge and a source of resilience for the entire community.

Here in the Pacific Northwest, we get about one or two mega-earthquakes every thousand years. Such a massive quake would disrupt most or all bridges, roads, and power lines. It would be at least months and possibly years before everyone had electricity and other services restored and full access to the rest of the world. Also, about once every thousand years, somewhere in the world there is a volcanic eruption large enough to cool the planet drastically for years, decades, or even centuries. Climate change in and of itself can create serious difficulties. The human population is probably already too high for long-term planetary health and is still rising. Concomitant with overpopulation go crises caused by pollution, war, famine, and disease. Pandemics also happen. Past pandemics have often involved communities isolating themselves or being isolated via quarantines. Oil might become unavailable, or too expensive for most purposes. Depressions happen. Stock markets collapse. Currency can deflate and become scarce or inflate and become worthless. Jobs can vanish. Financial or social instability or wars or terrorism can disrupt jobs or access to goods and services.

Traditionally, gardeners have played a major role in sustaining themselves, their families, and their communities through hard times of many kinds. Would you be able to do likewise? Or would your garden fail utterly because it depends totally upon electricity, irrigation, oil, agribusiness imports, and the roads and financial and social infrastructure needed to deliver them? Would your garden be able to actually feed you after you scaled up in response to the situation? Or would your garden be of limited value because you grow only flowers or salad ingredients? Would you be able to grow serious amounts of your own staples, because you've experimented and done a little of it in good times and have learned how? Have you identified the crops and varieties that would work well for you if you really had to depend upon them? Would you be able to grow them without electricity, irrigation water, and imported fertilizer or seeds? Could you do it without a rototiller or the services of the tractor guy? Could you scale up your production to feed more than just yourself and your family? Could you provide the seed and experience to help others to do so? Do you know how to save seed? Could you serve as a source of seed and knowledge for your community?

We gardeners love to experiment. In this book I invite all gardeners to do the kinds of exploration and adventuring that would prove most valuable if they or those they teach ever experience mega-hard times. You may never have to experience mega-hard times yourself. But if you build the appropriate knowledge base and pass it on to others, and encourage them to do likewise, it is likely that sooner or later—to someone somewhere over the next thousand years—that knowledge will matter.

I believe that the potential role of gardeners in

mega-hard times is more important today than ever before. In times past, a large portion of the population knew how to grow and preserve food and could survive on what they could grow and preserve. In the United States today, only about 2 percent of the population farms, and they farm largely in ways that are totally dependent upon imported oil and gas, electricity, irrigation, roads, national and international markets, and an intact financial and social infrastructure. In many kinds of mega-hard times, those farms would not be functional, and the knowledge of how to farm in those ways would be useless. In some of the mega-hard times of the future, what food we have may be a result of the knowledge and skills of *gardeners*. I challenge all gardeners to fully accept their role as a source of resilience for their communities in mega-hard times, and to play and adventure in good times so as to develop the kinds of knowledge and skills that would most matter.

It's easy to build knowledge and experience in good times. In good times, learning such things is a matter of enjoyable adventuring. In addition, learning how to garden with minimal inputs and minimal labor teaches us more than just how to deal with hard times in which the inputs might not be available. When we know how to minimize labor, water, and other inputs, we spend less, waste less, pollute less, and are more sophisticated and efficient gardeners, in good times as well as bad.

Special Dietary Needs as Hard Times— and an Invitation to Gardening Adventures

I can't eat wheat or wheat relatives (barley, rye, spelt, triticale). I have celiac disease, which is an intolerance to wheat gluten. I'm also severely allergic to wheat and mildly allergic to cow's milk and certain other foods. (Celiac disease breaks down the integrity of the gut, so one tends to pick up additional food allergies beyond the initial wheat problem.) Nearly all commercial prepared foods—everything from bread and canned soup to soy sauce and most condiments—contain wheat. Those who can't eat soy or dairy products have a similar problem. Wheat, soy, and dairy ingredients are so ubiquitous in our food that being unable to eat them deprives you of the food and food patterns of our culture. Being unable to eat most of the food of your culture creates a kind of ongoing personal hard times.

Like many others with celiac disease or other food intolerances and allergies, my attempts to get a medical diagnosis went nowhere for years. Modern medicine failed me. My gardening, though, did not fail me. Long before I knew why I was having problems, I found my gardening interests changing. I became increasingly interested in growing my own staples—delicious gourmet-quality staples—staples that made wheat superfluous.

I cooked and evaluated hundreds of heirloom and traditional corn varieties. I discovered that modern commercial cornmeal is all very poor-flavored compared to meal made from many traditional varieties, and that commercial cornmeal represents only one class of corn flavors. There are many other flavors that are powerfully delicious and dramatically different—so different, in fact, that people don't even know the grain in the bread is corn until they are told.

I found flint corn varieties that can be cooked into a delicious polenta (cornmeal mush) with just seven minutes of stirring. I found the best varieties for parching corn, a great, healthful snack and camping food.

As a gluten-intolerant person, one of the things I wanted most was bread. Most modern corn-bread recipes include wheat, and produce what is basically corn-containing wheat bread that depends upon the gluten and cooking characteristics of the wheat. Such recipes were no help to me. Older recipes were dependent upon particular kinds of corn, which are unspecified. The information about which varieties of corn go with what recipes and cooking methods has been lost. I rediscovered the uses of various kinds of corn and developed recipes for using them that didn't require wheat. My recipes make delicious breads, pancakes, and even cakes without wheat or any other grain, without milk, and without xanthan or other artificial binders. My standard corn-based skillet bread is more like a dense traditional wheat bread in texture than what most people think of as cornbread. It holds together so well it can be used to make sandwiches. It contains only corn, water, eggs, salt, baking powder, and butter (or fat or oil of some kind).

I also began breeding short-season corns for making polenta, cornbread, corn cakes, parching corn, and savory brown corn gravy.

I grew and tasted dozens of varieties of dry beans of several species and found varieties that are delicious, productive, and easy to grow. I also bred two new varieties, 'Hannan Popbean', a garbanzo that can be grown organically in the maritime Northwest without irrigation, and 'Fast Lady Northern Southern Pea', a very early maritime- and northern-adapted cowpea (Southern pea), also selected for organic production.

I became enchanted with gourmet winter squash, especially those that store well and that thus could become a major part of my diet for most of the year.

I also studied and learned to reproduce the Hidatsa Indian way of making dried squash—squash picked in the green summer-squash stage, then sliced and dried to produce a long-storing staple. I even developed a few modern variations on the traditional method. Then I expanded upon the Native American information by evaluating modern varieties for use as dried squash. Many were bland. A few varieties, however, produced unique, new, delicious flavors that are so good they are worth growing just to make dried squash. Delightfully, some of the varieties that make the best dried squash are among the best summer squash too. So we can have plenty of summer squash, and can dry all those that get past the prime summer-squash stage—producing an extra staple crop essentially for free. Dried squash has become one of the major bases for my winter soups and stews.

Trying to live and be healthy on an agribusiness diet is itself a kind of hard times, even for those who don't have special dietary needs. Being gardeners allows all of us to achieve greater control over our food supply. We can produce better, more nutritious, more delicious food than anything we can buy. For those of us with special dietary needs, our gardening is especially important. Having truly gourmet food of a quality that cannot be bought goes far toward making up for the fact that there are certain things we can't eat. In addition, we can focus our gardening to provide exactly what we need. Once I knew I couldn't eat wheat, I focused my gardening deliberately. My personal dietary needs became factors that informed, guided, and added originality to my gardening and plant breeding. My dietary

"problems," in other words, became a rich source of gardening and cooking creativity.

A Funny Thing Happened on the Way to Y2K

Many people got very worried toward the end of 1999 as the year 2000—and the so-called Y2K event—approached. They feared that a computer glitch would bring modern society tumbling down, at least temporarily. They spent a lot of money buying expensive and bad-tasting commercial dried food and expensive back-ups for their computers. I didn't. Bad-tasting food still tastes bad in hard times. One might have to make do with bad food in hard times, but I never arrange for bad food deliberately. Any arrangements I make involve eating well. As Y2K approached, I did precisely nothing. Because of my special dietary needs and how they had shaped my gardening interests, by 1999 I had a garden full of overwintering vegetables, bags of potatoes in the garage, and a pantry full of dry corns, beans, winter squashes, and dried squash—all of gourmet quality—plenty enough for my own family and neighbors besides, at least for a while. I already had equipment for grinding the corn. I had already developed the recipes. Growing and using these staples was an ordinary part of my life.

And as for my computer . . . it had always had a hard time with time. By Y2K, my computer was about two years behind. I figured what it didn't know wouldn't hurt it. Sometimes different kinds of hard times cancel each other out.

We gardeners already know that we can grow much better food than anything we can buy in the grocery store. This is even truer for staples than it is for the more ordinary garden vegetables. So I grow some of my own staple crops. It's deeply satisfying. Doing so enhances my emotional as well as physical resilience. It gives me greater control over my food supply. My small, private, individual resilience translates into resilience writ larger, however. I don't grow and store staples because I'm expecting civilization to collapse within the next season so that I need the stored staples in order to keep from starving. I do it primarily because growing and using those potatoes, corn, beans, and squash provides superb food of a quality I can't buy, personal satisfaction, and greater joy and health for myself.

If some kind of major disaster were to hit my world, though, a few hundred pounds of dry corn and the equipment and knowledge needed to turn them into human sustenance might make a big difference for me and my neighbors. The resilience of individual gardeners working for personal satisfaction and joy in ordinary hard times (such as having special dietary needs) can thus be transformed into resilience during more extraordinary hard times, for both the individual and his or her community. Life is full of hard times. By learning to garden our way through the small and ordinary hard times, and by passing that knowledge on, we can help our children, our children's children, our country, and our species through both the ordinary as well as the extraordinary hard times that happen through the generations.

Practicing Balance

As it turned out, pretty much nothing happened on Y2K. I don't know whether it was because all the major companies managed to fix their computers in time or not. This I do know: There are many kinds of disasters we can foresee, and many or most of them never materialize. Even if they do materialize, it might not be in our lifetimes. Disasters also happen unforeseen. But we don't get our choice of hard times. You could spend huge amounts of time and money stockpiling things for the disaster you expect, and instead get a disaster such as a fire, when what you need to do to survive is to forget all those supplies and evacuate. Furthermore, living too much in the future is emotionally unhealthy. It's important to position ourselves and our societies so as to enhance our resilience in good times and bad, and that requires some advance planning, learning, and exploration. We also need to enjoy life and to live fully. For that it's important to live primarily in the present.

In hard times, I might not have electricity for watering or irrigation. So I learn how to minimize the need for electricity and irrigation in my current gardening. But I don't try to do without electricity entirely. I have shifted my gardening so as to minimize the need for irrigation as well as to get the optimum use out of the irrigation I do apply. In this way, I enhance my ability to garden in any potential future hard times, but I also garden more efficiently in good times. I avoid wasting water, which means that I also minimize the electricity required to pump it and the labor involved in watering. Excess water leaches out some soil nutrients, also. So minimizing watering and avoiding unnecessary watering helps minimize my fertilizer needs. It allows me to have a smaller ecological impact on the land. It makes me a better, more ecological, more efficient gardener, in good times and bad.

Hard times might make fertilizer unavailable.

So I learn exactly how much fertilizer I need in what situations, when I can get away without fertilizing at all, and how I can best use the resources I have to retain and enhance fertility. This means if I suddenly need to do without any external inputs for a while, I'll know how. It also means that I avoid overfertilizing, thus saving money in good times. By not overfertilizing, I avoid polluting in good times and bad.

While mega-hard times are likely over the next thousand years, you personally may never need to deal with anything more than a broken leg or your city limiting yard and garden watering temporarily because of a minor drought. To the possibility of hard times of all sizes and kinds, I suggest a gentle, moderated response. Your current gardening is most likely based upon the assumptions that things will continue in the coming years as they have in the past, that society will remain intact and functional and bring you rototiller parts, gas, fertilizer, and seeds, that you will always have plenty of water and electricity for irrigating, that you can easily buy all the foods you want, and that you can consider growing and preserving food as primarily a recreation or luxury. I suggest you devote a portion of your learning and practice of gardening to all the *opposite* assumptions. Continue to focus primarily on your ordinary life and your ordinary gardening. But also learn and play and adventure in your yard and garden so as to increase the resilience of your yard and garden and yourself. Continue to give your primary attention to your ordinary life and to full enjoyment of the present, however. Your first job in surviving any possible future hard times is to survive long enough to get there.

Appropriate Self-Sufficiency

How independent should we be? How independent should we *want* to be? And of what and whom? Many people who become aware of the uncertainty of life and the reality that hard times happen respond by going somewhat overboard, I feel. They assume, for example, that a breakdown in the social fabric through social or physical disaster would mean that they would have access only to what could be provided in and by their immediate neighborhoods. In fact, humans have never been so limited. We weren't so limited before we had horses, oxen, and wheels. We aren't now. If a major disaster were to destroy our current means, methods, and patterns of trade, I am confident that it wouldn't take us long to create new ones. To err may or may not be human, but to trade definitely is.

Humans have been trading for millennia. For instance, the best obsidian and flint for making tools is found only in certain places. Throughout the world, it was always widely traded beyond those places. Here in the Pacific Northwest there were regular trade bazaars held at certain times of year. Coastal and Columbia River tribes traded dried salmon to inland tribes for dried camas-root cakes, dried elk meat, and other goods. Lewis and Clark passed over the mountains on a road made by Indian traders. Navigable rivers were major trade routes. Rivers and oceans have always been thoroughfares for trade, and many settlements grew up on and near waterways. Those waterways are still there. Even in the worst of all possible scenarios there would still be rivers, oceans, lakes, waterways, traders, and trade. I don't see humans having to depend more than temporarily upon only their own skills, talents, and immediate local resources. Instead, I imagine them rapidly rebuilding societies from whomever and whatever is left, and quickly setting about to do what they have always done—specialize, swap with neighbors, and trade over seriously long distances.

I think a worst-case scenario is not that a human family or community will be knocked back to totally local resources indefinitely. Instead they will be knocked back to local resources temporarily, or trade over long distances will become more expensive, difficult, or dangerous. In the latter case, communities would need to depend more upon resources nearby and less on those from long distances. People, though, will still have different personalities, inclinations, skills, and talents, and their land will still be suitable for growing some things and not others. People will still specialize. Individuals will not need to grow all their own food, make all their own tools and shelter, or provide all their own law enforcement and protection. Since well before the start of recorded history, humans have always had families, communities, societies, specialization, and trade to provide these things. In mega-hard times, however, your ordinary job may be irrelevant, and food production and food items to trade may be what matters. For such times, you want a repertoire of survival skills. Your gardening can be one of these.

Is "independence" even a virtue? It seems to me that, to be truly independent, I would have to love and care about no one, and be loved and cared about by no one. And I would have no one to learn from and no one to teach. It's a depressing image.

Humans are inherently social creatures. Even those of us who are relatively serious loners are only loners intermittently. We are all parts of a complex web of relationships and mutualisms. It isn't normal, natural, or healthy for us to be "independent." What is healthy is interdependence. In ordinary and good times, we don't really seek true independence, but rather, enough knowledge and skills so that we can build and hold up our end of honorable interdependence. I think the same applies to even mega-hard times. We don't need and need not bother wanting to be "independent." Instead, we need the kinds of knowledge and skills that allow us to be valuable and contributing participants in honorable interdependence in both good times and bad.

How Much Land Do You Need?

Owning good gardening land is a great joy. At least, I suppose it is. I hope to own some myself one of these days. I've never owned any land at all until recently, and what I have is nothing like good gardening land. It's about half an acre, mostly occupied by the house, heavily shaded by trees on adjacent properties or set aside as septic easements. All of it is heavy clay. Some is less than a foot of heavy clay over solid bedrock. Until the neighboring trees grew so high they shaded my backyard totally, I used the limited decent gardening space for vegetables on raised beds and for much small-scale experimenting. Then, as soon as I found a corn or bean I really liked, for example, and had learned how to grow it on a small scale, I made cooperative arrangements with other people who had more and better land. In some cases I actually contracted with local farmers to grow a variety I wanted. At a later stage, I grew some vegetables and experiments in the backyard, but also had a tilled field elsewhere on the property of a friend or friendly farmer for the corn, beans, and squash. Now that my backyard is totally shaded, I've expanded to two acres of leased land elsewhere, and the backyard is forage for the duck laying flock. The land is far more suitable for growing duck eggs than it ever was for vegetables.

You don't need to actually own any land. Over the years, I've gardened on ten different pieces of Oregon land, all but one begged, borrowed, rented, or leased. There is vulnerability in not owning the land where you garden, of course. But land ownership doesn't confer invulnerability. It doesn't guarantee that your neighbor won't ruin your garden by careless fencing of his herd of cattle. My first planting of my first garden in Oregon was killed by herbicide drift from spraying on the nearby power company right of way. "Ownership" is a strange concept, anyway, when applied to land. Given that we have to pay taxes on it and can't take it with us, "ownership" of land isn't really ownership; it's just one kind of leasing arrangement. What is critical isn't ownership of land so much as the knowledge and skills to use it. When and if the time comes that people in your region need more local food production in order to survive, if you have the knowledge, seeds, and tools, people will make the land available. Up until then, you only need enough land to play and learn on, and to produce what you care most about and what you most enjoy.

You can start your learning in a plot in a community garden, for example. If you're a university student, your school may have a garden club you can join and get access to land—usually prime agricultural land, already tilled. Friends and neighbors often share gardens. If your neighbors have a patch of great garden soil they aren't using,

offer to tend their pets or water their garden while they are on vacation in exchange for use of that patch. Sometimes a landless gardener just puts an ad in the local newspaper asking for access to good garden land in exchange for a share of the crop.

Finally, in agricultural areas you might be able to formally lease enough land for all the garden you would ever want. Leasing even prime agricultural soil here in the Willamette Valley—the prime agricultural land in Oregon—is cheap compared with land ownership. Leasing fees normally cover little beyond taxes and irrigation costs. Often, an owner needs to lease some land to someone who is doing agriculture on it in order to qualify for the lower agricultural property tax rate. Much ordinary agriculture involves leasing. People arrange for long-term leases and grow even crops like Christmas trees or raspberries. Your local agricultural newspaper may have a section that lists land for lease or wanted for lease. For many people, actually owning land is far from their first step down the road to gardening.

Last spring, after gardening together a couple of years and deciding we liked it, Nate France and I pooled our gardening efforts and obtained a long-term lease on two acres of prime soil just a five-minute drive from home. Our approach was simple. We used Benton County Soil Survey maps to identify every piece of prime agricultural land close to home. Then we put fliers in the boxes of all the people located on that land. "Wanted: Long-term lease on 2–5 acres for production of organic grains, vegetables, and seed crops. Payment in terms of money, labor, farm care-taking or management, or delicious organic vegetables."

Gardening on other people's land has its disadvantages, of course. But it also has advantages. You may get to learn firsthand from other experienced gardeners. In addition, every piece of land is different, and has different soil. When you garden on just your own land, you learn certain patterns, some of which work for just that one situation. You often don't realize how specifically your patterns are tied to that particular land and soil. Then when you move—even to another property nearby—you find that to some extent you have to learn to garden all over again. To really understand how to garden in your region you need experience with different kinds of land. Such experience is also the ideal preparation for buying or long-term leasing land for gardening or farming.

However, even leased or borrowed land isn't strictly necessary. You can raise amazing amounts of herbs and food entirely in containers. And if you are a student or a person whose life involves dislocations, container gardens have the advantage that you can just put them in a pickup truck or van and take them with you.

In addition, *growing* plants and food is only part of what this book is about. Learning to process and store food and use it optimally are equally important. I think it's a useful goal to learn to process and store all the crops produced in your region that are potentially good staples. This doesn't mean you have to grow them. Many more people know how to grow most fruits and vegetables than know how optimally to turn them into long-term staples that can be used as a serious part of their food supply. So if you learn and practice (and teach others) all about the storing, preserving, and using, that also contributes food resilience to you and to your community.

Anderson's blueberry farm is about two miles from my home. They sell perfectly picked berries (virtually all ripe and without stems) for $1.80 a pound. Just avoiding the time and labor of having to pick them myself is worth that much to me. I buy about forty pounds per week in season, eating many in savory dishes that are my main carbohydrate staple in July. Most I preserve to eat in midwinter and early spring when no local fruit is available.

What matters to me about blueberries—what enhances the quality of my life—isn't growing them. It was learning to use them—developing recipes for using blueberries in main courses (not just desserts) and learning to preserve them. To learn to preserve and use blueberries takes a kitchen, not land. We are not all situated to garden in every year of our lives. Nor can we grow every kind of crop that can be grown in our region. But we can be developing a repertoire of information about what is grown in our area, who grows it, and how to store, preserve, and use it. We can develop knowledge and patterns with respect to those crops that enhance our day-to-day quality of life, our personal resilience, and the resilience of our communities.

If you had to do everything—if you had to be "independent"—then you would need a lot of land to grow everything. But you aren't "independent," and don't need to be. You don't have to do everything. You just have to do something. You make a start. Then you do what you can, what you want to, what you most enjoy.

Gardening—an Essential Survival Skill

There are some things everyone should know in order to be a fully functional and productive member of society. Some of these skills define adulthood. Mastering them is part of becoming an adult. Others require decades of further living for full mastery, and mark the transition from mere adulthood to wisdom. Everyone's list would vary somewhat. Here's mine:

You need to be able to walk, run, stand, and crawl. You can read, write, do basic arithmetic, and type. You can drive, swim, perform first aid, use contraception, deliver a baby, tend the old or ill, comfort the dying. You are able to support yourself. You wash your hands. You are courteous. You function at least adequately in an emergency, perhaps excellently, and you know the difference between an emergency and an inconvenience. You can give orders, take orders, lead, or follow, and you know when to do which.

You either don't drink or can hold your liquor. You know when to speak and when to be silent. You know how to listen. You know how to say, "I'm sorry," and mean it. And "I was wrong," and mean that too. You can build a fire. You can cook a delicious meal from simple basic ingredients. And you can garden.

You can garden. You know how to grow food, including some staples. You may not garden every year of your life, but you at least know how.

Knowing these things promotes individual personal happiness and survival—survival physically, emotionally, and spiritually. A community in which many people know these things is a healthy and resilient community—a community that is maximally positioned to thrive in good times and to survive the rest.

CHAPTER TWO

The Plant-Gardener Covenant: 33 Golden Gardening Rules

*The Grand Alliance. The Covenant: The Contract between the Domesticated
Plant and Her Gardener. The 33 Golden Rules of Gardening.*

The Grand Alliance

We humans refer to certain plants and animals as "domesticated," as if they were passive players in a process we imposed upon them. In reality, humans are not unilateral actors in the domestication deal. Rather, we are part of what I call the Grand Alliance, a complex association of humans, plants, animals, and entire landscapes that have domesticated and shaped each other and co-evolved over the generations. In this chapter I give a basic overview of the relationship between humans and their primary food plants from an ecological perspective, and I outline how this relationship translates into the basic practices of gardening and farming. This chapter serves as an introduction to gardening for the newcomer as well as establishes the themes among which and upon which, for reasons of resilience, we make choices and create variations. The chapter is framed in terms of our primary food plants— vegetables, grains, and fruit and nut trees. These are the plants most dependent upon us and upon which we are most dependent. Later chapters consider other components of the Grand Alliance that are also most relevant to yards, gardens, and small farms.

The Covenant: The Contract between the Domesticated Plant and Her Gardener

I, _____, henceforth to be referred to as "The Plant," promise to produce more and more delicious food for you, my Gardener, than ever did my wild ancestors. I won't produce poisonous or noxious chemicals that prevent you from eating my foliage, stems, roots, tubers, fruits, or seeds. (Or I'll produce just enough to make distinctive delicious flavors.) (Or I'll produce poisons only in the parts you don't want to eat.) This means I will be more vulnerable to insects, herbivores, and disease. In addition, I will minimize my production of tough woody fibers you can't digest. I will focus on producing large edible portions for you instead of other things that might help me survive better by myself (such as a large aggressive root system). I will sacrifice tough seed coats and seed dormancy mechanisms that make my seeds inedible or harder to control or adapted only to limited geographical regions. All this makes me vulnerable. I won't stand up well when competing with wild plants and weeds. And without seed dormancy mechanisms, my seeds won't know when to germinate and grow.

I, _____, henceforth to be referred to as "The Gardener," promise to give you, my Plant, an extra nice place to grow, with more than ordinary amounts of nutrients and with ideal amounts of water. I will soften the soil to make things easier for your roots. I will remove competing weeds before I plant you. I will take the responsibility for planting your seeds at the right time and at the right depth. I will nurture you. I will give you enough space to grow and flourish. I will protect you. I will help you cope with insects, pests, herbivores, and disease. I will remove all competing weeds. Finally, I will save, cherish, distribute, and plant your seeds. Together we will prosper.

The 33 Golden Rules of Gardening

1. All Gardening Is Local
Buy one or more good gardening books that cover your geographic and/or growing region. Nationally oriented books, garden magazines, and Web site information can be a good source of general principles, inspiration, and ideas, but many of those ideas won't work in your region.

Also, call, write, or e-mail for the mail-order seed and nursery catalogs that represent your region. (Or dip into their online catalogs.) These companies are the best sources of varieties of seeds and plants that are optimally adapted for your area. Such catalogs can also be among the best of ways to learn about gardening in your region. Regional seed companies and contact information are listed in appendix B.

2. Plant Things That Grow Where You Live
You can learn a lot about which plants and varieties these are from your local and regional gardening books and regional seed company catalogs.

USDA climate zone maps can give you a rough idea of some of the basics. Most mail-order seed catalogs have a USDA climate map somewhere among the first few pages. You can find the USDA maps on the Web by searching for "USDA Plant Hardiness Zone Map." However, locally oriented seed and nursery catalogs often have maps that are much more fine-tuned and useful. That particularly matters in areas where a few miles might represent a vast difference in climate and growing conditions.

Sometimes, as garden explorers, we boldly venture where no one else in our region has gone before, and add new crops to the local repertoire. When you're just beginning, however, encourage yourself with plenty of initial successes by stacking the odds in your favor. In other words, plant things that are known to grow in your area.

3. Variety, Variety, Variety
The three most important factors in having a successful garden are: variety, variety, variety. Among crops of a given kind—squash, for example—only some varieties will perform well in your area. Some need more heat or a longer frost-free period than you have. Others may succumb to diseases prevalent in your region.

Agribusiness usually grows varieties that don't taste nearly as good as the best gourmet or home garden varieties. The highest-yielding and best variety for machine harvesting or long-range shipping is almost never the best in flavor.

A tomato variety can taste wonderful grown in one region and insipid when grown somewhere else. My favorite tomato varieties are 'Stupice' and 'Amish Paste'. 'Stupice' is very early but is full-flavored, which early tomatoes usually aren't. The fruits are only up to about 2 inches across, however. 'Amish Paste' is a great paste tomato that is also full-flavored and delicious raw. Most paste tomatoes aren't. 'Amish Paste' is a big tomato that is about three weeks later than 'Stupice'. After growing dozens of tomato varieties I have settled on these two partly because of flavor, but also because these varieties are capable of making their great flavors in partial shade and in cool weather. Many tomato varieties develop top flavor only with full sun or more summer heat than we usually have.

Heirloom varieties often have special characteristics that at one time were highly valued, and that may be just as valuable to home gardeners today. 'Russian Hunger Gap' kale, for example, bolts (makes flower stalks) a month or more later in the spring than most kale, thus providing greens during the "hunger gap" after most overwintering kales have bolted but before spring-planted greens are ready to eat. Many heirloom varieties are especially noted for their flavor. 'Green Mountain' potato is one of the oldest potato varieties as well as one of the most spectacularly delicious when baked. (But not when used any other way.)

Different varieties are often best for different purposes. Some pea varieties are for shelling to get fresh green peas. Some varieties have succulent edible pods. Some have neither great pods nor green seeds but are best for producing dry soup peas. The pods of soup peas are tough and stringy and inedible, and their seeds zip through the green stage too fast for you to harvest them for green shelling peas.

Varieties can be determinate or indeterminate. Determinate plants grow a certain amount of plant, then quit making vegetative growth (leaves, stem) and instead make fruits or seeds. Indeterminate plants continue making more plant as they make fruit or seeds. Determinate plants

tend to be bushes that mature all their harvest more or less at once. Indeterminate plants tend to be big sprawling plants or vines that yield more than determinate plants and yield over a longer period of time. Indeterminate varieties usually require more space than determinate ones, and they may also need support such as trellises, poles, or cages.

Some varieties store well and others don't. 'Yukon Gold' potato stores for months. 'Rose Gold' sprouts within a month of harvest.

Some varieties of fruits or vegetables are great for freezing; other varieties of the same crop may turn to mush or lose all semblance of flavor if frozen or cooked or canned. 'Benton' strawberry is great for eating fresh but loses all its flavor and most of its color if cooked or blanched and frozen. 'Totem' strawberry is great for making preserves but isn't sweet enough to eat fresh. However, for preserves, you can add as much sugar as you want.

Different varieties of the same crop may require different planting times. Some varieties of radishes can be planted in either spring or fall. Winter (storage) radishes like 'Black Spanish', though, can be usefully planted only in summer for a fall crop.

You gain in gardening experience from year to year only by keeping track of the specific varieties you plant. That way, when something succeeds, you can repeat it. If something fails, you can try something else.

It's harder to keep track of varieties than one might think. Birds, kids, and all of Nature have an irrepressible urge to pull up, rearrange, or remove those little markers you put in the rows. Experienced gardeners will have written notes somewhere indoors where they can look up the varieties after the little markers have vanished or the print has faded. I always record the seed or plant source as well as the variety, as one seed company's version of a variety may be quite different from the variety sold under the same name by some other company.

4. Plant Varieties That Grow Where You Live

Your regional gardening books and regional seed company and nursery catalogs are your main source of information about which varieties do well in your area. It's also useful to amble down alleys, peer over fences, and talk with anyone you see gardening. Most people love to talk about their gardens.

5. Buy High-Quality Seeds or Plants

Big-box chain stores are not the right place to buy seeds or plants. Chain stores usually feature nationally distributed seed racks full of packets of the lowest possible grade of seed labeled with names of varieties that are popular nationally. Often the real variety contents are not actually the same as the names, just whatever was the cheapest type that looks (but doesn't necessarily behave or taste) vaguely similar. The name on the packet represents what will sell as a name, not the actual contents. (Those experienced enough to know when the variety name and contents don't match aren't buying this seed.)

Such stores sell exactly the same stereotyped selection of varieties in Florida, Minnesota, and Oregon. Most of these varieties are not the best choice for your region. Some won't even grow or produce in your region. Even when the variety is appropriate, and that variety is actually what is in the packet, you won't usually be getting the best line of the variety, only the line whose seed was cheapest. And the particular line matters a lot in

many cases. The grade of seed also matters a lot. Those nationally distributed packets in the chain stores tend toward sweepings-from-the-seed-room-floor grade.

The fruit trees in the chain stores usually don't represent the varieties best for your region either, and may include varieties that don't *ever* actually produce fruit in your region. Sometimes you don't even get variety names. The label just says "Pear" or "Apple." There is no one whose reputation is on the line if the tree you buy is dead or diseased, or the variety isn't hardy enough to survive even your average winter. Chain stores buy from suppliers based mostly on the lowest possible price.

When buying seeds or plants look first to local or regional seed companies and nurseries. Many of these sell primarily or exclusively by mail order or via the Internet. Some sell only via the Internet. Become a fan of mail-order and Internet-based seed and nursery Web sites and catalogs. (See appendix B.) Nearly all "local" or "regional" seed companies actually have a national customer base. What makes them regional is that they emphasize varieties that perform well in their home region, and in their catalogs, they clearly indicate any varieties that won't perform well in that home region. Pick up a catalog from a generic national company, on the other hand, and many or most of the varieties may not do well for you, and you have no way at all of knowing which will.

Next, get all the catalogs from regions that share many similarities with your own. Most especially, if you live in the maritime Northwest, New England, or the Mid-Atlantic coast, get all the catalogs from companies representing all those regions. These areas have enough in common that many varieties that do well in one will do well in the others. In addition, most companies in these regions actually have much of their seed grown here in maritime Oregon, which is a better place for seed production than the East Coast. So many of the listed East Coast varieties actually grow well both there and here.

You can buy from seed racks where the racks represent one of your local or regional seed companies. Racks from your local company will usually be in locally owned feed and seed stores, nurseries, and garden stores, not in the national chains. Local food co-ops may have locally produced seed. You may also find good local seed and transplants in farmer's markets.

When buying plants or transplants, inspect the plants for signs of disease such as obvious mold, a stunted or miserable appearance, or wrinkled, curled, or splotchy leaves. The transplant shouldn't be too big for the pot. The transplant should not be root-bound. That is, the roots should still be inside the soil, not running round and round against the bottom or sides of the pot. The plants should be the color they are supposed to be, not pale yellow, for example, indicating (usually) nitrogen starvation.

6. Plants Need Sun

Some need more than others. Most fruit trees benefit by full sun. Most vegetables such as corn and tomatoes also prefer as much sun as they can get (in most regions). But most greens such as lettuce and kale can do well in space that is partially shaded. Generally speaking, most fruit crops, including tomatoes, squash, and melons need lots of sun. Where the crop is foliage, partially shady areas might work fine. Root crops tend to be somewhere in between greens and fruits. Different varieties can vary in how much

Heirloom and Open-Pollinated Varieties

Generally, I grow heirloom or other open-pollinated, that is, *non-hybrid* varieties of vegetables. Only these allow us to control and reproduce our own seed. Hybrids may or may not produce seed. When they do, the seed does not give offspring that are true to type. Instead, each offspring represents a different combination of the characteristics of the two parents. I usually plant heirloom and other open-pollinated varieties, varieties that breed true. In most cases I plant hybrids only occasionally for comparison. Many seed companies prefer to sell hybrids so we gardeners and farmers can't save the seed. (We can, however, use the hybrids to breed our own open-pollinated varieties, as described in my book *Breed Your Own Vegetable Varieties: The Gardener's and Farmer's Guide to Plant Breeding and Seed Saving.*) In most cases hybrids yield no better than the best open-pollinated varieties for our region, and the flavor of hybrids is often inferior. The advantages of hybrids are mostly to the seed companies and breeders, not to the gardener or farmer. And certainly not to resilient gardeners and farmers, who will usually want to be able to save seeds. For books that are good sources of information on heirlooms and OP varieties, see note 2-2.

sun they need. Many seed and nursery catalogs have a little symbol by each variety that tells you whether the variety needs full sun or can thrive in partial shade. If you live in an area that is very hot and dry during the summer, however, even fruit-bearers such as tomatoes and squash may prefer partial shade.

In planning the use of a yard, we usually reserve the sunniest spots for the vegetable garden and the fruit trees. In the vegetable garden we put a row of tall pole beans or tall corn north of shorter vegetables they would otherwise shade out.

7. Plants Need Warmth

Some plants can survive freezing weather. But no plant *grows* below freezing. Some plants can thrive in the cool weather of early spring. Others need more heat, and we wait until summer to plant them or transplant them into our gardens.

8. Some Plants Need Cold

Fruit tree varieties often need a certain amount of cold in winter in order to initiate flowering in spring. Part of what makes a fruit tree variety suitable for your region is that its need for cold is met by your winters.

Some plants require cold for the best flavor. Kale or collards don't develop their best, sweetest flavor without some cold weather. Parsnips require some freezing weather to develop sweetness in the roots.

9. Plants Need Soil

There is such a thing as hydroponics, which involves growing plants in greenhouses without soil. Hydroponics is very high tech, and depends upon access to agribusiness chemicals and infrastructure. This book is about low-tech gardening and farming and assumes organic approaches. We'll be growing our plants in soil.

10. Plants Need Nutrients

Plants obtain most of what they need from water, air, and the energy from the sun. The rest comes from the soil. Whether your plants need anything added to the soil in order to grow optimally depends upon the plants and the soil. Virgin fertile loam in the U.S. Corn Belt could grow good crops of corn, beans, and squash for five years or more without any fertilizing. After that, crops diminished, and Indians dug a new garden and let the old one go fallow for several years to rejuvenate. Few of us are gardening on virgin fertile Corn Belt–quality loam. Nor do we have unlimited new garden areas to dig up. As we remove produce from a garden or orchard, we remove nutrients that have to be replaced in order to maintain the land's productivity. So we need fertility-maintaining and -enhancing strategies, as covered in chapter 7.

11. You Must Prepare the Ground for Your Plants

To start a vegetable garden, you'll need to remove or turn under sod and loosen the ground with a shovel, heavy hoe, plow, or rototiller. We usually have to plow or till twice to start a new garden. After the first tilling, the soil ends up with a lot of lumps that have chunks of grass or weeds in them that will regrow. So we till the first time, then wait at least three weeks or so to let most of the grass-weed lumps die from being turned under. Then, when those clumps near the surface have just begun to regrow, we till again so that most of those will end up buried deeply enough to die. In addition, the lumps are further broken up in the second tilling. You can't go from lawn or pasture to garden in one tilling. It takes at least two, sometimes three. (If you do the second tilling without the wait of a few weeks, you turn under the clumps at the top of the soil but bring up just as many still living clumps from underneath, thus accomplishing nothing with the second tilling. You need the wait in order to let the deeply buried clumps die.)

The ground has to be at the right moisture content for tilling. If it is too wet, you end up with semipermanent clods and may damage the soil structure for years.

Tilling turns under the topmost layer of soil, the one that contains most of the weed seeds, and puts them too deep for them to germinate. A proper initial tilling can dramatically lower the overall weeding problem.

If you make a small garden by converting a piece of lawn to a garden bed by shovel, it's easiest if you remove the sod and put it in the compost pile. Then add any compost or other amendments and turn the bed over to the depth of a shovel and mix and break it up with a heavy hoe.

With fruit or other trees or bushes, we plant fairly big plants (one- or two-year-old trees) in places where they are taller than the surrounding grass and need only a chance to get re-rooted to be competitive. We usually dig a hole just a bit bigger than the root ball. We soften the rest of the ground only by adding fertilizer, compost, or mulch to the surface of the ground so the ground softens by itself (via earthworms, for example) as the tree's root system expands and needs the space.

12. You Can Plant in Beds or Rows; You Can Plant Intensively or Less So

There is no best choice. There are only advantages, disadvantages, and trade-offs of various kinds, as elaborated in later chapters. The gardening style profoundly affects weather resilience of

the garden, its water needs, and the kinds and amounts of labor you will need to do, as described in later chapters.

13. Plant at the Right Time

Wild plants often have complex seed-dormancy mechanisms that allow their seeds to germinate at the right time of year. We humans have selected against these mechanisms. They interfere with our ability to get the plant to grow when and where we wish, and in regions far away and far different from those to which the plant was originally adapted. Thus we must take responsibility for planting seeds at the right time.

When we plant a particular crop or variety depends upon several factors. One is when there is enough heat for that particular crop to germinate and to grow. Different crops and varieties need different amounts of heat. Pea seed germinates happily in ground that is so cold it just rots the seeds of corn. A second factor determining when we plant crops is how resistant they are to freezing. Young pea plants can take serious freezes. Young corn plants of most varieties can take some freezing (in the seedling stage only), but not such serious freezes as peas. Tomato plants die when exposed to the slightest freeze.

A third factor affecting when we plant is to what extent the plant can thrive in cold or cooler weather. We are often tempted to plant seeds too early. We find an early patch of weather that seems warm enough, and we plant our corn. If it is too cold, the seed rots instead of germinating. Sometimes the seed germinates, then cooler weather returns, and the corn seedlings fail to grow. They need it warmer to actually thrive. So the worms and bugs and molds take over, and the seedlings succumb. We can generally plant corn and have it germinate earlier than we *should* plant corn in order to have it actually survive and thrive. Meanwhile, while our corn we have planted too early is dying, our peas, planted even earlier, are growing rapidly and happily. Peas both germinate and grow well in cool weather.

All these factors add up to the following: We plant our corn later than the peas. And we plant our tomato transplants later still. Seed catalogs usually tell you when to plant particular crops and varieties. (Such information is sometimes also written on the seed packets.)

We plant based upon our expectations and understanding of the climate in our area. But what we get day to day and week to week in the garden isn't climate. It's weather. Climate is statistical. Weather is particular. Weather is fickle. May 15 is a good time to plant tomato transplants here, because it is after our average last spring frost. We could have a freeze in late May *this* year, however, and lose our tomatoes.

Welcome to the concept of replanting.

14. Plant Seeds at the Right Depth

The general rule usually given is that most seeds should be planted at about four times the depth as the seed is big. In actuality, the optimal planting depth for any given seed depends not just upon the size of the seed but also upon the soil, the season, and the current and expected weather. So tiny little dustlike seed is just barely covered with soil. Big seeds like corn and beans are usually planted an inch or more deep, depending upon soil and weather (see chapter 3). The most common reason for failure of seed to germinate is because it was planted too deep. ("Please, please, please tell people not to plant too deep," one seed-company owner pleaded. "They plant too deep,

the seed doesn't come up, then they blame the seed.")

15. Plants Need Water

Most of our domesticated plants came from regions that have ample rain during the growing season. If your region also has ample rain during the growing season, you may be able to grow your entire garden without irrigation, or with only occasional irrigation, depending upon the crops and the specific growing methods and plant spacing. If your region gets less water than the plants are expecting, however, you may need to irrigate to make up the difference.

16. Plants Need Room to Grow

If we plant fruit trees too close together, they will not grow as well as when spaced appropriately. Their roots will compete for resources. The fruits will be small or the crop will be inferior. Crowded garden vegetables will be stunted, and may grow so slowly or under such duress that the produce is tough or bitter.

17. You Must Weed

Plants need freedom from competition with weeds. In some cases weeds are wild plants native to our area. But not usually. The plants that give us the most problems as weeds are usually something else entirely. In gardens, they are often our own pasture, forage, or lawn plants. These plants are more competitive, aggressive, and vigorous than our vegetables. Our lawn and pasture grasses don't have to have tender parts; we don't eat them. And we do expect them to compete reasonably well with wild plants and weeds. Many compete so successfully that they overrun many or most native plants. The same grasses we plant happily in lawns and pastures are a huge weeding problem in vegetable gardens.

Sometimes our weeds are minor edibles that we tend to tolerate as weeds in gardens—chickweed, purslane, or lambsquarters, for example. However, our most pernicious weeds are often full-fledged members of the Grand Alliance in their own right—they are just not ones that we invited to join or are particularly happy about having. Dandelions are members of the Grand Alliance whether we like it or not, just like the Norway rat and house mouse.

18. Resist the Temptation to Do Unnecessary Things

The skillful gardener does *less* while the garden yields just as much or more. Things don't have to be perfect. The spacing doesn't have to be identical. The rows don't have to be perfect, just good enough so you can till or hoe between them. It isn't necessary to remove the suckers from tomato plants or corn. You don't need fungicides on seeds if you have the right varieties and the right seeds. If you do use fungicides on seeds, you will soon find that you *need* to use fungicides on seeds. Because everything has side effects, doing unnecessary things tends to lead to doing *more* unnecessary things to try to correct for the side effects of the first unnecessary things. Doing all these unnecessary things adds up to lots of extra work.

19. You Must Thin

Plants need freedom from too much competition with each other. With many garden vegetables that are direct seeded, we plant the seed much more densely initially than what the grown plants will need. We have to do this, because not all seeds germinate, and insects and other vicissitudes get many others. Indians taught the European settlers

to plant about five times as many corn seeds as plants wanted. "One for the bug, one for the crow, one to rot, and two to grow." If the bug, crow, and fungus don't claim their shares, we can end up with a thicket of corn that will yield only tiny stunted ears, and maybe nothing at all.

Produce from crowded stunted plants is never as succulent, tender, flavorful, or sweet as produce from plants with appropriate spacing. In addition, stressed plants tend to produce nasty chemicals that can make the produce bitter or tough. So we must thin if we end up with more plants than is optimal for the space.

It can take discipline to thin. Making the first cut, removing the obviously inferior plants, may be easy. But making the final cut—that is, pulling up or hoeing out perfectly healthy, vigorous, worthy plants that deserved to live as much as anyone but simply happen to be too close to other worthy plants—that can be hard. I have to grit my teeth and ask forgiveness from Heaven while I do it.

Getting big prime fruit often requires thinning fruits on the trees. I once watched an owner of a peach orchard do this. When the peaches were marble-sized and hanging in clumps of two to four, he went through with a plastic toy bat, and, with evidence of much practice, unerringly knocked all but the biggest baby peach out of each clump with one or two sharp taps.

20. Plants Need Protection from Insects, Pests, and Herbivores

I have to trap gophers in order to grow garlic. If I don't trap gophers, the gophers get every single garlic bulb. The same applies whether I plant a tiny patch of garlic or an entire field. The only difference is that an entire field of unprotected garlic will produce a far bigger crop of gophers. Willamette Valley, with its wet mild winters and many overwintering crops, is Gopher Heaven. When we ask garlic to grow in Gopher Heaven, our part of the contract includes dealing with the gophers.

Gardeners have several options as to how to deal with mega-pests such as deer, rabbits, and rodents. Sometimes we fence. Sometimes we actively trap or eliminate pests. Sometimes we call upon other members of the Grand Alliance to help with pest control. For example, cats and some dogs may deal with the gophers well enough to make trapping unnecessary. Many in my neighborhood must have a deer fence in order to have a vegetable garden at all. Those who don't are all people who have a dog outdoors at night.

We organic gardeners usually deal with insect pests by planting the right varieties, by planting with timing that avoids the worst of the problems, by using rotations and other tricks to minimize the populations of pests, and by enlisting and encouraging the predators of the pests with untilled places for them nearby or hedgerows that include a year-round supply of food and shelter.

I don't use sprays or insecticides, even those that are sanctioned for organic food crops. If you use sprays, you select for varieties and a Grand Alliance that depends upon the sprays. Instead, I try to choose (or breed) appropriate varieties and develop appropriate methods so as to strengthen the Grand Alliance to work and thrive without sprays.

Local gardening books, regional seed catalogs, and neighbors are the best source of information with respect to the pests in your area and what to do about them. Pay attention to your neighbors.

If all successful vegetable gardeners or fruit tree owners in your neighborhood have deer fences around their plantings, there is probably a good reason for that.

21. Plants Need Protection from Disease

We organic gardeners usually protect our plants from disease by practicing good crop rotation, by using timing to avoid growing in periods of heavy disease pressure, by appropriate watering, and by planting disease-resistant varieties.

22. Plants Sometimes Need Protection from Weather

This book is about plants that grow mostly outside, not those that require greenhouses. But even plants that grow mostly outside sometimes need a little help. They often evolved somewhere with different weather. Tomatoes are tropical perennial plants that are frost sensitive. To grow tomatoes at all in temperate regions with freezing weather in winter, we have to grow them as if they were annuals. And we need to give them an early start so they will have long enough to produce a crop before freezing weather. So we start tomato seeds indoors under lights or in a greenhouse to give them about a six-week head start on the season. We transplant the plants outdoors only after it's warmed up more.

It's becoming increasingly common to garden in plastic tunnels called hoop houses or to use plastic row covers of some sort. The hoop houses are metal or PVC tube or fiberglass hoops covered with plastic, arranged to cover one to several rows of garden. Hoop houses are usually open at the ends for ventilation. Daytime temperatures are much warmer inside the tunnels than outside, and there is usually an extra few degrees' worth of protection against freezes. Floating row covers are just a thin synthetic fabric of some sort put over a row of plants and supported by the plants themselves. Like the tunnels, row covers give more heat in the sun and a little protection from mild freezes.

23. You Can Use Transplants or Seeds

Using transplants instead of seeding directly into the garden can have many advantages as well as disadvantages, and many implications with respect to weather resilience, water resilience, and kind and amount of labor, as covered in later chapters.

Some crops lend themselves to transplanting. Others don't. Some can work well either transplanted or direct seeded. So we get a choice. Most people grow tomatoes from transplants. You get lots of tomatoes for each transplant grown, and the root system of tomatoes cooperates with transplanting. Most people direct seed corn, beans, and peas. If transplanted, each of these would give just a small amount of food for the labor of growing and planting each transplant. In addition, corn, beans, and peas make taproots that tend to outgrow the pot before the top is very big. And the roots are usually damaged by transplanting.

In order to plant transplants, you must have transplants. You can grow your own or buy them. If you grow your own, you need a greenhouse or lights indoors. If you buy your transplants, you are limited to crops and varieties that are commonly grown by others in your area and offered for sale. This truncates your individuality and creativity. Buying tomato transplants is a great way to start in vegetable gardening, however. Just keep track of the varieties you buy so if you love the tomatoes, you can get the variety again.

Fruit trees, vegetable starts, and other transplants are usually planted at the same depth as they had in their pot. However, there are exceptions. Tomato transplants are often deliberately planted deeper than they started. Tomato plants form *adventitious roots* from all buried stem nodes, and the extra roots are an advantage. If you plant fruit tree transplants too deep, however, the buried trunk rots. Also, if you plant a grafted fruit tree with the graft union between the top (variety part) and the rootstock below ground, the variety itself can send out its own roots and mitigate any desirable characteristics of the rootstock, including the control of final tree height. So when we plant a fruit tree, we take care to make sure it ends up at exactly the same depth as it was originally in the container.

Transplants should be *hardened off*, that is, given a few days in their pots to acclimate to outdoor weather before being taken from their pots and replanted in the garden. Both exposure to outdoor weather and being removed from the pot and having their roots disrupted is a shock. It's best to ask the plant to deal with just one shock at a time.

24. Some Plants Need Support

Pole beans like poles or trellises or nice tall cornstalks or sunflower plants to wind around and grow up. Without support, the pole bean plants don't yield many beans, and the ones they do yield are muddy and insect-eaten. Pole beans are just not worth growing sprawled all over the ground, a fact I established independently several times for myself as a new gardener. Indeterminate tomato varieties are sometimes tied to trellises too. However, most people prefer to cage them, that is, provide some structure that allows the vines to stay upright and off the ground without requiring tying or fussing with individual branches (other than to poke escapees back into the cage).

25. Some Plants Need Pruning

With fruit trees we trim out many interior branches that would produce heavily shaded small fruit. We may also trim the tree in such a way as to make it easier to pick the fruit. With blackberries we remove old canes that are through bearing fruit to give room to the young bearing canes.

26. Learn to Harvest and Store Produce Optimally

Many gardeners are much better at growing produce than at harvesting it or storing it. I know many gardeners who produce hundreds of pounds of tomatoes per year, for example, but never even one tomato of prime quality. Sometimes part of the problem is they are not growing the most delicious varieties. But in even more cases, the problem is that they don't harvest optimally. Most gardening books don't cover any crop in enough detail to include optimal harvesting and storing. In this book, I focus on just a few crops, but cover them thoroughly and include harvesting and storing information. This book is for people who love good food. Our object is not just to grow food. It's to grow, harvest, store, and eat spectacularly delicious food—food so delicious that eating it is one of life's great pleasures.

27. Experiment

Gardening is always a matter of trying things and experimenting. Trying things is just trying things. Experimenting is trying things using controls. Whenever I use fertilizer, I leave it off two or three plant positions or rows. Lots of times the fertilizer turns out to make no difference. That means

less work and expense in future years. Whenever I try a new variety, I always plant it intermixed with or in alternate rows with my basic standby variety. If a new variety planted alone does poorly, it could have been the fault of the land, weather, or other factors. You can learn just by trying things (without controls), particularly if you try a thing many times in different years. However, you can learn things much faster and more efficiently by experimenting, that is, trying things with controls. In my book on plant breeding and seed saving (*Breed Your Own Vegetable Varieties*) there is an entire chapter on how to get the most information out of the least space and work when it comes to variety trials and garden research.

28. Keep at Least Some Records

Many gardeners keep elaborate records. When I keep elaborate records, I tend to never read them, so keeping elaborate records for me is just like keeping no records. I'm usually better off with the minimal records that I am willing to review and read. I always write down the planting time, the variety, the seed source (if bought), and the year I bought or saved it, where I planted it in the garden, and when I started harvesting. Over the years, those have been the six things I am most likely to want later. Sometimes I do make elaborate notes, especially with variety trials, breeding work, or taste tests. But often my written records, other than those few things, contain just a line for results, or sometimes even just "yes" or "no." That is, plant it again or don't.

29. Think Small

Don't dig up more than you can take care of. It's much easier to till up and plant a garden than to keep it weeded. Once annual weeds go to seed or perennial weeds take over completely, gardening in that spot may be much more laborious or even unworkable for years.

Don't use a backhoe if a shovel will do, especially if you are at the shovel level of knowledge and experience. If you act out of ignorance and make a mistake, your mistake will be smaller and easier to correct if you used a shovel. And which of us isn't ignorant about at least some important aspects of virtually everything?

30. Everything Is Connected

Everything you do affects everything else. You can't do just one thing. Everything has unforeseen consequences. Results are never totally predictable or desirable. There are always trade-offs. The tiniest yard or garden is complex beyond anyone's science or philosophy. Whenever possible, try your idea first on the smallest scale possible and see what actually happens.

31. Slow Down

Gardening is like life. Getting to the end as fast as possible isn't the point. The point is mostly the process.

This cool dew-laden air, pregnant with the scents of the garden and of Willamette Valley, Oregon, in early spring—what can I know of it with my eyes closed? What can I tell of my garden and of this nurturing valley by inhaling their richness on the moist morning air? Which plants can I smell? What soil? What creatures? What can I hear? Listen. . . . First I hear birds in the trees, ducks foraging nearby, distant noise of traffic. I listen closer. I hear a bug munching a plant about a foot above the ground and eight feet away. Later I will go and look to see who is chewing so noisily. I hear a slight rustle under the mulch—a mouse probably, I think. I hear the soil-moving sounds of a gopher just beyond the garden fence. Opening my eyes, looking around at the lush new greenness of the garden framed by blue sky and deep green mountains, I know I belong to this place. We—gardener and garden—we belong together. We evolved to be together. We are meant for each other. We need each other. We are most fully ourselves only with each other. I belong here, here in this place, here in this time, here in this garden, here in this rich fertile valley in this magnificent bountiful gentle generous land.

32. Notice Everything

Look now, how that yellow jacket is dive-bombing the colony of aphids on that mustard plant. The ant seems to be defending. But defending what? Aphids? Honeydew? What's going on here? The yellow jacket seems to be trying to avoid the much smaller ant, and the ant seems to be attacking fearlessly. Over and over the yellow jacket swoops, dodges, and drops quickly into an ant-free area for a quick taste of stolen sweetness. It is the honeydew, then, not the aphids the yellow jacket covets. Over and over the ant charges fiercely, mandibles wide-gaping, and the yellow jacket retreats to the air. Timelessly I watch. Without any names in my head of "yellow jacket" or "ant" or "aphids" I watch everything and seem almost to be each creature. Wordlessly I merge with yellow jacket and ant and aphids and all within the four quarters, as I watch from somewhere removed in time and space but simultaneously totally now and here. Then words come—"yellow jacket," "ant," "aphids"—and ordinary perception returns. But that moment lives on in my memory. Such moments are an important part of why I garden.

33. *Save, Cherish, and Distribute Seeds of the Varieties You Care about the Most*

You don't have to save seeds, even of your favorites, every year. But you should at least know how. And you should keep a backup supply of seeds. Many a treasured variety is supplied to all retail seed companies by just a single grower. In such cases, the variety is just one mistake away from being lost forever. If you have seed of the variety stashed away and know how to do seed saving, then, if the variety becomes unavailable, you can start saving your own seed at that point. Up until then, you don't have to save seed of the variety if it is available commercially. But you should do enough seed saving to learn how. I like to save seed of all the varieties I care most about. Many gardeners never save seeds. But *resilient* gardeners want to be able to continue gardening if something interferes with their access to bought seed—which is likely to be exactly when gardening may matter most.

As long as you plant only seeds and varieties bred by others, you propagate their creativity and their values along with their varieties. You are a consumer, not a full participant. When you save seeds you become a plant breeder. You choose what germplasm to perpetuate. You select according to your own ideas and needs and values. If you are gardening organically, for example, you select for varieties that do well when grown organically, that do not need high inputs or seed coatings or pesticides in order to thrive. And you select for varieties that do well under your local conditions and for your purposes.

When you save your own seed you complete the circle. You fulfill in full measure the Gardener's Covenant with the Plant to save, cherish, distribute, and plant its seeds. You become a willing and creative partner in the further evolution of the Grand Alliance.

CHAPTER THREE

Gardening in an Era of Wild Weather and Climate Change

*Global Warming in Your Backyard. Adventures with Wild Weather,
and What Happened the Year the Californians Stole Our Rain. Lessons
from the Little Ice Age—a Model for Agricultural Resilience. Electricity.
The Hopi Rule. Evaluating the Resilience and Use Potential of Your Land.
Gambling on Global Warming—Strategies with Annuals and Perennials.
Planting Depth, Soil Type, and Weather. The Gambler's Guide to Transplants.
Presoaking Seeds and Germination Tests. Climate Change, Diseases, and Pests.
Overwintering Crops, Staggered Planting, and Resilience. Eggs, Baskets,
and Diversity. On Making Hay while the Sun Shines.*

Global Warming in Your Backyard

My house has been much hotter in the summer in the last decade than it used to be. Global warming? Probably not. The two huge Douglas fir trees south of my house died and had to be cut down. The effect of that loss on the temperature of the house in summer was immediate and dramatic. With the trees, we stayed cool in summer just by opening windows at night and closing them during the day—the traditional maritime Northwest form of air-conditioning. After the trees were removed, I was forced to mechanically air-condition one room, and I find at least some days most summers in which I need to retreat to that room. Local often trumps global. Two big trees may matter more (on an immediate, personal scale) than global warming.

Global warming is happening, however. It's been happening since the glacial maximum about 20,000 years ago, so it is nothing new. There is much argument about how fast global warming is happening and how much is caused by people;

that's not a subject for this book. What is directly relevant here I will summarize and elaborate upon in this section.

1. *An overall trend of global warming does not mean that the globe will be warmer today, tomorrow, this decade, or this hundred years, even on average.* Climatic trends are full of irregularities and hiccups. Any period of a thousand years in which the overall trend is in one direction has periods of years, decades, and even centuries in which the climatic trend reverses temporarily. The Little Ice Age (from about A.D. 1300 to 1850), noted for seriously colder weather in North Atlantic Europe and America, was a period of several hundred years that was part of the overall global warming trend that has been occurring since the last ice age. The Younger Dryas Interval was a period of about a thousand years during which the climate snapped all the way back to the frigidity of the glacial maximum,

after which global temperatures rebounded to where the overall warming trend would have taken them if the Younger Dryas had never occurred.

2. *Even if global warming prevails and the average global temperature increases during the next few years, your garden may not get warmer, even on average.* Climatic changes cause irregularities in the patterns of ocean currents and winds. The local effects of those changes are huge compared with the few degrees cited as likely increases in *average* global climate in the next few decades. A change in wind patterns that brings Arctic inland air masses to you instead of mild ocean air will matter much more than a few degrees higher average global temperature.

3. *In most cases of climate change, somebody loses and somebody gains.* The Medieval Warm Period was apparently lovely for Europe. Famines and diseases were rare. Populations swelled. Civilization and cities expanded and flourished. The same period was devastating for other areas, such as Mexico and the American Southwest, which experienced horrific droughts—droughts that probably contributed to the collapse of civilizations and the vanishing of entire populations.

The Little Ice Age is defined in terms of colder weather in North Atlantic Europe and eastern North America. But the Little Ice Age seems to have had little or no impact on the American West and many other parts of the world.

4. *For agriculture, water is often more critical than temperature.* Past periods of global warming seem to be associated with greater aridity and much more frequent and more extreme droughts in the American West. The Medieval Warm Period was cooler, less predictable, and marked with prolonged droughts in the Sahara. In many other parts of the world, the main impact of the Medieval "Warm" Period also seemed to be droughts. Says Brian Fagan in *The Great Warming*, "with respect to California, it's sobering to remember that the past seven hundred years were the wettest since the Ice Age." Pointing to prolonged droughts that lasted decades and even generations, Fagan says that, viewing the overall global situation, not just that of Europe, "it is tempting to rename the Medieval Warm Period the Medieval Drought Period." The American Northwest, California, the Southwest, the intermountain West, and the lower Hudson River Valley are all vulnerable to increased aridity and droughts.

5. *Patterns of volcanic activity and even individual volcanoes can trump and reverse existing warming trends and even trigger both minor and major ice ages.* Some mega-extinctions were probably triggered by volcanic activity. There was an extinction event about 72,000 years ago in which humanity was almost wiped out as a species. It was probably caused by a single volcanic eruption and associated climate change. To this day, the human species carries molecular-genetic and population-genetic characteristics that show that we were reduced to a mere remnant population once. That is, the human species shows much less variability than one would expect, to this day, because of that population bottleneck. None of

The Anthropology of Human Experience with Climate Change

As required reading for gardeners and farmers I propose Jared Diamond's book *Collapse: How Societies Choose to Fail or Succeed*. The larger the scope of a book and the more profound and original, the harder it seems to be to describe it. *Collapse* is not very well described by its title or any reviews I've seen and is basically not describable. *Collapse* presents a grand sweep of human beings throughout the eras experiencing and adapting to or being destroyed by various forces, of which a major one is climate change. One take-home lesson from *Collapse* is that in most cases, societies fail for multiple reasons. Damaging agricultural and environmental practices, deforestation, shortsighted social choices, overpopulation, bad government, and climate change are often all involved. Where a society

failed "because of climate change," in most cases the failure involved both climate change *and* inappropriate social and agricultural patterns and responses. Another take-home lesson—the factors building up to a collapse are an exponential function toward the end. Many societies go from their peak of population and affluence to their collapse in just a few years.

Reading and studying *Collapse* was invaluable to me for writing this book and this chapter. I viewed each issue, event, or situation Diamond considered from the point of view of a gardener, farmer, or plant breeder experiencing or preparing for it. I took *Collapse* as a definition of the potential problems and challenges, then asked the question, "So, as gardeners, farmers, and plant breeders, what can we do about it?"

the modern weather models include overall volcanic activity, let alone the activity of individual volcanoes, both of which are unpredictable. All our modern weather models, applied to A.D. 1300, would have predicted continuing global warming. What happened instead was the Little Ice Age.

6. *For the purposes of agriculture, the regularity of climatic and weather patterns may matter much more than the averages or overall trends.* Most of the famines in northern Europe during the Little Ice Age were as much or more associated with erratic, rainier, stormier weather than with temperatures. The Year without a Summer in New England (1816) featured freezes that were not particularly

outstanding, as New England weather goes. The problem wasn't the freezes. It was the fact that they happened right through the summer. The Year without a Summer was caused by the massive eruption of Mount Tambora in Indonesia in 1815; the resulting ash cloud spread over much of the Northern Hemisphere, blocking the sun's rays and cooling global temperatures. The crop failures in New England were serious, but the effects in parts of Europe were even worse, sparking starvation and bread riots in some countries and leading to what historians have termed "the last great subsistence crisis of the Western world" (at least until the next one happens).

7. *Climate change can be sudden.* In spring of 1315, it started raining in northern Europe and apparently stopped only briefly for the next several months. That spring marked the beginning of five years of colder, wetter, stormier, more erratic weather that was the obvious beginning of the Little Ice Age. Transition from one weather regime to another can be dramatic and fast enough to happen within a decade, a year, or even a single season, and it can be so dramatic it is obvious even to those who aren't keeping any weather records.

In summary, during periods of wild weather and climate change we gardeners and farmers need to be as ready for cold as heat, global warming or not. We need to be ready to deal with weather that is more erratic than "normal" and that shows greater extremes. In addition, we need to take into account the fact that regional rainfall patterns are also subject to erratic behavior and that temporary or permanent change can happen without notice.

Gardening and farming are critically linked to weather and climate. We plant what we plant and when and where because we believe we know, more or less, what kind of weather to expect. The last hundred years has apparently been unusually stable with respect to both weather and climate. It also has had an unusually low level of volcanic activity. Our current gardening and farming patterns depend upon a relatively stable climate and relatively predictable weather. We are most likely in for wilder and more erratic weather and climate change in the coming years and decades. As individual gardeners and farmers, we have learned to garden and farm in the context of unusually stable times. We now need to expand our perspectives and learn, or relearn, how to garden and farm in wilder times.

Adventures with Wild Weather, and What Happened the Year the Californians Stole Our Rain

In Oregon, it's traditional to blame every problem on the Californians. So when I stood looking at my garlic in spring of 2005—my garlic that wasn't growing because the ordinary winter rains had failed—I followed time-honored Oregonian tradition and declared: "Those #%&* Californians stole our rain!"

A day later, a Californian friend e-mailed me about their problems with their winter deluge. Indeed, it had been all over the national news—epic floods and mudslides throughout western California because of the horrific amount of rain. "Where in the world is all this #@%! rain coming from?" my friend's e-mail asked.

"From *here*," I e-mail-snarled in response. "That's *our* rain! Give it *back*!"

In winter in Oregon, the jet stream usually blows in from the ocean and across the coastal mountains and brings generous winter rains. In 2005, instead, a high-pressure area sat itself down over western Oregon and blocked the jet stream. The jet stream split. Half veered south into California. The other half veered north into Washington. In both California and Washington, those rains, more than normal or expected, caused massive flooding and mudslides. Agriculture was hampered by flooded fields and pastures and the need for more electricity to heat greenhouses and animal facilities. Meanwhile, here in Oregon, we expected those rains and our agriculture depends upon them. The rain that falls as snow in the mountains in winter replenishes the rivers and provides irrigation in summer. Furthermore, our overwintering crops are nonirrigated, and are often grown on land with no water rights or water access. We assume there will be plentiful rain in winter. In January and February of 2005 there wasn't. So there I stood in early spring of 2005 looking unhappily at garlic that wasn't growing because the winter rains had failed.

The big problem for agriculture in maritime Oregon is the fact that the warmth and the rain don't correspond. We have enough of both, but not at the same time. Almost all our rain falls in the winter. Summer vegetable crops must usually be irrigated. Furthermore, the amount of water that must be added is serious, as is the labor involved. Any crops that can grow in winter with natural rain are especially valuable. Hard-stemmed garlics can be planted in fall. They grow during winter and early spring using rain as their water supply, produce bulbs in late spring, then dry down naturally in early summer as the ground is drying out. I love the intense flavors of hard-stemmed garlics, and I love the fact that all I have to do is plant, weed twice, and harvest. Hard-stemmed garlics are a perfect fit for our climate. Our *ordinary* climate.

In spring 2005, standing in front of the dry garlic patch, for the first time in a decade of garlic growing I discovered the converse of such perfect regional adaptation: Any crop or growing method that is very fine-tuned to the ecology of a particular regional weather pattern is exactly what is most vulnerable if the ordinary weather pattern is broken seriously. When it comes to dealing with erratic weather, there is something to be said for

crops, varieties, and growing methods that have broader adaptation.

With my small backyard garlic patch, I simply grumbled a bit, rearranged the hoses to reach to the garlic, and watered it. It was a nuisance, but possible. But I sometimes have visions of a whole field of garlic as a cash crop. So this was a valuable warning. Even if a crop is ordinarily grown without irrigation, it could be valuable, I decided, to at least have the option of irrigating—even if it was laborious and inconvenient. Having the ability to water in a weather emergency might in some years make all the difference. Whatever the normal patterns, backup options can be valuable.

Another basic lesson illustrated by the garlic patch in 2005: Don't count on any single crop or growing pattern. Diversify.

Monoculture works best in periods of climatic stability. In periods of more erratic weather and climatic change, monoculture will be riskier.

In an era of wild weather and climate change, there will be more crop failures on most farms and in most regions. Farms will need to be able to survive occasional years with no income. The current pattern of farms borrowing money in order to plant or grow a crop will become increasingly unworkable. It presumes a reliability of weather, of acceptable harvests always following planting, which is likely to be increasingly unrealistic. The idea of farming being an ordinary business—agribusiness—is a misleading concept. The failure of any given crop at least once every five or ten years needs to be reintegrated into our concept and culture of farming. Once upon a time, farmers knew that *some years you don't get anything*. They had cultural patterns of not borrowing, of not buying anything they could make themselves, of never buying new if they could buy used, of always minimizing cash expenditures and obligations, and of growing and eating as much of their own food as possible, whatever their main or cash crop(s). Their lifestyle and philosophy helped them survive years in which they made no money at all.

Meanwhile, back in spring of 2005, I had made arrangements to grow my garbanzo beans and corn in fields on Sunbow Farm, the organic farm of my friend Harry MacCormack. Usually in March we hunt for a break in the weather for plowing. But in dry 2005, Harry had the field all nicely tilled and ready by early March, the optimal planting window for my particular variety of garbanzo bean. So I planted. My main worry was the dryness of the soil. Would there even be enough moisture to germinate the seed? The governor of Oregon just barely declared an official state of drought, however, when it started raining. It rained through the rest of March, and I rejoiced. My garbanzos would germinate.

It continued raining in April. The rains have usually stopped by May, but it continued to rain. I quit rejoicing. The field with the garbanzo beans turned into one big lake. Garbanzo beans do not grow in lakes. It was still raining in May. Now I was also losing corn-growing time. The cornfield-to-be, already tilled once, needed its second tilling before planting. It was now also a lake. You can't till a lake.

The rains did not let up until July. Most farms and gardens were delayed in planting by months on certain crops because the land was too wet to till. Even crops planted before the rains came and on high enough ground were delayed because there was so little heat. Tomatoes and squash were a month late. In addition, in gardens and on commercial farms throughout the region, many tree-fruit crops failed. Pollination didn't occur very well in many orchards because the weather was too cold and wet during the ordinary pollination window. A year of strange weather often affects many crops.

What had happened in late spring of 2005 again involved the jet stream. Normally in late spring, the jet stream swings north and away from Oregon, and we have dry weather. The soils dry out, and we till and plant our warm-season summer crops. In spring of 2005, the jet stream, absent in winter when we expected it, returned and remained stubbornly flowing right over Oregon in late spring, when we don't expect it. We not only had rain out of season, we had much more intense rains than usual. All the lower agricultural land flooded. So there I stood, looking at lakes on top of my garbanzo field and would-be corn patch. It was mid-July before the lake dried up. The garbanzo I planted is day-length critical. If planted too late, it starts flowering on tiny plants and isn't productive. It was too late to replant the garb.

By early July of 2005, the weather finally dried out enough so that Harry could till the prospective cornfield again. I planted 'Abenaki Indian Flint' (a.k.a. 'Roy's Calais'), a very short-season corn that is great for cornbreads and polenta. It did fine. When it comes to surviving weird weather, having short-season varieties is a useful tactic for enhancing resilience.

Lessons from the Little Ice Age— a Model for Agricultural Resilience

The lessons we can learn from the Little Ice Age in northern Europe are no less relevant because the Little Ice Age involved overall global cooling rather than global warming. While temperatures in northern Europe averaged about 4°F colder during the Little Ice Age, that was not the biggest problem for agriculture. It was more and worse storms, more rain, erratic weather patterns, drought, and the just plain unpredictability of the weather. By the end of the Little Ice Age, most northern Europeans had learned to deal with climatic unpredictability in ways that are highly relevant today. Now, after more than a hundred years of unusually stable weather and changed agricultural patterns that depend upon stability, it will be useful to remind ourselves of how Europeans in a prior era of climate change adapted to and transcended it.

A thousand years ago, Europeans were pretty much enjoying themselves as global warming happened. This warming was part of the recovery from the last ice age. About a thousand years ago, weather patterns were relatively regular, agriculture was flourishing over most of Europe, civilization was flourishing, and human population levels were at a high. In Europe of A.D. 1300, about 80 to 90 percent of the population were peasant farmers, and about 80 percent of what they grew was grain—wheat, oats, barley, and rye. Herders were mostly different people and ran separate operations. Herders owned flocks they grazed on marginal land, frequently public or common land. Vegetables, fruit, and meat were a very minor part of agriculture. Meat was mostly for the rich.

Most farmers were peasants who lived close to the edge of survival. Yields of grain were poor. A good harvest of wheat, for example, was ten bushels per acre. It took two bushels of wheat to plant an acre, so in a good year, the increase was only about fourfold. Fertility was restored to land largely by using fallows—that is, the land was allowed to rest uncropped for a year out of every two or three. Farming was mostly subsistence farming, that is, it was aimed primarily at growing food for the family rather than producing for market. Farmers went to market only with the excess.

This pattern worked well enough until about 1300. The last three hundred years of the period featured such regular and friendly weather (with the exception of one volcano-associated year) that frosts in May were receding into distant memory. Agriculture expanded at all the edges—people grazed animals higher in the mountains than they had in thousands of years, and had farms in places that had once been too cold for anything but grazing. The moderate and dryish summers also allowed the farming of lower and heavier land than had been the pattern in the past. The Norse expanded to and raised livestock in Greenland, which was actually somewhat green then.

By 1300, populations had expanded right up to or near the carrying capacity of the land in good times. Farmers were beginning to stint on fallows because of population pressures, thus harming yields. Then, all at once, starting with one horrific year followed by another four thoroughly bad years, the good times—that is, the stable times—were over.

The subsequent period, the Little Ice Age, lasted from about 1300 to about 1850. There isn't much scientific consensus on the causes. Summers were sometimes colder. Freezes in May became more common. There was much wetter weather during the summer growing season, and more storms. Especially toward the latter part of the period, some winters became unusually cold.

The Thames River froze over several years in one period. In one year, the New York harbor even froze over.

Grain is very vulnerable to wet weather. Heavy rains after the grain has begun to dry down can ruin the crop. Wind and storms can cause lodging of grain, that is, cause it to flatten onto the ground. Grains are basically just grasses with especially heavy seed heads on top. It doesn't take very much to cause those seed heads to droop down and touch the ground. Once that happens, the seed molds and is ruined. Grain crops were thus especially vulnerable to the weather problems associated with the Little Ice Age.

The Little Ice Age in Europe began dramatically in spring of 1315, when it rained in sheets day after day, week after week. Fields flooded. Planted grain and topsoil was washed away. The rains kept up for months. Storms flattened much of whatever grain survived. Five years of colder, much wetter, very erratic weather followed, which was prelude to several hundred years of more erratic weather. Famines started happening and became common. Most people who die of famines don't actually starve to death. Instead, weakened and malnourished, they die of disease. Or they die of increased violence or wars associated with desperate competition for food and resources.

The Black Death (plague) eliminated about a third of the population in its first sweep through Europe in 1348–50 and swept through almost every decade thereafter. People also died of cholera, typhus, dysentery, and diarrhea, the latter often the result of damage to the gut when starving people tried to eat rotting carcasses or inedible plants. More wars started and became the norm. Whatever the reasons or excuses people give for specific wars, overcrowding or famines are generally associated with wars. Wars, in themselves, tend to give rise to famines. Armies on both sides seize crops to use themselves and burn what they don't use in order to prevent opposing armies from using them. Harvested grain is ideal for armies to seize. Mature or near-mature grain in the field is especially vulnerable to being destroyed by burning. All at once in the year 1315, being a European peasant farmer growing primarily grain became an unattractive proposition, and it remained untenable for the next 500 years. Populations dropped dramatically.

Little by little, led by farmers in Flanders and Holland first, and then Britain, European farmers (except for the French) developed a new pattern. It constituted a revolution in agricultural patterns. It was this erratic-climate-adapted style of farming that was brought by European settlers and pioneers to America. It's a model for a maximally resilient farming community—one that I believe is highly relevant for most temperate regions today. Here are the basic features of the model:

1. There was much more diversity, on individual farms as well as regionally. Most farms raised vegetables, especially root crops, fruit, animal products, pasture, and forage crops as well as grain all on one farm. All these other crops were more reliable given erratic weather than was grain. Vegetable crops are less vulnerable to being burned by marauding armies. The diversification itself was a powerful tool for resilience.

2. Peas, beans, and other legumes were more widely grown. But the biggest change was the introduction and growing of legumes for animal fodder. Clover was introduced.

Alfalfa (lucerne) was added toward the end of the period. Both were used in pastures and as fodder crops. Improved (private) pastures including legumes and managed grazing replaced overgrazed public pastures (commons). Sophisticated crop rotation systems were developed.

3. Animals became much more important, and became an integral part of most farms. Pasture and animal forage crop rotations greatly enhanced the fertility of farmland and increased overall yields. The rotations involving pasture and forage were in lieu of rotations involving fallow. That is, where land was once taken completely out of production and allowed to "rest" one year out of every two or three, it was now instead used to pasture animals or grow forage or fodder crops for them. Rotations involving legumes, forage, and pasture did a better job of enhancing soil fertility than did fallowing, and produced a crop of meat, milk, or eggs as well.

   There was much more animal manure available, and it was used to further enhance the productivity of the land.

4. People grew lots more vegetables, especially lots more storable root vegetables. By 1850, the end of the Little Ice Age, common crops included turnips, beets, mangels, rutabagas, cabbage, kale, kohlrabi, cauliflower, rape, and potatoes. Root and tuber crops as well as kale and rape were grown both as fodder for animals and food for people.

5. During the later part of the period, the potato became important. The potato is less watery than other root or tuber crops, and is an excellent source of protein as well as

Livestock and Global Warming

There is a lot of talk about the raising of livestock being responsible for huge amounts of CO_2 release, thus being a global warming issue. We are even being told that the best thing we can do to prevent global warming is to eat less meat. To arrive at that conclusion, the global warming cost of deforestation of the rain forests in the Amazon and elsewhere is counted as part of world meat production, which is reasonable. But the tally goes on to apply that average number on an acre basis to individual pieces of land worldwide, which is completely unreasonable. To get the conclusion that livestock production in the United States is a serious factor in global warming, you must charge it for the rainforests burning in the Amazon in order to grow soybeans for South American livestock. However, no South American soybeans are used in North American meat. And little or no deforestation in North America is associated with livestock production. A fair estimate of the real CO_2 implications of all livestock production in the United States is that it is responsible for about 3 percent of our production of CO_2. (That includes the CO_2 costs of growing all the forage and feed U.S. livestock actually eat.) Given the large fraction of our food production and our diets meat represents, 3 percent is a modest figure. Go ahead and eat less meat or even no meat if you want. However, don't do it because of global warming.

carbohydrates. Potatoes yield better than all other root or tuber crops *and* grains and require much less labor to grow. Potatoes produce more carbohydrates per acre than all other temperate-climate crops, and more protein per acre than all others except for legumes. Potatoes can thrive in weather that is colder and wetter than that suitable for grains. Wherever the potato was adopted, it completely transformed the agricultural equation and allowed populations to stabilize and then grow again.

6. Global markets and transportation networks developed. Many farmers began producing primarily for markets. At its best, this pattern meant that land could be used more for what it was best at growing and there was less need to grow every needed crop on every farm.

7. Grain remained very important in most European diets. However, the diversified farm could buy grain from the world market when local crops failed, as long as the farm produced some marketable crops that could be sold for cash. Producing a diversity of crops, even when it didn't include grain, was a more reliable method of ensuring yourself of grain every year than growing primarily grain in an era of wild weather. Cash crops became an essential part of the viability of even the smallest farms.

8. Hunting, fishing, and harvesting from forests, wild areas, or commons remained important wherever such resources or commons were available.

9. Fencerows produced fruit, nuts, and habitat for wildlife, game, and pollinators, and also helped moderate wind patterns. In America,

a woods or woodlot was often part of the settlement pattern.

10. The orchard became an essential component of the small farm.

11. In most cases, one or more members of a farming family had alternate skills that made the family not completely dependent upon farming. They hunted, fished, trapped, logged, spun, and wove. They made clothes, shoes, furniture, wheels, and barrels. They worked as carpenters, as laborers on other people's farms, or kept shops or worked for shopkeepers in town. They put up and sold or traded jams, fruit, pickles, or sauerkraut. They made cider, whiskey, beer, or wine. They were healers, herbalists, or midwives. Successful farm families in the Little Ice Age had occupations that filled their time in off periods and provided some insurance against years of crop failures.

The agricultural pattern that developed during the Little Ice Age provided a high degree of resilience to uncooperative weather as well as hard times of all kinds. For modern gardeners and farmers in an era of wild weather and climate change, it's a pattern that deserves serious consideration.

Electricity

Many hard times great and small might involve lack of electricity. For many, no electricity would mean no irrigation. The ultimate survival crops—the crops you depend upon the most in hard times—need to be crops you can grow in your region in most years without electricity.

The Hopi Rule

Perhaps the all-time masters at farming in an era of erratic weather in North America are the Hopi Indians of the American Southwest. Hopi agricultural and cultural patterns developed during a period of overall aridity with highly irregular weather and serious droughts. Corn was their most important staple crop. Hopi culture called for storing enough corn for two years. As nations and individuals we might want to consider doing likewise.

Evaluating the Resilience and Use Potential of Your Land

In preparation for writing this book, I reviewed currently available computer-generated and other projections for the likely effects of global warming on various regions. Here is a summary:

First, many such studies admit that their models aren't reliable or useful at the regional level, and make no attempt to predict at the scale that matters in our backyards, farms, or even states or general regions.

Second, those studies that do make projections at the regional level do not give any insights that could not be inferred simply by knowing what has happened in that particular region in the recent and distant past. They give no new information.

Hence I will not refer further to these models and projections. Here are the questions and issues I consider most useful in developing an understanding of the resilience of our backyards and farms to climatic change and erratic weather.

What Is the Essential Nature of Your Soil?

Deep soils hold more moisture than shallow ones, and thus are less vulnerable to drought. Soils with higher clay content also hold more moisture. With too high a clay content, however, soils drain poorly and may be slow to dry out in spring, giving a slow start for plowing and planting warm-season crops. Heavy clay soils are more vulnerable to being too wet for agriculture if there are excessive rains. Sandy soil has little water-retention capability, so needs more irrigation and is more vulnerable to drought. A lot of your soil's virtues and liabilities come from the basic type (including depth) of soil.

The USDA cooperative soil survey program has mapped nearly every county and every bit of land in the United States with respect to soil types. The maps and accompanying information are invaluable. They give soil types, soil depth, available water capacity, limitations, appropriate agricultural uses and management (including fertilizing regimes for growing various crops), recreational uses, susceptibility to erosion, drought, and flooding, and much more. By the time you have looked up your own backyard or farm and studied its soil type and capability grouping, you will have an excellent concept of what potentials and problems have been associated with your soil in the last hundred years or so. You can find the soil survey maps and information online at http://soils.usda.gov/survey/. A specific illustration will demonstrate the value of these surveys and the kinds of information they contain.

When my farm partner and colleague Nate France and I decided we were ready for a long-term lease on a few acres of good agricultural land, we started our search in the pages of the old paper copy of the USDA Benton County Soil Survey I had. We studied the associated information, especially on all the Class I and Class II soils, the best agricultural soils. "Capability groupings" range from Class I to Class VIII. The Class I soils are deep loams with no limitations. Class VIII soils have such serious limitations they are only suitable for uses such as recreation or wildlife. The Class II soils are deep soils with specific limitations, which are part of the classification. A Class IIe-1 soil, for example, is a deep soil whose only limitation is susceptibility to erosion from being slightly sloping ground. A Class IIw-3 soil is a deep soil with the limitation that it experiences a high water table in winter, and thus is not appropriate for deepest-rooted crops such as tree fruits, and may not be appropriate for overwintering annuals, either. Nate and I eliminated the Class II soils that had a high water table in winter. (We want to grow a lot of overwintering crops.) We eliminated other soils that weren't well drained, were subject to flooding, were too shallow, and so on.

As mentioned previously, we identified every patch of soil of Class I or appropriate Class II types within a twenty-minute drive of the house and approached the owners. The result, after some lengthy negotiations, was a five-year lease on a lovely chunk of Willamette soil a mere five-minute drive from home.

Here's a partial description of Willamette soil taken from the soil survey: "The Willamette series consists of deep, well-drained soils that form in silty alluvium on broad terraces above floodplains in the Willamette Valley. . . . Where these soils are not cultivated, the vegetation is grass, hazelnut, wild blackberry, Douglas fir, and Oregon white oak. Elevation ranges from 200 to 300 feet. Average annual precipitation is 40 to 45 inches, average annual air temperature is 52° to 54°F, and the frost-free season is 165 to 210 days. In a representative profile . . . [a description of all the layers follows].

"Rooting depth is unrestricted. Permeability is moderate. Available water capacity is 11 to 13 inches.

"This soil is used for pasture, hay, small grains, orchards, grass seed, wildlife habitat, and recreation. It is used for vegetable and specialty crops when irrigated."

Level Willamette soil is capability Class I-1. Our particular chunk has a slight slope, thus is Class IIe-1 with the sole limitation of a potential for erosion. (The threat of erosion is easy to deal with by using cover crops, which we intended to do anyway.)

Additional information in the capability-group information gives us general fertilizer recommendations for our soil: "Small grain and grasses respond to nitrogen, row crops respond to nitrogen and phosphorus, and legumes respond to phosphorus and sulfur. In many places legumes grown on these soils also respond to lime."

Where Is Your Land with Respect to the Basic Topography?

Many vulnerabilities are obvious from topography. Hillsides are vulnerable to erosion. Land only slightly above waterways, lakes, or wetlands may flood. Land on natural floodplains may flood even in ordinary times, and even, occasionally, in an era of dams. What the three dams upstream from my hometown of Corvallis will do in the next mega-9 earthquake I don't know, but I can guess. Heavy clay soils at the bottom of depressions, being the results of floods, are likely to flood. If wetland plants are growing all over your land, it means that the plants think you have a wetland.

Limitations and Marginality

Every region and every piece of agricultural land has limitations. If climatic change or a year of erratic weather happens to affect a characteristic that is limiting in your region and pushes it in the wrong direction, there is a serious impact. For example, if you live in a region that is somewhat water-limited in the best of times, you can expect to be especially vulnerable to a change that brings less overall water or more droughts, or droughts of greater severity. If you have a short frost-free season that limits the crops you can grow, you would be especially vulnerable to erratic weather that decreases the frost-free season even more by bringing more late spring or early fall freezes.

Here in the maritime Northwest, we are limited on total summer heat. We don't have to take an advanced course in agriculture to figure this out. All we have to do is notice that about one summer in every five, our tomatoes don't ripen until September, just barely before cold winter rains end the tomato season. (Other heat-loving summer crops also lag in such years, with the longer-season varieties failing to mature.) Furthermore, you don't have to go very far north from here before you can't grow tomatoes reliably as an outdoor crop. Even within our region, you don't have to go very far up the mountains or into the cooler coastal mountains before you can't grow tomatoes well at all.

Anytime you are at the edge of the area where a particular crop can be grown, this represents a land-crop combination that is especially vulnerable to erratic weather or climate change.

Agriculture, in general, expands when conditions are stable and permissive, then becomes unworkable at the edges when conditions are

erratic or change in the wrong direction occurs. The Norse spread to Greenland during a warmer period and thrived for a while, then died off when things became colder. The Hopi Indians flourished widely in the American Southwest during wetter times, but survived in only a few of the wetter locations when the climate became drier again.

So if you are at the margins of where a particular crop can be grown, you haven't much resilience when it comes to growing that crop and should probably not bet the farm on it in an era of wilder weather.

What Is Grown Commercially in Your Region and Why?

Generally, any specific crop can be grown over a wider area than where it is grown commercially. A crop is grown *commercially* in the area where, from past experience, it has proved not only to grow and produce well *but also to be reliable*. Crops are grown commercially in the area that is at the core of the region of suitability rather than the margins. The core is less vulnerable to erratic weather than the margins. However, the same crop is often grown successfully in backyards and market gardens far beyond the core commercial region.

Most land-grant universities have lots of information about the commercial agriculture of specific regions and are a good source of insights as to what factors are limiting in your region and what commercial crops are grown there and why. Become familiar with the Web site of the agricultural extension service at the land-grant university closest to your home.

Of the crops you are interested in growing, which aren't grown commercially in your region, and why not? Where are they grown commercially, and why? What is easiest to grow in your region?

What Did the Indians Do with Your Land?

All along the East Coast, Indians engaged in extensive agriculture, and generally without irrigation. Corn, beans, and squash were the major staples. However, we also know that there was a multiyear drought during the period in which Europeans were trying to settle Jamestown. New England appears especially vulnerable to cold weather extremes when global climatic change causes erratic behavior in currents in the North Atlantic. In general, however, the East Coast of North America appears to be an area of great climatic resilience.

Indians also grew corn, beans, and squash along the Mississippi and other river valleys of the Midwest, again without irrigation. *Buffalo Bird Woman's Garden* (Wilson) offers a detailed description of the agriculture of the Hidatsa and Mandan Indians in the upper Midwest.

In the American Southwest, Indians farmed throughout the region with and without irrigation in the wetter eras, and dropped back to just the wetter spots and use of irrigation during the drier periods.

Indians in California and the maritime Northwest did not practice formal agriculture. They periodically burned land to keep it as savannah, however. Willamette Valley was burned every fall, which enhanced crops of game, acorns, and camas. Otherwise it would have been solid forest.

What Did the Pioneers Do in Your Region? What Did They Grow? Did They Use Irrigation?

In many areas of the country we find that modern commercial patterns as well as modern garden-ing patterns require irrigation, even though the pioneers did fine without it. If so, what were the pioneers in your area doing differently? (Often, part of the answer lies in gardening style and plant spacing, as discussed in chapters 5 and 6.)

When You Have Had Particularly Bad Gardening Years for Reasons beyond Your Control, What Happened and Why?

The answers to those questions tell you something about the practical limitations you are already experiencing, and suggest particular issues to focus on that might matter in an era of greater climatic irregularity. Extend your reach by talking to the oldest local gardeners you can find in your region and asking them about their all-time worst years for gardening. Ask about both bad-weather years in general as well as especially bad years for the particular crops you care most about.

Consider and Remember What We Know about All-Time Awful Years and Eras

These would include the 1930s Dust Bowl in the American West, the Year without a Summer in New England, multi-decade droughts in the American West, the Potato Famine in Ireland, and the Little Ice Age in northern Europe and Atlantic North America.

Gambling on Global Warming— Strategies with Annuals and Perennials

Even in the best of times, every act of planting involves a gamble. Now, with more erratic weather, every act of planting is more of a gamble. Much of this book is about how to reduce the gamble or spread the risks. But gambling can be fun. And climate change can represent opportunities as well as risks. The very name "global warming" tempts and thrills certain of us. *Hey, maybe I use some of that global warming in my garden*, we think, and immediately start looking covetously at crops and varieties that are recommended for the USDA zone one or two numbers warmer than our own—crops or varieties that have hitherto been forbidden. Where the plant is an annual, why not play around? The gamble may be well worth it, even if you lose one crop of every four to the weather.

More thought is indicated before planting large long-lived perennials, especially those that are biggest and longest-lived—trees. Because global climate change is often accompanied by more erratic weather, you might want to err on the side of caution. If you are zone 8, plant trees suitable for zone 7 or less instead of expanding in the warmer direction and taking on plants typical of zone 9. Even if the average of the winter low temperatures is going up, that doesn't help if winters are so erratic you now experience more extreme lows every few years. In order to avoid freezing out your trees, you need every single year to have a lowest temperature that is permissive, not just some years. The *average* lowest temperature isn't really what matters. Regional mail-order nursery catalogs often list the specific degree of freeze tolerance of every cultivar, at least every cultivar for which the information is known. Knowing that, in my own experience here in maritime Oregon, there have been at least a couple of winters in which the winter low was approximately 0°F, these days I would refrain from planting any tree with a freeze tolerance of less than −10°F. And I would prefer −20°F.

On the other hand, winter lows are not always

the characteristic that limits a perennial to a zone warmer than our own. Sometimes we plant or don't plant a fruit tree based upon characteristics such as whether there is enough summer heat for the fruit to ripen. In that case, we can better afford to experiment. The gamble over whether there is enough heat over any particular summer season risks only one crop, not the lives of the trees themselves.

So to make appropriate gambles with perennials, it's a good idea to know exactly why that more southerly variety you are lusting after isn't usually grown in your region. For varieties released in recent years or varieties commonly grown commercially, there is often excellent and precise information on the Internet provided by the breeder or by your local land-grant university. You can often find the exact degree of freeze-hardiness, the exact amount of summer heat (degree days) and length of growing season required, and many other advantages and limitations, including diseases that may be the factor that limits the geographical appropriateness for any particular variety. Finding and studying such information is well worth the effort when contemplating the kind of space big trees take up and the years of patient care (and ultimate productivity) they represent. When it comes to annuals, however, I literature-search less and play more. I tend to just buy some seed and try it.

Erratic weather can also make pollination more of an issue. In some years, your two different varieties of plum trees will flower simultaneously and pollinate each other just fine. But in a year with unusual weather, the varieties may respond differently and end up flowering out of synch. If the two varieties need each other as pollinators, you would then get no fruit on either tree. In an era of wild weather, there is increased value in fruit and nut trees that are self-fruitful.

My own approach in the years ahead will be to gamble more with annuals but less with perennials than I did in the era of more regular weather. There are some fruit tree varieties that have been favorites and dependable producers in maritime Oregon for *decades*. I'm figuring these are the place to start for main crop plantings, with the gambles limited in number, or limited to branches grafted onto varieties that are the established dependable favorites.

Before getting carried away with the possibilities suggested by the words "global warming," however, ask yourself whether your region and your backyard are actually warming. Mine aren't. At least not significantly. Not enough to notice. Rather, some summers seem warmer and others colder and wetter than I recall from twenty years ago. And the standard rain patterns have become less dependable. That is, I think I'm seeing much more erratic weather rather than weather that is changing in a consistent, uniform direction. Formal records suggest a small increase in average local temperatures, but that is tiny compared to the huge and obvious variability in the features of weather that matter most to gardeners and farmers.

Planting Depth, Soil Type, and Weather

As already mentioned, one version of conventional wisdom is that seeds should be planted about four times as deep as the seed is wide. Another version is that big seeds such as peas, beans, and corn should be planted about 1 inch to 2 inches deep. These versions don't add up to the same planting depth. And whether either rule of thumb works depends upon the soil type and the weather. We are also usually advised to tamp down the soil over the seed, but that may be unnecessary or even counterproductive, depending upon soil type and weather.

Let's suppose I want to plant pea seeds in the heavy clay soil in my backyard in early spring. If I actually plant them 2 inches deep in this heavy soil and tamp down the soil over them, I can guarantee that *none* will emerge. That much heavy clay soil tamped down is just too difficult for the pea sprouts to emerge through. In addition, the soil is colder 2 inches down than it is closer to the surface. Surface soil warms up much more, at least during the day. Planting that deep in early spring will mean that the seed just rots.

The tamping down in this case is unnecessary and counterproductive. The next of our frequent spring rains will compress the soil around the seeds more gently and as much as is needed. Under these conditions, I would guess the optimal planting depth to be about ¾ inch, assuming no tamping down and ordinary wet weather. However, if the weather is drier than expected, the top inch or two of the soil might dry out completely, killing the germinating seeds that are only ¾ inch down. If I knew ahead of time to expect dry weather I would plant deeper.

For planting peas at the same time out on our lovely Willamette loam, I would guess 1 inch to be the perfect planting depth. For a later planting after the rains have ceased, made with dry seed, I would estimate 1 inch to 2 inches to be just right, and tamping down would be needed in order to achieve close enough contact between the seed and the soil to allow the seed to imbibe enough water for germination. This loam soil isn't as gooey as my backyard clay. Seeds can emerge through it pretty easily even when it is tamped down. If I had sandy soil I would plant deeper still.

In short, the best planting depth depends upon both the soil type and the weather for the entire period of germination, and the latter we can mostly only guess. My basic approach is to hedge my bets. I use a combination of over-seeding and selective sloppiness. I make furrows that make it easy to seed at every depth between 2 inches and the surface. I plant about two to three times as much seed as the number of plants I want. So whatever the coming weather, some seed will be at the best depth. With a little luck, about the right amount of seed comes up. If conditions are permissive and the seed at nearly all depths emerges, I end up with a stand a bit too dense and must then thin. I describe exactly how I make my furrows and do direct seeding (with minimal labor) in chapter 5.

In late spring or summer, rains are few and far between or long gone, and I usually water seeds in after I plant them. Alternatively, I tamp down dry seed (on loam) or plant presoaked seeds. (I never tamp down on heavy clay. If moisture isn't readily available, I water the seeds in or plant presoaked seed.)

Planting tiny seeds such as lettuce, carrot, or cabbage or other brassicas is an entirely different problem from planting big seeds. There are two major issues. First, it's very difficult to get tiny seeds covered with the right amount of soil. What is easy is planting them too deep for them to come up. The second problem is that, when tiny seeds are planted shallowly enough to germinate, they are within the area of soil that dries out completely given even a day or two without rain or watering. This dries out and kills the germinating seeds.

If I make a furrow to plant tiny seeds, I find that I invariably plant too deep. They need to be just barely covered with soil. Anything more than about ¼ inch tends to be too deep already. And ¼ inch is probably too deep in heavier soil. So I generally sprinkle the seeds on top of the (tilled or prepared) ground, then rake the surface lightly to bury seeds at variable depths. Some will be right on the surface. Some will be too deep. But some will be just the right depth.

Tiny little seeds planted at optimal depth are terribly vulnerable to drying out. Any day the surface of the ground is dry means I need to water. A misting style of watering is ideal. Big drops tend to smash, uproot, or bury the delicate germlings that emerge from tiny seeds. (I describe another approach to planting tiny seeds under water-limited conditions in chapter 6.)

After you are familiar with how to plant the tiniest and the biggest seed, you can extrapolate and mix and match methods as needed.

The Gambler's Guide to Transplants

Transplants can take much of the gamble out of spring. In spring of 2005, while I was gnashing my teeth over a garbanzo bean planting that had become a lake, my farmer-host Harry MacCormack's operation was little affected. Harry grows vegetables mostly from transplants. His transplants were all growing happily in greenhouses while outside it rained every day and the fields flooded. Garbanzo beans are not suitable for transplanting. However, with many crops, such as squash, brassicas, and lettuce, one has a choice. More erratic risky spring weather increases the risks associated with direct seeding and increases the relative advantages of transplants.

However, transplants cost more in money or labor than does direct seeding. This runs up the cost of losing a gamble. Here in Oregon, many overwintered crops are a bit of a gamble. They might make it most years but tend to freeze out or fail occasionally. Most experienced farmers plant many of such crops by direct seeding. The crop is worth the gamble involved in the occasional failure only if the costs and labor are kept low by direct seeding.

The cost of gambling on transplants also depends upon the kind of transplant. Our tomato transplants are big, a foot high or more, in big pots, and they require digging a big hole or trench by hand for planting. There is considerable investment in those big plants. And if something kills one, it is too late in the season to grow a replacement. So we don't gamble with our tomato transplants. We put them out in the field well after the last expected freeze. However, we plant our overwintering brassicas in plug trays and transplant directly to the field when the plants are just a couple of inches high. The holes we dig for the transplants are only a few inches deep. It takes less than a minute to dig the hole and transplant one of the plugs. And if something kills the brassicas, it doesn't take much time or effort to grow up another tray of a couple hundred little seedlings.

Greenhouses don't always provide protection against weird weather. At least twice in the last decade or so, we had heavy snow here in maritime Oregon. Most local organic farmers were heavily invested in greenhouses and hoop houses. They lost thousands of dollars when the structures collapsed from the unexpectedly heavy snow. Generally, we build such structures pretty light, since that is what is cost-effective in a region in which only occasional light snows are the norm.

At least, that is what used to be cost-effective. In addition, severe winds sometimes blow greenhouses or hoop houses over or away or smash trees or tree branches into them.

Presoaking Seeds and Germination Tests

It takes a higher temperature to germinate seeds of a variety than to grow the seedlings or established plants of that variety. That is, the temperature required for the seed to break dormancy, imbibe water, and start growing is higher than the temperature required for vegetative growth. Furthermore, seeds require more water to germinate than the seedlings require to grow. When we grow transplants in a greenhouse or indoors under lights, we provide that extra warmth and water for germination. However, in many cases we can get most of the benefits of growing transplants without the extra work just by presoaking the seeds.

I often presoak pea seed for the first early planting. We usually make that planting in February, on land that was prepared for it the previous fall. Usually, somewhere in February, there is enough of a break in the weather to plant and grow peas fine . . . if they germinate. Frequently, the little break of warm weather just doesn't last long enough to germinate the peas. So I like to start with seeds presoaked indoors, where it is warm enough for them to wake up, imbibe all the water they will need to germinate, and do so.

To presoak pea seed (or corn, beans, or any big seed), I put the seed in a huge bowl or bucket so I can add much more water than seeds. The biggest danger in presoaking seeds is killing them from lack of oxygen. So I use a container that holds at least 2 gallons of water for up to a quart of seeds.

I do the presoaking in the kitchen, and put the bowl somewhere obvious so I will be reminded to stir the seeds and water frequently and to replace the water at least three times per day as well. The stirring and replacing helps keep the water oxygenated. In addition, replacing the water a few times limits the danger from bacteria that tend to start growing if the seed stays very long in one batch of water. (Some nutrients leach out of the seed into the water and will support the growth of bacteria if not washed away.)

I always start off with cold water. This gives the seeds a gentle start. If you start off with warm water, many seeds imbibe water so rapidly the seed coats break. Seeds with broken coats release more nutrients into the water, encouraging the growth of bacteria. Broken seeds also don't germinate as regularly or do as well in the field. So I rinse the seeds, then start them in cold water. After an hour or two, I replace the water with warm water, and use warm water from then on.

I usually soak pea seed about a day or two. (Older seed and some varieties might take a day or two longer.) The object is to get the seeds to fully imbibe and begin to germinate, but to plant them just before they actually do germinate. I like to see the *radical* of the peas, the little taproot, swollen under the skin of the pea and ready to break through but not emerged yet. At that point I can remove the peas from the water, rinse them a final time, and plant them just as if they were dry peas, that is, walk down the furrow and just drop them in. If the radicals have just barely emerged, that's also OK. But if the radicals are much more than just emerged, they are vulnerable to breaking off. This means I have to get down on hands and knees to plant—knee-breaking work I prefer to avoid.

Once dormancy is broken by proper presoaking, the pea seed will usually grow no matter our February weather. If there is a freeze after planting, the primed seed just waits and grows afterward. With dry unstarted seed, a freeze right after planting usually means the seed rots instead of germinates. The presoaked seed actually behaves more like a baby pea plant than a seed, and baby pea plants can take freezing; they just wait out the freezes and return to growing happily whenever the temperature is above freezing again.

Presoaking is also a way to get around limited water during planting. Sometimes there is plenty of water in the ground, but the upper couple of inches are subject to drying out. Presoaked seeds can extend their roots through relatively dry ground into deeper, moister layers.

The disadvantages of presoaking seed are the work involved, and the fact that once you start the presoaking, you must then plant when the seeds are ready, whatever the weather or your own plans. So I don't usually presoak seed without cause. I tend to presoak the first early planting of peas in February, for example, but plant dry seed in all the subsequent plantings. I plant dry seeds of corn in May when there is plenty of soil moisture and more rain is expected. But if I do a late planting in June, I presoak the seed.

An added disadvantage of presoaking seeds: If some seeds are moldy or contaminated with bacteria, presoaking can contaminate and ruin the entire batch. Where I suspect mold or bacterial contamination of the seed and the numbers of seeds are small, I presoak the seeds on paper towels so that any contamination is limited to just the seeds carrying it. In addition, I usually start weak or inferior seed on paper towels. I also use this technique for germination tests.

To start seed on paper towels I use Brawny brand towels. (This is because many brands smell like mold when they are wet. Sniffing helps me tell if there is a problem, so I want the wet paper towels themselves to smell clean.) I pull off two to four sections of towel (depending on the size), fold them so as to make a double layer in a large tray, then run tap water into the tray to saturate the towels. Then I place a couple dozen seeds in two rows near the top edge of the towels. I place another swath of paper towels a couple of towels deep over the seeds and saturate these with water too. Then I roll up the towels with the seeds, fold the roll over once, place it in a gallon-size Ziploc bag, seal, and label it. There is excess water in the bottom of the bag, so the towels stay thoroughly saturated that first day.

After the first day of soaking, I open the bag, unroll the roll, and examine the seeds. If they have all swelled up completely, I roll the roll back up and *wring it out thoroughly*. I also dump all excess water out of the bag. This wringing must be done before the seeds start to germinate to avoid damaging them. Keeping the paper towels somewhat dry limits fungal or bacterial contamination to just the seed it came on.

I open each bag, unroll each roll, and examine the seeds daily. Without this, they run out of oxygen and die. (With an unsealed bag, it's too difficult to control moisture, and evaporating water cools the germinating seeds.) With weak seed, I sometimes orient the seeds so that they will be root down when the root emerges if I put the bags upright in a jar. Then I can give the seeds a bit more time and let them turn into baby plants for transplanting.

Tiny seeds can also be presoaked. For example, if I want to presoak kale seed, I mix a chosen amount of seed into a bucket or bowl of moist potting soil and leave it long enough for the seeds to just barely begin sprouting. (How long this is varies with the crop. It can be a day or two with brassicas or three weeks with carrots.) I then plant little pinches of potting soil. With some attention to the amount of seed and potting soil, each bit of soil has a couple dozen seeds, the right amount to sow into each planting position. (The seedlings are later thinned to the best plant per position.)

Presoaking seed is a powerful technique for dealing with unfavorable or erratic weather.

Climate Change, Diseases, and Pests

Climate change can translate into changes in disease or pest patterns. Now would not be a great time to plant a thousand-foot-long hedge of just one kind of bush or tree to be the centerpiece and visual highlight along the drive to your home. I say this as someone who once lived in a section of St. Paul, Minnesota, where the streets were lined with the stumps of huge elm trees, victims of Dutch elm disease. Those trees must have been beautiful once. But the city did not have funds to remove so many huge stumps at once. So they remained, a depressing eyesore. And the street was unshaded. In the future it might be better to plant a diversity of trees so that no disease is capable of wiping out every street tree in a city, and so that all the trees lining the streets don't die and have to be replaced all at once.

With respect to annuals, we can afford to gamble more, even with annuals we grow as staple crops. However, because of the potential for diseases and pests, old and new, I suggest not depending upon just one crop as your staple food supply or cash crop. Nate and I love our potatoes. But the Irish already did the critical experiment of depending too much on just potatoes. They also did the experiment of growing just one variety. So Nate and I spread out our risks. We plant about twenty varieties of potatoes. But even more critically, we don't grow just potatoes for our staple food supply. We also plant two corn varieties, six dry bean varieties representing six different species, and several squash varieties of three different species. In addition, the garden is full of fresh vegetables in summer and overwintering vegetables in winter. And the ducks give us eggs year-round.

Overwintering Crops, Staggered Planting, and Resilience

A single planting of corn is not as drought-resilient as three plantings in succession, each one coming to its most water-needy stage—tasseling out and pollination—at a different time. A short drought or a heat spell might destroy one planting and leave the others unscathed.

A single large planting of a single variety of corn doesn't provide as much resilience as three blocks, one with an early variety, another with a mid-season variety, and the third with a late variety, even if the corns are all planted at the same time. All will be vulnerable to germination failure if the weather doesn't cooperate during the single planting period. But the two earlier types can be replanted. The three blocks will tassel out and need the most water at different times. So if a minor drought hits, it will be likely to impact only one of the corns severely. The mid-season variety will yield more than the early corn, assuming a good selection of varieties. The late-season

variety will yield more still, if nothing happens to truncate the season. However, if something does truncate the season and ruin the late-season crop, there will still be a substantial harvest from the earlier varieties.

We plant our fava beans (*Vicia fava*) in the fall, grow them through the winter, and harvest them in late spring, all without irrigation. Fava bean plants of the right varieties overwinter well here, and they grow happily whenever the temperature is much above freezing, that is, during most of our winter. We plant 'Hannan Popbean', a garbanzo (*Cicer arietinum*), in early spring and harvest it in late spring, also without irrigation. It is also freeze resistant. The favas and popbeans give us resilience to any disaster that might involve a loss of irrigation water or of electricity for irrigation. However, an extreme winter-weather event could wipe out the favas, and an extreme spring event could wipe out both the favas and the garbs.

We have four other species of dry beans we grow, however, that are planted in spring and grown in summer with irrigation. They wouldn't be affected by a winter or early spring weather event. These represent four more different species. Two, the tepary and the cowpea, are relatively drought tolerant; we are going to try growing them without irrigation next year. Having several different species of beans that are grown in different times of the year gives us much more weather resilience than having several different varieties of one species that are all grown in the same time of year.

Eggs, Baskets, and Diversity

Diversifying is one of the major ways we deal with uncertainty. It is traditionally one of the ways farmers and gardeners have dealt with the unpredictability of weather. "Don't put all your eggs in one basket," as the old saying goes. But when I collect eggs from my flock of laying ducks, I use just one basket, and so does everyone else I know who has a laying flock. Why?

I put all my eggs in one basket because I need one hand for the basket and one for picking up the eggs, and two hands is all I've got. After I've collected the eggs, it's easier for me to carry one basket than two. I need one hand for opening and closing doors. If I go up the stairs using one hand on the banister, I'm less likely to stumble or fall, which is the main thing that might destroy a basket of eggs. If I fall, I'm going to smash all the eggs in all baskets, so having more baskets wouldn't help. And if I fell I might break more than a day's worth of eggs. Anyway, it wouldn't matter much if I dropped a basket and lost a day's eggs. I have eggs from other days. I also have plenty of other things to eat besides eggs. That is, I have diversity at higher levels, which allows me to choose convenience, efficiency, and safety over practicing diversity at the lower level of the individual day's baskets and eggs.

Diversifying in various ways is one of the major strategies for protecting ourselves from the worst of the consequences of damaging weather and many other kinds of hard times. However, diversification doesn't *automatically* protect us. Only certain kinds of diversity help with certain kinds of situations. We might have both June-bearing strawberries and cherries for fruit, for example. One is a short-term perennial, the other is a tree. One requires ladders and climbing, the other stoop labor. Birds may get all the cherries. Many a gardener with both fruits ends up actually only getting strawberries for themselves. The two

types of fruit are grown very differently and add diversity to the landscape and to the diet.

If you have either cherries or June-bearing strawberries, however, adding the other may be the least useful fruit choice. Both bear in spring. The harvests and labor demands overlap. If you are doing the harvesting, and you can't do it that year, for whatever reason, you lose both crops. If instead you had June-bearing strawberries and November-harvested apples, many of the weather events or labor problems that affected one would be over by the next harvest of the other. If you broke an arm in June and couldn't tend or harvest the strawberries, your arm would probably be all healed by November and eager to pick those apples. And much of the labor of caring for the apple trees was done back in the winter before you broke your arm.

Traditionally, farmers and market gardeners tried to diversify based at least partly upon labor demands. I think the same concept is useful for enhancing resilience on even the backyard garden scale. If you have an important crop that takes a lot of work in July, for instance, ideally you would try to choose additional crops that have their primary demands at other times.

The monocultural mega-farm, where human labor is a major component, depends upon a supply of transient migratory labor. Anything that isolates the farm might eliminate that labor supply. In addition, a transient labor supply can vanish in a flash when laws or rules are changed, or whenever those laborers have better options. The resilient farm needs to be diversified in such a way that the labor needs can be met by local labor. A combination of crops that spreads the need for labor out over the year is one tactic.

Diversifying is usually considered a way to limit

the damages of unfortunate weather. And it is, to a considerable extent. However, severe weather of some kinds may affect all the crops. In the Midwest, many farmers rotate corn and soybeans. But a severe drought will kill both.

Many of my friends with home orchards have a mix of apple, pear, cherry, and plum trees. This combination yields fruit from mid-spring through late fall. Most years, even when one type fails, others produce. In 2005, however, many orchards produced little fruit. It was cold and wet for so long in spring that pollination of all the fruit trees was poor. The fruits mature over a long period, but their flowers all need to be pollinated in spring, and the weather that spring was too cold for most of the insect pollinators. The wet weather also interfered with the ordinary timing windows for planting corn and squash. But there was still plenty of time for late plantings or replantings of short-season varieties of corn and squash. And animal and forage crops were largely unaffected. My ducks laid happily all through the unseasonable spring deluge, delighted that the backyard was so soggy and full of little ponds and puddles.

Diversification can take place at many levels. Sometimes higher levels are especially useful. Many a young couple who have started a market garden have focused too much on the crop level of diversification, paying full and proper attention to markets, labor requirements, water, and so forth—only to discover that, if you have unexpected expenses or less than expected income and lose the farm, it doesn't matter what crops you planted. Money in the bank, an income based upon something entirely separate from the garden, or at least one person in the family with an "ordinary" job all provide diversification at that higher level.

On Making Hay while the Sun Shines

"Make hay while the sun shines." We've all heard the expression. Here is the underlying reality: To make hay, you let the grass grow until it is just starting to flower, but before it starts setting seeds. At that point, the grass has its highest nutritional value. Then you choose a window of dry weather, cut the plants with a scythe, then rake the hay into windrows. Windrows are long shallow piles or rows in the field that allow the hay plants to dry out with plenty of air exposure so they dry fast and don't mold. A few days later, you rake the windrows of dry hay into piles and fork them into a wagon for hauling to the barn. If you're a modern farmer with a big farm, you cut and windrow the hay with huge machines, let it dry, then come back and bale it with another huge machine. But the drying of the hay in windrows is just as basic and primitive as it has always been, and if rain happens while the drying or dry hay is in windrows or bales sitting in the field, it molds just as fast. Ancient times or modern, huge landowner or peasant, enough hay for just one ox or thousands of acres of it—one thing is constant: You need dry weather for the entire operation. If the drying or dry hay gets rained upon, it will mold in the stack or bale and be ruined.

Haying by hand is hard work. In addition, the timing is critical. When the grass starts to flower, you need to hay it off at the first opportunity, that is, the first break in the weather that offers a few days of dryness for the operation. If you hay earlier, you have less hay with much less nutritional value. Traditionally, farmers often had and needed more hay land than they were likely to be able to deal with themselves during the narrow harvest window. They handled the problem by using work parties. All the men and boys in the neighborhood dropped whatever they were doing when it was time to hay someone's place. They did it as a gang. The womenfolk made great things to eat, and after the day's haying came the party. Generally, one piece of land was ready to hay at a slightly different time from another. So when the neighbor's hay was ready, you dropped what you were doing and went to help, just as he did for you. Generally, the amount of labor required all at once during the weather break would have been limiting if just one farm family had to do it. Each family could grow much more hay and minimize the labor bottleneck if many families pitched in and helped when each family's fields were ready for haying.

"Make hay while the sun shines" means more than just that you can't make hay at other times. It means that when you have the right break in the weather and the plants are at the right stage, *you must make hay then.* You must drop everything else you're doing and forget about anything else you might have preferred to do that day and make hay. That break in the weather that's good for haying your field may be the only one you get. If it starts raining, and continues raining too frequently for haying, the plants go beyond the prime stage for haying and lose much of their nutritional value. If the weather never dries out enough for haying, you may not get a hay crop at all that year. If it rains on your cut drying hay, it will mold and be ruined. This means either buying hay, or butchering or selling animals you would have preferred to keep.

In order to be able to make hay when the sun shines, the entire rest of your life must be run in such a way that you can drop everything else when it's time to make hay, and when that is going to be is unpredictable.

Many gardening tasks are like making hay when the sun shines. They are optimally done during a particular type of weather. Many can be done *only* during this particular weather. Transplanting is best done when it is cool and overcast so that there is less water stress on the plants while they are trying to establish new roots. Seeds are most easily planted when the soil is soft right after tilling. Wait too long and weeds will get a head start, and you had best till again before planting. The ideal time to plant is right after tilling and right before a nice rain that waters the seeds in and gives them a quick start.

I pull perennial weeds by hand when the ground is wet, because this is when the roots come out of the ground easily. I hoe annual weeds when the ground is drier, because you can't really hoe mud. It clogs the hoe. Weeding can be easily done with a hoe if the weeds are tiny. In fact, if you know exactly where your rows are, you can do your first weeding with a rake before the crop seedlings even emerge. The bigger the weeds get before they are hoed, the more they interfere with the plants and the harder it is to remove them at all with hoeing. So often, weeding is a little like haying, though the timing isn't usually quite as critical. Good gardening involves having the attitude that when the weather is optimal for a particular thing, or a certain task is most critical, that's what you do. And you arrange the rest of your life to be flexible enough to allow and support this attitude and pattern.

For many gardeners, the most critical break in the weather is the spring tilling. If you rototill or have someone with a tractor prepare your soil in spring, you have to have the soil dry enough so that it can be worked properly by the machine. You have somewhat the same problem even if it's just a bed at a time that needs to be hand-dug. Here in western Oregon, it rains pretty regularly through winter and early spring, and gardeners and farmers alike watch the weather with intense interest, watching for a break that allows the soil to dry enough for tilling or digging. Often there is exactly one good break in March. You do your tilling then, or you may not get it done until far later than is optimal. Occasionally there is no good break. Or the only good break may have happened back in February, when only the most alert and experienced gardeners and farmers took advantage of it. Those most alert and experienced folks—expert gardeners—they're flexible and opportunistic. They realize that there are normal patterns, and also that normal patterns shouldn't really be counted upon.

In northern areas people are often waiting for the snows to melt off their gardens and farms in spring, *and* the ground to dry out well enough to work, *and* the weather to warm up enough in spring to germinate the seeds. Gardeners watch the weather with intense interest. We go out and turn over a shovelful of earth as the soil seems to be getting close to the right stage. The exact right stage and first possible point at which you can work the soil depends upon the weather and the land and the soil itself. Well-drained soil dries out and can be worked earlier than soil that is less well drained. Sandy soil dries out faster than soil with a high clay content. So we watch carefully, and "clear our schedules" so that when it is time to work the soil, we can work the soil. Then, when the "shovel test" in a few different spots indicates that the soil is at the right stage, we haul out the rototiller or shovel or call the tractor guy.

The gardener is attentive—attentive to the plants, the soil, and the weather. The gardener is flexible and opportunistic. The gardener leaves room in her life to take advantage of opportunities. Being a gardener is a different mode of existence. Becoming a gardener changes you fundamentally.

Before you became a gardener, you might have filled your schedule. Most non-gardeners do. But anything unexpected then results in overload. And most of life is unexpected. So you were always overloaded. You never had time for anything spontaneous or unscheduled. (And when your friend or a family member needs you most, it is likely to be spontaneous or unscheduled.) You also seemed to live from crisis to crisis. You might have even thought your going from crisis to crisis "putting out fires everywhere" was because you were so important. In actuality, being always too busy for anything unscheduled or spontaneous— seemingly always to go from crisis to crisis—these are signs of a life not being lived as well as it could be, a life full of missed opportunities, a life too full of busyness for most of what makes a life worth living.

Now, as a gardener, you leave time for the unexpected. You make flexibility in your life. You minimize scheduling. You take on only what is reasonable. You know the unexpected is always happening, so you don't make plans for every hour. You leave plenty of room in your plans, your schedule, and your life. You do this because you need to be ready to drop everything and tend the garden when it needs it. But now you find that you also, magically, seem to have more time for your child, or your elderly mother, or your friend. And when your friend or someone in your family has a crisis, it is easy to be there when you are most needed. You are a better gardener, a better friend, a better parent and family member, and a calmer, happier person. You are now an expert gardener. Your garden is transformed. Your garden is transforming.

For many gardeners, what we enjoy most about gardening is not so much what we grow as who we become. We gardeners are healthy, joyous, natural creatures. We are practical, patient, optimistic. We declare our optimism every year, every season, with every act of planting. We engage in regular, purposeful exercise. We eat a large variety of delicious foods we harvest and prepare with our own hands. We notice everything. We accept everything. We use everything that comes our way. We feel the birth and ebb and flow of everything. We are part of the pattern. We are rooted firmly in the natural world, as aware of the plants, soil, winds, and weather as any other natural thing. We gardeners are fully connected to the land of our living.

CHAPTER FOUR

Diet and Food Resilience

Two Orange Trunks and a New England Flood. Buying Patterns, Apples, and Resilience. The Nut Lady—on Nuts, Opportunism, and Oral Tradition. Trading, Swapping, Borrowing, and Gifts. Water. Choosing Your Calorie and Protein Staples. Wheat Allergies, Gluten Intolerance, and Celiac Disease. Ideal Storage Conditions for 49 Fruits and Vegetables that Keep Longer than Two Months. Milling and Storing Whole-Grain Flour. Using Whole-Grain Gluten-Free Flours. Asthma, Allergies, and Adventures with Omega-3 Fatty Acids. Buying Grass-Fed Meat and Dairy Products. The Missing Ingredient— Can What We Aren't Eating Make Us Fat? How to Let Your Body Tell You What It Needs. A Different Conceptual Framework for Understanding Obesity. Sugar. Salt, High Blood Pressure, and Edema. Other Oils and Fats. Vitamins, Minerals, Phytochemicals, and Fiber. Special Implications for Vegetarians and Those with Celiac Disease or Gluten Intolerance, or Who Can't Eat Dairy Products. Preserving and Storing Methods. Drying Fruits and Vegetables. Dehydrators. Drying Prune Plums (and Figs, Apricots, Peaches, and Nectarines). Hoarding and Saving Seeds.

Two Orange Trunks and a New England Flood

Part of the tradition of my family was the two orange trunks. Bags of rice and beans and other emergency supplies were stored in the trunks. The trunks could be quickly loaded into a car if an emergency required leaving. The rice and dry beans were a regular part of our diet and were turned over regularly. We kids (older sister Janice, younger brother Mark, and I) were taught to stockpile the basics. Food and water. It wasn't so much the specific contents in the stash as the principle that mattered, and the teaching of that principle to one's children.

My sister Janice, who lives in New Hampshire, has always stored rice and beans, certain canned foods she really likes, water, and other items. She always felt a bit chagrined about it, she admitted to me, but did it anyway. Then came the summer of 2006. It started raining in New England, and it forgot to stop. Janice's town got more than 14 inches of rain in a few days. The river flooded its banks and put water more than 10 feet deep in the downtown. The rains and floods washed out many of the roads. Furthermore, the dam was threatening to break, and residents in the endangered area had to be evacuated.

Janice lives on high ground and was in no danger from the floods. But most roads were impassable, power lines were down everywhere, and most grocery stores were flooded or unreachable. Janice didn't know whether any stores were reachable, even by circuitous routes, from where she lived—or whether, if reached, they would have anything in them, given the flooded highways and disruptions in deliveries. Because of her stash of water and food, however, Janice was in no danger from even worry. She just stayed home. She did not have to risk driving treacherous roads to try to reach stores that might have been inaccessible or empty. Janice no longer feels chagrined about her emergency stash of food and water.

The food in my parents' orange trunks, as I recall, was mostly scores of one-pound bags of white rice, navy beans, and kidney beans, all commercial quality. Those could be a blessing in a crisis. They aren't my choice today. But the basic principle still applies. That is, foresight suggests having a supply of food enough to last at least a few months, and that food supply should be things you like and eat regularly and turn over regularly, so that they are never much more than a year old. That way, in a crisis, you have food you know how to prepare and enjoy, which is both practical and comforting. And your stash never gets old and stale.

I've never experienced a huge disaster. But there have been lots of minor events that could have become emergencies if I had needed to travel for food or water. There was the week without electricity after a winter storm, with debris and power lines down on the roads everywhere. That was a week without electricity, heat, water, or a stove. (The water pump and stove are electric.) Fortunately, I had plenty of food, a stash of water, and propane camping gear for cooking. The power goes out for several hours at a time about three times a year. When it does, we never know whether it will be out for hours or days. Having the stash is reassuring. There have also been icy

enough conditions a few times so that the steep road between our home and the highway became impassable, thus isolating my neighborhood. These things can become emergencies if you try to travel. If you have the option of just staying home, they are merely inconveniences.

Buying Patterns, Apples, and Resilience

In the fall of 1972, shortly after I moved to St. Paul, Minnesota, one of my new faculty colleagues took me to The Apple Barn. There, with thousands of other city folk, I participated in a venerable tradition. I tasted a few dozen varieties of apples and bought a bushel of each of my favorites. That was the basic pattern for customers of The Apple Barn. We bought an entire winter's supply of apples directly from the farmer in the fall, then stored the apples in our cellars. Houses all had cellars for the furnaces, and the cellars were normally unheated except for the indirect warmth from the furnace. In such cellars, the right apple varieties would keep through the winter.

Imagine a city or town or region in which every family has several bushels of apples tucked away. Given a personal or regional emergency in the winter, those families would have at least some weeks of food, just based upon those apples. In addition, the local economy, as well as regional food resilience, is enhanced when all those apples are grown, bought, and eaten locally, and stored in thousands of separate cellars throughout the region. That apple farmer would still have customers and would still be in business, even if Minnesota was temporarily cut off from the rest of the planet.

Buying patterns profoundly affect food resilience. If you buy a few potatoes at a time, you never have more than a few. If you buy potatoes by the 25-pound bag, much of the time, you have enough for at least a few meals. If you go one step further and buy several boxes or bags of potatoes directly from the farmer right after harvest and store them yourself, you can get better potatoes, of gourmet instead of commercial types. And during much of the fall and winter, you have a serious stash of food. If you usually use 50 pounds of rice a year, consider buying a 50-pound bag each fall (after the harvest).

For the serious gardener, the delights and possibilities associated with growing and storing more of our staple foods are endless. You may never experience a serious, general, long-term disaster of the sort that makes it critical that your family has a hundred pounds or more of grain, a couple hundred pounds of potatoes, as well as bushels of fruit or vegetables or a 5-gallon bucket or two of sauerkraut tucked away. But if you lose your job, it will help if you can say, "Well, whatever else, we aren't going to go hungry any time soon."

Meanwhile, good times or bad, if an unexpected guest or two (or two dozen) arrive(s), you'll be able to provide a good meal. Or many good meals, if need be. And if that grain is a true polenta corn you've grown yourself, or the soup is unique and delicious because it's based upon the dry squash from an especially good drying variety, or the sauerkraut is the best anyone has ever had—these foods will add delight to your everyday life, enhance any feast, and become a conversation piece for company. This is the kind of stashing and storing I suggest: a style designed primarily to enhance the quality of our lives in ordinary times—which, secondarily, also serves to enhance our personal and regional resilience in hard times.

This is a gardening book, and part of what I want to encourage is more gardening, and especially, more growing of food, especially staples. However, growing food is only part of food resilience. Other critical components include buying patterns where relevant, storing patterns, and, most especially, the patterns of using. You can learn to grow staple crops pretty easily. It is actually much harder to learn to use them and reincorporate them into your diet. Many people have become used to highly processed and prepared food. When they go to grow field corn, the biggest problem isn't *growing* the corn. It's the fact that they don't know how to *use* the corn. What they are used to in the way of corn is store-bought corn chips or ready-made tortillas or muffin mixes. To grow and use staples is as much an exploration and education and reeducation in the kitchen as in the garden. For this reason, the chapters on staple crops in this book are as much about using them as growing them.

The Nut Lady—on Nuts, Opportunism, and Oral Tradition

Much of my hometown of Corvallis, Oregon, was orchard in the pioneer past. Many streets are still landscaped with apple, pear, walnut, and hazelnut trees. Huge walnut trees dump hundreds of pounds of walnuts in the fall and make myriad dents in the tops of any cars parked under them. European filberts, which are especially large, delicious hazelnuts, thrive in the maritime Northwest. In 1981, shortly after I moved to Oregon, I found myself jobless and gardenless in a neighborhood full of old walnut and filbert trees. The walnuts were bitter and the filberts were all full of worms. No one wanted the nuts. They just accumulated under the trees and became debris. The trees hadn't been tended in decades. No one I knew who collected the nuts ever tried to eat more than a few. Apparently, every walnut tree in Corvallis produced bitter nuts and every hazelnut tree, wormy hazelnuts. Yet pioneers must have delighted in those nuts. I figured they must have known something I didn't. Just what that was didn't seem to be in the books. Books acted like walnuts and hazelnuts were edible. Why weren't ours? I was a new Oregonian. But there were plenty of long-time Oregonians walking around. If I asked enough of them, maybe I could figure out what was going on with the nuts.

I knocked on three doors within two blocks of my apartment and got permission to collect nuts. The owners of the trees agreed readily after warning me that the walnuts were bitter and the hazelnuts all had worms. I started with a pair of hazelnut trees on 5th Street, because the sidewalk there was busiest. I decided that I would take my bags there and stop every passerby and ask what he or she knew about harvesting, processing, and storing nuts. The bags and collecting was just theatrics, initially. I was really after information.

The very first person I stopped was a woman who, it turned out, had, with her husband, run a walnut and hazelnut orchard back in World War II and before. We sat in the shade under the trees for more than half an hour, and she instructed me.

The walnuts that accumulate under city trees are perfectly good walnuts, the Nut Lady told me. The problem is, the nuts need to be removed promptly from their husks. The nuts mature during our rainy season. Some nuts fall free of the husks, but most fall with the husks on. The husks

are usually somewhat gooey and partly rotten. They are very bitter. You need to collect the nuts and remove the husks within a day or two of when they fall. If you leave the husks on a while, the bitterness leaches through the shells and into the nutmeats. So all I needed to do was discard the nuts that had already fallen, come back every few days to harvest freshly fallen nuts, then remove the husks promptly. (The trees were too big to shake.) The husks on the fallen nuts are easy to strip off by hand. Then you dry the nuts. They are green at first, don't taste good, and will give you indigestion. The Nut Lady's farm had commercial dryers, but they aren't necessary for a family-sized crop. I could just do what the pioneers did, and put the nuts in mesh bags such as onion bags, and hang the bags anywhere indoors, and allow the nuts to dry naturally. So said the Nut Lady. And she was right.

The situation with the hazelnuts was a bit more complicated. A few hazelnuts get worms in them while on the tree and fall prematurely. But most of the nuts are ruined because of a different worm that gets into the nut from the ground under the trees. Neglected trees have such high concentrations of these worms that virtually every nut that is dropped and left on the ground ends up with a worm. So said the Nut Lady. So you start by clearing all the fallen nuts out from under the trees and discarding them. Then you shake the trees and pick up the newly fallen nuts.

Filbert trees are small and easy to shake. I put a couple of old sheets under the trees to catch many of the nuts as they fell, then crawled around on my hands and knees to collect the rest and toss them on the sheets. I went back daily for a week or so, each day discarding the few fallen nuts and shaking off a fresh batch.

There is an additional trick the Nut Lady told me. Nuts that drop prematurely because they have a worm in them don't release from the cap easily. Most nuts fall free or can be removed from the cap by a flick of the finger. Those that don't should be discarded. With these two picking tricks, nearly every nut I collected was worm-free and perfect, even though the trees had not been tended in years. The hazelnuts, like the walnuts, needed to be put into net bags and allowed to dry for a few weeks before being ready to eat.

With the wisdom of the Nut Lady and a couple hours of work a day for a week or so, I put away several big onion bags of walnuts and hazelnuts—80 pounds of walnuts and about 200 pounds of filberts—all prime nuts. I ran a rope between two walls in my tiny two-room apartment and hung the bags of nuts in such a way that they were fully visible but out of the way. This was back in the early 1980s. Not much was going well in my life at that point. Being able to look up and see nearly three hundred pounds of prime, gourmet-quality, nutritious food provided both meaningful food security and emotional comfort.

What nuts grow in your yard, your neighborhood, your region? What fruits? What grains? What other agricultural crops? Do you know how to harvest, store, and use them? Have you ever done it? *Reading isn't doing.* Many food-harvesting and storing problems and techniques are regional. Are there older people around who know things that you might want or need to know some day? Better get them to teach you now. No one lives forever. In addition, the knowledge and skills involved in storing and processing food are most easily learned when times are good, and when learning the skills is a matter of fun and exploration.

Trading, Swapping, Borrowing, and Gifts

Humans have been specializing and trading for thousands of years. We *enjoy* it. It greases the social wheels, and we are social creatures. In addition, no one piece of land is suitable for all the crops that can be grown in a particular region. Even now, when Nate and I do grow most of our food and we could grow nearly everything, we don't. We specialize in certain things, sell or trade those, and buy others. We sell or trade potatoes, duck eggs, and seeds, for example, and buy or trade for fruit. We also forage wild fruit as well as offer to pick other people's fruit in exchange for a share of the harvest. (Fruit trees don't fit as well as annual crops into a regime of leased land.)

The pioneer settlers in the Willamette Valley were not "independent." They did not smelt the iron for their tools or make their guns or even grow all their food. They grew certain things, made certain things, had certain skills, and swapped, gifted, and traded for the rest. The Kalapuya Indians who lived on this land before European pioneers weren't independent either. They were camas specialists. They went to the regional bazaars on the Columbia River and traded camas cakes and dried elk and venison for dried salmon and other things. Nate once discovered an obsidian flake in our leased field when he was hoeing. The closest sources of obsidian are in the southern Cascades. That flake came from a chunk of trade obsidian in the hands of an Indian, who at some point, in some era, sat on the high ground above the camas field in the wetland below, right where we are gardening now, and made a tool. He wasn't independent, and neither are we.

Trading is sometimes called "trading" and is formal and exact. Sometimes the trading and sharing is called "gifts." The categories overlap. You share your bounty of one thing. Friends and neighbors share their bounty of other things.

When you first move to the countryside, accept all presents joyfully. This person's pie. That person's bushel of apples after they've just been harvested. Someone offers to help you get in your firewood. Another offers to take care of your kids while you go to town. They are showing off their skills and meeting you with expressions of goodwill. In addition, as your new neighbors, they are trying to work you into their trade and labor-exchange network. You need to do your part. Figure out what you can share, what you can produce extra of, and what skills you have (or can develop) that are worthy of sharing. You share the delights of the good things you have in life. Part of the good things others have comes back to you. Everyone enjoys the fruits of a larger variety of crops and skills and land than they have themselves. Each trade or gift helps create and reinforce the social bonds and the goodwill among friends and neighbors. Then, when one person or family gets in trouble, they are not alone or abandoned. They are part of a network of people who know and care about each other, who can and often will step in and help each other. Our friends, neighbors, and communities are an essential part of our resilience.

Water

The most important food is water. Most people can survive weeks without food. We may not be optimally happy or functional, but we wouldn't die. Water is much more critical. Potable water is a problem in many kinds of emergencies and lesser situations. I keep ten gallons of water—just tap water, which is well water for me—in half-gallon glass jars on a shelf near the sink. I turn it over regularly by using it as part of my ordinary patterns. (Half-gallon jars are the biggest that can be handled and poured with one hand. I use wide-mouth jars, which are easiest to wash. For storing water I use plastic screw-on lids, which are bought separately.) There is another 50 gallons or so of water in plastic containers in the garage that isn't turned over and tastes heavily of plastic. It's a backup supply. I've also rigged part of the drainage from the roof so that it runs first into a 50-gallon barrel and keeps it filled. That's pretty foul stuff but is backup emergency water for the ducks.

I would like to have a well with a hand- or foot-driven mechanical pump for a backup system for a longer disaster. (I'll look into it the next time I need to replace the well pump.) A system to collect and store rainwater and a gray-water system would also be useful. But the basic water stash, good for about a month, is as far as I've got. The rest will happen as opportunity and finances permit.

My 10 gallons of prime water in glass half-gallon jars is all I've needed so far in my life. It's useful to have, even in the best of times. When I cook, I start with the room-temperature water; it comes to a boil much more rapidly than cold well water. Instead of having to run the tap for a while to clear the pipes and get fresh water each time I want a glass, I reach for the jugs in the refrigerator or the supply of room-temperature water on the shelf. I like having both chilled water and room-temperature water available. On hot summer afternoons, I like the chilled water from the refrigerator. In winter I prefer water at room temperature rather than drinking it as cold as it is fresh from the well.

Choosing Your Calorie and Protein Staples

After water, the most important characteristic of food is calories. It is lack of calories that will put you in the most trouble the fastest. After water and calories, protein is next in importance. As gardeners, we grow a variety of greens and vegetables. But to be *resilient* gardeners, we need to be skilled at growing more than just salads. We need to be able to grow some of our calorie and protein staples.

When people find out that I am breeding gourmet specialty field corns and use these as my major grain staple, they often immediately ask me how much corn I grow to provide all the carbohydrates and calories I need for a year. My response? *I don't approach diet or staple crops that way.*

In summer, my calories come primarily from fruit. In fall, potatoes and fall squash and fruit are the main calorie staples. Through most of winter the main staples are potatoes and winter squash. I depend upon dry grains (corn) and dry grain legumes (garbanzos, beans, cowpeas, favas, teparies) primarily during late winter and early spring before new potatoes and fruit again become available. The corn products— the polenta, cornbread, corncakes, savory brown gravy, and parching corn—are essential during this "hunger gap," as are the dry beans and squash. The rest of the year they add variety but play secondary roles. There are greens from the garden and duck eggs year-round as well as

tomatoes and other warm-season vegetables in summer. There is overwintering kale and other overwintering vegetables in winter. This pattern provides lots of variety and lets me fully enjoy and celebrate the bounty of each season. I think it is a more practical diet for most gardeners in most areas of the country than a diet based upon day-in-day-out unrelenting emphasis on dry grains. In addition, this approach to staples brings the amount of dry grains and grain legumes needed by a family down to what it is relatively easy and fun and manageable to grow and store.

Here are some possible excellent high-calorie crops: potatoes, sweet potatoes, winter squash, fruit, nuts, corn, beans and other grain legumes, wheat, other small grains, alternative grains, and sunflower seeds. Meat, milk, eggs, game, and fish can also deliver lots of calories in addition to being excellent protein sources.

Grains also contain significant amounts of proteins. Grain legumes are richer in protein than grains and also have substantial amounts of carbohydrates and calories. Grain legumes don't yield as much as the better-yielding grains on a field basis. But on a backyard scale, grain legumes are easier to thresh, clean, and use than grains (except for corn). Nuts and sunflower seeds are also good sources of protein.

Potatoes are unexcelled as a carbohydrate *and* protein source. A 2,000-calorie all-potato diet actually contains as much or more usable protein as a 2,000-calorie all-wheat diet and considerably more than a 2,000-calorie all-rice diet. In addition, it's *much* easier to grow 2,000 calories of potatoes than 2,000 calories of any grain (even corn). Furthermore, potatoes can be grown in areas too cold or too wet to grow grain. Potatoes have so many varieties with distinctive flavors and lend themselves to such a diversity of cooking methods that it is easy to eat potatoes every day for months and never get tired of them.

Corn, other grains, dry grain legumes, and nuts have a unique role, however. These are the crops that can be stored for years without electricity, so they are our ultimate backup crops. Stored supplies of these would be critical should we ever experience any worldwide mega-disaster that destroys all agriculture for an entire season or more. In routine years, these crops get us through the "hunger gap" in spring as well as provide year-round variety. I cover potatoes, corn, beans, and squash in detail in separate chapters. In this chapter, I will outline the basic agricultural and nutritional roles of all of our major staple crops as well as touch upon certain relevant aspects of other crops that are sometimes used or considered for use as staples.

Corn is usually the first choice of the grains for growing on the homestead scale anywhere it can be grown. It is much easier to grow than other grains and yields better. It is native to this continent and isn't so inclined to disease as wheat and its relatives. Corn is also *immensely* easier to process by hand.

Pioneer settlers in Oregon, for example, grew corn first because they could plant it using just a large hoe in land between girdled trees and tree stumps. They didn't grow wheat until the stumps were removed and the land could be tilled with draft animals. (Wheat and other small grains need a fine seedbed.) Even after the pioneers began growing wheat, it was enough harder to grow that they tended to use it as currency and ate the corn. And even later, after they had enough wheat to eat themselves, pioneers still didn't have bread. They ate their wheat in the form of cooked whole wheat berries or crude porridge, because they still didn't have wheat mills. Mills good enough to mill wheat into bread flour were a community-scale development. Farmers normally needed to cart their wheat to the local mill and bring back the milled flour. Corn, on the other hand, was ground on every homestead with small inexpensive hand mills, readily available then as now. Lewis and Clark carried a corn mill with them.

Wheat and wheat relatives—rye, barley, triticale, spelt, farro, and emmer—are good grain choices for many people. Wheat, rye, barley, and triticale can be overwintered in many places. They can be grown in regions too cold for corn. Wheat is the easiest of the small grains to thresh. Rye is next. Rye can be grown in areas that are too cold for wheat. Triticale (a wheat/rye hybrid) seems to be more theoretically interesting than practical. It doesn't yield well enough to compete with wheat and rye, and is harder to thresh than both. Barley has a hull that isn't easy to remove using home methods. Barley, though, is especially useful for making beer because its starch-digesting enzymes, unlike those of most grains, are water-soluble. To make barley malt for beer, you don't need to remove the hulls.

Wheat and all these wheat relatives contain gluten, so for those with celiac disease or wheat-related allergies or gluten problems of any sort, none of these grains is a viable choice. Spelt is a kind of wheat. It has less gluten than most wheat but not none. So spelt, contrary to what is often claimed, is absolutely *not* a good choice if you have problems with wheat or gluten. Beer made from barley, alas, also contains gluten and should usually be avoided by those with wheat or

Wheat Allergies, Gluten Intolerance, and Celiac Disease

Many people simply don't do very well with a diet that includes wheat. Some people are allergic to wheat proteins, and experience asthma, allergies, hives, rashes, or other allergic reactions when wheat is part of their diets. Others have celiac disease, in which an allergic reaction to wheat proteins in the intestine itself causes an auto-immune reaction that destroys the villi, the nutrient absorbing structures in the intestine. This damage leads to malabsorption for many critical nutrients and vitamins.

Celiac disease is diagnosed by intestinal biopsy. The trashed and degraded villi are obvious. The treatment is simple. Avoid all wheat and wheat-related grains. In the United States, celiac disease is widely under-diagnosed. It takes people an average of nine years from when they start having serious enough problems to seek medical help to when they get a good diagnosis. My impression is that you are much more likely to get that diagnosis by reading or hearing about celiac disease yourself and going to a specialist for testing than by getting the information and diagnosis from the general (non-specialist) medical profession.

The definitive book on the medicine, biology, and treatment of celiac disease is *Celiac Disease: A Hidden Epidemic*, by Peter H. R. Green, M.D. and Rory Jones. (See note 4-20.) Green, who is director of the Celiac Disease Center at Columbia University, lists characteristic symptoms of celiac disease as bloating, gas, stomach cramps, diarrhea, constipation, joint pain, numbness or tingling in hands or feet, itchy skin lesions, fatigue, and headaches or migraines.

Celiacs are often diagnosed as having irritable bowel syndrome, eczema, unexplained dermatitis, fibromyalgia, chronic fatigue syndrome, or nervous stomach (non-ulcer dyspepsia). (These words are basically just descriptions of symptoms instead of a real diagnosis of causes. The underlying cause may be celiac disease.)

In addition, according to Green, many people with the following diseases may have celiac disease as an underlying cause or a related problem: lactose intolerance, osteopenia, osteoporosis, peripheral neuropathy, non-Hodgkin's lymphoma, small intestinal cancer, psychiatric disorders or depression, anemia, infertility, and all autoimmune disorders including thyroid disease, type 1 diabetes, Sjögren's syndrome, chronic liver disease, or an immediate family member with celiac disease or any other autoimmune condition. So Green recommends that everyone with any of these conditions be tested for celiac disease.

Some people are intolerant of wheat and have digestive upset when they eat it, but don't show the classic sign of degraded villi that is characteristic of celiac disease. Whatever the cause of a person's difficulty with eating wheat, however, ceasing to eat wheat, taking control of our food supply, and expanding our repertoire of other delicious staple foods is the solution.

gluten problems. There are hull-less barley varieties available, but I have no experience with them.

Many gardeners here who experiment with wheat often sneer at the traditional northwestern soft white winter wheats because they are lower in protein than hard wheats. However, we cannot grow high-protein wheat in winter, whatever the variety. Winter rains leach so much nitrogen from the soil, there isn't enough to support growing a wheat with a high protein content. So growing higher-protein hard wheat here requires using spring varieties, which doesn't take advantage of our natural cycle of rain. However, there is no reason to get so carried away with protein content. Keep things in perspective. Soft white wheat still has considerably more protein than rice. Furthermore, any kind of wheat can make good bread. The breads with lower protein content have a heavier, denser texture than those made from flour with a higher protein content. But all the extra air in fluffier loaves doesn't have any particular food value. If you like wheat and like making bread, any wheat you can grow in your region is a good choice.

You don't have to choose between the extremes of agribusiness wheat versus growing your own. If you live in a wheat-growing region, consider buying a few bushels of cleaned wheat (a year's supply) from a local farmer and just doing your own milling. Fresh-milled whole wheat is going to be much tastier than commercial flour, even when it is of the same variety. And as an emergency food supply, having a year's supply of wheat matters lots more than who grew it.

Oats can be grown in regions that are too cold for wheat. Some varieties can even be overwintered in some areas. Most varieties, spring or fall types, will overwinter in the maritime Northwest. However, oats are not easy to thresh on a home scale. They are not even threshable by large farms with combines and lots of grain-handling equipment. However, there is considerable new interest in home-scale grain growing and handling, so check the Internet for updates. As it stands now, however, oats are generally grown on a small scale as cover crops or hay or for use without dehulling as animal feed.

Most commercial oats are contaminated with wheat grains and wheat gluten because they are grown by the same people, combined with the same machines, and milled in the same mills as wheat. So commercial oats and oat products are treacherous and unpredictable for people with gluten or wheat problems. However, pure oats are gluten free.

There are "hull-less" oat varieties available. Most varieties I've seen have too many hulled oats among the hull-less ones to work for me. We are advised to "float the hulled grains away in water and then redry the grain." That might work for a handful of grain, but certainly isn't scalable to amounts needed for a serious staple crop. In addition, everyone I know who has grown hull-less oats ended up with fatter and happier birds but no oats. I invite anyone who has information on growing hull-less oats or dehulling regular oats on a home scale to contact me.

Other grains. Some people grow and use tiny grains such as amaranth or teff. These have the disadvantage that they can't be milled in the electric mills or hand mills available for home use. They have to be boiled up into whole-grain porridge. I don't find the porridges particularly enticing in flavor or texture. In addition, the main thing I want from a grain is bread. For that I need flour. Buckwheat is easy to grow but impossible to thresh on a home scale. I've grown quinoa. I still have a bucket of uncleaned seed full of debris. Cleaning it without some kind of thresher is torturous. I cheerfully process hundreds of pounds of corn and beans every season, but I will be happy to never clean another pound of quinoa again in my life.

I don't grow teff. I do use teff flour, though, since it can be bought directly from the farm, the Teff Company, in Idaho. (See note 4-3.) The Teff Company produces both brown and ivory teff, mills it daily on dedicated mills, and doesn't produce wheat. So their teff flour is totally gluten free. They ship immediately after milling. I store my flour in the freezer. Bought in 25-pound amounts, their teff flour is reasonably priced for a gluten-free flour (a bit over $2 a pound, including shipping). Brown teff flour is pretty strong flavored. It is generally preferred for *injera*, the traditional fermented teff-flour pancake, a national dish from the homeland of teff, Ethiopia. Teff flour makes spectacularly delicious sourdough or standard pancakes. I prefer it to all other flours for pancakes. Teff flour also makes a good Universal Skillet Bread.

Gene Logsdon's classic book on homestead-scale grain growing has recently been released in a new expanded second edition under the title *Small-Scale Grain Raising: An Organic Guide to Growing, Processing, and Using Nutritious Whole Grains for Home Gardeners and Local Farmers.* This book is the *Small Is Beautiful* of grain growing, and Gene Logsdon is one of the founding curmudgeons of modern garden farming and sustainable agriculture. *Small-Scale Grain Raising* covers all major and most minor, new, or alternative grains, including corn, wheat, rye, triticale, sorghum, milo, buckwheat, rice, wild rice, amaranth, and others. Of particular value is the information on threshing and dehulling. For many grains, it is the problems with threshing or dehulling that limit the grain's role or usefulness when grown on a home scale.

Fruit is underrated as a calorie staple. Apples can be worked into salads, added to stir-fries and soups, served as one ingredient in sweet-and-sour dishes, and basically treated as a high-calorie vegetable as well as a fruit. One of my favorite salads in winter is what I call Winter Salad. It is just a mix of sauerkraut, apples, daikon radishes, and whatever else that is around that is crunchy. The fermented kraut juice keeps the apples from browning. Winter Salad will keep several days in the refrigerator. Apples go great in most salads. I love apples and daikon radishes in my tuna salads. Any sandwich is improved by a layer of thinly sliced apples. When we learn to use fruit in savory dishes, we greatly extend its usefulness and versatility. Virtually any sweet-and-sour dish can be made with fruit or fruit purée as the sweet component.

Some varieties of apples and pears keep well all winter long in root cellars. Some varieties even require such a period of storing for optimal flavor. (Many russeted varieties of apples taste starchy when first picked and become sweet and spicy and delicious only after a month or more of storage. 'Comice' pears should be stored at least a month before eating.) Fruit also lends itself to both canning and drying. In addition, you can build a tree house in an apple tree but not in a corn plant.

In the shell, many *nuts* are prime from harvest until considerably after the next nut crop is in and

Table 1: Ideal Storage Conditions for 49 Fruits and Vegetables That Keep Longer Than Two Months[1]				
	°F	°C	Relative humidity (%)	Storage life
Apples	30–40	-1–4	90–95	2–7 months
Asian pear	34	1	90–95	5–6 months
Beets (topped)	32	0	98–100	4–6 months
Boniato	55–60	13–15	85–95	4–5 months
Cabbage (late)	32	0	98–100	5–6 months
Calabaza	50–55	10–13	50–70	2–3 months
Carrots (topped)	32	0	98–100	7–9 months
Celeriac	32	0	97–99	6–8 months
Celery	32	0	98–100	1–3 months
Chinese cabbage	32	0	95–100	2–3 months
Cranberries	36–40	2–4	90–95	2–4 months
Daikon radish	32–34	0–1	95–100	4 months
Dates	0 or 32	-18 or 0	75	6–12 months
Garlic	32	0	65–70	6–7 months
Ginger root	55	13	65	4–6 months
Grapes (Vinifera)	30–31	-1– -0.5	90–95	2–6 months
Horseradish	30–32	-1–0	98–100	10–12 months
Jaffa orange	46–50	8–10	85–90	2–3 months
Jerusalem artichoke	31–32	-0.5–0	90–95	4–5 months
Kiwano	50–60	10–15	90	6 months
Kiwifruit	32	0	90	3–4 months
Kohlrabi	32	0	98–100	2–3 months
Leeks	32	0	95–100	3 months
Lemons	50–55	10–13	85–90	2–3 months
Limes	48–50	9–10	85–90	6–8 weeks
Lo Bok	32–35	0–1.5	95–100	2–4 months
Malanga	45	7	70–80	3 months
Onions (dry)	32	0	65–70	1–8 months
Onion sets	32	0	65–70	6–8 months
Oranges	32–48	0–9	85–90	1–3 months
Parsnips	32	0	95–100	6 months
Pears	29–31	-1.5– -0.5	90–95	2–8 months
Persimmons, Japanese	30	-1	90	2–4 months
Pomegranates	41	5	90–95	2–3 months

	°F	°C	Relative humidity (%)	Storage life
Potatoes (early)	40	4	95	3–5 months
Potatoes (late crop)	40–55	4–13	95	5–10 months
Pummelo	45–48	7–9	85–90	2–3 months
Pumpkins²	50–55	10–13	50–70	2–3 months
Quinces	31–32	-0.5–0	90	2–3 months
Radishes, winter	32	0	95–100	3–4 months
Rutabagas	32	0	98–100	4–6 months
Salsify	32	0	95–98	2–4 months
Scorzonera	32–34	0–1	95–98	6 months
Squash, winter	50	10	50–70	2–6 months³
Sweet potatoes	55–60	13–15	85–90	4–10 months
Tamarillos	37–40	3–4	85–90	2–3 months
Taro root	45–50	7–10	85–90	4–5 months
Turnips	32	0	95	4–5 months
Yams (true)	61	16	70–80	3–6 months

¹Selected data from Welby and McGregor, USDA Agriculture Handbook 700. See note 4-16.
²Probably means only the standard orange Halloween pumpkins.
³With the right varieties, more than 6 months is possible, in my experience.

are still palatable and good for years. (At least, hazelnuts are. Walnuts probably aren't as long-storing, but here I admit I'm guessing.) Store nuts in the shell. They begin going rancid once shelled. Most nuts also provide generous amounts of oil. In fact, most nuts have too much oil to be a primary protein source, as getting all your protein from the nuts involves consuming too many calories. But nuts can play secondary roles. Sunflowers can also be an excellent source of protein, calories, and oil if you live where they can be grown and dried readily without the birds getting them all. (I don't.)

Turnips, beets, rutabagas, and onions have all sometimes served as European calorie staples. They are watery compared to potatoes, so aren't as concentrated a calorie source. In addition, they don't have the higher protein content of potatoes, grains, or grain legumes. Also, with all the varieties and flavors of potatoes and ways of cooking them, you can eat potatoes as your major carbohydrate and protein staple and delight in eating potatoes every day for months. I don't know of anyone who voluntarily eats beets, turnips, rutabagas, or onions as their major carbohydrate staple for very many months and delights in it. However, beets and rutabagas can be overwintered in gardens in mild areas. (The turnips get eaten by pests if you do that here.) Onions serve as both food and condiment. These foods add variety to the diet. So while they may not be most people's primary staple crops for calories, they can play a significant auxiliary role. For Jerusalem artichokes (a.k.a. sunroots) and camas as carbohydrate staples, see note 4-5.

I recall reading somewhere that turnips could be used to "clean the land up" from weeds. Ever optimistic, I immediately broadcast turnip seed, figuring that they must grow faster than weeds and would produce turnips with minimal care. Wrong. Turns out, turnips traditionally "cleaned up" the land from weeds by virtue of being planted in rows and hoed repeatedly and meticulously all season long. All the hoeing is what cleaned up the land. The way I figure it, the hoeing would be much easier to do without the turnips in there.

Milling and Storing Whole-Grain Flour

The main reason our food system deals in refined flours instead of whole-grain flours is because whole-grain flours go rancid. Refined flours store better at room temperature. When a grain kernel is broken open during grinding, the fats in the germ are exposed to air, and those that are unsaturated begin to oxidize. The finer the flour is ground, the more fat is exposed to air, and the faster the flour becomes unpalatably rancid. When fatty acids are oxidized, trans fats are among those produced. So rancid fat is not merely unpalatable; it also is bad for us. Corn has a higher fat content than wheat, so cornmeal goes rancid faster than wheat flour. We can sometimes buy whole wheat flour off the shelf in a grocery store and get good flour—if it was milled and shipped promptly and the store's turnover on whole wheat flour is high enough. But we are unlikely to get whole corn-meal that isn't rancid off the shelf. With corn, our choices are usually degermed meal (that is less nutritious and tasteless) or whole meal (which is rancid). In addition, whole wheat flour is from varieties specifically grown for people food. The cornmeal found in the grocery store, however, is from the same varieties grown for animal feed and industrial purposes. It isn't ordinarily from varieties that have great flavor. To get good cornmeal, we usually need to grow and grind our own. (For a couple of small commercial mills that produce and sell gourmet-quality cornmeal fresh-ground from heirloom corn varieties, however, see note 4-7.)

An added problem for those who must avoid wheat is that most non-wheat flours are milled on the same commercial mills as wheat and contain some cross-contamination. This gives those of us who need to avoid wheat added reason to grow and mill our own grains. (Bob's Red Mill grinds some non-gluten flours on dedicated mills but not the cornmeals and flours.) If you need to avoid wheat, don't let anyone grind wheat in your mills.

To have good whole-grain flour, we do one of two things: We order whole-grain flour directly from a farm/mill or mill that mills regularly and ships promptly; then we refrigerate or freeze the flour as soon as we receive it. Or we grind the flour or meal ourselves from whole grain, then either use it immediately or refrigerate or freeze it. The whole grains can be ones we've grown ourselves or ones we have purchased.

I usually grind a half-gallon or so of flour or meal at once, put it in Ziploc bags, and store it in the freezer.

For milling on a home scale I suggest starting with a home grist mill. The classic is the Corona mill, which is still available for about $50 new, and appears to be sturdier than the knockoffs I have seen. The Corona is a hand-cranked mill in which the grain slides past and is broken up by two rotating steel plates with burrs on them. The Corona can grind anything in the size class of rice to the biggest corn or beans. In two passes, you can get a coarse but workable flour fine enough for coarse (but delicious) bread from most grains. Tiny grains such as amaranth or teff are too small to mill without getting metal powder in the grain and wearing down the steel burrs. With one exception, Corona mills are limited to producing a coarse flour. True flour corns, as I cover in chapter 12, are the easiest of all grains to grind, and fall apart into fine soft flour, even when ground in a Corona mill. Even though I now have an electric impact mill, I still always use my Corona mill to make polenta meal from flint corn. Polenta meal should be fairly coarse. It's easy to get it exactly right on the Corona mill.

To grind corn, I set the burr plates so that they crack the corn into coarse chunks on the first pass. Then I dump the grain back in the hopper after resetting the burr plates as fine as I want, and run the grain through again. Smaller grains can be ground in one pass. (Corn can too, but it's easier cranking if you grind corn in two stages.)

In order to make really fine flour, you need a different mill. For most households, the affordable choice is an impact mill, an electric mill in which needles strike and explode the kernels of grain. Impact mills give a very fine flour, similar to commercial wheat flour in texture. There are two models I have used. One is the K-tec, which I do not recommend. It has a tiny feed hopper, is painfully loud (even with ear protection), and jams frequently. The model I have (and recommend) is a Grainmaster Whisper Mill. The new name of the Whisper Mill (reflecting changes in the business world) is the WonderMill, which appears to be identical except for brand name. WonderMills are about $250 new. The Whisper/Wonder Mill has a large grain hopper, runs quietly, relatively

speaking (you still should use hearing protection), rarely jams, and is easy to unjam with a flip of a knob if it does. Impact mills do not give you any control over fineness of grind. You can only grind very fine. (The size settings are to adjust the needles for the size of grain you are milling, not to influence the fineness of the flour. People who write the advertising information on these mills don't always realize this and sometimes assume the size control affects flour fineness. It doesn't.) So you can't turn out the desirable coarse grind needed for polenta on an impact mill. You also can't grind anything much smaller than rice or much bigger than big-kernel varieties of corn. And you cannot grind anything with substantial oil content, such as soybeans or peanuts.

I do most of my grinding on the Whisper Mill, because I usually want fine-grained flour for bread, and electricity is nice when you're grinding more than a few cups. But I would not want to be without the Corona Mill. I grind all my polenta meal on it and also use it to crack corn for ducklings. And if there was a long-term power outage, I would need a nonelectric mill for everything. The Corona is my nonelectric backup.

For producing larger amounts of fine flour than you would need on a home scale, such as for a restaurant or bakery, a farm selling flour, or an entire town or city, I recommend Meadows Mills (www.meadowsmills.com). These have granite grindstones and range in size from stones 8 inches across to many feet and prices of about $2,000 up to many thousands. Meadows Mills people will consult with you to help you choose the right mill. If you are gluten intolerant, tell the Meadows Mills people that, and ask them to do their routine testing on your mill with corn (instead of the usual wheat). Meadows Mills will

Using Whole-Grain Gluten-Free Flours

Most recipes for making bread or other baked goods from gluten-free flours involve complicated mixtures of many flours, usually refined flours. I think baked goods should be based upon whole-grain flours for everyone, but especially for people who have digestive system or malabsorption problems. The strategy behind the complex mixtures appears to be necessitated by the fact that the flours have off-flavors. The processed bean flours, for example, intended to add protein to the other refined flours, are distinctly bitter. The potato flour, used to help hold the baked products together, tends to taste like subprime poor-grade potatoes, which is exactly what it is. Potato flour gives baked goods a slimy texture. The sorghum flour has a weird bitter taste. (And that's the white "sweet" sorghum touted for not being bitter.) By combining various flours with various bad flavors, one is supposed to end up with a flour that doesn't taste bad enough in any particular way to notice. Unfortunately, I can still taste all the bad flavors in the final baked products.

Pure whole-grain flours made from gourmet corn varieties, teff, oats, buckwheat, and brown rice, on the other hand, have *wonderful* flavors. There is no need to mix or dilute them. All we need is to have recipes that take advantage of the essential natures and flavors of these grains.

An additional problem is that most recipes for gluten-free baked goods include xanthan gum, a product made by a bacterium. It gives me (very slight) indigestion. It also has its own flavor, which I taste in the baked goods and don't like.

Xanthan gum is used as a binder to make up for the fact that gluten-free flours have no gluten. Xanthan gum gives baked goods a slimy texture. The best I can say about it is that it doesn't taste as bad as potato flour.

I find bread made from these gluten-free flour mixes and recipes pretty unpalatable stuff. Sweet breads, cakes, brownies, and cookies are better. The sugar helps mask the off-flavors.

I've developed my own recipes for gluten-free bread and baked goods based upon just pure whole grain, water, salt, a little fat or oil, baking powder, and eggs. The sweet breads and cakes also contain sugar. There is no xanthan or any artificial gums, and no dairy products unless the choice of fat or oil is butter. I developed my recipes in the context of corn, so they are described in the corn chapter. However, the recipes are universal. They will work with any gluten-free flour such as oat, buckwheat, teff, brown rice, or corn. They merely require adjusting the amount of water added. In some of these recipes, the binding power is generated by making a paste with part of the flour and boiling water, and combining the paste with the other ingredients. In other cases, such as for the Universal Sponge Cake and Universal Pancakes, eggs are the binder. My Universal Skillet Bread recipe is fast and easy to prepare and bake, and holds together well enough to make sandwiches. In the corn chapter, the recipes with "universal" in the title apply to any gluten-free flour. (They would presumably also work with wheat, rye, and other wheat-related flours.)

allow you to grind all the way from very fine to as coarse as you want.

For a variety of home and farm mills (electric and not), including those with capacity sufficient for animal feed, see *Lehman's Non-electric Catalog* of household appliances, tools, and gadgets (www.lehmans.com).

Asthma, Allergies, and Adventures with Omega-3 Fatty Acids

For two decades, roughly the 1970s and 1980s, I had serious problems with asthma and hay fever. My ducks healed me. At least, they gave me the critical clue. After I started producing my own free-range duck eggs, I noticed two major effects that they seemed to have on my health. First—my problems with asthma and hay fever seemed to vary inversely with the duck eggs. When I was eating a lot of free-range duck eggs, I had little or no problem with asthma and hay fever. When I didn't have the duck eggs, or when forage was poor and the eggs weren't really free range, the asthma and hay fever returned.

A much more dramatic and obvious effect of the duck eggs, however, was that they satisfied my craving for meat and fatty foods. No amount of commercial meat or fatty food had actually ever satisfied that craving. I could put away a two- or three-pound steak, and stop eating (temporarily) only because there was no more room. I would still want more half an hour later. The steak didn't satisfy the craving, not in any amount. But after just a couple of free-range duck eggs, I was completely full and satisfied—for the first time in my life. It was a completely new feeling. A daily diet with a duck egg or two in it allowed me to eat modest, ordinary amounts of food and be satisfied. The effect was dramatic and immediate enough so that I could experiment with it easily. It took only about twenty minutes after eating the eggs for the feeling of satiety to appear. This made it easy to test which foods had whatever it was that gave me the feeling.

I tried other kinds of eggs. Commercial chicken eggs didn't work. "High-omega" chicken eggs didn't work. Duck eggs worked only if free range, but not if from confined ducks, and not from "free-range" ducks on poor forage. Wild-caught salmon satisfied the need very well, but not farmed salmon. Commercial meat never satisfied the craving. As locally produced meat became available, however, I found that it sometimes satisfied the craving. Grass-fed, grass-finished lamb and beef did a great job of satisfying the craving. Pastured pork did not. Pastured poultry provided only a little of that feeling of satiety, at best, and sometimes none at all, though it sure tasted wonderful compared with the commercial kind. Most fish didn't help. Canned tuna didn't help. But the New Brunswick kippered herring snacks listed as having 1 gram of omega-3 fatty acids per can did the trick. So did canned sardines. Cod liver oil was *very* effective. For the amount or the money it was far more effective than anything else. No amount of walnuts or flaxseed meal or oil or canola oil helped a bit. A good inference is that what I was craving was one or more omega-3 fatty acids, and it was getting enough of certain omega-3 fatty acids that gave me the feeling of satiety.

The fact that I didn't respond much to pastured poultry meat is not surprising when you consider that the birds are confined in small pens that are moved around so as to give the birds mostly just sun, air, and salads. With so many birds and so little space, birds get few bugs. Most of the diet of the birds is actually their feed of commercial-style chow and grain, not what they forage. Pastured pork hogs are usually raised in fields with little for a hog to forage. Their diet is nearly all commercial feed or grain. Canned tuna has almost no fat, as indicated on the label. So whatever the books say about tuna being a good source of omega-3s, the canned tuna brands I have seen are not.

The fact that I did not respond to flaxseed meal, flaxseed oil, walnuts, or canola oil was puzzling initially. These are rich plant sources of omega-3s. It is often stated that we can make all the long-chain omega-3s we need from the short-chain plant types. So I was expecting the plant sources to work. They didn't. Only after I got into the subject a bit did I come to realize that only *some* people can do the conversions from the 18-carbon plant omega-3s to the 20- and 22-carbon omega-3s we human animals need. I am apparently one of the people who needs to get her 20- and 22-carbon omega-3s already made for me by other animals such as fish or grass-fed ruminants or a laying flock. In addition, the conversion reactions may not work when there is excess omega-6 in the diet. Most Americans have huge excesses of omega-6s in their diets. Apparently, for at least some, and maybe many of us, eating meat or animal products is not optional.

After increasing the omega-3 content in my diet, most of my problems with asthma and hay fever went away. After I in addition eliminated milk products from my diet, as recommended by Andrew Weil (*Eating Well for Optimum Health*), all traces of both asthma and allergy vanished.

Essential fatty acids are certain polyunsaturated fatty acids we need in order to live, and which we are not capable of making ourselves. Essential fatty acids are of two basic kinds, omega-3s and omega-6s. The most biologically important omega-3 and omega-6 fatty acids are 18, 20, or 22 carbons long. Brain cell membranes are made mostly of the 22-carbon omega-3 fatty acid abbreviated DHA. Omega-6 fatty acids are readily available in vegetable oils and commercial meat and dairy products, and are present in excess in the agribusiness diet. Omega-3s have been almost completely eliminated from the agribusiness diet.

Omega-3 fatty-acid deficiencies may cause or be associated with or exacerbate asthma and allergies of all kinds, immune and autoimmune diseases, rheumatoid arthritis, joint pain, colitis, heart disease, cancer, high blood pressure, and a huge variety of brain and mental health problems such as depression, postpartum depression, bipolar disease, schizophrenia, general emotional instability, and even inability to control rage. Omega-3 deficiencies may also play a role in autism, ADD, ADHD, Alzheimer's, and aging. High omega-3 diets, on the other hand, are associated with better heart health, less risk of heart attacks, lower blood pressure, lower platelet clotting, and less inflammatory disease of many kinds, including less asthma and allergies. It is reasonable to speculate that a lack of adequate omega-3 fatty acids in people's diets may actually cause many cases of these diseases, and may be a major reason why some of these diseases are increasingly prevalent. For those who have, or think they may have, any of these problems, I recommend Andrew Weil's *Eating Well for Optimum Health*, as well as the books on omega-3s I list in the chapter notes. The other general nutrition book I recommend is *Eat, Drink, and Be Healthy: The Harvard Medical School Guide to Healthy Eating*, by Walter Willett.

Omega-3 and omega-6 fatty acids are critical components of cell membranes, but are also transformed into substances that have somewhat opposing regulatory effects. So the balance between omega-3 and omega-6 in the diet is important. An excess of omega-6 relative to omega-3 in the diet is associated with all of the diseases and symptoms listed above under omega-3 deficiencies, that is, more asthma and allergies, inflammatory diseases, blood clotting, high blood pressure, and so on. I think most of us will want some good animal sources of omega-3s in our diet. The easiest and most workable backyard approach to growing our own long-chain omega-3s is to have a laying flock. (For more on keeping a home laying flock, see chapter 9.)

The essential fatty acids in eggs are in the yolk, along with the fat-soluble vitamins. The white contains the protein, but there are plenty of vegetable sources for protein. So if you must throw away some part of the egg, throw away the white and eat the yolk. Eating eggs with the yolks does *not* increase the cholesterol level in people's blood in any studies that have been published on that subject. The idea that people should avoid egg yolks as a way of controlling their blood cholesterol levels was based upon a series of unwarranted assumptions and speculations, which have turned out to be untrue every time they have been actually tested.

The most important role of meat for most of us may be as a source of omega-3 fatty acids, not as a source of protein. Protein is readily available from many sources, including plant sources. Long-chain omega-3 fatty acids are not. Note well: it is the fat in the meat that contains the omega-3s. With grass-fed meat, you should eat the fat. If you must throw something away, throw away the meat and eat the fat. When I buy commercial meat, I trim away and eliminate excess fat. (The fat of commercial meat is mostly saturated, and the unsaturated fat is overwhelmingly omega-6.) When I pay the extra price for local grass-fed meat, however, I get meat that is as fatty as possible, and I keep and eat all the drippings and every tasty nutritious fatty morsel.

Cod liver oil of the right brands can be an excellent source of exactly the long-chain omega-3s we need and is far less expensive than grass-fed meat, wild-caught salmon, or canned fatty fish. For many, cod liver oil is the practical route to a diet with enough long-chain omega-3s. I use cod liver oil in addition to duck eggs and occasional treats of grass-fed meat. The cod liver oil is also a rich source of vitamins A and D. (See note 4-13 on choosing a good cod liver oil.)

Buying Grass-Fed Meat and Dairy Products

Nate and I hope to have a small farm someday, and to be able to produce our own meat. In our mind's eye, a flock of sheep and some water buffaloes as well as our duck flock provide all the eggs, milk, meat, and draft power we need. Right now, what we can produce is duck eggs and the occasional roasting or stewing bird. So when we eat meat, we have to buy it. Buying good meat is not trivial.

Organic meat isn't necessarily grass fed. And most "free-range" poultry isn't genuinely free-ranged on good enough range for long enough so that the meat has useful levels of omega-3s. When it comes to omega-3s, "grass-fed" or "pastured" or "free-range," not "organic," are the critical words to me. I always buy from local vendors of whom I can ask the necessary questions.

Ruminants produce meat or dairy products with good levels of omega-3s only if they are fed green grass with no grain. Grain causes the ecology of the rumen to change entirely so that omega-3 production is almost eliminated. Hay and silage don't have much omega-3 content. So meat from animals butchered in or after a winter of hay may have little more omega-3s than commercial meat. When I buy local meat, I always ask the vendor what kind of animal it was from (breed, age, sex, condition) and when the animal was butchered. I want meat from a fat animal (which, being grass fed, is still not as fat as commercial meat). With beef, I want an animal that is at least two years old; meat from younger animals doesn't have as much flavor. *Lean* grass-fed meat defeats the nutritional purpose. It is also less succulent and tasty. The real skill of the all-grass grazier is in getting enough fat on the animals for highest quality and nutritional value, not in producing lean meat. I also want an animal that was butchered right off grass, not after feeding for some time on hay or silage. The omega-3 content of the meat of an animal on hay, silage, or grain drops rapidly. (The most spectacularly flavorful roast is the shoulder roast, which has the most fat.)

In the United States, commercial dairy animals (organic or conventional) are virtually always fed grain-based supplements, even when they are grazed. To get milk with good omega-3 levels, you need to feed the cows pretty much just forage. This means an unacceptably low level of production except on the scale of the home milk cow. And in the northern parts of the United States, even the home cow would need to be fed on hay or silage during the winter. I know of no source of commercial dairy products in the United States that have a good level of omega-3s. (Please contact me if you are such a source.) I'm a big fan of Kerry-Gold butter, though. In this book, when I say "butter," I mean Kerry-Gold butter. It's imported from Ireland, where it is produced from grass-fed cows milked in summer only. The flavor of Kerry-Gold butter is spectacular. And my body can tell the difference. Kerry-Gold butter makes it obvious why so many people in so many parts of the world have been willing to do the work involved in keeping a cow and speak so much about and so value their butter.

Most pastured poultry broiler chickens are of the same commercial Cornish cross lines that commercial producers use. They develop rapidly and are butchered at seven or eight weeks. They spend about five weeks of this time in the brooder, eating a commercial diet, not on pasture—not even on limited pasture in little portable pens. The flavor of pastured poultry is much superior to that of conventional poultry. But with an eight-week-old bird, my body's evaluation is that it doesn't contain enough omega-3s to be significant. (It doesn't trigger my satiety mechanisms.) With a twelve-week-old pastured bird, my body usually says there are at least some omega-3s in the bird, though not much. And the twelve-week-old pastured bird has much more flavor.

Good pastured turkeys are a better bet, nutritionally speaking. Ask and make sure that they are being grown to full roasting size, that is, are butchered at four months. (Processed birds for sale may be younger than this but just of a larger-sized breed. You need the older bird for full flavor as well as omega-3 content. Once upon a time, dressed turkeys were sold with a few wing feathers intact to prove the bird was four months old and thus full-flavored.) I ask specific additional questions and make sure I am getting an animal that was allowed to forage in big fertile fields, not confined in a little mobile pen. Genuinely free-range turkeys that are four months old and butchered off of good range are spectacularly delicious, and my body says they have good levels of omega-3s.

The Missing Ingredient—Can What We *Aren't* Eating Make Us Fat? How to Let Your Body Tell You What It Needs

During my childhood, I had uncontrolled celiac disease. I ate huge amounts of food, especially lots of meat and fat. Yet I was painfully skinny. There was a tradition in my father's family that we simply needed several times more food than anyone else, and especially needed meat. We were actually proud of how much we ate. Undiagnosed celiac disease, as well as a family tradition that made it survivable, were probably both being passed down in the Deppe family.

Decades later, after the celiac disease had escalated to the point of being near lethal and obvious, I completely eliminated wheat and gluten from my diet. That improved my health profoundly. But I suddenly gained about a hundred pounds in only a few months' time. Now that I was digesting food better, I didn't need as much as I was used to. I struggled with controlling my weight thereafter. For years, however, all I could do was simply avoid gaining more. I had horrific cravings for huge amounts of food in general and for fatty meat and other fatty things in particular. The situation changed completely once I figured out the relationship between omega-3 fatty acids and my food cravings. Once I got the omega-3 levels in my diet up, I no longer had food crav-

ings. Now, when I eat a normal amount, I feel full. This hasn't meant I've instantly lost all the extra weight. But it has meant that I am slowly, essentially effortlessly, going in the right direction.

My body apparently knew it wasn't getting omega-3 fatty acids and knew that I should be able to get them from fatty meat. I think my cravings were my body ordering me to eat the things it knew should correct the problem. It was a healthy response, not an unhealthy one, I now believe. Unfortunately, I believe, my body was sabotaged by the fact that the omega-3s had been removed from the meat and fatty products where it expected to find them.

Can what we *aren't* eating make us fat? Can some of us be overeating because our diets aren't giving us what we need?

I have noticed other situations that can override my satiety mechanisms and interfere with my ability to experience satiety and feel satisfied when I have had enough food (including enough omega-3s).

"Sugar jags" can cause food cravings. I'm carbohydrate sensitive. If I eat too much sugar or high-glycemic-index carbohydrates, especially in the morning, it throws my energy metabolism off and sets up a pattern of food cravings that lasts all day (and that invariably results in serious overeating). "High-glycemic-index" foods are those that are digested rapidly and cause a rapid rise in blood sugar soon after they are eaten. The high blood sugar levels trigger a spike in insulin release, which then drives sugar levels down so rapidly they end up abnormally low. The abnormally low sugar levels cause shakiness, fatigue, and food cravings. I discuss glycemic index and avoiding sugar jags and carbohydrate-sensitivity problems in the chapter on potatoes, but the information applies to all high-glycemic-index foods with substantial amounts of carbohydrates in them.

The shakiness, fatigue, and sick feelings that result from abnormally low blood sugar (and the associated desperate food cravings) are not hunger. True hunger is actually a mild symptom. It is just a slight sensation in the back of the mouth and throat that feels almost identical to what we experience when we are just starting to get a sore throat from a cold (but before we actually feel bad). True hunger doesn't cause shakiness, fatigue, or food cravings. The hungry person still feels fine and is perfectly functional, just a bit more motivated toward food than otherwise. And the food tastes more spectacularly delicious than otherwise. Many Americans have never experienced true hunger. I often experience true hunger when I wake up in the morning, before breakfast. The true hunger symptoms clearly occur when I have had fewer calories during the last day than usual. My body apparently signals me to go out and hunt and gather more, and simultaneously, or perhaps a little later, realizes that it has quite a few pounds of fat it could be using. Occasional symptoms of real hunger don't inconvenience me or cause any discomfort. They are reassuring. Given that I am overweight, if my *average* intake is appropriate, it should be less than my requirements part of the time so that my body, little by little, uses up and eliminates its excess fat reserves. (Actual starvation is a different issue.)

Caffeine also seems to completely mess up my energy metabolism and cause food cravings. I can afford the small amount of theophylline in a cup of tea or two in the morning. But that is about as much caffeine-class substance as I can afford. Chocolate, which contains theobromine, another caffeine relative, is another substance that seems to mess up my energy metabolism and lead to cravings and overeating. The conventional nutritional wisdom is that caffeine and caffeine analogs are harmless in moderation. But no one seems to be noticing or evaluating the effects of these substances on food cravings and satiety.

The absolute worst thing I can do, the way I can guarantee horrific food cravings and overeating all day, is to start the day with a cup of coffee with sugar in it (with or without breakfast). Both the coffee and the sugar lead to deranged satiety mechanisms, desperate food cravings, and invariably overeating.

Based upon my personal experience, for my body to be able to tell when it has eaten what it needs and to be happy to stop—for my satiety mechanisms to work:

1. I have to limit consumption of caffeine and its relatives.
2. I must avoid big spikes in blood sugar levels.
3. I need to be fully hydrated. If I allow myself to become even slightly dehydrated, that tends to be mistaken for a need for food. I need to drink plenty of water in the first half of the day for my satiety mechanisms to work. Water later in the day isn't as effective.
4. My satiety mechanisms do not work at all on liquid food. Not even fruit juice. I don't know why. I have noticed liquids go through my stomach fast compared with solid food. (As evaluated by simply eating a pint of solid food or liquid quickly, then noticing the swelling. The liquid passes lower down in minutes. The solid food takes a while.) I avoid or limit all liquid foods. In my case, the main issue is apple cider in fall. But undoubtedly the same would apply to

beer, wine, other alcoholic beverages, all fruit juices, and soda pop. It's amazing how much weight one can gain by simply substituting cider (great cider made with a blend of apples, including genuine—bitter—cider apples) for all water. In my case, all the calories in the cider simply get added onto the total I eat that day. I don't eat less food to make up for them. My body doesn't "see" the liquid calories at all. They do not trigger my satiety mechanisms.

5. My satiety mechanisms do not work at all on dry food like cookies, crackers, corn chips, potato chips, or even dry fruit. I don't know why. I use such foods only occasionally and with caution.

6. I have to eat slowly enough for my satiety mechanisms to work. It seems to take about 20 minutes for my body to know whether it has had what it needs. If I bolt my food, my satiety mechanisms don't work. I need to wait at least 20 minutes after finishing a meal before deciding upon seconds. (The hormone ghrelin, produced in the stomach and associated with hunger and satiety control, is said to take about 20 minutes to work. I had noticed that 20-minute lag, though, long before I knew anything about ghrelin. This 20-minute timing suggests to me that the satiety mechanisms I have noticed might involve ghrelin.)

7. My body seems to expect some carbohydrates, some protein, and some omega-3s with every meal. Dietary advice makes it sound as if our bodies think in days. Mine doesn't. It thinks one meal at a time. If I eat a meal without some carbohydrates, some proteins, and some omega-3s, I will not feel full. I will either want seconds, or want another meal sooner than usual. I take some of my daily quota of cod liver oil with each meal. This is far more effective in creating satiety and making me happy with less food per day than when I take the cod liver oil all in one meal. The cod liver oil does the best job of creating satiety when I take it about a third of the way into the meal, not at the end.

8. Finally, my body seems to needs some serious roughage in *every meal*. Even breakfast. So when I eat cornbread and a duck egg for breakfast, for example, I include a carrot. The carrot makes a huge difference in the satiety.

I think the basic concept of a "meal" might be counterproductive. How can our satiety mechanisms work if we eat all the foods at the same time? We probably often overeat everything when we really need more of just one thing. I learned about my own satiety mechanisms partly by eating one food at a time, then waiting before eating the next food. Even now, I prefer to keep the carbohydrates separate from the rest of the food. If my stew contains potatoes as well as meat and other vegetables, I may have to overeat carbohydrates when all my body wants and needs is a little more meat or vegetables. So I serve potatoes, rice, polenta, or bread separately rather than combining them with everything else in single dishes. I also leave the meat in soups or stews in big chunks. (Whole turkey thighs go in my turkey soup, for example.) That way I can cut up the right amount of meat into each bowl of broth and vegetables, as satiety mechanisms of the moment suggest. Often, for the second bowl of soup or stew, I really only want the broth and vegetables. My satiety mechanisms work best when I have a long, leisurely meal with different foods in individual courses and with plenty of time between courses or before seconds.

What my body seems to be able to evaluate are carbohydrate, protein, vitamin C, and omega-3s. That is, a lack of any of these can create cravings for foods that are approximately reasonable (though not necessarily effective). When my vitamin C levels are too low, for example, I crave sour things like oranges, hot and sour soup, salads with vinegary dressing, and things with ketchup or spaghetti sauce. Which exact food my craving fixates upon varies. The oranges satisfy the craving very well. The ketchup and spaghetti sauce are sour, but don't satisfy the craving. Apparently, my "vitamin C tooth" knows to look for vitamin C in sour things, but is not capable of learning that some sour things don't have much vitamin C. (Just like my "omega-3 tooth" wasn't capable of learning that commercial fatty meat didn't work.) But I can intervene intellectually. If I respond to an apparent spaghetti craving with spaghetti, I'll end up overeating, probably because I'm really craving vitamin C, and I don't get enough vitamin C from spaghetti sauce to satisfy the craving. However, I can completely cure the craving for spaghetti sauce in twenty minutes with a little pure vitamin C (or with a couple of oranges). Or I can indulge my craving for spaghetti sauce but add a little vitamin C to it, and cure the craving with a reasonable amount of spaghetti sauce and without overeating. (I add pure vitamin C to my morning tea. I also occasionally add it to soups. I don't use vitamin C in the evening, as it has some stimulant effects and causes me insomnia when ingested then.)

If my sweet tooth starts acting up, what it focuses on is something with jam or maple syrup. Sometimes I indulge it a little, especially in the evening after dinner. The rest of the time, I buy my sweet tooth off with some (unsweetened) cornbread, polenta, or potatoes. The right amount of cornbread or potatoes satisfies my "sweet" tooth just as well and as fast as some sugar, and doesn't cause the additional problems. My "sweet" tooth isn't really a sweet tooth. It's a carbohydrate tooth.

There may be other nutrients my body can evaluate that I'm not aware of, or that are always present in adequate amounts in my diet and thus give me no signals. Vitamin D deficiency, for example, is said to be associated with food cravings and inability to feel satiated. However, I wouldn't know. By the time I have eaten enough cod liver oil or animal-based omega-3s, I have plenty of vitamin D.

It is well known that both wild and domestic animals can evaluate the nutritional quality of their diets and choose accordingly. It is not likely that we humans would have lost this ability; in fact I've become convinced that we do still possess it. However, we may need to rearrange certain aspects of our diet in order to allow our own personal satiety mechanisms to work properly.

A Different Conceptual Framework for Understanding Obesity

The modern conceptual framework for understanding obesity assumes that humans are not really designed to be able to deal with a world with excess food. Famine and starvation, not feasts and excess, were the situation we evolved with, the idea goes. I challenge this assumption.

Every successful animal species that has survived, thrived, and expanded its populations over large parts of the planet had an average access to food that was adequate, or more than adequate, by definition. An average that is adequate means there is sometimes too little and sometimes too much. Both feasts and famines are normal. Animals have to be able to deal with both. Wild animals generally become fat only when it is desirable. Bears must accumulate fat in order to hibernate through winter. Whales have layers of subcutaneous fat to provide insulation from cold water. So do ducks. Most temperate animals, in good times, accumulate some fat through the summer to help them make it through winter. Wild animals become sleek and accumulate a little fat in times of plenty. But they don't become counterproductively obese. They clearly have mechanisms for evaluating and choosing not just the right intake of specific foods, but also the overall intake of calories. Is it likely that humans, of all animals, would have lost their ability to deal, physiologically, with both feast and famine? Let's assume not. Let's assume that humans, like other animals, have superb mechanisms for evaluating the nutritional characteristics of their food and regulating their food intake during periods of both feast and famine. If so, why are so many people obese? The basic reason, of course, is that these people are eating more calories than they need. The question, however, is *why*. If people have the ability to evaluate their food and regulate their intake, then why are they overeating? Something (possibly multiple things) must have gone wrong. Here are some possibilities I can think of:

1. Our modern food supply might be too low in one or more critical nutrients (such as omega-3 fatty acids), as I already discussed. We respond in a healthy fashion and eat a larger volume in order to get enough of the critical missing nutrient, and are thus forced to overeat total calories.

2. Our modern food supply might have poisons in it that interfere with or override our satiety mechanisms. Caffeine definitely acts this way for me. So does sugar (unless there is a fruit around it).

3. The concept of meals, that is, eating lots of foods at once, might interfere with our satiety mechanisms' ability to evaluate what we need. Once upon a time, we had to climb the tree and eat the fruit, then walk to the termite mound and fish for termites. The fruit and termites didn't come all mixed together. We may need to eat foods one at a time in order to be able to evaluate them.

4. We might not have evolved to have satiety mechanisms that work with liquid foods, dry foods, or sugar that is outside of the fruit. We certainly did evolve with sugar. Sugar is the great communication mechanism between plants and animals. The plant produces sweet fruit to signal to the animal, "This is good to eat, and spread my seeds around, by the way." But fruit is mostly water and secondarily roughage, a safe package for the sugar that dramatically limits the amount we can eat and slows its absorption.

    Our natural food is mostly water. Even our grains are mostly water by the time we cook them. Our satiety mechanisms may work optimally only with water-saturated foods, and may require adequate roughage and volume. Our satiety mechanisms may not work, for example, with cookies, which are almost pure sugar, grain, and fat, and little water. My satiety mechanisms don't work with any dry food—not crackers, not chips, not cookies, and not even dried fruit.

5. Our satiety mechanisms may work only when we are getting adequate exercise.

6. During our evolution, the fact that we had to walk (and carry any excess weight we had along) in order to forage might have mattered. This might have made getting seriously overweight difficult just on mechanical grounds. But there may be more than just mechanics involved. I speculate that exercise of the big leg muscles might be integrated into energy metabolism and weight control. That is, we may need to walk (or run) in order for energy metabolism to be optimally controlled. (See the discussion of restless leg syndrome in chapter 5.)

7. Maybe our jaw muscles have needs too. Sometimes I want some crunch. I used to reach for crackers or chips in response. That was fine when I was underweight. It's not fine now. However, while I think of crackers or chips when my "crunch drive" kicks in, my desire for crunch is satisfied just as happily by carrots or apples or a salad full of crunchy vegetables.

   I've also found that a chunk of chuck roast cut into steaks satisfied me much more than a cut of meat that is more tender. It takes much more time and chewing to eat the chuck.

8. Maybe we need to play with our food. Sometimes I find myself heading into the kitchen with a strong drive for . . . well . . . nothing in particular. And I'm not even hungry. I just want to fix something. I want to prepare some food. That's all. I want to mess with food. And that can lead to an extra unneeded meal. These days, when I feel my drive to play with my food kicking in, I go prepare something that's going to take a while. Beans. A complex stew. An oven full of big baking spuds. I satisfy the drive to mess with food now by preparing a meal that won't be ready until much later when I will actually be hungry.

Why is it that when you are the person who prepares the Thanksgiving feast, it doesn't taste nearly as good as when someone else prepares exactly the same things? Whenever I spend all day preparing food, I am just not very hungry when dinner comes, even if I have eaten nothing all day. We humans do more and more complex food manipulation and preparation than any other creature. I speculate that the drive to play with food—to shell, peel, pound, grind, cut, cook, carry—is now built into us genetically. I think we need to play with our food to feel fully satisfied. I think that playing with our food contributes to satiety, even before we eat the first bite.

Today, however, many people are being deprived of the opportunity to play with their food. Once upon a time, everyone would have picked and peeled their own bananas and fished for their own termites. These days, one person usually cooks the meal. And even that cooking is often minimal because of the wide availability of prepared and processed foods. Also, increasingly, people eat out, order take-out, or go to fast-food restaurants.

9. Perhaps occasional famines are essential. The process of using our body fat and turning it into energy may involve enzymes or regulatory mechanisms that are induced by starvation. That is, perhaps we need occasional periods of starvation for our bodies to keep activated all the mechanisms we need in order to be able to use our fat stores. Without these mechanisms, we might be able to deposit fat but not use it very well. If so, our bodies might demand more food any time we undereat a little instead of resorting to fat stores. Without occasional periods of starvation, our fat metabolism might become one-way. We might be able to lay down fat stores but be unable to utilize them.

While I suppose that feasts were a normal part of our evolutionary lives, famines undoubtedly were also. Perhaps we actually need a bit of serious belt-tightening occasionally for optimal overall health. Perhaps we need both the feasts and the famines.

Sugar

Our bodies are designed to run on the 6-carbon sugar glucose ("blood sugar"). Potato and grain starch are polymers of glucose. Sucrose and high-fructose corn syrup are about half glucose and half fructose. Every cell in the body can use glucose, so when we eat glucose, most of it is used for energy production. Furthermore, glucose stimulates the release of insulin, and glucose triggers our satiety mechanisms. When we eat glucose, most is used up by all the other cells in the body before reaching the liver. Only a little needs to be metabolized by the liver. And most of that is made, not into fat, but into glycogen, a safe store of ready energy.

Fructose can be utilized only by the liver. It doesn't trigger insulin. It is invisible to our satiety mechanisms. When processed by the liver, most of the fructose ends up as body as well as liver fat. Lipid droplets in the liver are not any more natural when derived from fructose as when derived from alcohol. Both cause a fatty, damaged, less functional liver. Basically, fructose is metabolized more like alcohol than like glucose. And fructose is largely converted straight to fat. (Go directly to jail, do not pass go, do not provide any energy for the body, do not satisfy hunger, do not collect $200.) The only safe way to eat fructose is with a fruit around it. Eating fructose without a fruit surrounding it is more like eating pure fat than eating most foods (such as grains and potatoes), in which the starch is made up of units of glucose. Table sugar (sucrose) and high-fructose corn syrup both contain about half fructose. Whether the high-fructose corn syrup is worse for us than the sucrose, given that both contain comparable amounts of fructose isn't yet obvious. What is obvious is that neither does us a whole lot of good.

The preceding analysis of the metabolism and dietary implications of sugars is drawn from a lecture by Robert H. Lustig, M.D., who is on the faculty in the Department of Pediatrics and Weight Assessment at University of California, San Francisco. The lecture is available on the Web. Look it up under the author's name and "Sugar: The Bitter Truth." Dr. Lustig said, "Pass it on." I'm convinced by his arguments, and hereby do so.

Sugar is said to be a flavor enhancer. I think it is a flavor enhancer only in small concentrations. Larger amounts seem to mask and overwhelm rather than enhance other flavors. It seems to me that our taste buds have a set point for sweetness based upon what we are used to. One reason why I have virtually quit eating candy is because it ruins the experience of eating fruit. Fruit, to the tongue not jaded by high doses of sugar, is exquisitely delicious and intensely sweet, as sweet as I would ever want anything to be. Even if I only eat candy occasionally, fruit doesn't taste very sweet to me, and I can't taste the explosion of complex flavors I experience when eating fruit on a mostly sugar-free diet.

I'm suspicious of artificial sweeteners. I suspect that, like real sugar, they raise the set point of our "sweet tooths" so that natural amounts of sugar don't taste good, and we eat more real (caloric) sugar in the rest of our lives. If my suspicion is correct, drinking diet sodas or eating products with artificial sweeteners could be fattening, even though the artificial sweeteners have no significant amount of calories.

Salt, High Blood Pressure, and Edema

Most of us would get all the salt we need from our ordinary food before we added any extra salt to it. For many or most of us, our problem is limiting our salt intake rather than getting enough.

My body can evaluate and regulate its salt levels, but there seems to be a huge learned component to the process. Perhaps it was entirely learned. Like some (but not all) people, my blood pressure goes up in response to too much salt intake. High blood pressure is said to be asymptomatic, that is, to be invisible. In me, high blood pressure is not asymptomatic. It makes me lethargic, sleepy, weak, uninspired and uninspiring, and

somewhat depressed. The effect of salt intake on my blood pressure is dramatic and totally predictable. Overeating salt leads to a blood pressure rise about twelve hours later, which lasts about a day. The lethargy also lasts about a day. Once I got a blood pressure monitor and figured out the correlation, and once I learned that too much salt makes me sick, I developed a (clearly learned) aversion to overeating salt. I can tell when I have had enough salt and should limit intake the rest of the day because the saliva in the back of my throat becomes noticeably salty.

I couldn't figure out anything about my blood pressure from going to the doctor's office, by the way. I always have high blood pressure in a doctor's office. This is called "white-coat high blood pressure." *Nota bene*: Don't assume you really have high blood pressure unless you know you have high blood pressure outside the doctor's office. I know several people who have been on high blood pressure medications for years, drugs that have side effects (as all medicines do), without their ever finding out whether they *really* have high blood pressure.

Like sugar, salt has an escalator effect. The more you eat, the more you need for something to taste salty enough. If you transition to less salt, once you have adjusted, less salt tastes good, and the amounts in all processed foods make them taste so salty as to be almost inedible. All the cooking and recipes in this book assume a low-salt diet, a diet with only about 1,000 milligrams of salt per day. (If you are used to and can tolerate the ordinary American high-salt diet, you will probably want to use more salt than I do.)

Salt is said to be a flavor enhancer. I think the situation is more complex than that. I think salt, like sugar, enhances flavors in small amounts but masks them in larger amounts. When I rub the salt off a potato chip, I can taste the relatively unpalatable oil and the fact that it is clearly somewhat rancid and unappealing. With the salt, the chip tastes much too salty to my tastes but good otherwise. I think agribusiness puts so much salt in their processed food partly because the food doesn't taste very good otherwise. Maybe they need the salt so we don't taste all the preservatives and other off-flavors.

When I assumed responsibility for caring for my mother, she was experiencing routine swelling of her feet, ankles, and legs that was painful and sometimes so severe as to cause her skin to bruise or split. She was wearing special constricting socks for the condition, and was supposedly (but not actually) on a low-salt diet. Within a few days of eating my food and cooking, which is genuinely a low-salt diet, all my mother's edema (swelling) had disappeared. Sometimes thereafter, though, she experienced some very mild edema. It correlated completely with diet. It always started within about six hours of certain meals and lasted about a day. The things that caused the edema were too much salt, processed meats such as bacon or sausage, and anything with MSG. In addition, if I served major amounts of protein in more than one meal per day, my mother would also get a little edema. The salt, bacon, and sausage didn't surprise me. The MSG and total protein did. Kidney function in older people may not be as good as when they were younger. Lower protein intake is often recommended for people with kidney disease. It is the kidneys that have to process and excrete the waste products from digesting meat. And it is the kidneys that are responsible for excreting salt. Perhaps lowered kidney function was the mechanism in all my mother's responses.

Many elderly people have edema. How many of them, I wonder, could find profound relief in just a change in diet?

Other Oils and Fats

We need only a few grams a day of omega-3 and omega-6 polyunsaturated fatty acids. Our bodies can make all the rest of the oils and fats they need from other components. However, most of us would be hard-pressed to do without other oils and fats to grease our pans, stir-fry our vegetables, and add more succulence, calories, and flavor to many of our foods.

It's pretty easy to grow canola (rapeseed) or soybeans or sunflowers. However, it isn't so easy to process them into oil on a home scale. In most areas of the world, processed oil is a relatively recent product. Humans need processed oil most in countries where they have developed cooking styles that require it. China has long had soybean oil and stir-frying as a major method of cooking. Italy has long had olive oil and vegetables fried or drenched with it. These cuisines were the exceptions, though. For much of the temperate-zone world, animal fat was what was used to grease the pans and add texture and succulence to the bread. Most domestic animals were at one time grown as much for their fat as for the protein they provided.

Native Americans had no processed oil. When they wanted to bake and had no animal fat, they used the "skim" off the top of the water after boiling ground corn or sunflower seeds. That is, when you boil ground corn or sunflower seeds, a little oil is released and floats to the surface. You can use that oil to grease your baking stone (or pan). This low-level extraction can give you enough oil for baking. It would not support a cooking style involving lots of frying or stir-frying. As yet, I don't grow most of my cooking fat or oil, and don't know how to do that without raising more serious amounts of meat. However, I don't use much cooking fat or oil.

The main thing many of us need oil for is salad dressings. I have a simple approach to that problem. Instead of using refined oils, I use maximally unrefined ones. I sliver nuts and use them as ingredients in salads instead of oil. Or I use hard-cooked eggs with the yolks in the salad. Then I dress the salad with just a few herbs, salt and pepper, and lemon juice or vinegar. Or I mash cooked egg yolks with vinegar and herbs to make a salad dressing.

Vitamins, Minerals, Phytochemicals, and Fiber

As gardeners, we eat lots of fruits and vegetables of many kinds, and this big variety satisfies our needs for most vitamins, minerals, phytochemicals, and fiber. Those nutrients that might be lacking in the fruits and vegetables are generally found in whole grains or beans. So a diet based upon staple whole grains and beans, fruits, and vegetables is likely to be a healthy diet.

Getting enough iodine used to be a problem for many inland people once. Now, with iodine added to commercial salt and fish available even to people far from oceans, lack of iodine isn't common.

Plant foods don't provide any vitamin B_{12} or long-chain omega-3 fatty acids, however. For this reason, this book includes a chapter on the home laying flock.

Many people in temperate climates don't get enough vitamin D. The sun isn't intense enough in winter. Indoor lives, clothes, and sunblock further exacerbate the situation. Eggs may provide vitamin D, but it depends upon what the laying flock is eating and how much sun they are getting. I take a daily (standard, not super-potent) vitamin pill as well as cod liver oil, both of which include vitamin D.

Special Implications for Vegetarians and Those with Celiac Disease or Gluten Intolerance, or Who Can't Eat Dairy Products

Those with celiac disease or other malabsorption problems are the last ones on the planet who should be eating refined grains or highly processed foods. Malabsorption in celiacs is not always entirely corrected once gluten is eliminated from the diet. Much more so than most people, we cannot afford empty calories. Our situation is exacerbated by the fact that gluten-free flours are not vitamin-supplemented, as is ordinary refined flour.

Since celiac disease most affects the absorption of fats, we can expect omega-3 fatty acids and fat-soluble vitamins (A, D, and E) to be a particular issue. But other vitamins and nutrients can also be affected.

Over the years I've become convinced that I don't digest raw vegetables very well. Whether this is related to celiac disease I don't know. I enjoy salads, but I eat most of my vegetables cooked, and for my vitamins, it is cooked vegetables I depend upon. Whenever I steam or boil vegetables, I always keep and use the cooking water. I use it in soups, stews, or gravies, or make my tea with it the next morning. (I always boil vegetables without salt and salt the vegetables later so that I can use the cooking water.) We humans have been cooking since we were *Homo erectus*. I toss out here the idea that some of us humans may be "obligate cookers." For us, cooking much of our food may not be optional.

Cow's milk is good food for some people. However, cow's milk is *not* a very good food for most human beings on the planet. Fully three-quarters of the world's adult human population is lactose intolerant to some extent. That is, after childhood, they quit producing lactase, the enzyme needed to break down lactose, or milk sugar. As Walter Willett notes in *Eat, Drink, and Be Healthy*, "Half of Hispanic Americans, 75% of African Americans, and more than 90% of Asian Americans can't tolerate a lot of lactose. For them, drinking a glass of milk can have unpleasant consequences, such as nausea, bloating, cramps, and diarrhea."

Even among those who aren't lactose intolerant, cow's milk can produce problems. Many are allergic to milk proteins. And even in those not allergic to the milk itself, milk can exacerbate asthma, allergies, and sinus problems. I spent my entire life breathing through my mouth until I read about the involvement of milk in allergies in Andrew Weil's book *Eating Well for Optimum Health*. In my case, it is clearly cow's milk protein that is involved. I can eat sheep, goat, or water buffalo milk cheeses. I can also eat cow's milk butter as long as it doesn't contain milk protein (casein) or whey. But if I eat cow's milk cheeses, ice cream (which always contains milk), milk, or anything containing milk protein, in about fifteen minutes my nose is stuffed up. If I eat more the next day, I get short of breath too, the beginning signs of asthma. If I eat cow's milk protein a third

day, I'm short of breath and start having mild asthmatic attacks, which get worse if I persist. Even a tablespoon of milk in my coffee or tea daily is all it takes to keep me in the mode of being asthmatic. (As long as I had a little milk in my coffee daily, I couldn't tell milk was a problem. I simply always had problems with asthma and hay fever and a stuffed-up nose. It is only after I completely eliminated the milk from my routine diet that I could see the correlation when I occasionally added it back.)

However, if I eliminate cow's milk protein from my diet completely, I can get away with eating a major amount about once per month. (I love butter, but need to choose carefully to get a brand that is just butter and salt and doesn't include whey.) So I avoid milk completely in my routine diet, but do have it as a special splurge occasionally.

In an appendix section on dietary recommendations for ameliorating disease, Andrew Weil in *Eating Well for Optimum Health* recommends eliminating dairy products as being useful in treating or ameliorating all of the following: allergies, arthritis, asthma, bronchitis, diarrhea, infections, inflammatory bowel disease (ulcerative colitis, Crohn's disease), sinus problems, and ulcers.

A recent book, *Devil in the Milk: Illness, Health, and the Politics of A1 and A2 Milk*, by Keith Woodford, raises the interesting possibility that it is only some, not all, cows that produce milk protein that is problematic. Unfortunately, most of the breeds used for commercial milk production in Europe and North America have cows that are mostly the wrong type, the A1 type. A1 and A2 are alleles of the gene associated with the production of the milk protein beta casein. A2 beta casein is the "ancient" form of the gene. A2 or an equivalent is the allele in humans, goats, water buffalo, most sheep, African cattle, some but not most European and American cattle, and many but not all New Zealand cattle.

The A1 form of the beta casein gene apparently rose in European cattle about 5,000 years ago. It has a different amino acid at one particular position in the protein chain of the beta casein molecule and, as a result, breaks down to create a seven-amino-acid peptide called beta-casomorphin-7, or BCM7. BCM7 is resistant to digestion and is capable of getting across the intestinal wall into the bloodstream, at least, of anyone who has a leaky gut. All newborn mammals have leaky guts so as to be able to take up maternal antibodies, which are proteins. Celiacs have leaky guts. People with intestinal infections sometimes have temporarily leaky guts. Once in the bloodstream, BCM7 crosses the blood-brain barrier and has opium-like and other effects. *Devil in the Milk* is a documentation and analysis of evidence suggesting that BCM7 might be implicated in diabetes, autism, schizophrenia, allergies, intolerances, and autoimmune problems of many sorts. *Devil in the Milk* is one of the most thorough and best-presented arguments I have ever seen of any scientific issue in a book for a lay audience. (See note 4-18.)

Some heirloom breeds have a high proportion of cows that are of the A2 type. Individual cows as well as bulls can be tested for their beta casein genotype using a few hairs from their tail switches. Nate had a Dexter cow, but was unable to use the (unpasteurized) milk because it gave him indigestion. Even making yogurt didn't help. A housemate ended up milking the cow and using the milk. I've had unpasteurized milk from a couple of different small local herds. It was sweet and the flavor was fantastic. Obviously pasteurization

really affects flavor. But the unpasteurized milk gave me exactly the same problems as pasteurized milk. Pasteurization isn't the issue. So, blaming cows in general, Nate and I have been thinking in terms of getting water buffalo for milk, meat, and draft. However, maybe only some cows are to blame. We are now eager to try the milk of individual heirloom-breed cows to see if our beef is with just some cows. (We will most likely remain primarily interested in water buffalo, however, for various other reasons, even if it turns out that we can drink milk from some cows. See note 4-19.) Given the availability of a simple inexpensive test of beta casein genotype, it should be easy to identify A2 cows for the home milk supply as well as to breed commercial dairy herds that produce all A2 milk. (See note 4-18.)

Meanwhile, for whatever reason, many of us cannot drink commercial cow's milk as it exists presently. Not drinking milk regularly has secondary dietary implications. For many people, the vitamin D added to commercial milk is their main source, and vitamin D deficiency is potentially a problem, even for gardeners, as already discussed. The only reliable way around the problem for those who don't drink milk may be supplements such as taking a vitamin pill or cod liver oil daily.

A second problem with not drinking milk, at least theoretically, is calcium. If you buy the idea that we need 1,000 milligrams or more of calcium per day, there is almost no natural way to get that without drinking milk. I don't buy that idea. That number may more reflect the power of the milk lobby in America than anything scientific. In actuality, we apparently don't know how much calcium humans need. A good review of the calcium issue is Willet's chapter, "Calcium: No Emergency," in *Eat, Drink, and Be Healthy.*

Calcium uptake and metabolism is affected by vitamin D and vitamin K. Many people with low bone density may be suffering from a lack of D or K to help them deal with calcium rather than lack of calcium *per se*. Getting both D and K is easy with a daily multiple vitamin. As for whether supplemental calcium is necessary for most people, the jury is still out on that.

Most vegan vegetarians can generally get their protein pretty easily from plant sources. Protein needs of individuals seem to vary widely, however. I suspect some people need too much protein to thrive as vegetarians. But clearly some people do fine as vegetarians. Most vegetarians, with a full diet of whole grains, beans, and many vegetables, especially dark green leafy vegetables, probably don't need to worry about either protein or calcium. However, there are three nutrients that are potentially problematic for those who don't eat at least some animal products. Vitamin B_{12} is found only in animal foods. Vegan vegetarians are advised to take a B_{12} supplement or a general daily vitamin containing B_{12}. Vegetarians may also lack vitamin D. That, too, can be solved with a simple once-daily all-vegetarian vitamin pill. The third potential problem is omega-3 fatty acids.

If we could all convert the short-chain plant form of omega-3 fatty acid into the longer-chain animal forms that we need, omega-3 fatty-acid needs of vegetarians could be provided by plant sources such as flaxseed, walnuts, canola oil, and, to some extent, greens. However, as already mentioned, not everyone can convert the short-chained plant-derived omega-3s into the longer-chain ones. Those who cannot need to eat animal products containing the long-chain omega-3s. That is, not everyone can survive and thrive as a vegetarian. For some of us, of whom I am

undoubtedly one, eating meat or animal products or fish is obligatory.

Vegetarians with any of the problems associated with a lack of omega-3 fatty acids (asthma, allergies, depression, bipolar disease, mood problems, schizophrenia, ADD, autism, heart disease, etc.) might want to reconsider eating fish or at least taking a cod liver oil supplement. I suspect that people in good health who don't have any of the omega-3 deficiency associated problems, and who feel better when they don't eat meat, can do the omega-3 conversion reactions and don't need the meat. That doesn't mean their diet is appropriate for everyone else. Those who cannot do the conversion of short-chain omega-3s to longer-chain forms will need some meat or animal products in their diets.

Preserving and Storing Methods

What you choose to store and how will depend upon what you like to grow and eat, where you live, and how willing you are to do which kinds of processing work. My main approach to storing staple crops is *natural storage*. Dry corn, beans, and in-shell nuts keep well indoors. Winter squash is shorter-lived than the grains and beans, but stores indoors at room temperature for months, given appropriate varieties. Natural storage requires no extra work beyond harvesting the crops.

Our secondary storage method is cool, moist storage for potatoes, that is, *root-cellar storage*. In our case, our "root cellar" is a wall of shelves in an unheated attached garage. Nate and I stored about 800 pounds of potatoes in 2008 and about 1,200 pounds in 2009, and in both years, ran out of potatoes before we ran out of desire to eat them. Here in the maritime Northwest with our mild winters, we use *winter gardening* and *in-garden storage* and *overwintering* to supply many winter vegetables instead of a root cellar. On our wish list, however, is a full orchard, and bushels of apples and pears in cool storage along with (but in a separate room from) the spuds. In areas with more severe winters, where winter vegetable growing is impossible, in-garden storage becomes less practical, and root-cellar storage is more important.

In the northern tier of the United States, potatoes and apples are by far the most important root-cellar storage crops. Other commonly root-cellared vegetables include carrots, turnips, beets, rutabagas, leeks, daikon radishes, cabbage, Chinese cabbage, and parsnips. These vegetables all need cold or cool, moist storage conditions. Onions and garlic, on the other hand, like cool, dry storage.

I recommend the book *Root Cellaring: Natural Cold Storage of Fruits and Vegetables*, by Mike and Nancy Bubel. It covers both formal root cellars as well as many informal equivalents such as our attached garage, and describes how to grow, handle, and process various fruits and vegetables for root-cellar storage. I particularly exhort everyone to read *Root Cellaring* before building any structure intended for root-cellaring. Many people consider temperature properly in their building plans, but don't know enough about humidity and ventilation issues.

Canning, fermenting, and pickling are also popular storage methods. These methods haven't been my choice, and I have little experience with them. I freeze some fruits and vegetables, but not more than I can afford to lose. Information on these subjects is readily available elsewhere.

Drying fruits and vegetables can give us additional long-storing staples, often with delicious flavors that are distinctively different from those of the fresh produce. Furthermore, with drying we can make our own travel and camping foods. Dried fruits and nuts are some of the best emergency foods; they are portable and can be eaten without cooking.

Drying Fruits and Vegetables

I dry substantial amounts of certain varieties of squash, as I describe in the squash chapter. There are a number of books on drying fruits and vegetables. The one I have found most useful is *Preserve It Naturally II: The Complete Guide to Food Dehydration*, which is published by and available from the company that produces Excalibur dehydrators. Fruits that can be of excellent quality when dried (using appropriate varieties) include apples, apricots, cherries, coconut, dates, figs, grapes, kiwi, nectarines, peaches, pears, persimmons, pineapples, prune plums, and strawberries.

Commercial dried fruit is normally treated with sulfur, sulfites, or metabisulfites. Some people with asthma or allergy problems can have reactions to such fruit, ranging from a stuffy nose to lethal attacks of asthma or anaphylactic shock. Organic processing excludes such additives. But organic dried fruit is expensive. If you can't eat commercial dried fruit, it's especially nice to be able to make your own.

These days, the best way to dry foods is with an electric dehydrator. Sun drying, shade drying, and most solar drying take much longer, create lower-quality dry produce, and give erratic results depending upon the weather (unless you happen to live in a desert). In addition, dirt and flies can be a problem. Oven drying uses a lot of energy and produces inferior, overcooked dried foods, when it works at all. Often it burns the produce. Ovens are not designed to run at temperatures low enough to dry food reliably.

The modern electric dehydrator with its heat source and fan is actually cheaper than either canning or freezing by the time you consider, properly amortized, the costs of equipment and supplies. I believe that, these days, the electric dehydrator is the place to start learning about drying. Then one might move up or back to more natural methods, if desired. (A solar dehydrator, for example.) I use an Excalibur dehydrator for most purposes and strongly recommend it. I suspect, though, that much of the drying done by the American pioneers involved just hanging produce near the wood stove, and those with a wood stove today might explore that possibility.

Many books, especially older books, spend a lot of time talking about pretreatments of produce to be dried with metabisulfites, ascorbic acid (vitamin C), or lemon juice in order to prevent brown-

Drying Prune Plums (and Figs, Apricots, Peaches, and Nectarines)

Prune plums are plums of varieties that are especially good for drying. They are also my favorite plum varieties for fresh eating. ('Italian', 'Brooks', 'Stanley', and 'Imperial Epineause' are some good prune plum varieties.) I dry prune plums by picking or shaking them off the trees, then collecting them in monolayers in flat cardboard trays (such as are discarded by grocery stores after they remove the six-packs of soda). The plums will shake off the tree when they are ready to ripen, but will still be hard enough at the shake-off stage to be quite resistant to bruising. I've harvested immense amounts by shaking the trees every two or three days and collecting until the harvest is over. I let the plums ripen to perfection indoors, examining them daily. It's easiest to tell prime ripeness by squeezing each plum very gently.

To process for drying, I rinse the plums (if necessary), cut them in half, and flip the seed out with my finger. Then I pop the backs as I place each half in the dehydrator (cut side up). "Pop the backs" simply means pressing against the skin side of each half to turn the half inside out. No pretreatments are necessary. The optimum temperature for drying is 135°F. The drying takes place from the cut surface, not through the skin. So it isn't necessary to turn the plum halves over, and they don't stick to the drying surface.

The same process is used to dry halved figs and freestone varieties of apricots, peaches, and nectarines. All other fruits require additional work to remove cores or seeds and/or to slice for drying. Sliced fruit takes much more space in the dehydrator than fruit that can be dried in halves. And sliced fruit must be turned over piece by piece part way through the drying; plus it sticks to the drying surface. So if you love dried fruit but are as resistant to processing labor as I am, look first to prune plums, figs, and freestone varieties of apricots, peaches, and nectarines.

ing of cut surfaces. Metabisulfites, as I mentioned, can cause dangerous allergic reactions in some people. Generally, such pretreatments are not necessary if you are using a modern electric dehydrator. Apple slices, it's true, may turn brown and unappetizing if dried without an antioxidant such as vitamin C or lemon juice. However, it depends upon the variety. Many varieties of apples dry fine without browning with no pretreatment.

Prune plums, figs, and freestone varieties of apricots, peaches, and nectarines are the easiest to dry, and will give you the most excellent-quality dried fruit for the least labor. In each case, you need the right varieties. Some fruits, such as grapes, blueberries, and whole prune plums, have enough surface wax so that they must be "checked," that is, subjected to a brief dip in boiling water, before they can be dried (whole).

Use prime produce for drying. Blemished is OK if the blemishes are cut away. Fruit should be fully ripe or very slightly underripe (by about half a day), since some ripening occurs during the drying process. Tasteless underripe fruit will be inferior dried. Eat your cull fruit fresh or turn it into jam or feed it to livestock; don't bother drying it. (Somewhat underripe fruit goes well in curries or in sweet-and-sour dishes.)

The optimum temperature for drying is 125°F for most vegetables, 135°F for most fruits, and 145°F for tomatoes and onions. If dried at a temperature less than optimum, the process takes longer. If dried at too high a temperature, however, a fruit or vegetable may case-harden instead of drying properly. That is, it forms a hard impervious dry outer shell over cut surfaces, and the interior doesn't dry at all.

Vegetables are usually dried until crisp. Fruits are usually dried until leathery. For optimum reliable storage, I dry fruits beyond the point of optimum moisture for pleasurable eating, then re-hydrate them a little before eating. This can be done by just leaving the bag open for a couple of days before you plan to eat the fruit.

Dehydrators

For the resilient gardener, a dehydrator is not optional. We may or may not dry fruit or vegetables. But we need a dehydrator to dry seeds for long-term storage. The dehydrator is an essential part of our seed-saving (and seed-hoarding) repertoire. The most relevant dehydrators for the home scale are of three types: poorly designed little round-tray dehydrators, workable little round-tray dehydrators, and far superior but more expensive Excaliburs.

The poorly designed little round-tray dehydrators push air up through the lowest tray to the next. So the produce in the second tray gets moist air that has already gone through the first tray, and dries considerably slower. Produce in the third tray gets even moister air and dries even more slowly. Avoid dehydrators with this design.

The other kind of little round-tray dehydrator has an airflow pattern in which the air comes up through a central column and goes out over the trays. This is a better design. The moist air from one tray doesn't pass over any other tray. However, the total amount of air is divided among all the trays. So while you can stack up four trays, for example, each will get only one-fourth the airflow as does a tray used singly, and the batch will take roughly four times longer to dry. I got my start seed saving with two small round dehydrators. They are most useful in drying things that are already nearly dry to start with, such as seeds. That is, they are best when being asked only to put the finishing touches on a drying job. Lower trays tend to get more air, so it's important to rotate the trays occasionally when drying seeds. I don't want to mention brand names here, because they seem to change every few years. There are several brand names with nearly identical designs and interchangeable trays. For seed saving you need a reliable thermostat that goes down to 95°F. (Some don't have a setting that low.) For drying fruits and vegetables it's useful if the thermostat and temperatures go up to at least 145°F.

The amount each tray will hold is pretty limited, and the fact that there is a large hole in the center of each tray is inconvenient. The big advantage of these small dehydrators is that they are inexpensive and readily available both new and used. New ones cost about $50. Used ones are often available in yard sales for about $10. I don't find them very practical for drying more than a single tray of fresh produce at once, about a pound or less. But that's all you need to experiment with and learn on. And one of these little dehydrators with half a dozen trays is enough to support a serious seed-saving habit.

Anything a little round-tray dehydrator can do an Excalibur can do better. The Excalibur has a more powerful fan and heater and a much better design. The airflow is divided and a constant portion flows over each tray. Each tray gets the same amount of air, no matter how many trays are in use. So a full load dries as fast as a single tray. The Excalibur trays are square with no hole in the middle. A single Excalibur tray holds as much as a small round dehydrator loaded with six trays. It also dries a full batch in about a quarter of the time (or faster). So even the smaller four-

tray Excalibur model has the production capability of about sixteen round-tray dehydrators with six trays each. The smaller four-tray Excalibur costs about $200; the deluxe nine-tray model costs about $300. The deluxe model, in addition to temperature controls, has a twenty-six-hour timer.

Hoarding and Saving Seeds

Seed saving is much talked about. It involves growing plants in such a way that the seed is genetically pure and genetically what it should be, then cleaning and processing it. There are several books on seed saving, including my own, *Breed Your Own Vegetable Varieties: The Gardener's and Farmer's Guide to Plant Breeding and Seed Saving*. In addition, I discuss seed saving specifically for corn, beans, and squash in this book in the appropriate chapters. *Seed hoarding*, however, isn't generally discussed. By seed hoarding, I mean laying down a supply of seed for long-term storage. The seed may either be seed you have saved or seed you have bought.

In my freezer are gallons of seeds, specially dried and sealed in glass jars. Most of it is seed I have grown. Some is seed I have bought. I can expect that seed to last as long as the freezer and the electricity last plus (for the corn, for example) at least another ten years. I think it is a good idea to have such a backup supply of seed for all varieties that really matter to me. Whenever I come to appreciate some new variety, my first step isn't saving the seed. My first step is simply buying extra, drying it properly, and freezing it. I don't save seed of every variety I use. But I have learned how. And I do try to have a stash of every variety I use. Should it become impossible to buy the seed, I would have enough hoarded seed to grow a crop and to start saving the seed myself from that point on.

To freeze seed you need to be able to seal it in jars or other airtight containers. Much commercial seed is not dry enough for that. The seed continues respiring slowly, and needs oxygen. The seed needs to be dried more thoroughly, which puts it into a deeper state of dormancy. After the more thorough drying, the seed can be sealed in airtight containers and frozen. To get the seed dry enough to seal in glass jars or freeze requires a lower humidity than is found naturally in most places. So I dry our seed in a dehydrator at 95°F for the right amount of time, until the indicating criteria say that it is dry enough. The biggest indicator for corn and beans and other legume seeds is the "hammer test." That is, take some seeds out to the sidewalk or driveway and hit a few of them with a hammer. If they shatter, they are dry enough to seal in airtight containers and to freeze. If the seeds smash instead of shattering, they are still too wet. The indicating criteria for dry-enough squash seed are a little more complex; I discuss them in the squash chapter.

After you remove a jar of seed from the freezer, always give it a day to warm up naturally before you open it. Otherwise, moisture condenses on the seed, and it is too much of a shock.

An added benefit of freezing seeds is that it kills insects and insect eggs. So freezing the seed for a few weeks is useful even if you don't store any that way permanently. (A shorter freeze may or may not be sufficient.)

If you don't have a freezer you can still hoard seeds. Dry them as described and seal them in airtight containers. Then replace each lot of seed with fresh seed occasionally. (For most seed, once every five years will do.) Store the containers of seed in as cool a place as you have. Hidatsa Indians hid caches of seed in the ground as they left summer villages for winter villages. I haven't quite figured out how to store containers of seeds in the ground for more than a few years. (The metal lids would rust. Most plastic disintegrates.) But even a few years might be useful.

I prefer to hoard seed I have saved myself. It is possible to produce hand-saved seed that is prime beyond anything possible on a commercial scale. Such seed has astonishing longevity and vigor. For example, six-year-old corn seed of mine that has been fully dried and stored in a glass jar at room temperature germinates faster and more vigorously than most freshly bought commercial seed. Last spring Nate and I planted six-year-old flour corn seed, most of which had been stored at room temperature. It was a breeding project, and we wanted every seed to count. So we spaced it carefully. Nearly every seed came up. I doubt if we were "missing" more than a dozen seeds in the entire field of a few thousand.

Of course, I do save seed (and breed) for crops and varieties I care about the most. I breed my own varieties so I can select for varieties that have spectacular flavors, and that do well under organic growing conditions, that thrive without seed treatments and on modest levels of water and soil fertility, that are resistant to everything relevant in my garden, and that are optimally adapted to my region and my growing methods and purposes. To do my own plant breeding I have to be able to save seeds. In addition, I save my own seeds because that gives me the best quality. And so I don't have to worry about other people crossing up or changing the varieties. Or about importing diseases. I also save seeds because the price is right. And because saving seeds is such fun. I love to harvest, thresh, and clean seeds. I love to run my fingers through them, play with them, and array them in jars on shelves where I can see and take joy in them.

To save seeds is to complete the circle. When we save seeds, we are plant breeders, choosing which germplasm to perpetuate. We incorporate our values into our seeds. We spread our values along with our seeds. Thus do we help create and shape the next generation of the Grand Alliance.

CHAPTER FIVE

Labor and Exercise

Purposeful Exercise. The All-or-Nothing Problem. Warming Up and General Conditioning. Basic Safety. Restless Leg Syndrome, Walking, and Gardening. Gardening Styles and Labor—Beds versus Rows. Choosing Gardening Styles, Planting Methods, and Tools to Fit Your Body. Garden Beds: Double-Dug, Single-Dug, Sorta-Dug, and Worm-Dug. The Peasant Hoe. Spacing and Labor. Planting. The Furrowing Plow. Varying the Kinds of Labor. Weeds. Buying Tools. Using the Peasant Hoe. Using Light Hoes. Sharpening Tools. Mulch. Transplanting versus Direct Seeding, Revisited. Selective Sloppiness. Knowing When to Stop. Easy on the Back (and Knees). Helpers.

Purposeful Exercise

Once upon a time, most people got all their exercise by creating and maintaining their homes and food supplies. These days, it's common to see people hiring someone else to maintain their yards, then walking or running long distances to nowhere and exercising hard doing nothing in order to stay fit. Meanwhile, many of us have trouble with our weight. We just don't seem to have the "discipline" to walk or run strenuously for no reason or to work hard doing nothing. I think we humans, like other sensible animals, have been evolutionarily selected to avoid unnecessary work. We save our energy in case we need it later, when something might be chasing us. People who were inclined to wear themselves out needlessly were more likely to already be tired when the saber-toothed cat showed up, and got themselves eliminated from the gene pool a long time ago. We thus descended, I believe, from the sensibly lazy. So when we resist artificial exercise, it's not because we "lack will power." It's because we have good instincts.

In order to stay fit, however, we *need* to exercise. We know that. But what we need emotionally in order to be willing to *do* the exercise is legitimate, purposeful exercise—exercise that accomplishes real things, and during which we get our needed physical activity as a by-product.

Tending yards and gardening can be excellent purposeful exercise. It is *not*, however, *automatically* excellent exercise. For many people, yards and gardens are where they go to get heart attacks, strokes, carpal tunnel syndrome, or other injuries, acute or chronic. This chapter is about how to design and organize our gardening so as to optimize its role in encouraging healthful exercise while at the same time minimizing total work, unnecessary work, inefficient work, "unfun" work, and the probability of injury. This section is also about how to design our gardening so that it is more resilient to the loss of our labor input, as can happen when we or those we love experience injury, illness, or other emergency, and the garden must do without our labor for a while.

The All-or-Nothing Problem

The main difficulty with gardening and yard work as exercise is that they tend to be too all or nothing. There is no exercise of a given type for a long time, then a huge amount all at once. That pattern is better at exhausting or injuring bodies than strengthening and conditioning them. We need to better understand the labor implications of our garden design and planting patterns so that we can better spread exercise of various types over time. In that way, our gardening provides more useful conditioning exercise and fewer all-at-once chunks of work and labor emergencies.

By "labor emergencies" I mean situations such as needing to harvest all the dry corn and beans all at once before a sudden rain. Or needing to harvest 1,500 pounds of squash *today*, because a freeze is expected tonight. Making hay while the sun shines is one thing. Needing to harvest all the dry beans and corn or all of a huge squash planting at the same time suggests a need for better planning. Some people like labor emergencies, however. If you're in your twenties and in great condition, you may be able to garden any old which way, abuse your body for as many hours as you like, and still recover without serious inconvenience beyond a few days of soreness. You may even use your gardening to create physical challenges for you to overcome. And that's OK—if you're young and fit. Have at it. I once swam kitty-corner six miles across Long Lake in the Adirondack Mountains in early spring, just to see if I could. I understand.

If I gardened now as I did once, however, I could pretty easily injure or possibly even kill myself. Furthermore, if I strain myself too badly by doing a single type of gardening work for too

many hours, I'm unable to garden over the next day or two or maybe several. I just don't snap back afterward as quickly as I did when I was younger. Generally, though, I garden much better and more efficiently now than I did a few decades ago. And my gardens do better. They produce gloriously and abundantly, on amazingly little labor. With gardening, experience matters.

Warming Up and General Conditioning

I've seen many books and articles that espouse the idea of doing warm-up exercises before gardening or even walking. If this works for you, that is fine. It doesn't work for me. I dislike purposeless exercise enough that requiring myself to do some before gardening or walking tends to mean less gardening or walking. In addition, many of the most glorious walks or gardening sessions happen spontaneously. I have never injured myself by gardening or walking. So if I want to take a walk, I just go walk. And when I want to garden, I just go and garden. I start slowly, however. My walks start off as ambles. They speed up automatically as I warm up and feel inclined. I tend to start each type of garden task slowly too. The beginning of the hoeing, for example, constitutes its own gentle warm-up. If you like to plunge into activities at full speed, however, some warm-up stretches beforehand are probably a good idea.

Many books and magazines also suggest exercising indoors specifically to be in shape for the gardening season. I don't do that either, with two exceptions. The exercises usually recommended don't match the kinds of labor I need to do with the tools I generally use. What muscles you use for gardening depends a lot upon your garden style and your specific choice of tools. In addition, the exercises are usually focused upon strengthening the back in preparation for straining and trashing it while gardening. I instead have developed methods for gardening that are easy on the back.

I do a few minutes of gentle stretching in the mornings, however, to maintain overall limberness. I also walk regularly. I use short walks for breaks, or when I want to think about something, or when I'm just feeling restless. Walking is an excellent way to maintain the cardiovascular health that enhances overall fitness and endur-

Basic Safety

Carry tools with the edges and tips pointed down and/or away from you (and others) so that if you stumble and fall, it won't be on a sharp point or edge. When you put a tool down, even for an instant, always place it with the point or edge down/away. Don't place tools in such a way that if someone steps on any part of them, they can get impaled or cut or cause the tool to flip up.

Don't get macho about how much you can do or how fast you can work or how long unless you're young enough and fit enough to not have to be concerned about heart attacks and it's too cool for heatstrokes. Don't let someone younger or fitter than you goad you (directly or accidentally) into competitions. Don't goad anyone else into trying to keep up with anyone else.

Fatigue can lead to carelessness and injury.

Drink water before you "need" it. Our body's thirst signals lag behind our actual need for water. Thirst signals become less obvious as we get older. Even slight dehydration is associated with muscular weakness and fatigue, and can raise the probability of heat stress or heatstroke.

Not everyone can work in the heat of the day on hot days. Many of us need to limit our gardening to the cooler hours.

"Go soak your head in a bucket of water" is great advice on a hot day. There are lots of blood vessels very near the surface on our heads. Dumping water on our head or running the hose over our head can cool the entire body and can make a big difference when we are feeling overheated. Running cold water over the wrists and hands also helps. They, too, have many blood vessels near the surface.

Hats matter.

On cold days, wear layers you can shed as the heat from exercise and the weather require. A hat (or balaclava), neck muff, and warm shoes and socks can make your hands warmer, which matters if it is cold and you need to work without gloves. (I chop the end off a balaclava cap to make a great neck muff.)

Pay attention to your body. Pay attention to your heart. Notice what it does when you are simply getting a good workout versus overextending. If your heart seems to be struggling, stop and lie down in the shade for a while, way before you push yourself into a heart attack. You may be able to work much longer and harder some times than others, depending upon how hot it is, whether and when and what you have eaten, whether you are adequately hydrated, whether you are coming down with or recovering from something, and other factors.

ance. This translates into being able to garden for hours when I want or need to. In addition, walking takes care of lower-body strength.

There are many gardening tasks that require upper-body strength. The gardening tasks themselves tend to be too seasonal or too all-or-nothing to build the basic strength and endurance in the muscles involved. I don't have anything in my life except gardening that builds or maintains upper-body strength. So I resort to a little minor weightlifting. I use a couple of 8-pound barbells and a couple of 1-pound ones. For the heavier weight, I chose ones big enough so that I can feel ten repetitions and don't need to do more than twenty, to build the capability of my muscles to work through heavier tasks. I lift the barbell above my head several times with one hand, with my arm oriented different ways on different sections of lifts (so various different muscles are used). I also put one arm on a table, bend over, and lift the weight from below with my arm oriented different ways. I do an equal number of reps with both hands.

I do most of my weightlifting with the 1-pound barbells, which simulates the muscular effort needed for hoeing and most other garden tasks. I do lots of repetitions, usually while doing something else, like listening to the news. I do the lifts various ways to exercise the muscles generally. But I especially lift with my palms down and hands and thumbs both tucked over the barbell, the lift starting with arms hanging down. This lift strengthens exactly those arm muscles involved in using the peasant hoe. I also do some wrist exercises, that is, just wriggling the 1-pound barbells up, down, and around using my wrists. This exercise is designed to strengthen my wrists and protect against carpal tunnel syndrome.

Back when I did a lot of pulling of weeds by hand, there was another exercise I found useful. I kept a towel by the chair I sit in to watch TV. While watching TV, I would loop the towel around one foot, grasp it with the fingers of both hands in exactly the same orientation as is used in pulling weeds, and make corresponding pulling motions.

Restless Leg Syndrome, Walking, and Gardening

I sometimes get restless leg syndrome (RLS) when I don't walk at least every other day. That is, in the evening, my legs are twitching and jumpy and uncomfortable. Sometimes my legs get so twitchy it is impossible to sleep, and I get up and walk up and down the stairs several times. I hate that sort of thing, it's much harder on my knees than walking, and it runs my pulse up to where it still takes a while before I can sleep.

When I take walks every day, I never have a problem with RLS. I can do enough gardening or yard work to get obviously tired and have sore legs and still have RLS symptoms in the evening if I have skipped walking for more than a couple of days. The health and fitness pundits speak as if all exercise types that get your heart rate up high enough for long enough are equal. I don't think so. I speculate that the style of muscle use involved in walking is uniquely tied into our overall physiology, and that walking *per se* may have significant effects upon overall energy metabolism, fat utilization, and weight control. Other exercise, even other leg exercise, might not be so physiologically integrated. (I would guess that running or jogging would work as well as walking, but haven't confirmed this.)

What is restless leg syndrome? Nobody knows. I do know that I tend to get restless in the late morning or early afternoon if I have been doing nonphysical things all day. So I take a break and take a walk. The walks are not long enough or intense enough to tire me (or, probably, to please the exercise pundits). However, I come back refreshed mentally and physically. I get classic RLS symptoms in the late afternoon and evening, and always on days when I have skipped walking for two days or more. Restless leg syndrome is generally considered a medical condition, and some people take medication for it. In me, though, it seems to be a sloth indicator. It means I need to walk more, and that I have missed or ignored the cues. Sometimes I have developed a pattern of jumping in the car and going off to run some errands instead of walking when I get restless. RLS symptoms serve as a reminder to readjust my patterns. In me, RLS seems to be a useful health-encouraging cue, not a medical problem.

Perversely enough, I only have RLS symptoms when I'm in basically good shape or returning to good shape. When I'm completely out of shape, I have no RLS symptoms. The general restlessness cue, as well as the RLS I get from ignoring the cues, seems to require a basic level of fitness to work. I also don't seem to get RLS when I'm genuinely sick and have quit exercising because I can't.

I relate my personal experiences here because I think there are probably others who, like me, can avoid RLS just by walking. Since we don't know what RLS is, however, we don't know if all RLS has the same causes and cures in all people. It might not. My observations, though, might suggest something worth trying if you have RLS.

Meanwhile—back in the garden—I would love to tell you that I think gardening is wonderful all-around exercise and that it can substitute for everything else. And I think it almost is . . . almost . . . except for walking. I think we still need to walk. Or at least amble.

Gardening Styles and Labor— Beds versus Rows

How many gardens start thus? First, we haul out the rototiller (or hire the tractor guy) and till up the entire garden. We let the buried thatch decompose for three weeks and hire the tractor guy or rototill again. Then we try to plant the whole thing all at once, preferably before it rains. Rain will compact the soil and make it harder to create furrows for planting. In addition, if a couple of weeks go by before we plant, weeds will have such a head start that we really should rototill again or hoe the entire area before planting. So after the second plowing or tilling, we tend to want to plant everything all at once. Planting becomes a bottleneck. Needing to plant everything all at once creates an emergency.

Once we have successfully planted everything all at once, it will all need to be weeded all at once. And the entire garden is in seedlings needing maximum watering care all at once. Many a garden fails because, once planting has been turned into an all-at-once emergency, the gardener collapses (exhausted but happy) and forgets the garden for a while, during which time the seedlings fail to germinate or die from lack of water, or weeds get too far ahead.

For small gardens, there is much to be said for beds. In many situations they are the only option. A garden bed is a soft place where you don't walk. You don't walk on beds even when weed-

Choosing Gardening Styles, Planting Methods, and Tools to Fit Your Body

The style of gardening as well as your particular choice of tools determines what parts of your body you use (and possibly abuse). Some choices of gardening styles mean that you will need to spend much time on hands and knees to weed instead of hoeing. Planting transplants requires getting down and rising up again for every plant, which is hard on the knees. Some styles of hoes allow you to work with a straight back and straight wrists. Others require a bent back or bent wrists. The way most people "instinctively" grab a hoe translates into a bent back and bent wrists. It is much easier on your wrists if the tools you choose and your style of using them allow you to work with straight wrists. Consider the effects of using the tool on your back and wrists when you choose a garden tool.

Longer handles are usually associated with tools meant to be used without a need for bending the back. Short-handled peasant hoes, shovels, or garden forks require a bent back. The D-grip on my furrowing plow and the grip-piece on my diamond hoe are designed so that these tools can be used with a straight wrist (see photo insert).

It can be useful to have different kinds of tools—different light hoes, for example—that represent different designs. That way, when the job is big, just shifting tools changes which muscles are involved. My diamond hoe, for example, is held by the grip in one hand and uses a forward-and-back movement of my arm (with a straight wrist). I shift between arms at intervals. If I then shift to the Coleman hoe, I will be using entirely different movements of my arms. A shift to the peasant hoe means I'll be using primarily the lifting muscles of my arms. (None of these hoes, *used properly*, require bending my back. But if my back was stronger than my arms, I might choose a stirrup hoe.)

ing, harvesting, or digging to renovate them. This means the width must be limited to what you can comfortably reach across from the sides—a maximum of about 5 feet, generally. Beds may be any length, however.

We usually create or rejuvenate beds by digging. Someone, of course, has to do the digging. But you don't have to dig all the beds at once. Gardening in beds particularly lends itself to areas with long growing seasons, mild winters, and year-round gardening, with different beds being planted at various times throughout the year. Gardening in beds is also typical for perennial or ornamental plantings. I had no choice about gardening in beds when vegetable gardening in my backyard. Various concrete walls and fences and property lines made it impossible to drive a tractor into the yard. So there was no option of hiring the tractor guy. Also, there were so many septic easements and shady areas that the space available for gardening was limited to small areas here and there. Even rototilling with a walk-behind tiller isn't practical with tiny dispersed beds.

When we garden in beds in the backyard, it is often automatically in raised beds. When we start with poor soil or the subsoil typical of many

Don't Put Sides on Your Beds

Do not build garden beds with wood or other artificial sides unless you are on a slope so steep that the soil will fall out of the bed otherwise. The minute you put sides on a garden bed you totally change the labor situation. You can't hoe effectively near the artificial side. So you now must do that weeding by hand on your hands and knees. Furthermore, you can't run a tiller or mower between the beds very near to the sides, so you have to hand-weed around the outer sides of the beds also, and perhaps all of the paths in between the beds. Make your raised beds as gentle, natural mounds with no artificial sides.

backyards, we usually add bulky organic materials (leaves, compost, etc.) to help create a decent garden soil. These added materials plus any dug soil translate into a raised bed. Raised beds have special advantages and liabilities. They dry out and warm up faster in the spring than planting areas that are level with the ground around them. This is a big advantage for early plantings in areas that experience cold, wet springs (such as Oregon). In addition, if the water table is high or the soil is shallow you may need raised beds to provide deep enough soil for plant roots. However, when there is little or no rain (such as in Oregon in summer), the fact that raised beds dry out faster means they need more frequent watering.

Beds don't need to be raised, though. They can be level with the rest of the ground. You can, for example, start by tilling a garden area, then just designate certain areas as beds and others as paths. Beds also do not have to be permanent. Temporary beds are not walked on throughout the growing season but are tilled up at the end of the season; and next year's beds may not be in the exact same places. Even raised beds need not be permanent. You can till up the entire garden area first, then hoe or till the soil up into beds. Then you plant and tend the beds as beds (and avoid walking on them) for just the one growing season. Several large organic farms around here operate largely or completely with a style of temporary raised beds. They till a field, then shape it into raised beds with a tractor-drawn bed-forming implement. Then they treat the beds as beds (and don't walk on them) for a season before tilling the entire field again.

For many years, I used a mixed strategy. I grew the crops that needed to be harvested almost daily for summer meals in permanent raised beds in the backyard. Then I had a larger tilled garden elsewhere for field corn, dry beans, and winter squash. In my backyard I planted about one bed every three weeks as the breaks in the weather permitted. I planted the bed for first-early peas in February; greens in March and April; tomatoes, summer squash, and green beans in May and June; overwintering brassicas in July and August; and garlic, fava beans, and overwintering peas in October. My plantings of corn, dry beans, and winter squash were too large for me to be able to deal with as hand-dug beds. They also needed to be planted approximately all at once in May, fitting perfectly with the pattern of just calling the tractor guy to till up a field. These crops also did not require tending or harvesting daily. So these are the crops I grew in the tilled field away from home.

Gardening in intensively planted beds, as described in the next section, is the way to get the most yield from small spaces. In order to obtain those high yields, however, you must have very fertile soil, must water regularly, and must plant intensively. You really crowd the plants compared to traditional plantings in rows. I found that such intensive plantings did not work for me. The crowded plantings must be watered almost every day it doesn't rain. Here in maritime Oregon, that is every day starting in June and going right through the entire summer.

I am not the sort of person who, given my druthers, wants to water or do any other chore every single day, even in the best of times. During the period I was caring for my mother, absolutely all of my ability to do those kinds of tasks was taken up with the caregiving situation. Garden beds do not have to be planted intensively, however. If I planted my beds with about 50 percent more space than typical for intensive beds, I didn't have quite the watering pressure. I found I could water every other day or even skip two days without much problem. Nevertheless, I still lost entire beds here and there whenever an emergency in my mother's medical situation took me totally out of the garden for a while. I learned to minimize the impact of these emergencies on my gardening by not planting more than one bed every three weeks. That way I had only one bed at a time at its most vulnerable stage with respect to either watering or weeding. Whenever the unforeseen deprived the garden of my labor for a while, if I lost something, it was usually only one bed, not all of them.

These days Nate and I garden entirely in a tilled garden arranged in traditional rows, and our spacings within the rows are on the generous side. We space things so as to allow ourselves to water only the most moisture-dependent plants (tomatoes, full-season sweet corn, melons, and kale) once per week and the least water-needy plants (potatoes) not at all. This cuts down on the total amount of water needed as well as watering labor. This garden can survive and thrive when left completely alone for a week, even during the worst heat waves in summer, and considerably longer the rest of the time. Nate doesn't like must-do-every-day chores any more than I do. Until I had expanded to a much bigger leased garden elsewhere (and a collaborator), however, garden beds in the back-yard were an essential part of my strategy. And I simply did not have the room to give the plants as much space as they needed for once-per-week watering and greater water resilience. Gardening, like the rest of life, is full of trade-offs.

Garden Beds: Double-Dug, Single-Dug, Sorta-Dug, and Worm-Dug

There are two kinds of vegetable gardeners. There are those who garden in beds of some kind, and for whom John Jeavons's classic *How to Grow More Vegetables* is the ultimate foundation book, a must-read, and an essential reference. Then there are those who don't garden in beds, for whom *How to Grow More Vegetables* is *still* a must-read and an essential reference. The full title of the current (7th) edition is *How to Grow More Vegetables (and Fruits, Nuts, Berries, Grains, and Other Crops) Than You Ever Thought Possible on Less Land Than You Can Imagine*. The title actually understates the contents. The book is about how to grow pretty nearly all your food and your garden's fertilizer on a modest amount of land.

John Jeavons gardens in California on double-dug raised beds. He describes everything about the process, from what kind of tools to use and how many minutes every stage takes to the yields of produce obtainable for virtually everything. This book is crammed with hard numbers. I still refer to it frequently, even though I no longer garden in beds at all and have actually never made a double-dug bed.

A double-dug bed is dug and worked 2 feet deep. I've never made one in part because my back argues about digging even ordinary beds and simply vetoes out of hand the concept of 2-foot-deep ones. In addition, parts of my current backyard have bedrock less than 2 feet down. And parts of an earlier backyard had the winter water table less than 2 feet down. However, you can make shallower, less perfect beds than Jeavons's bed and simply space things a bit wider to make up the difference.

My favorite way of starting a garden bed is to begin in fall and make a huge pile of leaves or duck-poopy straw bedding in the area where I will want the bed. A layer about a foot deep is ideal. I just dump the layer right on top of the (mowed) grass. All winter long, huge night crawlers work on the pile and transform and soften the ground underneath with worm burrows and enrich it with worm castings. By spring there is only a little layer of leaves or straw about an inch or two thick left on the surface. This is easily turned under into the already soft soil beneath. That is, the bed has been dug for the first time by the worms. So all I have to do is the less demanding sort of "turning over" needed occasionally with an established bed. This pattern depends upon the fact that we have big night crawlers and mild, wet winters. However, the basic pattern that time and natural processes can be substituted for much of the digging labor applies everywhere.

I often only "sorta-dig" a garden bed, even when I am starting in spring. For example, I sometimes turn over the soil only about one shovel deep. I start by removing the sod using my peasant hoe (see sidebar). Then I add the compost or other amendments (manurey straw, for example) and turn the soil over and break it up, again with my heavy peasant hoe. (I may water the soil and come back two or three days later before digging or hoeing. A key to minimizing digging effort is to have the right moisture content.) Then I plant something I intend to harvest within about six weeks, such as eat-all spring greens. The softened bed is only a few inches deep, but the greens are harvested before their roots need more. Then I hoe down the residue and plant something else. (Using the peasant hoe again; you need a heavy hoe, not a light one, to do these sorts of jobs.) By then, worms and other soil life have been working on the bed for two months, and the layer of softened and fertilized soil is significantly deeper than what I originally dug. By the time the second crop has germinated and grown enough to need a deeper bed, the cooperating critters (worms, sow bugs, and myriad others) in the bed have had three or four months to soften the soil beneath and extend the layer of better tilth and fertility.

My all-time favorite bed started with a couple cubic yards each of sand and compost, just mixed and dumped on the mowed grass on the hillside where I wanted the new bed. Underneath the grass was nearly solid clay. This gave me a raised bed about 6 inches deep of sandy compost on top of sod over clay. (I didn't remove the grass sod or dig anything.) Then I planted an eat-all 'Green Wave' mustard crop for freezing. Six weeks later, I harvested the mustard. The 6-inch bed was deep

The Peasant Hoe

If I needed to grow substantial amounts of food and could have only one store-bought tool, I would choose my heavy hoe, my "peasant hoe." Oregon settlers built and maintained their gardens and corn patches primarily with this tool. We peasants the world over always have some version of this tool. Buffalo Bird Woman's model was made from the shoulder bone of an elk. It was her only hoe as well as her shovel. My peasant hoe was made by Bob Denman at Red Pig Garden Tools (See note 5-4.)

The peasant hoe is what's known as an "eye hoe," but there are many different designs of eye hoes. Eye-hoe heads have a ring through which the handle is fit and a hole or eye in the ring for a screw that helps hold the head on the handle without wobbling. My peasant hoe has a 2-pound head with a 7¾-inch width and a 9-inch length. That is the size, weight, and dimensions I recommend. The sides of the head are *not* parallel. They expand toward the blade end. I sharpen both the end and the first inch or so of the sides to make points. During the stroke, I cant the blade slightly so that it slices into the soil or weeds with one point first.

My peasant hoe has a 60-inch handle. You can get a similar hoe head from many sources by just looking under "eye hoe" and choosing the one that fits my description. However, most do not come with a handle as long as is needed to use the tool the way I do—that, is with a straight back, using the lifting power of the arms and the weight of the tool instead of the muscles of the back. I use my peasant hoe for general digging, removing sod, breaking up soil, knocking down residues, and weeding.

enough because the plants weren't in the ground long enough to need more.

After I harvested the mustard, I hoed down the residue, then planted tomato transplants. This involved digging a hole for each transplant, so I was automatically softening and digging the bed a bit deeper in each transplant position. The digging was considerably easier than it would have been earlier, as the grass sod had mostly vanished and the clay beneath was already softer and was beginning to resemble actual soil. After the tomatoes' had grown for about a month (and the rains had quit), I put down 3 inches of straw mulch so that the tomatoes' roots could fully occupy and use their still-less-than-ideally-deep

bed. (Without mulch, the top few inches of soil dry out occasionally, killing roots and making the bed effectively shallower.) We had all the tomatoes we could eat that season from this half-dug bed. By the end of the season, the bed was worm-dug much deeper than I ever did.

Spacing and Labor

If I plant corn and thin to 8 inches apart in the rows, there isn't enough room between plants for me to use my favorite hoe, my peasant hoe, which is 7¾ inches across. I instead thin to 12 inches and use the peasant hoe. If I plant anything else at

4 inches apart or less, even my light hoes won't fit between plants. I would have to do all the weeding between plants by hand on my hands and knees. If I broadcast lettuce or mustard seed over a bed, the seedlings will be close enough together so that I will have to do all weeding by hand. This is workable only when the soil is relatively free of weed seeds and the seeds I'm planting germinate and grow fast enough and vigorously enough to compete with weeds.

Gardens arranged in rows with traditional spacing make it easiest to tend the plants with a hoe from a comfortable standing position. However, there is more empty space that has to be tended than with beds.

The spacing of the paths between garden beds or the space between rows also has major labor implications. If paths are too narrow for a garden cart, you have to hand-carry all amendments and mulch in and produce out. If the paths are too narrow to run a tiller or mower down, you may end up spending a lot of time hand-weeding or hoeing paths. In addition, if you are going to hoe your beds, you need wide enough paths between the beds to get the right angles on the work. I find even comfortable weeding by hand requires having generous room between beds or rows. Hand-weeding from tiny paths requires contorting one's body, back, and wrists in ways that are unnecessary when there's more space between beds. I consider 3 feet between beds minimal.

The space between rows in traditional row-style plantings is often highly integrated with the tool to be used in weeding between the rows. Nate and I use 3½ feet between rows, partly because that gives enough space for hoeing and weeding. But in addition, that spacing is as little as we find comfortable when it comes to tilling between the

rows with a 26-inch-wide rototiller. That size rototiller was chosen, in turn, because it works well with 3½-foot row spacing.

All of our crops are happy with 3½ feet of space between rows except for big viney squash. For those, we use 7 feet. We find it easiest to use 3½ feet or multiples of 3½ feet, and adjust space in the rows to accommodate that row spacing rather than trying to change row spacing for individual crops or varieties.

Planting

Back when I was gardening mostly with beds, my initial approach was to try to dig as many beds as possible when the first break in the weather came and the soil dried out enough to dig. It didn't work. Digging is very hard on the back, which is my weak link. I usually wore out my back and my enthusiasm simultaneously and quit at some point to take a break. Then I often never quite got back to the garden that day. Sometimes I would end up missing the rest of the weather break and end up with no beds that were actually completed and ready to plant. So I learned to restrict my digging to no more than about an 8-foot length of a 4-foot-wide bed. I turn over that much, hoe it with my heavy peasant hoe to break up clods, then plant it. It is much healthier and more workable for me to deal with the digging, hoeing, and planting of a small bed or section of bed in a day than to try to get more area dug, great digging weather or not. The different tasks exercise different muscles and are thus less likely to exhaust any one group. And I tend to quit if I assign myself the task of doing lots of straight digging. I detest the digging. On the other hand, I enjoy the hoeing and planting. I can get through the digging easiest when it is a small amount, and when I have the enjoyable hoeing and planting coming along soon. When I have a bed that is longer than 8 feet, I dig, hoe, and plant it in 8-foot sections. (I simply make a little ridge between sections worked and planted on different days and treat each section as if it were an independent bed.)

These days, Nate and I plant everything in the tilled field we lease a short distance from home. We hire out the primary tillage. Planting and harvesting of our biggest crops—corn, squash, dry legumes, and potatoes—are the labor bottlenecks. We grow several varieties of dry legumes with different maturity times. For the larger plantings of single varieties, we use staggered plantings to additionally spread out the harvest dates. The planting of the potatoes is spread out over two months, and we have many varieties of all possible maturity times. So we usually don't have planting or harvesting bottlenecks on the potatoes or beans. Our two big plantings of corn (flint and flour types, in separate fields) and our planting of winter squash each take a half day of work for two people, however. These are our marathon plantings. Nate and I can plant about a third of an acre of corn or squash by hand in about four hours (which includes plenty of breaks as well as the time spent recording everything). Here's how we do it.

For marathon planting, I take into the field seeds, garden tools, a hat and jacket (or warmer clothes if appropriate), drinking water, a folding cot and folding chair, a shade canopy, and an equivalent of a chamber pot (which sits in the van). Without the pot, I find I generally tend to stay somewhat dehydrated to avoid frequent trips to inconveniently distant bushes. It's better to stay somewhat over-hydrated and have a means

of relief handy. Being even slightly dehydrated causes general fatigue and lowered physical strength and endurance.

It takes as much or more time to plan the planting of a big plot with several varieties than it does to plant it. So for major planting sessions it pays to do the planning ahead of time. I also gather everything and load the van the day before planting so as to be able to start the planting day early and fresh, and spend it actually planting rather than just preparing to plant. It also takes longer than one would suppose to do the recording of what is planted. (There are always modifications necessary when you get to the field. So the plans are at best only general. The specifics and any modifications need to be recorded.) I used to do all this recording standing in the sun or sitting awkwardly on the ground (which was hard on my back, even when I was considerably younger). These days, I do the recording sitting comfortably in a chair in the shade. When we marathon-plant, we do it in style.

It pays to put extra time into planning plantings so that harvesting will be easy later on. I alternate varieties of different colors or kinds. All the white or gold potato varieties alternate with varieties that are blue or red. Round-podded pole bean varieties alternate with flat-podded varieties. That way it is easy to see where one variety stops and the next starts without the need for stakes or field markers, which tend to get lost or obscured during the season. (And stakes and markers get in the way of weeding.) These kinds of tricks make harvesting much faster and easier.

I do all my direct seeding walking comfortably with my back straight. To sow heavy seeds such as corn or peas or beans, I usually just make a furrow using my furrowing plow, walk down the row and drop the seeds in, then turn the furrowing plow over and drag it down the furrow again to cover the seeds. Most people use a hoe to make and close the furrows; the furrowing plow makes better furrows and is several times faster. Dropping seeds into furrows from a standing position only works with heavy seed, and only if there is little wind. Winds here are pretty predictable. There usually isn't much wind in the morning. In the afternoon, it's often so windy and the wind is so variable that it takes backbreaking bending over to get the corn or peas or beans in the furrow. So I always plan so as to do my planting in the morning.

For bigger plantings when there is seed enough to waste, we use an Earthway seeder. The Earthway seeder is supposed to make a furrow, drop in the seed, and cover it as the seeder rolls along. In my experience, it does not make furrows deep enough or well enough, and it fails to properly cover even the inadequate furrows it makes. We use the furrowing plow to make and cover furrows, and use the Earthway seeder just to disperse the seed into the opened furrows. (There are furrowing attachments for rototillers, but they are expensive. And we hope to replace the rototiller with oxen or water buffaloes one of these years, so don't want to invest more in rototiller-based systems.) Earthway seeders have a variety of plates for different sizes of seed. By choosing the right plate, you can seed just about anything. However, generally, you can set the seeder to

---

The Furrowing Plow

You can make and cover furrows using a hoe. I use my furrowing plow, which is several times faster. The furrowing plow is designed to open a broad, shallow furrow. The head is about 9 inches across and 13 inches long. In freshly tilled soil it makes a furrow about 6 inches across and 2 to 3 inches deep. This furrow is easy to hit when dropping seeds from a standing position. The flip side of the head of the furrowing plow is designed to cover furrows (see photo insert).

I simply walk down the row dragging the furrowing plow. After I have a few hundred feet of open furrows, I stop and seed them. Then I flip the furrowing plow head over and drag it down the seeded furrows, covering them. Furrows, however they are made, start to dry out and become crusty after they are opened, so it is best to seed and fill furrows promptly after they are opened rather than making all the furrows first.

The furrowing plow is custom-made by Bob Denman at Red Pig Garden Tools based upon a European design. I know of no other source for the tool. There are two different sizes, each of which has various options for handle length and style. I recommend the 9-inch head, the 72-inch handle, and the D-shaped handle addition. The length of handle in this case relates less to height of person and more to angle on the work. The D-handle transfers motion directly from your body through your straight arm to the handle with no bending of the wrist. The D-handle on my furrowing plow is set very slightly off from vertical so as to be perfect for a right-hander. If you are a lefty, say so when ordering. At the moment, the 9-inch tool with the 72-inch D-handle costs about $70 plus shipping.

deliver only too much seed or too little. We choose too much. When we don't have seed enough to waste, we seed by hand. However, when we have enough seed to waste, the seeder saves a lot of time. Neither the seeder nor dropping seed from a standing position gives you seed in exact positions or at very exact spacing. Appropriate spacing is established during thinning.

To direct-seed into exact positions I used to bend over or squat. Not any more. Now I use "planting tubes." These are pieces of ¾-inch PVC tube that are long enough to reach from the ground to my hands when I am standing comfortably with my back nicely unbent. When I am seeding kale at 3 feet apart in the row, for example, I don't bend over or squat every 3 feet. Instead, I use my 1-tube planter (see photo insert). The 1-tube planter is just a PVC tube attached with rubber bands to a rod. The rod is lightweight fiberglass and is 5 feet long. It is meant to hold up movable electric fencing and costs about $2.75 at my feed and seed store. The rod projects a bit beyond the end of the PVC tube, marks the planting position on the ground, and holds the tube up off the ground so that it doesn't get plugged up with soil. The upper end of the rod rests on my shoulder so I have both hands free to mess with seeds. When I want a seed to fall into an exact position, I set the PVC tube about two inches above the end of the rod and drop the seed down the tube.

For planting kale, I want a little pinch of seeds every 3 feet in the row. And I want the seed dispersed in a ring about 4 inches across. I set the PVC tube and rod so that the end of the PVC tube is about 6 inches above the ground when the rod rests on the ground. Then I drop pinches of seed down the tube at each planting position. (I carry a plastic cup with the seed in a fanny pack

turned around to my front. All the bags of seed of different varieties are in the fanny pack so I don't have to make extra trips back to the car, or bend over to shuffle packs of seed in a box on the ground.) I don't make a furrow for fine seeds such as kale. I just amble down the row and drop a little pinch of seeds onto the surface of the soil every 3 feet, then walk back down the row with a rake and run the rake a couple of times over every marked position to bury just enough of the seed. (The seeds are sloppily buried at variable depths. Some depth will be just right.) After the seedlings have germinated and grown up to about an inch high, I thin to the best plant in each position.

For squash seeds I plant three seeds 6 inches apart in a linear hill (just an 18-inch-long spot in the row). The hills are 3 to 8 feet apart depending upon the variety. I thin later to the best plant in each hill. To seed the 3 seeds I use my 3-tube planter, which Nate has dubbed "Carol's 3-tube planter version 3.0." The 3-tube planter is three pieces of PVC tube supported by two fiberglass rods and braced with a cross bar of wooden dowel with notches sawed in it to hold the tubes the right distance apart (see photo insert). By sliding the cross bar up or down or moving the tubes from the inner to the outer notches, I can adjust the planting distance from 6 inches to 18. The whole thing is held together with strapping tape. When I want to change the planting distance, I just cut the tape, shift the crossbar, and retape.

For planting squash I set the rods so the seeds drop from about 2 inches above the surface of the furrow. After I drop a seed into each of the three planting tubes and they fall into positions 6 inches apart, I move to the next hill position. I usually just guess the distance between hills. That is much less critical than the spacing of seeds within the hill.

Varying the Kinds of Labor

Resist completionism. It's emotionally satisfying to finish a job. It's so satisfying that I am strongly tempted to try to do huge chunks of one kind of work at once. "Today I'll hand-weed within the rows in all the garden beds," I tend to want to say. And if I actually do that, I'm likely to strain or overwork something or other. It is far easier on the body and is better conditioning to instead weed one of the beds by hand (on hands and knees), then do some hoeing with the peasant hoe (standing comfortably and exercising primarily my arms), then switching to another hoe that uses primarily different muscles, then loading a cartload full of mulch and hauling it down to the garden to be ready for spreading on the morrow, and finally hand-watering whatever needs it (which requires just standing there with the hose, feeling satisfied).

Whenever possible, change sides of the row, angles of approach, and which arms or hands you are using frequently. Make your gardening workout as bilateral as possible.

It's best not to do a lot of any one kind of garden activity when you haven't done it for a while. I figure an hour with the peasant hoe is enough in early spring when I haven't used it for a while. Then I skip a day or more before the next session with that task or tool. A pattern of exercising every other day gives me faster body conditioning at this point in my life than exercising every day. When I was younger, bigger sessions and every-day exercise gave me faster conditioning.

Weeds

There are several basic approaches to weed control. Smaller gardens are often weeded entirely by hand on hands and knees by pulling weeds or disrupting them with small hand-cultivating tools.

With traditional row-style plantings you can do most of your weeding with a hoe. You still have to do some weeding squatting or on hands and knees, at least the weeding immediately around the plants. However, the weeds between the rows are controlled by hoeing, or with a wheel hoe or rototiller, or by cultivating with draft animals.

Some plants and situations lend themselves to weed control by hilling up, as described in the chapters on potatoes and corn. To hill up, soil from between rows is hoed up onto the rows in such a way that weeds in between rows are uprooted and those within rows are mostly buried. This works only for plants that don't mind having the lower part of their stems buried.

A fourth approach to weeding certain crops on a commercial scale is to use selective herbicides. Herbicides have serious environmental costs and are not permitted in organic gardens. I don't cover them here.

A fifth approach to weeding is flaming. I haven't much experience with it as yet. I have bought the backpack propane tank and flame-throwing attachment, though. You walk through the field and run the flamer over the weeds near the ground, essentially boiling the stems at ground level. Some friends of mine swear by flaming for carrots, which take about three weeks to germinate. They plant the carrots, then flame the surface of the soil lightly after about two weeks, killing all the germinating weeds, which generally germinate faster than the carrots. Then the carrots come up.

The sixth approach to weed control is to try to avoid or minimize weeds and weeding by using mulch, as discussed in the separate section that follows.

Sometimes we can broadcast certain crops thickly enough to outcompete weeds. I do this with 'Green Wave' mustard in March. At that time of year with that particular variety, the mustard generally outgrows and shades out any weeds.

A related approach is to use smother crops to control weeds. Cover crops can help shade out weeds and thus act simultaneously as smother crops. Big vigorous viney squash are especially good at shading out weeds.

With weeding, timing is everything. Weeds that are just emerging from germinating seeds are easily handled by cultivating, hoeing, or even raking when they are caught early enough. The earlier you catch the weeds, the easier it is to deal with them. Planting immediately after the ground

Buying Tools

Efficient weeding requires quality tools that are made of quality steel. They are forged, not stamped. They are tempered. They will take and hold an edge. You usually buy them from a local hardware store, a feed and seed store, a mail-order or specialty tool company, or a seed company's section on garden tools. You usually don't buy them from a big-box discounter. Discount stores usually have cheap tools—tools that cost little and are worth even less—tools with cheap metal that won't hold an edge, cheap attachments of heads to handles, cheap design that doesn't transfer your energy to the tool optimally, and cheap handles that are too short and that will break your back. Good tools aren't cheap. Sorry.

My shovels are all good-quality but standard tools. They came from a local hardware store or from my local feed and seed store. The blades are forged and tempered and are contractor's grade, and it says so on the tool. The tops of the shovels have a wide rolled-down section so I can jump up and down on them without injuring my feet when I work in light shoes. (The edge rolls forward, not back, so it helps hold things on the shovel.) I also bought my pitchforks, garden forks, hay hooks, and other such tools from my local hardware store or the feed and seed store. My hoes have all been mail-ordered.

I like shovels with pointed blades, long handles, and some angle between the blade and handle. The latter allows putting both feet and all your weight on the shovel. Straight shovels with straight blade ends make straight-sided garden beds but are harder to get into the ground. And you can't get your full weight on them. I can't make myself dig garden beds using such tools. I settle for scalloped edges (and bottoms) on garden beds and a digging job that is easier to do.

For heavy hoeing you need a peasant hoe. For light weeding, there are many designs of light, sharp hoes made from quality steel, and each gardener tends to develop a favorite. Get tools with handles long enough so that you can work without bending over unnecessarily.

Using the Peasant Hoe

The classic way we see the peasant hoe being used in photographs portrays a tool with a short handle held in the hands with the same grip as is used in holding a baseball bat. The tool is applied to the weeds directly in front of the person, whose back is bent so much that just looking at the pictures makes my back hurt. The power stroke of this short-handled hoe involves the muscles of the arms *and back*. I got my long-handled peasant hoe mostly by accident, and only learned by experience that it permits a different grip and angle on the work that allows one to work with a straight back and minimal effort. Here's how I use my peasant hoe:

First, I grip my peasant hoe handle with both palms down and both sets of five fingers curled over the hoe. The position of the thumbs is optional. They can be curled under the handle. However, if you curl the thumbs over the handle, as I do, you can work without gloves and never get blisters (see photo insert).

Using this grip, the hoe is positioned off to one side and only slightly in front of me. And my wrists are straight.

I hoe using primarily the lifting muscles in my arms to lift the hoe. Then I merely drop it. My arms and hands serve merely to control and aim the drop. They do not impart any power. Gravity alone does the work of the power stroke. (This is why it is essential that the peasant hoe have a heavy head.) I sway a little from side to side (not front to back) as I hoe. The swaying is from my ankles and hips (but not back) as I lift and drop the hoe.

I cant the hoe slightly so it enters the ground or cuts into the weeds with one point a little ahead of the rest of the blade. This gives a better slicing action and gives more penetration for the same amount of power.

I switch sides regularly. That is, I'll start with the left hand lower on the handle and the hoe working off to the left. Then, a few minutes later, I shift my grip to make the right hand lower on the handle and have the hoe working off to the right. I like to exercise my body evenly when I have the option.

And of course, I stop regularly to rest and to sharpen the hoe.

---

is turned or tilled is optimal so weeds don't have a head start.

Once weed seedlings are more than just barely emerged, you can't kill them with a rake or tined tool anymore. Instead, you need a hoe. However, a very light hoe will do. When the weeds are bigger, you need a heavier hoe. The bigger the weeds, the harder the weeding job.

For weeding with a rake, tined tool, or hoe, you need to have the surface of the ground a little dried out. You can't rake or hoe mud. In addition, with too much moisture in the soil, many disrupted weedlings will just continue growing in their new positions. With drier soil, they die.

Perennial weeds emerging from established roots are a different problem. They will just laugh at rakes or tined cultivating tools. Perennial weeds usually resprout vigorously from root

Using Light Hoes

Choose a hoe that permits you to hoe in a comfortable, erect, standing position. Avoid the standard rectangular American hoe. The blade meets the handle at an angle appropriate for digging, not hoeing; but the blade and tool are too light for heavy hoeing or digging. It is also usually made from poor steel that won't hold an edge. Were twenty expert gardeners to have a speed-hoeing contest, they would probably be using fifteen different hoes, but none would be the standard rectangular hoe.

The Coleman hoe is Nate's favorite. My favorite light hoe is a diamond hoe from Red Pig Garden Tools that has a 72-inch handle and a special grip piece that allows one to use the tool with both a straight back and straight wrists. All well-designed light hoes have blades set so that the angle of attack of the blade upon the ground is very close to parallel. You shave rather than dig. The sharp hoe skims just below the surface of the ground.

The best grip for hoeing isn't obvious. The obvious power (baseball bat) grip usually involves a bent-over, backbreaking posture. You should be able to hoe standing up comfortably.

To hoe with the Coleman hoe, grip the hoe with the left (lower) hand palm down on the handle, the left fingers curled over the handle, and the left thumb tucked under. The right hand grips the hoe handle palm up, with the right fingers tucked under the handle and the right thumb tucked over. (Alternatively, the thumbs may be rested on the hoe, both pointing up. This grip puts the hoe somewhat to the left and in front, but quite near the feet, and the blade of the hoe enters the ground at an angle that is only slightly off from parallel to the ground. The wrists are kept mostly straight. The muscles in the arms are used more for fine control than to deliver power. Switch from right-handed to left-handed use frequently. (In the photo, Nate is hoeing left-handed, with one palm up and one down, as before, but with the left hand uppermost with palm up and the right hand lower with palm down and the hoe off slightly to his right.)

pieces. This means that even tilling deeply with a rototiller or moldboard plow doesn't kill them. It does break them up into smaller (weaker) pieces, but it also spreads these pieces around. It often takes tilling or hoeing *regularly* for several seasons before the perennial weeds are set back often enough and hard enough to die. If you don't have perennial weed roots in your garden, one of your main tasks as a gardener is to keep it that way. If you do have them, one of your main tasks is to hoe or pull them persistently until you don't have them.

With smaller plantings, it's usually best to pull perennial weeds by hand. Since we want to remove as much of the root as possible along with the top of the plant, the best weather for pulling perennial weeds is weather in which the soil is as wet as possible—but dry enough so that you will still be able to get into the garden to work without sinking up to your eyeballs in mud.

Pulling weeds by hand is excellent exercise for the arms, wrists, hands, and even fingers. I shift from hand to hand frequently, and I'm careful not to overdo it. It's easy to get carpal tunnel syndrome from too much hand-pulling of weeds. I pay attention and monitor the condition of muscles whenever I do much of any such repetitive tasks. Pulled perennial weeds may need to be removed from the garden area, especially in wet weather, as they tend to re-root readily. Pulled or hoed purslane fragments need to be removed from the garden area even in dry weather. The succulent leaves store enough food and water for the fragments to actually flower and set seed without re-rooting.

If you import the leaves and lawn clippings from your neighbors, you will also be importing their weeds. In theory, by composting such material you can eliminate weed seeds. In practice, a good composting job eliminates at best *most* of the weed seeds.

My favorite tool for weed control is my peasant hoe. I design my gardens in part so as much as possible can be done with my peasant hoe. My favorite tools for hand-weeding right around the plants are the Korean hand plow (EZ digger) and a simple one-piece steel knife I call my "planting knife," which is equally a "weeding knife" and "transplanting knife." The Korean hand plow is available from most mail-order seed companies that sell tools. (Red Pig Garden Tools has both right- and left-handed versions.) My planting knife is a "Bushman" knife available from Cold Steel. It's inexpensive and easy to sharpen, and has a coating to deter rust.

Many people's favorite long tool for light weeding is a good-quality stirrup hoe such as the Glazer. But not me. And not, generally, other

people with back problems. Stirrup hoes have a real advantage, however, where bindweed or other weeds that reroot readily are the problems, such weeds need to be removed from the field. With a stirrup hoe you can slice the vines from their roots and simultaneously gather the vines in to piles for removal.

Sharpening Tools

To weed efficiently you need to stop regularly to sharpen your tools. I sharpen hoes, shovels, my brush hook, and many other tools with a file. At one point, before I really got the hang of using the file, I succumbed to the siren song of power and bought a bench grinder. It's hard to get the correct angles on tool edges with the grinder. And the grinder can't go to the field. Doing serious amounts of hoeing easily depends upon stopping regularly to sharpen the hoe. So depending upon an electric grinder means sloppy edges and tools that are only sharp at the beginning of the day, at best. Sharpening garden tools with a file is actually much easier than using the grinder. There are five tricks to using the file.

1. You need the right kind of file. The right kind is flat on one side and curved on the other. The flat side is ideal for the hoes. The curved side is great for curved edges such as those of shovels. Such files can be found in any good hardware store. You need to replace the files every so often when the abrading surfaces get too worn.

2. The file goes to the field along with the tool, the peasant hoe, for example. After every fifteen to thirty minutes of hoeing,

take a little break, have a drink of water, and sharpen the hoe. It only takes about nine full strokes, each of which covers about one-third of the edge of the hoe, and a few light finishing strokes to sharpen the 7¾-inch blade on my peasant hoe. (I sharpen the last inch or so of the sides of the hoe too, but not as regularly as the blade.) Sharpening the peasant hoe only takes about a minute when the hoe is being sharpened as frequently as is optimal.

3. However, for this fast, efficient sharpening, the tool must be solidly braced so that the full power of the stroke transmits into removing metal rather than wiggling the tool. The tool must not move at all during the sharpening. (In addition, you can't get a consistent angle on the edge if the tool moves.)

4. You need an angle on the work that puts your arm, hand, wrist, and weight above the file and tool so that you can put the power of your arm and the weight of your body into the stroke (without straining your wrist). When you have the tool and yourself properly positioned for sharpening, it takes only about three strokes on each part of the tool to do the job, and the metal powder flies off obviously with each stroke. The major motion of the stroke is along the length of the edge. Ideally, the stroke is somewhat counter to the edge, but if the configuration of the tool and situation make it much easier to do the opposite, I do so.

5. I don't oil my file. Metal clippings and dirt stick to and clog an oiled file.

These days, our gardening is all in our leased field a few minutes' drive from home. So my file stays in my van. The peasant hoe and shovel and any other needed tools are loaded into the van before each trip to the field. I have positions for sharpening each that involve leaving the tailgate open and wedging the tool with blade up and braced against the open end of the van. Then I sit on the tailgate and sharpen.

On the peasant hoe I like an edge with an angle of about 30 degrees (that is, one-third of a right angle). On lighter hoes I like a somewhat sharper angle, about 22 degrees, or about a quarter of a right angle. With shovels, I like a 45-degree edge (half of a right angle). I chose these angles somewhat arbitrarily and partly because they are easy to approximate visually. The sharper the tool, the easier the work while the tool is freshly sharp, but the faster the tool dulls, and the more susceptible the edge is to major dents if it hits a rock.

There is no reason to sharpen both sides of most tools. A very light finishing stroke on the unsharpened edge is useful to take off feathered edges and burrs, however. I sharpen first and hardest on the outside edge of my peasant hoe. I finish by drawing the file lightly over the edge in the direction with the edge, and I do that on both sides. The object is to break off the wire edge that has formed. About three such light double strokes does it. The tool is noticeably sharp to the finger after, but not before, the finishing strokes. With shovels, I sharpen the inside edge using the round side of the file. Then I use the light finishing stroke on both sides of the edge.

Garden shears, fine sickles, and other such fine-bladed tools should be sharpened with knife-sharpening equipment, not a file.

Mulch

I once had a conversation with a wannabe farmer who had just moved to Oregon from the East Coast. He wanted to try growing vegetables in permanent raised beds with deep mulch, as was often touted in the *Organic Gardening* magazines he had been reading. My response was: "But it doesn't work here." He touted it some more. I responded again with, "But it doesn't work here." And so it went, until we put in a test plot of mulched and unmulched potatoes side by side. The mulched potatoes took weeks longer to sprout and then grew slowly and were stunted and obviously miserable. In the maritime Northwest, you have to really screw up to make potatoes miserable.

Here in Oregon, any heat in the springtime is usually limited. Soil that lies beneath a deep layer of mulch stays soggy and cold. Pull back the deep mulch to make a row to plant something, and the something will take longer to germinate and will grow much more slowly than the same thing planted in bare soil, even though the soil over the seed is left exposed until the seeds have germinated. And the worst is yet to come. After the first couple of years of deep-mulched permanent beds of vegetables, there are so many slugs, sow bugs, and other such critters that everything is eaten up as soon as it germinates. Our winter freezes don't go deep enough to kill pests in the soil under a deep mulch. Admittedly, the deep mulch does take care of the weed problem. Here, beds with permanent deep mulch are most useful for perennial and ornamental plantings, not for vegetables.

Deep permanent mulches have worked for some people in some places and certain situations, even in the vegetable garden. But they aren't for everybody. However, mulches can be thin or deep, temporary or permanent. In the era in which I gardened with raised beds in the backyard, I often used a light or late-applied mulch as a way of adding to soil fertility or moderating water loss.

"Deep" mulch usually means a layer at least 6 inches deep after the mulch has consolidated. For loose material such as straw or leaves, this generally means a layer 8 to 12 inches deep initially. A thinner layer doesn't do the intended job of preventing weeds from growing. If there are perennial weeds with large roots, even the deep mulch won't work. You need to get rid of perennial weeds first.

Most people who use a permanent deep mulch successfully in their vegetable gardens seem to be located on the East Coast or in the Midwest, and also to have gardened for years or even decades using conventional methods, and have already eliminated all perennial weeds and built up soil fertility and tilth. Apparently, one can garden successfully using permanent raised beds with permanent mulches, even with vegetables, and even starting from scratch, at least in some areas. A good book on gardening in beds with permanent deep mulch is Lee Reich's *Weedless Gardening*.

Once you have mulch on a garden, you can't use an ordinary hoe any more. (With light mulches, I can still use my peasant hoe, but not light hoes.) So if you have perennial weeds coming up through the mulch, you may need to pull them all by hand. Ideally, with a deep mulch there are few or no weeds. Light mulches prevent some but not all of the weeds from germinating; those that grow have to be hand-pulled or hoed with a heavy hoe. So light mulches may either increase or decrease the weeding work.

Here in Oregon where it doesn't rain in summer, it can be unworkable to try to provide water by overhead-watering with a deep mulch. You can't get the water down through the mulch. So deep mulch tends to work best with permanent landscape plantings where drip irrigation lines are installed under the mulch. You can readily overhead-water through a 3-inch layer of mulch, however.

I have used mulches of various kinds with my raised garden beds, primarily to add fertility or reduce water needs. I used light mulches, not deep ones. My favorite mulched gardens were my tomato beds. Tomatoes need lots of water and are sensitive to changes in hydration, which cause the fruits to split. I planted transplants into raised beds and left them unmulched the first month or so, when the plants needed every bit of soil heat possible. After the plants were established and the soil had warmed up, I put on a layer of straw about 2 to 3 inches deep. With this light mulch, I could overhead-water my raised beds just once per week instead of twice a week. By the end of the season, most of the mulch had vanished into the soil, leaving just a little to be turned under.

Nate and I grow a 150-foot row of tomatoes these days. We grow them unmulched and level to the surface rather than in raised beds. They need to be watered only once per week. We could water even less if we added a thin mulch after the first month, as I did with raised beds. But where would we get the mulch? On large plantings, mulching is often impractical because there isn't enough mulch available. We could get enough free city leaves to mulch our entire two-acre garden, but not without bringing in bindweed seeds. We leased our current garden land partly because it doesn't have bindweed. We want to keep it that way.

Straw is commonly used as a mulch. On small garden beds, I often used a thin mulch of an inch or 2 of grass clippings, which served as both light mulch and fertilizer. (Deeper layers of fresh clippings turn to rotting goo instead of drying out into a nice layer of mulch.) Hay is fertilizer as well as mulch, but it is usually full of weed seeds. Ruth Stout, the Grand Lady of the permanently deep-mulched (East Coast) vegetable garden, used salt marsh hay. Salt marsh hay is from salty coastal marshes. It has few weed seeds of the kinds that matter in terrestrial gardens, and might have been an essential component of Ruth Stout's success. When she added another twenty-five bales of hay to her garden each season, she was adding both mulch and fertility. If we try to do the equivalent with straw, we are adding an excess of carbon and very little nitrogen. If we try to do the equivalent with our hay, we are bringing in weed seeds, which turn into a solid layer of grass and weeds on the surface of the mulch.

Mulches may or may not mean less total labor. As Robert Heinlein's characters in *The Moon Is a Harsh Mistress* were wont to say, TANSTAAFL, or There Ain't No Such Thing as a Free Lunch. You may get out of much or all of the labor of weeding as well as some of the watering. But you replace it with the labor of finding, hauling, and applying mulch (and tucking it up around each established plant).

In desert areas where every drop of water counts, mulches of some sort—deep or thin, permanent or temporary—may be obligatory. In areas with some but limited or erratic summer rain, even light mulching may mean you don't need to irrigate at all, thus saving in both water and watering labor.

Transplanting versus Direct Seeding, Revisited

If I direct-seed summer squash I can make furrows, drop seed, and cover it all from a comfortable standing position. If instead I transplant, I have all the labor of starting and tending seedlings in a greenhouse or indoors. Then, in addition, I will need to transplant a plant into each hill position on my hands and knees. The direct seeding is faster than transplanting by at least an order of magnitude. However, with direct seeding, I then have about a month of weeding of a field that is largely empty. That requires two extra full rounds of weeding not required when the field is planted with transplants. When the planting is in the summer, there is also extra watering needed to support germinating seed and seedlings spread out over an entire field. It is easier to water the few square feet of space the same seeds take when started in flats.

Transplants can facilitate getting more crops per area of land per season, meaning that less total land has to be tilled, watered, and weeded. Those with limited land often use transplanting as a strategy to get the most from the land they have.

Transplanting may increase or decrease the total amount of labor. What it undeniably does is change the kinds of labor.

Selective Sloppiness

Only some things are worth doing well. Most things that are worth doing are only worth doing sloppily. Many things aren't worth doing at all. Anything not worth doing at all is certainly not worth doing well.

During the era when I gardened largely in beds in the backyard, I initially started by digging and then hoeing to break up clods. Then I spent significant time moving the surface of the bed around to get it nicely smoothed. The smoothing made the beds look more elegant. It also meant that water tended to run off the beds instead of soaking in. Occasionally, however, I was too lazy to do the smoothing. I just dug, hoed, and planted. The result was beds that ended up with an uneven surface with little depressions here and there. They didn't look as elegant. But they worked better. All those irregularities helped the bed hold and absorb water better. The beds were less vulnerable to erosion in winter rains. In summer, the beds with sloppy irregular surfaces saved water and cut down on the watering labor. I soon learned to do my soil prep with the peasant hoe in such a way as to make the most useful irregularities in the bed surfaces (with no additional labor).

In the vegetable garden, groomed manicured paths all nicely mulched with bark dust in between garden beds mean that you must collect all the weeds as you pull them and cart them off somewhere else in order to keep your paths pristine. It's lots easier to leave the bark dust off and toss the weeds in the paths. They mulch the path and retain fertility in the garden area. (If the weeds threaten to re-root, you can run a mower over the paths occasionally.)

When I hand-weed newly emerged or emerging seedlings, I leave clumps and piles of weeds spotted judiciously around the garden bed. If I am neater and remove the clumps of weeds, sow bugs and slugs do a lot more damage to the seedlings. There are always some slugs and sow bugs just below the surface of the bed. When the bed is weeded and the weeds are all removed, the pests have nothing to eat but the planted seedlings. Slugs and sow bugs prefer to hide in and eat the piles of pulled weeds if given the option. I sometimes move the weed piles to the paths later, fauna and all. Sometimes I forget them. Either way, the planted seedlings have a better chance.

When I first started gardening, I got down on my hands and knees and planted a neat row of peas at a uniform depth and 2 inches apart in the row. But as described in chapter 3, there is no way to know the ideal planting depth, which depends in part upon the weather. So often only part of my row would emerge and do well—the part that was accidentally a bit deeper or shallower than I intended. These days, as I described, I deliberately plant excess seed sloppily at variable depths. And I generally get a lovely solid stand of peas, whatever the soil type or weather.

Spacing between plants in rows doesn't need to be anything like perfect. Measuring takes time. I usually just guess. (Spacing between rows *does* matter enough to measure if you are tilling between rows.)

There isn't any way to get exactly the same amount of water on the plants at the edge of the watering pattern as those in the center. Accept it. Some plants get more water this week, and some get less. I don't know what the perfect amount of water any particular week would be anyway. To set a sprinkler to roughly the right position takes much less time than trying to get it exactly right, which is impossible anyway. "Hey," I tell the plants. "We all have our ups and downs. My life isn't perfect either. So I'd better not see any whining or wilting around here."

Eschew unnecessary symmetry. It's often much easier to create an aesthetically pleasing curve than a straight line. If a line looks like it was meant to be straight, it will look like a mistake if it is even slightly curved. An obvious curve that looks like it's meant to be curved will be more attractive than an almost-straight line. A curve can be curved just about any way you want, and it looks like it should be just what it is. This means you can make curves fast and imprecisely and they still look good. Hand tending especially lends itself to graceful curves. You can mow or till either straight lines or gentle curves. Sharper curves are harder to mow or till.

When rototilling, the hardest part is turning the tiller around at the end of rows. So when a rototiller will be used for cultivating between rows, it is much easier when the space is laid out in fewer numbers of longer rows.

Trees or bushes or other immovable objects here and there in the yard each have to be mowed around. Consolidated areas of bushes or trees (such as an orchard) are usually easier to care for. Consider mowing implications in all landscaping decisions.

It often isn't necessary to weed the vegetable garden later in the season. Crops are already established and less vulnerable to competition, and late-starting weeds don't usually have enough time to go to seed before they are tilled in fall. They can usually just be ignored.

Knowing When to Stop

Some people make a big deal out of "Never quitting." Never quitting is no virtue if you are going in the wrong direction. As we live we learn more and gain greater perspective. To "never quit" would mean never allowing that new wisdom to inform our actions and choices.

Beginners often till way more garden than they can weed or water. Even the most experienced gardener can suffer an injury or an emergency elsewhere in her life, however, that brings the amount of garden out of balance with her available labor. The right amount of garden and gardening work provides good exercise, relieves stress, and enhances your resilience. A garden that you are in danger of losing entirely because you don't have enough time to tend it creates stress instead of relieving it. The sensible solution is to till under or mow over most of the garden before the weeds go to seed. Then we can concentrate all our energy on what we care about most, or what is most salvageable. Life is full of situations that don't go as expected. Sometimes we have to retrench. Sometimes we should cut our losses.

When I first started caring for my mother, my gardens tended to be all-or-nothing gardens. The most important things were spread out. I thought this minimized my risks. It didn't. In order to successfully grow the quarter I cared about the most, I had to properly weed and water and maintain everything. There was no way to retrench. In more than one gardening season, when some emergency with my mother changed the availability of my labor, I lost the entire vegetable garden for the year.

These days, when I decide how much garden to plant, I take the basic unpredictability of life and hence my labor into account. I prioritize. Then I organize, plan, and plant partly in terms of what could be written off if need be. I *don't* scatter all the things I care most about all over the garden. I have sections that are most important and other sections that I think I'll have enough time to tend but can sacrifice. I weed and water the sections I care most about first. I tend the rest if and when

I have time. Usually I have time for everything. Sometimes I don't. When I don't, I don't beat myself up over it. I just write off certain sections to bring the amount of garden into balance with my available labor. When I write off a section, it's the section that I care least about and that has the least time invested in it. The smaller successful garden that I am able to handle with my lessened labor then cheers me, reduces my stress, and feeds me physically, emotionally, and spiritually.

Easy on the Back (and Knees)

As we get older, our backs and knees tend to become the weak link when it comes to our ability to garden. Here are some of my tricks and approaches.

1. Many standard tools don't have long enough handles to allow you to use the tool without bending over. Get tools with long enough handles.

2. See the sidebars and photo insert for how to grip and use hoes so as to be easy on the back.

3. Frequent breaks matter for both you and your back. Getting the most out of breaks also matters. I keep a light folding cot in the van and stretch out for at least a minute or two on every break. Whenever the hoe or other tool starts getting dull or I feel tired, I amble over to the van, take a swig of water, sharpen the tool, take a few more swigs of water, then lie down and wriggle and stretch my back vertebrae out and gaze at the clouds or listen to the birds for a minute or two. Such breaks make it possible for me

to work longer and more enjoyably than if I just worked straight through.

4. I avoid the bending or hands-and-knees work most people do while planting by dropping seed into furrows from a standing position, as described in the "Planting" section in this chapter.

5. I hoe weeds instead of squatting to pull them by hand.

6. I direct-seed anything that can be direct-seeded, and resort to transplants only when direct seeding isn't an option. Transplanting requires getting down on hands and knees for each plant, which is hard on the knees.

7. Whenever there has been money available to hire anything out, I always hire out the digging or shoveling. Those tasks are harder on the back than other gardening activities.

8. I also minimize the digging requirements by using a tilled field instead of hand-dug beds whenever possible.

9. When lifting anything, I squat and lift with the knees. I don't bend over and use back muscles to lift (which can easily leverage a spinal disc out of place). Beware of objects that are too bulky or irregular in shape to hold close. These objects force you to hold them way in front of your body and then lift with the back. Even a light object so lifted can cause back injury. I get someone to help me lift anything that is too bulky or irregular to hold close and lift properly, even if the object is ridiculously light.

10. Squash and sweet potatoes occupy somewhat the same flavor and use niche. We grow lots of squash and no sweet potatoes. Sweet potatoes don't keep well under the conditions we have. That's one factor. But

in addition, sweet potatoes have to be dug. Squash plants are considerate enough to put their bounty up there above the ground where all we have to do is pick it up.

11. Picking pole beans can be done from a comfortable standing position. Picking bush beans requires much squatting or bending.

12. Some tools can be used with arm or leg or body power. Others require back power. Stirrup hoes use arm and back muscles. They are beloved by some and intolerable after just a few seconds by others.

13. Wheel hoes can be even easier on the back than hoeing and much faster if the weeds and soil conditions are right. Under ideal conditions, a wheel hoe can replace a roto-tiller for cultivating between rows of plantings up to a few acres. Wheel hoes get hopelessly entangled in bindweed, however, which is one of the most common weeds in Willamette Valley. And wheel hoes aren't much use if you need to deal with perennial weeds such as Canada thistle or wild blackberries, or even clumps of grass from shallow or inadequate tilling. The low-slung wheel hoes are a much better design than the high-wheel types. They transfer your muscle power more directly to the tool rather than primarily to the wheel.

14. Tables and chairs matter. If I take uncut potato seed to the field and cut it on the ground, my back will be killing me by the time I have cut enough seed for just the first 150-foot row of our planting. If instead I take a folding table and chair to the field and cut potato seed sitting down, it doesn't hurt my back, and I can do as much as I need to.

If we husk our field corn sitting on the ground, it is fun, but surprisingly back-breaking. If instead the corn is in the back of Nate's pickup, and we husk it sitting in chairs and dropping it into crates on the ground, it is fun and not backbreaking. Anything done sitting on the ground is surprisingly hard on the back. Even just writing down gardening records. Sitting on the tailgate of a truck or van helps. Sitting in an actual chair helps even more.

Helpers

Buffalo Bird Woman and her women family members did most of the gardening work. Among the Hidatsa Indians of North America, all the women in a family—which normally included multiple generations and more than one wife per generation—worked their family's garden together. Each age had its tasks. Younger women harvested the squash, for example. That takes a lot of bending and stooping. Older women sat in the shade and sliced the squash for drying. The men normally stayed out of the gardens, but came in to do certain heavy chores, such as clearing land for new gardens and hauling harvested corn back to the village.

Many women with extensive gardens have the rototilling done by their husbands or sons. Then they do the rest. Some women make the basic decision about whether to garden in beds or roto-tilled plots based upon what they can get help with. Many husbands will do rototilling but not digging. It's also harder to hire out digging than rototilling, and it's more costly. Tilling is a service that is generally offered and advertised. Garden-

bed digging isn't. It requires a specific personal arrangement.

Nate and I don't do our own primary tillage. We hire "the tractor guy," as does everyone else I know with gardens the size of ours. Rototilling such a big garden is too laborious and doesn't do as good a job as can be done with a tractor. The walk-behind tiller is better for secondary tillage and weeding in between rows than for sod-busting or primary tillage.

Some people are very labor-proud about their gardens, proud of the fact that they do everything themselves, by themselves. Some are people who could afford to hire help at critical points, and they have less garden than they want and could have with a little help. Some who love gardening stop or cut back drastically when they get older because of difficulty with certain tasks, where, again, a little help with certain tasks might be all that is needed. An Argentine friend tells me that, in Argentina, those who can afford to have servants are *expected* to have them. People need the jobs. An affluent woman who does all her own housework is not praised. She is instead considered selfish and miserly. There are different ways of looking at such things. I view my garden as a balanced expression of both independence and healthy interdependence. I thoroughly enjoy most of my gardening. The tasks I don't enjoy or have trouble doing physically, I minimize or get out of when I can.

My gardening involves lots of experiments and plant breeding. This increases the overall complexity of planting, tending, and harvesting. I often have people come visit, gardening-type people, who offer to help in the garden while we visit. In times past, I have had to say no. My garden was so complex that no one could help me with it. In addition, I couldn't even have someone present while I worked, because I needed my full concentration. Then came the year that I injured my foot. My right foot. I couldn't drive. I used a staff to hobble up and down stairs to take care of my mother. The garden was a short drive away and required walking some distance from the parking area. I had a friend who was willing to pitch in and help with the garden, but the garden was so complex there was no way to describe what needed to be done. Never again. My gardens these days are bigger, but they are *much* simpler. And I design my gardens so that I can make use of help as available or if needed. I consolidate plants and projects that will require my personal attention so that there are major sections that can be tended with less skilled or less attentive labor. If you are going to hire help or have helpers available, you need to design that possibility into the planting. Being able to accept help, even if it isn't usually needed, contributes to the resilience of both gardener and garden.

Planting and harvesting often present labor bottlenecks. If you have as much garden as you want and have just the right amount of gardening work most of the time, you might need help with the planting and harvesting of certain crops. Harvesting, especially, can represent a bottleneck, since there is often time pressure because of impending weather. Friends are often willing to help with the occasional bottlenecks, and most especially the harvesting.

I think of the harvesting when I design the plantings. I try to spread out the harvests with multiple varieties that have different maturities, or by breaking the planting of a variety into two blocks with different planting dates. In addition, I make my planting patterns simple enough so others *can* help with the harvest. If every row of corn has to go into a separate bin because it represents a different variety or treatment or lot of seed, it's hard enough to harvest it myself, even with infinite time. Given time pressure, things go wrong. So I spend extra time designing the plantings at the beginning of the season so that they are easy to harvest, and so that I can say "yes" to friends who want to help.

Even if we don't need help with the harvest, help often appears. Offers of help with the harvest should always be accepted. Harvesting is so joyful it wants to be shared. The desire to share harvesting and participate in harvesting runs deep. Harvesting is sacred. So we harvest the flour corn with our friends, then sit under a tree shucking the ears and exclaiming over every particularly large or beautifully colored one. It's hours of hard work, but utterly soul-satisfying. After we're done, there are hugs all around. Then comes a simple celebration. A block of cheese, late sweet corn that tastes delicious raw and straight from the plants, some good beer perhaps, and plenty of good cheer. Friends helping friends with the harvest—what could possibly be better?

CHAPTER SIX

Water and Watering

*The Essential Water-Nature of Your Land. Fruit and Nut Trees. Ornamental
and Landscape Plantings. Grass. Water and Spacing. Water and Fertility.
Water and Erosion. The Threefold Effects of Mulch. Why I Hate Drip Irrigation.
Soil Capillarity and the Pot Effect. Planting in Dry Conditions. Overhead
Watering. Water Resilience and Vegetables. Water Resilience and
Heirloom Varieties. Becoming Native to the Land of Our Living.*

The Essential Water-Nature of Your Land

What is the essential water-nature of your land?
Do you have enough total rain? How is it distributed over the year? What kinds of plants are
native to your area? What kinds of plants, native
or not, thrive in the unirrigated places? What are
their strategies with respect to water?

Here in Willamette Valley, Oregon, we get
about 60 inches of rainfall per year. That's
plenty. We get all of it in winter and early spring,
however, not during summer when most garden
crops need it. The Douglas fir tree, a dominant
species here, has the water problem all figured
out. An evergreen, it keeps its needles in winter.
It does photosynthesis whenever the temperature is much above freezing. The Doug fir grows
actively in the late fall and winter and in early
spring when there is plenty of rain. In late spring
and early summer it continues growing on the
residual moisture in the soil from winter rain. By
late summer, many soils provide little water. The
Doug fir on such a soil simply goes dormant. It
starts growing again after the winter rains return.
The Doug fir is perfectly adapted to this environment. Native annual grasses and forbs here

make their seeds and die in early summer. Native
perennial grasses typically turn yellow or brown
and go dormant in August. Perennial herbs
make tubers or storage roots as well as seeds by
midsummer. Then the tops die back, or they go
dormant until fall. All these native plant strategies tell us that, in August in Willamette Valley,
water is a problem.

On much of the East Coast and in the eastern
Midwest, there is enough rainfall to permit many
or most crops to be grown without irrigation. Part
of what makes the Corn Belt the Corn Belt is
the rich, deep loam soil; but part of it is the fact
that adequate amounts of water usually fall from
the sky during the growing season, and usually
at workably appropriate intervals. If you live in
one of these regions, the water issue for you may
simply be a matter of designing your gardening
patterns so as not to need irrigation at all except,
perhaps, as a backup plan.

If you live in a more arid region, though, you
may not have enough annual rainfall to support
vegetables. In these lands, vegetable gardening
automatically means irrigating. Your water issue
will be how, not whether, to add water to the situation. In addition, you will want management

strategies that allow you to minimize the amount of water you need to provide.

Here in Oregon we have the odd situation of plenty of water, but at the wrong time of year for summer crops. That essential water-nature of our land allows for a variety of approaches. One is to look for and emphasize, where possible, crops that grow mostly in the winter and early spring rather than the summer. Second, we can make optimal use of the residual soil moisture left after winter rains. Finally, we can irrigate summer vegetable crops that require it, and focus on management strategies that minimize the amount and frequency of the watering.

Nate and I employ all three tactics. We grow overwintered hardneck garlics as our main allium (onion family) crop rather than summer-grown onions. We are expanding our interest in overwintered fava beans instead of summer-grown legume species. (We would plant at least some overwintering wheat and rye, too, were I not gluten intolerant.) We also focus on our 'Hannan Popbean', a garbanzo I have selected specifically for production in Willamette Valley without irrigation. It is planted in early spring, then finishes on residual soil moisture and dries down in early summer. And one of our main staple crops is potatoes, which can be grown completely without irrigation with appropriate soil and spacing, making highly efficient use of residual soil water during the summer. We haven't given up irrigated crops, though. We love our tomatoes and squash. We simply consider water needs seriously when we choose what to grow, and set the bar higher for crops that require irrigation.

Soil type and topography both affect the basic water-nature of your land. Clay holds water better than sand. Organic matter also holds water. So lovely loam soils with adequate amounts of clay hold water better than sandy soils. And deeper soils hold more total water than shallow soils of the same type. As detailed in chapter 3, soil surveys are available for nearly every bit of land in the United States, and these surveys give the soil types, water-holding capacities, and soil depths.

Organic matter content is an especially noteworthy aspect of a soil's water-holding capability because we can change it. If we grow and till in a cover crop, for example, it increases the organic matter content of the soil. So does adding other kinds of organic matter, such as leaves or mulch. More organic matter content translates into more water being held by the soil, and more drought-resilience. Plowing or tilling land burns up and reduces organic matter. So tilling or turning under bare or sparsely covered soil can be counterproductive for water-holding capacity, soil fertility, and tilth. Unnecessary plowing or tilling should be avoided. When tilling between rows for weed control, we set the rototiller or other implement to work on just the top couple of inches of soil.

Creating garden beds changes the essential water-nature of the situation. Raised beds dry out faster and need more water than level soil or level beds. Beds can also be sunk below the surrounding soil surface. Sunken beds retain moisture better than level beds, and are especially useful in desert areas.

Don't, by the way, put vegetable garden beds under trees. Tree roots compete fiercely for water. In addition, tree roots can grow right up into the bed and turn it into a mass of tree roots by the end of the season, making the bed almost impossible to rework or renovate.

Dependence upon electricity-powered irrigation is a vulnerability. If you must irrigate, consider putting in a backup watering system that doesn't depend upon electricity. Throughout history, various cultures have used wind, flowing water, or draft animals to lift and pump water without electricity. These days, a human-powered treadle pump is being widely used in Africa and India. It can irrigate gardens up to an acre or two with an hour or two of daily walking. (For more details, look up 'treadle pump' on the Internet.) Lehman's sells hand-operated pumps suitable for household-sized water needs.

In regions where water is a limited resource, it doesn't make a lot of sense to shunt rainwater from the roof down gutters and into pipes designed to take it off the property as quickly as possible. Consider running the gutters into a water storage tank or a mini-pond for use in the yard or garden. (This isn't legal everywhere, amazingly. Here in Oregon it actually requires special permits.) Likewise, encourage any water flowing over the land to stay longer by making swales, that is, shallow ditches running along the contours of the land. In water-limited regions, consider adding a gray-water system. Gray water is the wastewater from the kitchen and laundry and sinks, but not from the toilet. (Using gray water to irrigate the yard or garden may also not be legal, depending upon local laws.) An excellent book on gray-water systems and using gray water is Robert Kourik's *Gray Water Use in the Landscape*.

Fruit and Nut Trees

Pioneers grew fruit and nut trees throughout most of the East, Midwest, and maritime West, and they usually grew them without irrigation. Here in maritime Oregon, I know several people who have "old-time" orchards, and they never irrigate except for newly planted replacement saplings. However, the trees are planted on deep soils, not shallow soils over bedrock or other impervious layers. In addition, the trees have generous spacing, usually about twice what modern recommendations call for. Modern commercial orchards, with dwarf trees on a tight spacing, need regular watering here. I strongly recommend planting fruit and nut trees with the generous, traditional, pioneer-style spacings.

Here in western Oregon, young fruit trees must be watered for the first couple of years to get a good start. My friend Harry MacCormack plants replacement trees in his old-time orchard as needed, and irrigates the babies with buckets. He places two to four 5-gallon plastic buckets with pinholes in the bottoms around the young tree. This tactic avoids the necessity of hooking up a hose or irrigation system for the orchard just for one or two replacement trees.

Dwarf fruit trees may be less water resilient than standards. Many people suppose or speculate that they are, but I haven't seen actual data. My own guess is that specific varieties, as well as different rootstock varieties, may matter as much as or more than the size class of the tree, which is a bit arbitrary. In addition, the specific situation might matter. Where the soil is contiguous with a water table or moist soil below, I would imagine that standard trees with large, deep root systems may have the advantage. On the other hand, if the situation is more like a large pot because of impervious or only dry layers a few feet down, and all the water is provided from the top (by either rain or irrigation), I can imagine that dwarf trees might actually sometimes have the advantage. Their smaller root systems would stay within the watered layer.

Among the various types of fruits, figs, apples, and grapes need the least water. Apricots, plums, and pears need somewhat more water. Then come cherries, peaches, and nectarines. Raspberries, strawberries, blueberries, and domestic blackberries all need a lot of water. I have never seen these latter four fruits grown successfully here in the maritime Northwest without irrigation. Wild blackberries do fine here without irrigation, however. So do wild serviceberries.

Fruit trees usually need water most at two periods. The first is when they are flowering. The second is as the fruit is expanding and ripening.

Old-fashioned, traditionally spaced orchards usually have grass-forb understories, not bare soil or mulch. A grass-forb understory makes good forage for the chickens or ducks, which are invaluable for pest control. The old-time orchard model was a production system for both fruit and poultry, and sometimes also provided forage and windfall fruit for a milk cow, sheep or cattle. (But not for goats or geese, which eat fruit trees. Geese are vegetarians; thus, contrary to what is often said, they don't contribute to pest control.) With widely spaced trees, there is plenty of light for the grass. Here in Willamette Valley, there is also water enough for both grass and trees without irrigation in orchards with traditional spacing. However, grass does compete with the trees for water. If your regional water situation is more stringent than ours, consider mulching your orchard instead of growing a grass understory.

The modern crowded orchard model undoubtedly gives you the most fruit per area of land *in good times*. However, the more widely spaced trees will give you more fruit *per hour of labor* in good times and bad. And in bad times such an orchard may continue giving you fruit while the modern crowded orchard dies from lack of water, or lack of your watering labor. With the old-fashioned orchard, there is the additional crop of eggs, milk, or meat. And what could be a more delightful sight than a flock of ducks or chickens on green grass cleaning up pests or feasting on the windfalls under orchard trees?

If you are experiencing a drought so serious that you are in danger of losing a tree entirely, here's a rescue method: Prune the tree back *drastically*. That is, remove one-third to one-half of the top of the plant. This reduction in leaf area dramatically decreases the loss of water through transpiration from leaves, thus reducing the water needs of the plant. The tree will be shocked and set back, but that is not necessarily a disadvantage in a drought. Growth increases water needs. Within two or three years the plant will probably have replaced all the top growth and be back to normal.

More modest pruning during a drought can be counterproductive, as it encourages new growth.

Ornamental and Landscape Plantings

I don't water what I can't eat. That is my basic rule. I believe a time will come when it will be illegal in most places to water non-food-producing crops and land. I'm getting a head start. (It isn't, ahem, because I'm just lazy. . . . OK, it is. But not entirely.)

Choose your landscape and ornamental plantings primarily from among those plants that do not require irrigation in your area. These may be native plants. Or they may be plants from areas in the world with a climate that's similar to yours. When you choose, consider the value of plants that provide food and shelter for beneficial insects and pollinators.

What if you are in love with some ornamental or landscape plants that are going to need watering in your region, however, and feel you just have to have them? If so, group such plants by water needs. That is, put together all the plants with similar water needs so that they can be watered with just one or two settings of the sprinkler, or with a single section of drip lines.

Rows of trees or bushes can make windbreaks that translate into lower water needs for the plants they are protecting. The traditional hedgerows on pioneer farms broke up wind patterns and ameliorated wind speed (and its desiccating power), as well as provided fruit and nuts for people and food and homes for wildlife.

Grass

Growing huge swaths of lawn in places where grass needs watering doesn't make a lot of sense unless you really need the lawn for something. You might. Your lawn may be the only place for your kids and all the other kids in the neighborhood to play baseball or soccer, for example. Many people have much more lawn than they need, though. Most of us don't actually need *any* lawn, by which I mean that pristine, very short-clipped golf-course-like, highly chemicalized and pollution-creating swath of green. But most of us do need some *grass*. Grass has unique properties. We can walk on grass without hurting ourselves or the grass. The growing point of the grass is basal, that is, down near the ground instead of

at the top of the plant. This means grass can be mowed or grazed without being too badly set back as long as not too much of the plant is taken off at once. Most of us want some visual openness to our landscapes, but not complete emptiness. We like both some grass and some trees in our home environments. In such an environment we feel most at home.

Pristine grass such as that grown on golf courses requires serious and regular fertilizing, watering, and mowing. It is ecologically unsound. It produces considerable pollution of surface and groundwater. However, you don't have to choose a golf-course-style lawn. Many of us here in western Oregon, for example, don't water our grass. It goes brown in August, just like much of the natural landscape. Then, along with the rest of nature, our grass returns to a beautiful, brilliant, vivid green color in fall with the coming of the winter rains.

If you want a pristine-style lawn, you will have to look in some other book as to how to install and maintain one. I've never had one. I don't particularly want one. I would prefer to have something other than tall fescue in my backyard, however. An eco-lawn, maybe, that stays short with just a couple mowings per year and is full of flowers. (See the Internet and local seed companies for eco-lawn mixes appropriate for your region.) But tall fescue is what came with my yard, and it does manage to grow in solid clay with no watering or fertilizing. I just mow it twice each spring to keep the wild blackberries and poison oak from taking over and making the yard impassable. That is the main reason that most of us need some grass. We prefer it to what would grow if we didn't have the grass. Pristine lawns are high maintenance, but grass itself is low-maintenance. So we put the vegetable garden and fruit and nut trees in the sunniest or best spots. The rest of our yard—the more shaded areas, the steep slopes, and the areas over septic drainage fields—is kept open and passable by growing grass there.

Mowing once per year is all that is necessary to keep trees, brush, and most weeds from taking over. Willamette Valley Indians burned the whole valley each fall to keep it as savanna. Additional mowing is needed to keep the grass at some particular length, or to keep it from flowering and releasing pollen, which may be illegal in some areas. Unkempt grass itself is sometimes locally illegal. More often the pressure toward pristine lawns is merely neighborhood tradition. If your neighborhood has strong traditions but no actual laws against "natural grass," you might consider a compromise. Consider maintaining a small pristine lawn right near the front door and walk, a symbol to neighbors of your willingness to try to meet social norms and get along. Then maintain all the rest of your grass as natural grass or eco-lawn.

If grass cannot grow at all in your region without irrigation, you shouldn't be growing grass. (Grass grows very well without irrigation in Willamette Valley. It just goes temporarily yellow in August.)

If you do maintain a section of irrigated lawn, water it deeper and less often rather than shallower and more often. The deep, less frequent watering makes the grass root deeper and be more drought resistant. Don't overwater. It wastes both water and fertility.

The more you fertilize, the more you will have to mow.

It's best to keep your grass higher than golf-course lawns. Such short cutting is very hard on the grass, which then requires more frequent watering and fertilizing. Mow frequently enough

so that you are taking only a small part of the plant with each mowing. Use a mower with sharp blades so they cut the grass rather than tear and mangle it. A mulching mower is advantageous. It cuts up the grass and puts it back on the lawn, thus mulching the grass as well as retaining the fertility and tilth the clippings represent.

Here in maritime Oregon, you need a mower with at least a five horsepower engine in order to cut wet grass. Lower-power mowers only cut dry grass. We usually have only two kinds of grass—wet grass that needs mowing and dry grass that doesn't.

If you are committed to a pristine lawn, consider a few compromises. First, don't automatically reach for the bags of "weed and feed" in the big-box stores. If you feel you must use chemical fertilizers on your lawn, buy just the fertilizer, without the herbicides, insecticides, moss killers, and fungicides. Second, consider going entirely organic with your lawn. Instead of the chemical fertilizer, apply an inch of compost a year. Chemical fertilizers, herbicides, fungicides and insecticides from lawns form a substantial fraction of the pollution that enters our surface and groundwater.

Here in western Oregon, we need grass over our septic drainage fields. "Septic drainage fields," though, is a misnomer. The septic drainage field is designed to have grass growing over it and won't work properly without it. Grass roots are needed to remove the excess water and nutrients. The transpiration and growth of grass is what drives the system, not passive "drainage." Grass roots don't expand in girth and clog the drainage field. Most trees, if planted over or near a drainage field, will grow so much root biomass in the drainage field that they clog it. Digging up a tree and renovating a drainage field can cost thousands of dollars. So plant grass over your septic drainage field.

Water and Spacing

Plants transpire, that is, they lose moisture from their leaves. Water loss from soil covered with plants is mostly from transpiration of the plants. The equivalent area of bare soil usually loses much less water. The more plants you have in a given area, the greater their water demands on the soil. So a densely planted crop may be stunted from lack of water, whereas the same plants with more generous spacing may have all the water they need. This means that we may vary plant spacing to fit the available water.

As I mentioned in the last chapter, I found intensively planted raised beds unworkable for me because they needed to be watered more frequently than suited me and my situation. Raised beds dry out faster than level soil. Intensively planted, they need watering every day. By allowing about 50 percent more space per plant, I found I could water every second or third day. A level bed of tomatoes could go about four or five days between waterings. A level bed of tomatoes with the same spacing and also 3 inches of straw mulch could go a week.

These days, in our leased garden field, Nate and I grow most crops in rows with 3½ feet between the rows. We are experimenting with different crops to find out how much space they need in the row, given that constant space between rows, our particular soil, and a management plan that involves watering no more than once per week for even the fully irrigated crops.

We plant our potatoes at a 16-inch spacing

instead of the ordinary 8 to 12 inches, given that we don't irrigate them at all, and they are usually irrigated here. However, we don't know whether this amount of extra space is necessary. We suspect it might not be for all varieties. We'll figure out what is actually needed by experimenting.

How much you need to water different kinds of plantings depends upon your region, soil type, soil depth, organic matter content, when and how much it last rained, and many other factors. Other local gardeners with similar soil can give you a rough idea of where to start. Beyond that, you too will have to figure out what your various plantings need by experimenting.

If a drought hits your vegetable garden and you can't water and are in danger of losing all the plants, eliminate every other plant. That will give the remaining plants more water, and hence a better chance at surviving and thriving well enough to be productive.

Water and Fertility

Sometimes, when plants seem to be growing slowly because of limited water, they could do better if the soil were more fertile. If upper roots have died because of soil drying, the plant may need to support itself only on the smaller volume of soil colonized by the deeper roots. With growth based upon a smaller volume of soil, it helps if that soil is more fertile.

Very high amounts of soluble fertilizer can actually draw water out of plant roots and cause the plant to wilt. (The correction is to massively overwater to wash away the excess.) You are unlikely to have this problem with organic fertilizers, which are not very water soluble.

If you fertilize your grass or trees or vegetables just ahead of a drought, you make them less drought hardy and water resilient. Fertilizing tends to create a spurt in growth. Rapidly growing plants need more water.

Water and Erosion

If you allow wind to blow unchecked over land that is dry and loose, you can lose topsoil. Even if you don't lose topsoil from bare ground in ordinary times, a bad year (or even more prolonged drought period) could completely remove all your topsoil if you don't guard against the problem in all your routine practices.

The other main erosion problem comes from slopes. If you have slopes, rain or irrigation water flowing over them can erode away topsoil. Gentle slopes should be tilled only along the contours so as to create mini-ditches that help hold water and soil on the land. Plowing up and down the slope creates myriad ditches that facilitate loss of topsoil and that can turn into major ditches and then into gullies. Gullies grow bigger the more water flows down them. Gullies dry out all nearby land to the depth of the gully. So a deep gully on one part of your land may make all the land too dry for ordinary gardening.

Protect your gentle slopes by minimizing tillage, by contour plowing when plowing is required, and by keeping the land covered with crops or cover crops during any times it is likely to be exposed to water erosion.

Avoid plowing or tilling steeper slopes. Plant them with perennial plants such as fruit, nut, or other trees, permanent ornamental or landscape plantings, grass, or perennial pasture.

The Threefold Effects of Mulch

Deep mulches prevent you from overhead watering effectively in most cases and, as noted previously, may work best with perennial plantings in which permanent drip lines are installed under the mulch. However, in some cases deep mulch may mean you no longer need to water at all. Even thinner layers of mulch are very effective at reducing water loss, and it is possible to overhead-water through them easily. In desert areas, vegetable gardening may require mulching.

Mulching has another effect not generally mentioned. Without mulch, the top 2 to 4 inches of soil dries out between waterings or rains. Often the tilled or plowed depth of soil is little more than this. If the top 4 inches of soil dries out, that kills nearly all the plant roots in the soft soil with the nicest tilth and the best fertility. The plant is then mostly dependent upon the roots it has sent deeper into harder, less fertile soil.

A 3-inch mulch on top of the soil protects it from drying out. The top inch or so of mulch dries out, but the entire depth of soil stays moist enough to support plant roots. This means the entire soft, fertile layer of soil is available for supporting the plant. In addition, under mulched soil, worms and other creatures that convert mulch to soil thrive. While the plant is removing fertility, these creatures are restoring and building it. It is much easier to maintain fertility and tilth when soil is mulched.

So-called "green mulches" are not real mulches. Green mulches are just an understory of growing greenery—clover between the rows in corn, for example. In my experience, green mulches are useful only when neither water nor fertility are limiting factors. They compete with the crop plant for both. Land with corn plus any additional swath of growing plants will need more water, not less. Sowing a cover crop between the rows before the main crop is finished is often useful, however. The cover crop doesn't compete significantly during the first month when it is germinating and starting to grow. After that, the main crop is harvested.

Why I Hate Drip Irrigation

I have used drip irrigation five times, on four different soil types, and in four different garden situations. All five times I regretted it. I tried it that many times because I had already spent $400 on the equipment, and I really wanted it to work. (And I'm stubborn.) But it didn't. Not for vegetables anyway. So this isn't going to be the book that teaches you how to do drip irrigation. (For that, see Robert Kourik's *Drip Irrigation for Every Landscape and All Climates*.) Instead, I will try to counter some of the extravagantly positive PR drip irrigation has by grumbling, snarling, and complaining about my experiences with it. Weigh my tooth-gnashing, hair-tearing, and garment-rending over drip irrigation together with the pro-drip PR, factor in your specific needs, and you just might be able to make an optimal choice for your situation.

Here's why drip irrigation didn't work for me:

1. Drip lines in the vegetable garden (or row crop fields) have to be put down after and lifted before tilling. It's a lot of work.
2. Drip lines are *not* labor free. Rodents like to bite into them and expand the little seep into a luxurious creek. With a bigger garden

(or a field of row crops) you have to walk the lines twice a week or more to repair leaks. In addition, you will need to trap or otherwise eliminate the water-loving gophers and other rodents you have attracted and succored.

3. The plastic types of irrigation lines are good for just a year and aren't cheap. In theory they can last two or even three years. In practice they last one. Plant roots grow into and around them. In addition, you trash the lines badly enough when you pick them up so that you can't reuse them.
4. How do you hoe without spending more time and work moving the lines than the hoeing takes? Hoeing can be done standing up comfortably. Moving drip lines requires bending over every few feet. It's backbreaking.

   Once plants get big or spread, good luck moving the lines. Viney squash plants grow over lines fast and don't like to be moved.

   After trying drip on bigger plantings, I decided it was likely to be workable for me only on small beds at home, and only at the cost of having to do all weeding on hands and knees. So I tried it. Even in that limited context it didn't work.
5. It's nearly impossible to direct-seed. Each drip line creates a little downward expanding cone of moist soil under each emitter *only*. The surface of the ground is dry between emitter positions to a depth of several inches. Optimally, the cones of water merge a foot or two beneath the soil surface to create an even moisture pattern. But even under ideal conditions, the surface of the soil is dry between the lines and

between the emitter positions within lines. You need the *surface* of the soil to be moist in order to germinate seeds. The spreading pattern beneath each emitter depends upon soil type, with soils with more clay having faster spread. Whatever the soil type, the only place you can germinate a seed or grow a small seedling is right under the individual emitters. Using drip lines works much better when all the plantings are transplants, and good-sized transplants at that, each of which can be positioned right at an emitter location.

6. Brassicas grown without overhead watering here get so aphid-infested and coated with aphid goo and poop, there are few edible leaves. From my kale plantings in two of the drip-irrigation years, there were big plants with plenty of leaves but *no*, count them, *zero*, edible leaves. Overhead watering or rain helps keep aphids in check by washing them off the plants. (I can end most aphid infestations just by hand-watering the plants hard, for example. You can see the aphids washing off. Some get carried back up the plant by ants, but most never make it.) Here in Willamette Valley with no summer rain, I want my brassicas overhead-watered. Even the squash plants become heavily aphid infested when watered only with drip irrigation, but with squash at least I'm not trying to eat the leaves.

7. Plants look dusty and dirty and less lush with no rain or overhead watering. They don't look as happy. Maybe they are as happy, but I'm not when I look at them. I'm depressed. I don't garden in order to get depressed.

8. The reason the plants look dusty and dirty is because they *are* dusty and dirty. They are dusty and dirty because the dry topsoil from between the drip lines blows off in great billows every time the soil is tilled. And this is in only ordinary afternoon wind. A single serious dry windstorm could probably remove inches of topsoil from the field in a day. Any time I see soil billowing from the land, I know something is wrong.

9. The drip lines don't actually water the soil between the lines unless you have lines placed very close together. For example, my friend Mike Hessel, the one grower I know who uses drip lines, puts down thousands of row feet of plastic drip lines each year, covered with thousands of feet of black plastic. He grows melons as well as delicata squash, which have relatively small vines. When I planted some squash in his setup, only the small squash such as delicatas did well. The drip lines, even covered with black plastic, essentially created long, moist pots about three feet across surrounded by dry soil. Big squash vines running out 10 to 20 feet in all directions couldn't get enough water from a root system restricted to those narrow pots.

10. Big viney squash put down roots at some of the nodes and support themselves on multiple root systems, not just the root system that formed from the seed. They can only do this when overhead-watered. They can't root from the nodes in the dry surface soil present in a drip-irrigated field. And they couldn't produce very many high-quality fruits on just the small root system of the initial plant. They could only produce inadequate numbers of squash of poor

flavor. I have never gotten prime squash of big-fruited varieties from a drip-irrigated garden. (The delicatas, admittedly, grow fine and taste great.)

11. One of the much-touted basic ideas behind drip lines is putting the water just where you want it, and not in aisles, paths, or elsewhere. If this works anywhere, it should have worked when I tried it in my backyard raised beds. It didn't. It turned out that, given my soil type, it was essential to water the entire garden area with the beds in it, not just the beds.

First, if I didn't water the entire area, the garden beds dried out almost instantly. I think when I watered just the beds, I ended up turning each bed into a moist pot surrounded by dry soil, which could absorb any water added to the pot almost immediately. If I watered the entire area I still had a pot, but it was much larger. It was the entire area of beds from topsoil to bedrock. Little pots dry out faster than big ones.

Second, if I didn't water the entire garden area, by late spring I got an "attack of the cracks." The clay soil in the rest of my yard and underneath the garden beds contracts as it loses moisture after the rains stop. Huge cracks form and run through the soil. The cracks are deep; they are a couple inches wide as well. If I water just the beds, the cracks forming in the area go right through the beds. I've tried to fill the cracks with soil when they run through beds, but it doesn't work. I've tried to block the cracks off with little dikes. That doesn't work either. Once a bed has a crack in it, it dries out so fast that it generally isn't possible to grow vegetables. Most beds developed at least one major crack.

If, instead, I overhead-water the entire area with the garden beds, that entire area stays hydrated, and it is big enough to stop the cracks near the edge of the watered area. So no cracks run across the garden beds.

My clay soil and cracks might have been an extreme situation. However, I think in many cases watering just the beds and not the paths and general area creates a "pot effect," to the overall detriment of the growing situation. The soil in the beds and the aisles is connected. You can't fail to water one without dramatically affecting the other.

I also had much more trouble with slugs and sow bugs whenever I watered just the beds. They are attracted to the wet areas. If I water the general area, most of such critters are just as happy to stay in the aisles and grassy border areas.

If I had ornamental or perennial plantings that required irrigation, I would consider permanent beds, however, with permanent deep mulch, and permanent drip lines installed beneath the mulch. Many people use that system with perennial plantings here. Just not with vegetable gardens.

Soil Capillarity and the Pot Effect

My mental image when I first started gardening and watering was of garden soil that was continuous with deeper soil down to some hypothetical water table. I think very often a better analogy is that we are gardening in a big pot. One of my farmer friends has low land with a water table about 2 feet down in winter. In winter, he is effectively growing everything on his farm in a wide shallow pot. Sometimes there is bedrock under your garden area, in which case you are gardening in a big pot. Sometimes there is a water table under your garden but an impervious layer between. Sometimes our gardens are large pots for reasons that are unavoidable, that derive from the essential nature of our land. Many such pots have successfully supported all the plants the gardener desired. However, where our garden soil is contiguous with deep, ever-moist soil or a water table, it is a huge advantage. It's a good idea to avoid creating pots unnecessarily.

Repeated plowing with a moldboard plow or a rototiller can create a "plow pan," a layer of hard, impervious soil at the lower limit of the tilling, thus creating a shallow pot out of the land. On a small scale, deep-digging with a shovel or spade or broadfork is the cure. On a large scale, the hardpan can be broken up with a chisel plow.

Plowing or tilling even once sometimes creates a temporary pot effect. It can destroy the capillarity of the soil so that moisture no longer moves from the water table up through the plowed layer to the surface. It may take a while for the ground to settle and the capillarity to be restored. Here in the Northwest, we usually plow or rototill early in spring. Substantial following rains moisten all the tilled soil, compact it a bit, and restore capillarity through the tilled layer to the underlying water table.

Last year, however, Nate and I finished the negotiations for our new garden-land lease quite late in the spring planting season. We immediately had the land moldboard plowed. We waited only three weeks before planting because we were getting such a late start. We irrigated after planting, since the rains had stopped and the soil was clearly too dry to germinate seeds. But we soon started noticing that the plants were showing signs of water stress, and the land seemed to be drying out much faster than we expected after

irrigation. Nate started muttering about "capillarity," then went out and dug several deep holes down to below the plowed level in the field. What he found was moist soil under the plowed layer and moist soil at the surface where our watering was reaching. But the bottom of the plowed layer was dry, disrupting capillarity with the moist soil beneath. The soil was drying out so fast at the surface because no replenishing moisture was coming from below. The water applied from above was all the water the top layer was getting. Nate responded by watering the entire field very heavily (once) to moisten the plowed soil all the way down to the underlying moist soil and to restore capillarity. (Even the section with the potatoes, which we usually don't water.) After that, the field needed only ordinary amounts of water. (And the potatoes needed none for the rest of the season.)

Planting in Dry Conditions

When we plant seed, we often must act to restore soil capillarity, especially in dry weather. When Nate planted beets in our field last August, he made a furrow, sowed the seed in the very bottom of it and covered it lightly, then walked down the furrow to compress the soil tightly around the seeds and restore capillarity between the disturbed soil and the ground. Nate's walking on the row made a narrow footprint-wide sunken bed out of the row. The next morning, the soil in the narrow sunken row was actually damp, even though he didn't water, and it hadn't rained for months. The beets germinated and thrived.

When I need to direct-seed under dry conditions, I often presoak the seed, as described in chapter 3.

When planting transplants under dry conditions, we need to change the dry conditions. For the somewhat disturbed roots of a transplant to expand rapidly in the soil, the soil must be moist. If it isn't, we often start by watering the hole the transplant is to go in, then "mudding in" the transplant. This is how I plant big tomato transplants.

Sometimes it is useful to leaf-prune transplants before planting. This reduces the water needs of the plant. Last spring, our tomato transplants were ready to plant two months before we completed negotiations on the land and had anywhere to put them. The transplants were 2 feet high in 4-inch pots, and were severely pot-bound and nearly dead. We pruned off all the leaves except for the top three or four and all the suckers. We also ripped off the exposed brown damaged roots. We planted the tomatoes slanted in trenches with only those top few leaves exposed. That way the plants had most of the nodes of their stems buried and would start new vigorous roots from every buried node. The tomatoes were late but still produced all the tomatoes we wanted.

For small transplants (such as 3-inch-high kale seedlings in small rectangular soil blocks) I prefer to water the row for the transplants with a hose or sprinkling can the day before transplanting. Then I make a clean cut into the soil with my planting knife at each planting position and loosen and push aside soil on one side to make the hole. Then I press one side of the transplant's soil plug (which is square) up against the compact, undisturbed soil on the clean-cut side of the hole so as to get one area of maximum restored soil capillarity where the roots of the seedling are as undisturbed as possible. Then I gently backfill the loose soil under and around the other sides of the transplant. I got this technique partly from my friend Mike Hessel, who grows twelve acres of melons a year, all from transplants—transplants that he plants himself with only his own labor. Mike, however, uses a trowel, not a knife, for making and filling the holes. He is a fan of a trowel he bought from Home Depot that is intended to work concrete. It has a blade of good steel with parallel sides and a squared-off end. It also has a conformation that Mike feels is easier on the hand for transplanting than typical garden trowels.

It's best to transplant on cool, overcast days. When those aren't available, transplanting in the early evening is best, so the transplants have the cooler night to begin to repair and reestablish effective root systems. If very hot weather is all you have, you may need to place temporary shade barriers over the plants. On a small scale in my backyard, if I need to transplant tomatoes on a hot day, I put a 5-gallon bucket south of each tomato transplant initially. That way the transplant will be protected for the several hours of most intense sun for the first few days. I also water the tops of the transplants daily for the first three days if the weather is hot. (Most plants can absorb water very effectively through their leaves.)

Overhead Watering

In the vegetable garden, we organize by water needs. We put the potatoes, which we don't irrigate, in a block separate from crops we do irrigate. The summer-grown drying beans need some water during the season but should have the water held off them after they start to dry down. We put them in separate patches or blocks. We water our early field corns two or three times but let them finish off and dry down in August. The tomatoes and squash and melons all need a lot of water, so they go best when planted either by themselves or with each other.

Most people who are watering a garden from a household water system will do their watering with ordinary oscillating or circular sprinklers of the same kind as are used for lawns. Before buying sprinklers, find out the flow rate and water pressure of your water source. Get a sprinkler rated for the right range and pressure. To run more than a sprinkler or two at once usually takes an agricultural well with greater pressure and flow rate than most home systems have available. You generally want a sprinkler that delivers no more than about 1 inch of water per hour. You want the ground to be able to absorb the water, not for it to puddle or run off.

You usually need to monitor and check on the amount of water you're delivering. We are usually advised to put some empty tuna cans round about in our watering pattern to figure out how much water we are delivering how fast. And that's useful. But it is no substitute for digging holes occasionally a day after watering to see what is moist and how far down.

We invariably have to overlap sprinkler watering patterns in order to cover all the ground with any degree of uniformity.

It is always best to water less frequently and deeper rather than often and shallow. Shallow watering encourages shallow root systems, making the plants more drought sensitive.

The more water-needy vegetables in Willamette Valley in August need no more than about 2 inches of water per week. They need considerably less in late spring and early summer. General advice is to give yards and gardens 1 inch per week, but that clearly is too generic to be useful. What is needed depends upon the kind of soil, when it rained last, how hot or dry it has been recently, whether your soil has capillarity to a water table or to moister soil, the soil type, whether it is mulched, and many other factors.

One trick in corn fields is to plant occasional sunflowers as water status indicators. The sunflowers need more water than the corn. When the sunflowers wilt, it's time to water the corn.

Plants aren't supposed to wilt. There is lore that it is normal for squash plants to wilt in the afternoon, and that it doesn't hurt them. That isn't so. Wilted leaves mean that the plants are conducting desperate measures to survive and aren't doing much photosynthesis. Squash that are wilting in the afternoons are water-limited and are not growing and producing as well as they could be.

Put stakes or heavy objects of some sort at the ends of beds and rows where you will be dragging hoses to keep the hoses from dragging over rows or beds and trashing plants.

Tall-growing plants can block the water from a sprinkler. A trellis full of pole beans works well on the outer edge of the watering pattern but not in the middle. The pole beans block and catch all the water, creating a "rain shadow" behind them.

Most plants, even desert plants, absorb water very efficiently through their leaves. Leaves absorb water and re-hydrate the entire plant, and water seeps out through the roots and moistens the surrounding soil. That moisture can be reabsorbed later. (This has been shown recently by using radioactive water.) In addition, roots can absorb water in a wet area and release it through the roots to other areas of the soil that are less moist. (This is called "hydraulic redistribution.") So you don't have to water every part of a plant or every square inch of soil to do an adequate job. There is room for a certain amount of sloppiness in our watering patterns.

When hand-watering, we are often advised to water the ground, not the tops of the plants. I water both. I water the leaves to rid them of aphids and leave them looking all bright and beautiful as well as to let the plants do their water absorption through the leaves and their hydraulic redistribution tricks. But I do put most of the water on the soil.

The ability of plants to absorb water through their leaves means that dew or fog that moistens plants can add considerably to the water balance. Here in maritime Oregon we don't have rain in August, but we ordinarily have cool night temperatures and heavy morning dew. Thus our plants experience conditions that are far from those of true desert in August, even though we have no more rainfall than true desert during this month.

There is a best time to water. If you run a sprinkler when it is hot and windy, you waste a lot of water from evaporation, and many of the fine drops blow away. When the wind is variable, it's hard to get the water even approximately where you want it. We are generally advised that it is best to water between evening and late morning for best water use efficiency. However, to avoid spreading fungal diseases, sometimes we want to water only in morning; we try to avoid having the plants wet in the cool nights.

The best time to water here in Willamette Valley is usually in the morning, when the relative humidity is high and there is little loss of water from evaporation. In addition, in morning there is little wind. In afternoons there is almost always some fairly variable wind.

When watering by hand with a nozzle, it's easy to underwater. I've found it's hard to adequately water more than about four small beds by hand. When hand-watering, I water each bed a little, then come back and water again when I've done them all. By then the first dose of water has seeped into the ground by capillarity. I give each bed several doses of water rather than watering one bed at a time.

I keep beds watered by hand by virtue of making them with irregular surfaces and deliberate swales, so I can put a lot of water on a bed, then go on to the next bed while the water on the first sinks in, and so forth. For more than a few small beds, I've found hand-watering more useful as a supplement to overhead sprinkler watering than as a replacement. That is, I run a sprinkler over the entire area occasionally. Then I hand-water the beds with higher water needs in between sprinkler waterings.

When watering with a sprinkler it's easy to overwater. I've tried several brands of electric or hydraulic timers, all of which worked only erratically. I've reverted to the old reliable but inconvenient standby of paying attention to the watering and setting a timer to remind me when to move the sprinkler or cut the water.

For all my watering I prefer using good-quality heavy hoses that resist getting kinks.

Water Resilience and Vegetables

If I had to grow a garden entirely without irrigation, I would grow fava beans, hardnecked garlic, and overwintering snow peas, all of which can be planted in October and grown entirely on fall and early spring rains. And I would plant 'Hannan

Popbean' (a garbanzo) and more snow peas in early spring. Both of these give a crop before water becomes an issue in midsummer. I would also plant a variety of fast-growing, early-harvested spring greens such as mustard greens and shun-giku (edible chrysanthemum). These plants and crops are not particularly water-resilient. The tactic is to grow them at a time of year when water is naturally abundant. In the Northeast and upper Midwest, soils tend to be fully water charged in spring because of melting snow. Maritime West soils are saturated from winter rains. So many water-needy vegetables with short maturity times and good growth in cold weather can be grown in many areas in early spring.

Growing full-season or warm-season crops is another issue. As mentioned previously, there is one and only one warm-season crop Nate and I grow entirely without irrigation. That is potatoes. We prefer to grow potatoes without irrigation, even when irrigation is available.

There are three other crops we plan to try completely without irrigation next year, because we have reasons for thinking they might yield enough to be worth growing that way: the tepary bean 'Black Mitla', the cowpea 'Fast Lady Northern Southern Pea', and the common bean variety 'Gaucho'. In addition, we want to try certain very early flint and flour corns. (See the bean and corn chapters, respectively, for more on these varieties.)

There is a lot of information available on the "general" water needs of vegetables, but little information on their *relative* water needs. In other words, which vegetables are good candidates for producing adequately with little or no irrigation? Which are best at surviving summer droughts? The best information I've seen on this subject is in *Water-Wise Vegetables*, by my friend Steve Solomon. (Some of it is also reported in his more recent book *Gardening When It Counts*.) Steve did some deliberate testing of different vegetable crops under conditions of no irrigation as well as when he "fertigated" with the leaky 5-gallon bucket method. This is the same method as I described for starting fruit trees in unirrigated orchards, except Steve usually puts some soluble fertilizer in the water. All his vegetables were grown in rows and with generous spacing. Steve reports the following:

1. Potatoes grow so well and taste so good unirrigated that Steve prefers to grow them that way, even when water is available.

2. Beets, chard, kale, leeks, rutabagas, and giant kohlrabi are good enough at scrounging water and are drought resistant enough so that it is possible to grow them without irrigation in the maritime Northwest, though all do better with at least some irrigation. Growing them without irrigation requires good deep soil and wider than recommended spacing. Midseason and late cabbages require a bit more water. (Spring cabbages are too wimpy for this situation.)

3. Squash, melons, and indeterminate tomatoes need more water but can be grown with some fertigation.

4. Bulb onions, celery, Chinese cabbage, and the summer and fall crops of lettuce, radishes, scallions, and spinach all require heavy irrigation.

The spring Nate France and I worked together for the first time, he had just moved to a house on a farm and had just broken his arm. Furthermore, there was no water in the prospective garden area. He was eager to garden, however. What could he grow without water? This would be a good year to find out. We know Willamette Valley pioneers grew vegetable gardens, but information about how they watered has been lost. (We do know that they grew a lot of wheat, corn, leeks, and cabbage, however.) So Nate started by reading Steve Solomon's books. Then he planted a little bit of lots of things. A few remained completely unirrigated. Some were fertigated. He planted everything in rows, and with more generous than ordinary spacing. There were additional problems, however. He had moved onto the land late and gotten a late start in spring. In addition, he was turning under a heavy sod pasture with a huge thatch buildup. The thatch could be expected to tie up most fertility. And fertilizing was minimal, some seed meal or nothing, mostly. (He had lifted samples for a soil test, but they take weeks to process.) But this year was all about what could be grown under lousy conditions generally, not optimally. (Steve's dry gardens were optimal except for water.) Here are the results.

1. The potatoes made a nice crop, in spite of being hilled up too little and too late. They were the only unmitigated success in the vegetable garden.
2. The nonirrigated bush drying beans 'Black Coco' and 'Indian Woman Yellow' really weren't worthwhile. But they yielded well enough to suggest they might be worthwhile if water limitation was the only problem. My early flint corns didn't yield well, given no fertilizer, no water, shallow soil prep, and heavy weed pressure from bindweed. However, they did make enough of a crop to get a successful additional year of plant breeding done, and to suggest that they might work without irrigation, given earlier planting and better weed control.
3. Some varieties of the fertigated summer and winter squash did make crops that were marginally worthwhile and that probably could be worthwhile under slightly better conditions. (See the squash chapter.)
4. The melons and cukes were fertigated but were a bust. The kale grew and survived but didn't produce worthwhile amounts of leaves.
5. The row of fertigated tomatoes made stunted plants with tiny tomatoes, whatever the variety. If all the water for the row had been put on two plants, that would have represented full irrigation, and there would have been severalfold more edible tomato biomass.
6. Brown teff, which is supposedly drought-resistant, was stunted and miserable and did not make any seed.

The real winners for the summer were the potatoes, the orchard, the milk cow, and the wild blackberries. The Dexter milk cow gave nice family-sized amounts of milk and cream all summer on nothing but grass. In Willamette Valley, grass is much easier to grow than vegetables. In general, plants with big root systems have more ability to scrounge water from deeper soil levels as well as to survive periodic droughts than do plants with small root systems. Even dwarf orchard trees have much bigger root systems than any of the vegetables.

Water Resilience and Heirloom Varieties

Traditional vegetable varieties, grown in rows with traditional wide spacings, can be grown in most regions of the world without irrigation. The space between rows should not be considered as "wasted." In fact, that space is what makes it possible to grow vegetables without irrigation in areas that have only adequate *average* summer rainfall. This planting pattern enables the vegetable patch to survive the inevitable periods when there is more time between periods of rain than is optimal.

The modern planting pattern, on the other hand, assumes unlimited water through irrigation. It crowds the plants. And it often features compact or even dwarf varieties. Dwarf plants can be crowded, so it's true they can yield more if given unlimited water and unlimited (chemical) fertility. Dwarf plants usually have dwarf root systems. In general, they aren't the best choice for growing in a more widely spaced traditional pattern under conditions of more limited water or fertility.

Big sprawling heirloom varieties of yore were generally planted with more generous spacing than we allow modern hybrids, and they were expected to be able to scrounge their own water and root deep and thrive on somewhat lower levels of fertility. When testing varieties for use under less than optimal conditions of water or fertility, always include some heirloom or heirloom-style modern open-pollinated (non-hybrid) varieties.

Taller varieties usually have larger root systems than dwarf types. Pole beans are likely to have deeper roots than bush beans. When Steve Solomon tested tomatoes under conditions of limited water, it was the indeterminate varieties

that performed best. When I have direct-seeded and grown squash under relatively dry conditions, it is the vine and half-bush types that survive. Varieties that have a strictly bush growing habit usually don't thrive.

Some *species* are highly drought tolerant. Tepary beans (*Phaseolus acutifolius*), native to the American Southwest, are generally highly water efficient and drought resistant. Cowpeas (*Vigna unguiculata*) are also generally more drought resistant than common beans (*Phaseolus vulgaris*). Bush varieties of water-resilient species may be more water resilient than pole varieties of less water-resilient species. Furthermore, individual varieties may override general plant form. The half-bush hybrid winter squash 'Sunshine F_1', for example, is more drought resistant than all the big-vined types we have tested it against except for 'Katy Stokes Sugarmeat' (which performs equally well).

If your conditions mean you are doing the equivalent of growing plants in a large pot in the field, bush types may perform better. Their root systems are more likely to be concentrated in the limited area you are watering and fertilizing.

Becoming Native to the Land of Our Living

The seasonality of "green" varies with the region. The true New Englander expects his densely planted landscape to be green and lush all summer. In fall, when much dies, he celebrates the "fall colors." When the ground is covered with snow, he doesn't complain about the lack of green, but rather, comments upon the pristine cleanness of the white blanket that covers all summer sins. Nor does he bemoan the naked, leafless, dormant deciduous trees in winter. Instead he notices their essential shapes and comments on the myriad patterns and shades and kinds of bark.

I'm a westerner, a scion of the Willamette Valley of Oregon. I appreciate the lush greenery of spring as much as any New Englander. But by midsummer, I expect the natural rhythms to be changing and slowing down. By August, I expect the dominant shade in the landscape to be the yellowish-brown of grass doing what it makes sense for natural things to do at this time of year … to go dormant. Like most Oregonians, toward the end of August, however, I am getting restless and eager for the return of the winter rains. I watch and evaluate those first few sprinkles in September. In response to each, I am asking whether it is just a sprinkle or a real rain—a rain that begins to re-hydrate the soil and wake up all the sleepers. I sniff every breeze for rain. When the first real rain comes, like most Oregonians, I rejoice, as humans often do, by running around and exclaiming over the rain and commenting about it to everyone who will stand still long enough. Sometimes I even go for a walk in that first real rain. I welcome it back by getting thoroughly and happily drenched, an act that is impossible in summer.

The leaves begin to fall from the deciduous trees. Most don't turn any spectacular color first. Yellow is usually the best we get. But I don't mind. The few swaths of bright red on the hillsides don't arouse any particular emotions other than a reminder to avoid those places. That's the poison oak. Our fall color isn't red or even yellow so much as green, the green of everything waking up, coming to life, germinating. Our winter, too, is mostly green. The occasional few days here and there with snow on the ground

are fun but get old fast. What I want is green. There are at least a hundred shades and kinds of green. I love them all. Spring is green and the rains cease. Early summer is still green, but the natural cycle (and the natural yard) is winding down. Then comes August in soft yellows and browns, a time of rest.

There seem to be more garden writers from New England than from elsewhere. Those of us who live elsewhere need to be careful not to be bamboozled into trying to impose a New England pattern on places where it doesn't belong. The Oregonian or Californian or Washingtonian who wants a green lawn in August is, in essence, saying to that lawn: "Be a New England lawn!" We lowland westerners should be landscaping with appropriate natives and adaptable imported plants that can thrive on our natural cycles, not trying to impose the patterns of alien regions.

National and state boundaries don't mean anything to plants. I will do better with lowland-adapted, dry-summer-adapted Mediterranean natives than native plants from eastern Oregon or even natives from a few miles away—but a mile higher. What plants care about are specific climates and temperatures and patterns of rainfall.

Those who live in truly desert areas have additional problems. They need desert-adapted plants. But in addition, they need a different concept about planting densities in their landscapes. A commonly stated rule is that most plants have roots that extend about as far down and around as the top growth of the plant extends up and around, or a bit beyond. That isn't true of desert plants. Desert plants often have root systems that are manyfold wider and/or deeper than the aboveground plant. Some have very deep roots specialized for reaching deep reservoirs of moisture. Some have huge expanses of shallow roots designed to grab every molecule of rainwater the instant it touches the ground. A yard landscaped with desert plants must mimic desert plant spacings. The desert-living human gardener adopts the patterns of the desert and learns to appreciate the spaces and rocks and sand as much as the plants in his sparser plantings.

One of the most joyous things we can do is to find our place, the land we fit into, the land where we belong. Having found our place, we snuggle into it, learn about it, adapt to it, and accept it fully. We love and honor it. We rejoice in it. We cherish it. We become native to the land of our living.

CHAPTER SEVEN

Soil and Fertility

The Big Picture. The Soil Test. Experiment. Stockpiling Fertility. Add Fertilizer to the Right Place. Retaining Soil Fertility. On Not Buying Things. Growing Our Own Fertility with Legumes. Growing Our Own Fertility with Azolla. Manure. The Power of Pee. Leaves. Fertilizing with Grass Clippings. Squanto and the Raw Fish, Revisited. Why I Don't Compost Anymore. A Debris Pile Addendum.

The Big Picture

There are two basic approaches to soil fertility. One is feeding the plant. The other is feeding the soil and allowing the soil to feed the plant by natural processes. As an organic gardener, I'm a practitioner of the latter approach.

A second major consideration for vegetable gardens is whether they are permanent or rotating. In the Northeast and upper Midwest, people can make permanent vegetable gardens. In many areas of the country with mild winters, we can't garden one piece of land perpetually because of a buildup of pests or diseases. Here in maritime Oregon, for example, most gardens get a buildup of symphylans after being gardened and irrigated in summer continuously for several years. The symphylan is a small arthropod that is up to about ¼ inch long and looks like a tiny white centipede. Symphylans eat both decaying organic matter as well as plant root hairs. In fields with a modest symphylan infestation, there are spots that are bare or full of stunted plants where the crop plants didn't survive long enough to emerge, or emerged but were so badly eaten they could not thrive. In badly infested fields it can be impossible to grow any of the plants that are most symphylan sensi-

tive. (Symphylans are a major issue for organic gardeners and farmers in the maritime Northwest. There is much information on them available on the Web as well as in Steve Solomon's book *Growing Vegetables West of the Cascades*.) Planting potatoes or unirrigated grass, hay, or pasture are the main organic ways we know of to lower the symphylan levels. Summer dry fallows or summer crops that don't require irrigation may help. In areas with mild winters, where winter freezes are rare or shallow, we may (in the long term) need two garden areas so that we can rotate between them.

A third issue is the level of fertility required for any given purpose. A grain field needs to be more fertile than most land for the farming to be worth the effort. A vegetable garden needs to be more fertile still (except for the potato patch). There are a few places in the world that have soils so rich that they can be used as vegetable gardens with little or no additional improvements in fertility. The Corn Belt of the United States has deep, rich loam soils, the best soils in the world. Native Americans farmed the floodplains of the rivers in the Corn Belt without using any kind of inputs. However, the yields they got were low compared to those we expect today. And in addition, after they had farmed a piece of land for a few years, they got decreasing yields. They then abandoned the land and cultivated a new piece. After several years of fallowing the land, growing grass, brush, and small trees, the old garden would be usable again.

Virtually everyone elsewhere in the world has less fertile soil than these native farmers had in the Corn Belt. Nor is there enough prime land available to simply mine the soil for a few years and then move on to another equally prime piece. As a result, most of us need to enhance the fertility of our land before it will grow vegetables optimally. And we want to maintain the fertility of the land rather than exhausting it.

Most of the bulk of plants that we remove from our soil when we harvest consists of carbon, hydrogen, and oxygen, which plants get from air and water. The soil minerals plants need make up only a small part of their biomass. To feed the soil and keep it in good tilth, we provide compost, tilled-under cover crops, or other organic matter to the soil. In addition, we provide those tiny amounts of minerals for that minor component plants get from the soil (if they aren't already there or have been used up). Plants create everything else from air and water. (I omit nitrogen, which is a little more complex.)

Willamette Valley has soils as good as any in the West. However, the base rocks in our soils have little or no calcium in them. In addition, heavy winter rains cause serious leaching of soluble nutrients. Nitrogen, calcium, and sulfur are all highly to somewhat soluble. Generally, these prime Willamette Valley soils are only prime if we add some ground-up rocks containing calcium and sulfur to the soil. These rock powders don't have to be added every year, however.

There are many books available on managing soil fertility in good times, when it is possible to import ground-up rocks, seed meal, and other things. In this chapter I will focus upon less common tactics aimed at getting us through hard times when inputs may not be routinely available.

There are three basic approaches to maintaining soil fertility. One is to retain as much as possible of the soil fertility we have. The second is to grow some additional fertility using cover crops or green manure crops, especially nitrogen-fixing legumes. The third is to replace lost fertility with additions from outside. On the small scale of a few garden beds, you may have many options. On a larger scale, we usually use some combination of all three approaches. We retain fertility and grow as much fertility as we can, then use certain additions of fertility from outside where needed or practical.

The Soil Test

USDA soil survey maps, which I have discussed in prior chapters, can be a starting point for understanding the fertility issues of your land. However, past history may matter as much or more. If the topsoil was removed or buried when your house was built, that will matter a lot more than what the fertility characteristics of your topsoil might have been if you had any. What the land was growing before you moved onto it, how it was managed, and what the former owner did or didn't add all matter.

Some lands have an excess of particular minerals, either because the soils contain too much of them naturally or because fertilizers have been added blindly and inappropriately in the past. We need to know what our land actually needs as well as what may be in excess. If we blindly add things our soil doesn't need, we are wasting money, and may be creating imbalances or toxicity problems that can be long term.

A soil test can give us hard data about our land. I don't recommend home soil test kits. They generally aren't very accurate, don't cover all the elements you need to know about, and can't give you specific recommendations as to what or how much to add when there is a deficiency. I suggest getting a good professional soil test on your land at least once. If you are gardening or farming organically, the standard tests based upon agribusiness assumptions and solutions aren't appropriate. My farm partner, Nate France, a soils specialist, recommends getting your soil test from the folks at Peaceful Valley Farm Supply, who are organic specialists. He recommends buying the interpretive booklet too. The soil test plus the booklet cost about $40.

When you get a soil test, ask for an analysis for nitrogen, phosphorus, potassium, sulfur, calcium, and magnesium. The more common analysis of just the first three (NPK) is not enough. Likewise, ask for an analysis for anything known often to be missing or present in toxic amounts in soils in your region. Send in your soil test six weeks or more before you need the results. It can take a while to get your report back, especially in late winter or early spring.

Collect several soil samples from different parts of your land and pool them. Collect from below a sod cover. Exclude leaves and roots.

After you have your soil test, you will learn what simple things you can do to correct basic mineral imbalances and deficiencies.

You don't have to add the ground minerals (such as lime, gypsum, or rock phosphate) every year.

Most are good for three to five years. However, the ground-up minerals don't become available instantly. Only a little is available the first year. Generally, somewhat more is available the second and third year, and diminishing amounts thereafter.

A good place to buy limestone, gypsum, and rock phosphate by the 50-pound bag is your local feed and seed store. For large amounts you usually buy from a wholesale source, and sometimes have the option of having the materials delivered or even delivered and spread.

Experiment

Even if you have done a soil test, don't assume that the results are actually correct. Test them on the ground. That is, put the gypsum or the rock phosphate on just some rows or sections and leave it off at least three rows or sections.

I don't advise mixing different rocks and fertilizer components together to make a "complete" mix. If you do that without a soil test, there is a good chance you will at least be wasting money, if not actually creating imbalances or toxicity. And if you mix everything together, how will you ever find out what is actually necessary? Learning what your land actually needs in good times is part of our essential strategy in preparing for all times, good and bad.

Let's suppose my soil test suggests adding rock phosphate, lime, and gypsum, for example. I would add all three in half the amounts suggested for the initial year. But I would leave the rock phosphate off three rows, the lime off three rows, and the gypsum off three rows. (Those three rows each time need to be in different sections of the field.) By the end of the year, I would know whether all three fertilizers are necessary. In a subsequent year, I might do an equivalent experiment to figure out what amounts are optimal.

Stockpiling Fertility

Once you have the result of the soil test, and have actually tested it on the ground at least one year, you'll learn what some of the basic fertility limitations of your land are. And you can add, for example, gypsum and lime and rock phosphate, or whatever you need, to your land to make semi-long-term improvements. However, here in Willamette Valley, the calcium and sulfur continue to leach away every winter. So at least once every five years, we know we should add more. Once you know what the long-term fertility characteristics of your land are, I suggest some judicious stockpiling. Tuck away enough bags of lime, rock phosphate, or whatever—enough for the next two additions. That way, you will have at least ten years beyond any loss of ability to buy ground-up minerals from elsewhere.

My friend Merry Youle, who gardens halfway up a volcano in Hawaii, feeds her garden soil mostly with compost made from macadamia nut hulls and dairy cow manure. She stockpiled both. Soon after, the dairy farm where she got the manure folded. Merry is glad she has enough manure to last her for a while.

Add Fertilizer to the Right Place

The soluble chemicals typically found in agribusiness fertilizers can be spread on the surface of the soil (away from the plants). Synthetic fertilizers are water soluble, and wash down to where the roots are. (These fertilizers will burn the plants if applied directly to them.) However, the ground rock powders beloved of organic gardeners, such as ground limestone or rock phosphate, are not very soluble. To be effective, they need to be down where the roots are. They must be tilled in. Compost and composted manure are also much more effective when incorporated into the soil, where moisture and microbial action do a better job of decomposing them so as to release their nutrients to plant roots.

You can add fertilizer to the entire field if you have as much fertilizer as you need. If you need to make the fertilizer stretch farther, it's more effective to band it in the row where the plants will be instead of spreading it uniformly. The problem is, you have to fertilize first and till the fertilizer under before you plant the crop. So how can you get the crop rows to correspond to the fertilizer rows? What I do is put bands of fertilizer down every 3½ feet, and extend each band a bit beyond where the land will be tilled. That way, I can see the fertilizer marks at the end of each row and know where to put the rows of seeds.

Retaining Soil Fertility

The first step in retaining soil fertility is retaining the soil. That is, do everything possible to keep your soil from blowing or washing away:

1. Don't leave soils bare during periods in which they may be vulnerable to wind or water erosion.
2. Plow along contours, not straight up and down slopes.

3. Don't plow steep land. Use it for perennial crops that don't need plowing, such as orchards, ornamental plantings, poultry (or other livestock) pasture or forage areas, hay, or grass.

Also, avoid wasting fertility:

1. Timely weeding conserves the nutrients for the crop.
2. Avoid overwatering, which washes away fertility unnecessarily.
3. Use cover crops to trap nutrients so that they will not be washed away in winter, where this is a problem.
4. Plow or till only when necessary. Tilling aerates the soil and encourages bacterial activity that eats up fertility.

The more biomass we remove from the land, the more fertility we will ultimately need to grow or import from elsewhere to make up for it. So if I remove just the ears of corn, and till under the corn plants, that holds most of the fertility of the corn plants on the land. If I remove both, it's more costly.

Weeds have a lot of nutrients in them. I like to leave the hoed or pulled weeds right there in the garden to return those nutrients to the soil. The only case where I remove weeds is with bigger perennial weeds that would re-root if left on the surface of the garden.

I like to do most of the trimming of vegetables right in the garden as I harvest. I leave the aphidy cabbage and kale leaves in the garden. I could compost them and return the compost to the garden, but there are nutrients lost at every stage of the transformations that take place off-site. I keep more of the nutrients on the land by leaving as much biomass in the garden as possible.

On Not Buying Things

Manufacturers of fertilizers, pesticides, and soil amendments tend to hate organic gardeners and farmers because we tend to not *buy* anything. We use things like manure and compost, obtained free or bought locally, not the nationally manufactured and advertised stuff. Now, with larger numbers of organic gardeners and farmers, there is an ever-increasing number of companies trying to convince us that we can't do organic gardening without their products. I tend to just say no. Mostly. I will buy products once to test them. So far none have been necessary except the legume inoculants.

Legume inoculants contain the spores of certain species of bacteria that can fix atmospheric nitrogen into forms plants can use. The bacteria bind to and invade the roots of appropriate plants, that is, legumes such as peas, beans, or clover. The plant and bacteria collaborate to form nitrogen-fixing nodules on the plant's roots. If you dig up a bean or other legume plant, you can tell whether the bacteria are present. The nodules are little lumps up to about ¼ inch across and are clearly visible. The bacteria share fixed nitrogen with the plant, allowing legumes to grow with little or no nitrogen needed from fertilizer or other sources. The plant, in turn, provides other nutrients to the bacteria.

We can buy commercial inoculants containing the appropriate bacteria for various legume crops. We then wet the seeds and roll them in the inoculant just before planting. Generally, the bacteria don't thrive when there is a lot of nitrogen available in the soil. So if you have used nitrogen-rich commercial fertilizers or lots of manure or compost, you may not see any root nodules on your legumes, even if you have inoculated.

Sometimes legume inoculants matter and sometimes they don't, depending upon whether the soil has grown legumes of relevant sorts in recent history. The legume inoculants also tend not to matter on long-term organic soils.

Almost all plants (brassicas being an exception) also form symbiotic relationships with various fungi. The plant provides nutrients. The fungus extends the reach of the root-fungus unit much farther into the soil and is especially useful in taking up certain minerals. Fungi that form such cooperative relationships with plant roots are called mycorrhizal fungi. There are preparations of spores of mycorrhizal fungi, that is, mycorrhizal inoculants, available for treating seeds. So far the mycorrhizal inoculants haven't mattered in any of my gardens. The wild plants that were growing on our leased field before we tilled it had roots full of mycorrhizal nodules.

The compost starters I've tried don't contribute anything useful.

The fancy aerated compost tea, when actually tested by using it on every other row, turns out not to do anything, either.

Always do an experiment—*a real experiment with controls*—before deciding you need to buy special, fancy, expensive products in order to garden or farm organically. Whenever I inoculate legume seed with a legume inoculant, for example, I always start by planting a few sections of uninoculated seed.

Growing Our Own Fertility with Legumes

On larger gardens and farms, using green manure crops and cover crops to grow some of our own fertilizer in situ is usually part of the strategy. For this, legumes with nitrogen-fixing bacteria are especially valuable. Here in the maritime Northwest, we often plant crimson clover or fava beans or both in the fall to tie up and protect soluble nutrients from being washed away in winter rains as well as to fix additional atmospheric nitrogen into the plants, which is then released to the soil when the plants are tilled under. Exactly what crops work best to build fertility in different seasons depends upon your region. Regional seed companies usually carry cover-crop seed and provide information about how to choose and use it.

People sometimes think the legumes can be interplanted with growing nonlegume crops and will provide nitrogen to them. They do not generally provide enough nitrogen to be of practical significance. Interplanted beans, for example, compete with the corn for water and the other nutrients (besides nitrogen). And they release no meaningful amount of nitrogen to the corn. The nitrogen isn't released until the beans are killed and turned under. So the nitrogen the beans fix is available to the crop that comes after the beans, not a crop that grows along with them. Corn is a heavy nitrogen feeder, however, and nitrogen is often the limiting factor in a corn field. Legumes growing with the corn where nitrogen is the limiting factor will compete less with the corn than will other corn or nonlegumes. So growing legumes with corn is an especially advantageous combination. I love to grow my pole beans on late-season corn. In addition, Nate and I plan to experiment with interplanting legume cover crops with our corn.

It is frequently useful to think in terms of limiting factors, by the way. For example, if water is the limiting factor in our corn field, and we interplant legumes with our corn, there will be less water for the corn, and the yield of corn will suffer. The legumes will directly compete with the corn for water. The fact that legumes compete less with corn for nitrogen than do nonlegumes isn't relevant unless nitrogen is the limiting factor.

Growing Our Own Fertility with Azolla

Azolla is a small nitrogen-fixing water fern. That is, like legumes, Azolla has a special arrangement with certain bacteria it harbors in its leaves that fix the nitrogen. The immense productivity of traditional Asian rice paddies was partly based upon the fact that they were bi-cultures of rice and Azolla. The Azolla occupied the top of the water, fixing nitrogen and not competing at all with the rice roots in the soil below. When the paddy dried up and the rice was harvested, the rice stubble and the Azolla were turned under to provide fertility for the next crop of fall-planted small grains or vegetables.

I got interested in Azolla back when I was living in the middle of Corvallis with just a few garden beds, a lawn controlled by a landlord (which is why it hadn't all been turned into vegetables), and a handful of ducks. The ducks had to stay in the garage most of the time and only got to come out and roam around the yard when I was gardening. There wasn't much to forage on the lawn. So I started growing Azolla in the little kiddy pools I used for duck bathing pools. I was thinking of it as duck forage.

Azolla of one species or another is available in

nearly all of North America. Just look it up and learn to recognize it, then go out and find some and bring it home. The species I have is *Azolla mexicana*. It makes plants about a half an inch high with dangling roots about 2 inches long. But any species of Azolla will do.

Azolla grows fast and makes a solid mat about an inch thick across the surface of the water. I moved about a quarter of the Azolla to a new kiddy pool, let it grow a week or two, and had another solid mat. The remaining three-quarters, of course, I left right there and let the ducks at it. They love Azolla and promptly gobbled every bit from the surface of the pond. I kept three kiddy pools busy growing Azolla.

One day, as I peered at and patted the thick mat of Azolla in preparation for harvesting, it occurred to me that it might make a great mulch. So I just picked up sections of the mat and arranged them around vegetables. It worked great. The vegetables with the Azolla mulch also became noticeably greener. They were clearly getting some nitrogen as the Azolla died. Furthermore, weeds just couldn't come up through the thick mat.

For a few small garden beds, I think I could easily grow all the fertility needed to replace what the harvested vegetables remove by using Azolla as a mulch or worked into the soil, or as a component of compost.

To grow Azolla, toss a shovelful of earth into the kiddy pool or other container. Azolla doesn't grow well in pure water. Azolla does fine in either full sun or partial shade, but it grows much faster in full sun. Azolla doesn't like excessive amounts of nitrogen. I let Azolla grow in the duck bathing ponds before the ducks bath in them. After the ducks have been in a pond a while, and have added soluble, nitrogen-rich fertilizer of their own, duckweed (if it's present in the pond) will outcompete the Azolla. (In cleaner water, Azolla by far outgrows duckweed.) Azolla grows happily in summer. As the temperatures get cold in fall, the plants turn purple, then die.

For a number of years, after I had a bigger yard and more ducks, I skipped Azolla. Now I've started experimenting with it again. I don't have good duck forage in August, and I am thinking a half dozen kiddy pools growing Azolla might help. This last winter, I overwintered a bucket of Azolla indoors in front of a window to get a faster start on the Azolla season. The Azolla grew only slowly with the poor light, but it did survive. I'll use that Azolla to get a fast start on the Azolla season as soon as it's warm enough outside.

Manure

Manure is the traditional organic fertilizer supreme. Its big disadvantage is it can spread diseases. However, we usually spread manure on gardens before spring tilling quite cheerfully, figuring that most noxious organisms will die before we harvest the crops. Up until recently, manure was often the only fertilizer on farms in Europe and pioneer America. A typical regime in New England, for example, would have called for heavily manuring the land, then growing corn, the crop whose yield is most dependent on relatively high levels of fertility. Then, the second year, you would plant squash or other things, which grow well on the moderate fertility left after the corn. The year after that, you plant potatoes, or perhaps beans. The beans can fix their own nitrogen. The potatoes don't need much fertility and in fact can get scab in recently manured soil. So you would

manure any given piece of land about once every four years. If you have access to manure, it can represent the main source of your garden fertility.

When I was gardening in beds in the backyard, I developed a duck-manure-based pattern of fertility. I had been importing compost of highly variable quality, sometimes still hot (that is, unfinished), sometimes exposed to rain and leached of every soluble bit of nutrition. Instead, I began importing straw to use as bedding for the ducks' night pen and commercial poultry chow. The ducks cycled those materials into eggs and manurey bedding which I call "straw-poo." For years, "straw-poo" was my only garden fertilizer.

A second disadvantage of fresh manure is that it is "hot," that is, it can burn plants. So we either dig or till it into the soil before planting so that the manure is dispersed over a wide area. Alternately, we use it carefully. I got quite expert at using straw-poo. I added it to beds when I created or renovated them. I also used it for a quick plant pick-me-up as needed, especially in spring. When the corn patch looked a little yellow, for example, I distributed clumps of the most potent straw-poo—the clumps of straw with lots of fresh manure—between the rows, far enough from the plants so that the plants would not be burned. Then I would water the clumps immediately so that their soluble nitrogen would wash into the soil instead of dissipating into the air. If I wanted the bed mulched and some extra fertility too, I used the hot straw-poo between the rows, the medium-hot straw-poo closer to the plants, and pure straw directly adjacent to the plants. If I wanted to add mulch to a bed without any extra nitrogen or fertility, I used just straight straw.

Back in that era, we ate all our vegetables ourselves, so I didn't worry about diseases. I figured that if the ducks ever got a disease that was transferable to people, we would probably catch it a lot faster and more directly than via contamination on vegetables.

Horse manure is hotter than manure from ruminants, who digest a much larger part of the plant material in their feed. Pure poultry manure is especially hot. Most manure, however, is usually a mix of bedding and manure, so it is substantially diluted. Of even greater concern to me back when I was buying compost is the fact that the manure and compost were often left out in the rain, so all the soluble nitrogen would be leached out. If you have access to manure, get it as fresh from the back end of the animal as possible, haul it home, and cover the pile to protect it from rain.

When you spread manure on land, dig it in right away. Much of the immediately available nitrogen can dissipate into the air as ammonia.

In days of yore, people used manure spreaders and spread the manure directly on the land before tilling or digging. These days, those operating on a smaller scale often instead turn the manure into compost to get around any potential problems with disease.

In traditional agriculture in Japan, China, and Korea, *humanure* was never wasted. In Japan, for example, every bit of human waste went into "honey pots" and was used on the gardens and farms. This pattern has to be viewed along with the cultural patterns in which all vegetables were cooked, and all water was drunk boiled into dilute tea. I was a school-kid in Japan in 1958. One day the science teacher brought in and dissected pig organs he had obtained from a local butcher shop. The display of fluke worms, tapeworms, and other parasites was memorable.

However, with humans being such a large part of the biomass of the planet, it isn't going to be workable to wash valuable sources of nutrients like human excretory products into the waterways for much longer. But to use humanure, you need a thorough composting process for it. See Joseph Jenkins's *The Humanure Handbook* for information on making and using humanure.

I find the fact that I waste my own waste inefficient and philosophically displeasing. I hope to have a composting toilet some day. And pastures and a home orchard to put the humanure compost on. But as for putting humanure, even properly composted, upon vegetable land any time soon—that isn't in the cards. We sell some of our vegetables. Using humanure compost on them wouldn't be legal. And even if it was, who would buy humanure-compost-fertilized vegetables? If you are eating all your own crops, you have more options.

The Power of Pee

Using human urine is a much simpler proposition than using humanure, which also contains feces. Urine from healthy people generally doesn't contain pathogenic bacteria or parasites and is in fact sterile at the time it's excreted. With our current vegetable garden, pee is off limits because we sell some of the vegetables. I feel pretty confident about the safety of pee, but using it on other people's vegetables isn't something I would want to have to explain to anyone. But during prior eras of my gardening life I used pee regularly, though intermittently. I was never so short of fertility as to need to collect all the pee. Instead, I just used it in situations where it was particularly advantageous.

All-American food security—corn, beans, and squash. 'Parching Lavender Mandan' corn, 'Mandan Red Flour' corn, and 'Futtsu' squash against a background of 'Gaucho' beans.

Seedsman Tom Stearns harvests 'Lacinato' kale. 'Lacinato' takes about 10 minutes to cook in boiling water, is resistant to over-cooking, has a rich hearty distinctive flavor, and makes incredible boiled greens, soups, and stews. CREDIT: HIGH MOWING ORGANIC SEEDS

This 'Russian Hunger Gap' kale overwintered far better than all other kales in our relatively harsh winter of 2010. 'Russian Hunger Gap' produces lots of incredibly sweet delicious greens, and continues producing long after other kales have bolted in spring. It is my favorite kale to eat raw in salads in spring. 'Russian Hunger Gap' takes about 3 minutes to cook in boiling water and overcooks readily. So I love it raw, steamed, stir-fried, or barely boiled, but not in soups or stews.

'Amish Paste' tomato is bigger and earlier than most paste tomatoes and, unlike most paste tomatoes, is delicious both fresh and processed. And like just a few tomato varieties, 'Amish Paste' develops its full, rich flavor even when grown in partial shade or cooler weather. CREDIT: HIGH MOWING ORGANIC SEEDS

These 1-tube and 3-tube planters allow precision seeding into specific locations without kneeling or bending over.

These long-handled tools are all easy on the back. *From front to back:* peasant hoe, diamond hoe, Coleman hoe, and furrowing plow. Note the special grips on the diamond hoe and furrowing plow that allow the use of the tools with straight rather than flexed wrists.

Here I am wielding the long-handled peasant hoe, my favorite gardening tool. I hoe off to the side and sway from side to side (from the legs) as I work. It is the lift stroke (using arm, not back muscles) that is the power stroke. I merely guide the tool as it drops, with gravity doing the work on the downstroke. Note how I grip the handle, with both palms face down and all fingers as well as the thumb wrapped over the handle. This grip allows me to use the tool with a straight back and straight wrists.

Here's my farm partner Nate France demonstrating the Coleman hoe, his favorite gardening tool. Note the distinctive way of gripping the hoe that allows him to work with a straight back. The light weight and acute angle of blade to handle are essential to the design of the Coleman hoe. You can tell it's early spring in this photo because Nate's feet aren't suntanned.

Certain crops can be broadcast so as to suppress weeds so thoroughly that no weeding is necessary. When it is possible, this method is the most productive way of growing many leafy green vegetables. This 4' × 18' bed was broadcast-seeded in mid-March with 'Red Giant' mustard in the near 2 feet and 'Green Wave' mustard in the rest. In eight weeks, the bed produced a measured 18 pounds of 'Green Wave' mustard for the freezer as well as a few added pounds of 'Red Giant'.

This field was infested with bindweed. So we planted buckwheat in the field at the same time as the squash to shade out the bindweed, then hoed the buckwheat back as the squash took over. Both buckwheat and big viney squash are good smother crops that help suppress weeds with their shade.

Ancona ducks have various colors and patterns that allow you to identify each individual, even at a distance. Here is part of my flock snoozing between bouts of foraging. Ancona ducks are the best layers of the medium-sized duck breeds, laying up to 270 huge cream- or green-colored eggs per year.

Ancona ducks are the best foragers of all dual-purpose ducks and possibly of all laying poultry. Anconas are calm and sensible and have very sophisticated flock behavior and communication skills. Flocks are led by female leaders chosen by the consent of the led. The behavior of Anconas lends itself ideally to egg production under free-range conditions.

'Sweet Meat–Oregon Homestead' is the squash to grow for a serious homestead food supply. I reselected this line of 'Sweet Meat' to recover the intense flavor, big size, thick flesh, excellent storage life, plant vigor, and ability to germinate and grow in cool weather that characterized the Oregon heirloom of thirty years ago—virtues that had been lost from the commercial variety. It took five years and raising more than a ton of squash to do the reselection. But it sure is great to have *real* 'Sweet Meat' back again! CREDIT: KEANE MCGEE/NICHOLS GARDEN NURSERY

'Sunshine F_1' is sweet, full flavored, high quality, and early. In addition, unlike most squash, it is capable of yielding prime fruit even when short on water, fertility, or summer heat. CREDIT: JOHNNY'S SELECTED SEEDS

Mike Hessel maintained his own line of 'Sugar Loaf' squash and continued to select it while the commercial material deteriorated. I had given up on 'Sugar Loaf' until I obtained some of Mike's seed. Mike's line, 'Sugar Loaf–Hessel' was introduced to the seed trade in 2008. CREDIT: KEANE MCGEE/NICHOLS GARDEN NURSERY

Hand-Pollinating Squash.
Tools for hand-pollinating squash: waterproof strapping tape for sealing buds and flowers, stakes to mark taped buds for pollination, and surveyor's tape to label hand-pollinated flowers.

Male and female squash buds ready for hand-pollination. Squash plants have separate male and female flowers on the same plant. The female flower buds have a baby squash at the base; the male flower buds don't. The baby squash reflects the shape and sometimes the color of squash that the plant will produce. *Left to right:* Female and male buds of 'Sugar Loaf' and female and male buds of 'Jersey Golden Acorn'.

Both a male and female bud of this 'Jersey Golden Acorn' plant are ready for taping. This is late afternoon the day before the buds will open. Tape-ready buds have a yellowish color lacking in younger buds and often gape open a bit at the tip. Note the younger bud between the two that are ready.

Gently apply tape to both female and male buds to keep them from opening.

Mark the taped buds with stakes so you can relocate them in the morning.

The next morning, pick the taped male bud and carefully tear off the tape. Then tear the petals off, leaving only the anthers with pollen attached at the end of the stem, a nice brush to use to daub pollen onto the stigma of the female flower. Tear the tape and ends of the petals off the female flower. Then gently roll the anthers full of pollen over the stigma of the female flower.

Close the pollinated female flower with a fresh piece of strapping tape. Then label the pollinated flower with a piece of surveyor's tape placed loosely so that it doesn't strangle or break the flower stem. (These days, I just loop the tape around the stem next to the bud rather than tying it around the bud's stem.)

When you harvest the fruit, tie the tag to the stem. In addition, label the fruit before or as you harvest. Some tags always fall off.

This modern squash-drying rack can be used in the sun outdoors or in front of a fan or near a woodstove indoors.

Small round-tray dehydrators are inexpensive and do a good job at drying seeds.

'Withner White Cornfield Bean' growing in the deep shade of 12-foot-high 'Bloody Butcher' dent corn. Note the size of the bean leaves, many of which are more than a foot across. (That's a ruler laid across one leaf.) 'Withner' has ordinary-sized leaves in full sun.

'Fast Lady Northern Southern Pea' is a very early northern- and maritime-adapted cowpea (a.k.a. 'Southern pea'). 'Fast Lady' started as a single mutant plant in a growout of 'Lady' peas. The 'Lady' peas were too late to be practical for me, but the mutant was a little more determinate and almost a month earlier. So I saved seed from the mutant plant and selected for earliness for a few years.

The search for popbeans—the beginning of an odyssey. Rich Hannan, then curator of the USDA garbanzo bean collection, told me that some garbanzo beans popped. But he didn't know which. He said he would send me a few to try. What soon arrived on my doorstep was one of the four existing copies of the entire 500-accession USDA core collection! Here are two or three seeds of each accession, a delightful display of garbanzo diversity. My work was cut out for me.

After seventeen years of plant exploring and breeding, I'm releasing this 'Hannan Popbean', a new variety I named after Rich Hannan, whose suggestion started it all. Garbanzo popbeans, like common-bean popbeans (*nuñas*), swell just a little and break open when parched, cook completely, and have a rich nutlike flavor. In the corner are microwave-popped beans; the rest are unpopped.

Three sister varieties of early productive flint corns I bred for flavor, cooking characteristics, and ease in seed saving—'Cascade Maple-Gold Polenta', 'Cascade Ruby-Gold', and 'Cascade Creamcap'. The 'Cascade' corns give us the most delicious and fast-cooking polenta as well as three different flavors of traditional (no sugar need apply) cast iron skillet cornbread. These sister lines may be grown in adjacent blocks in a single corn patch. (Just save your planting seed from the middle of each block, and eat the rest.)

'Parching Red Supai' flour corn, complete with clear evidence of genetic unruliness. The white patch on the middle ear is the result of jumping genes.

A handful of parched corn with a few nuts makes a great breakfast or snack. Parching corn kernels expand slightly and split or break open when parched. Left of the line of cashews are raw kernels of 'Magic Red Manna'; to the right are microwave-parched 'Magic Red Manna' kernels (with cashews). Parched parching corn will keep for three months, so it makes a great travel or trail food.

'Magic Manna' is a very early and productive flour corn I developed specifically for culinary characteristics and versatility for seed savers. 'Magic Manna' produces solid ears of four different colors, each with its own flavor and cooking characteristics. 'Magic Manna' gives you four different flavors of cornbread, pancakes, sponge cakes, angel food cakes, parching corn, and savory brown gravy—all from one corn patch.

Once upon a time I did various experiments on nutrient-poor grass. I found that a 1:10 dilution of pee did not burn the grass, and it made it green up within a few days after just one dose from a watering can.

I collect my first pee of the morning in a bucket. Later pee is pallid stuff. Both color and odor suggests that the first-early pee is more concentrated. My guess is that there are more nutrients in the first batch of pee after waking than in all the pee put together for the entire rest of the day. So I collect the first pee and forget the rest.

I use the pee right away. It has a strong ammonia smell, which indicates nitrogen escaping from it that I would rather have in the garden. In addition, within a few hours of sitting around, the pee grows bacteria. I doubt the bacteria would hurt anything, but I do know they are eating up the nitrogen I want for the plants. When I use urine, it is usually because I want a quick shot of soluble nitrogen, not nitrogen tied up in bodies of bacteria. So whenever I've used pee, I have used it promptly.

When I use the diluted pee in the garden, I dilute it in a watering can and water both the plants and the ground. Plants can take up nutrients through their leaves as well as their roots. I didn't use the pee on plant parts I was going to eat, such as lettuce or green onions. It was probably safe to do so, but I didn't think it was appetizing. But the pee sure worked well on the corn and squash.

If I were short of fertilizer and needed to save and use all the family pee, I would encourage people to pee in buckets and defecate elsewhere. It's just so much easier to use pure pee.

If you have plenty of leaves in fall, just pile them up and wet them with diluted pee. The extra nitrogen is all they need to compost beautifully.

Leaves

In chapter 5 I described how to make soft garden beds using just leaves and the labor contributions of night crawlers. Well-decomposed leaves can provide all the organic matter necessary for a garden. Mowed leaves make better mulch. Leaves make good poultry bedding, especially mowed leaves. Leaves can also be the high-carbon component of your compost. All you need to make great compost from your leaves is something else with a lot of nitrogen in it. Animal manure works fine (as does pee).

Fertilizing with Grass Clippings

One morning when I went down to a far section of yard to weed the multiplier onions, I noticed they looked a bit peaked and yellowish. The grass around the onion bed was a foot high or more and threatening to shade out the onions, and also needed to be dealt with. So I quickly cut the grass from immediately around the onion patch with a sickle and spread it between the rows of onions. A week later, when I next looked at the onions, they had colored up nicely. When freshly cut grass or weeds are watered or rained upon, useful amounts of fertility leach out. This soluble nutrition provides a quick but gentle jolt to the growing plants just when they need it the most. Afterwards, the rest of the grass remains on the surface of the garden soil and provides additional longer-term fertility as it decays.

Nitrogen is a particular problem in spring. It's very soluble, so any free nitrogen tends to wash out in our winter rains. Microbial action can release nitrogen from organic matter later in the year, but there is little microbial activity in cold weather. Agribusiness devotees use soluble chemical fertilizers containing nitrogen, so for them the cold-weather/low-nitrogen problem isn't such an issue. But for organic gardeners, low available nitrogen in spring is a major problem. My general tactic when gardening on a modest scale on beds in the backyard was to add something organic that would provide a little soluble nitrogen. Leachings from grass, weeds, or hay, some dilute urine, compost tea, manure tea, or a little manurey duck bedding can all provide a quick jolt of soluble fertility. For small corn plants, I could have used any of these. For a vegetable to be eaten raw in the immediate future, I prefer the leachings from grass, weeds, or hay.

When I gardened in town and had a landlord who regularly mowed the lawn and made a great stack of lawn clippings, I quickly learned to take advantage of those clippings. The clippings in spring and early summer are nitrogen-rich. I could just put a layer about an inch thick on the garden. That amount dries down nicely without forming a matted green goo. And it releases significant amounts of fertility the first time it is watered. Those spring clippings were also so nitrogen-rich that they composted with no additional ingredients. If you have a bigger lawn than a vegetable patch, grass clippings might be able to supply most of your replacement fertility. You are effectively allowing the grass to mine fertility from deep down in the soil on other parts of your property, then transferring that fertility to your garden.

In developing countries, grass and weeds scythed or collected from the property as well as those hauled in from roadsides and public lands are a major source of fertility.

Hay also releases soluble nutrients when it is rained on or watered. However, hay often contains weed seeds. The first cutting of hay, though, may not contain weed seeds. Nor does salt marsh hay. You can also make a tea by soaking hay, thus avoiding the weed seed problem.

Squanto and the Raw Fish, Revisited

As school children, we learned that Squanto taught the Pilgrims to use pieces of fish or small fish to fertilize corn. If so, he didn't learn it from fellow Indians. Native North American agriculture didn't include any deliberate fertilizing. Instead, only good soils were gardened, and they were gardened until they didn't yield well anymore, then abandoned for a several-year fallow. Squanto was no provincial, however. He was a politician and world traveler. He had been to Europe before the Pilgrims made it to New England, and when they arrived, he greeted and spoke to them in English. It's possible Squanto picked up the fish-fertilizing trick in Europe. It's also possible that the entire story is apocryphal.

When I first moved to Oregon I lived in the Alsea area, and I had a steelhead creek in my backyard. After the steelhead runs, the dead spawned-out fish—about 2 feet long, most of them—began washing up all along the creek in my backyard. I was building a garden just then and remembered the story about Squanto and the fish. Maybe I should have chopped the fish up or something, not just planted whole raw fish. Maybe I should have planted them deeper. Maybe I shouldn't have planted so many. . . .

I wish to report that a garden with lots of huge dead fish buried in it doesn't smell very good.

Also, critters dig up the fish and wreck the garden. And the dog digs up the rotting fish and rolls on them, then comes inside and rolls on the carpet. I ended up digging the rest of the fish out myself. However, that garden never really smelled quite right for the rest of that year.

Nate took a more restrained approach and planted just fish heads in his garden one year. Whatever else, at least the fish heads didn't attract creatures and stink. But Nate's garden soil was drier, and he planted the fish heads deeper.

Where crops can be planted in hills, the situation particularly lends itself to adding a lump of fertility in the middle of the hill. Butcher wastes, fish heads and entrails, trapped rodents and other pests, and pieces of roadkill all ought to be workable. Corn and squash both work well when planted in hills with several plants surrounding a fertile spot such as represented by a shovelful of manure . . . or possibly other things.

Why I Don't Compost Anymore

For many gardeners, making compost is a matter of religion. That it is wondrous stuff for gardens is undeniable. As with manure, compost, if you have enough of it, can be the main basis of a garden fertility program, without the potential disease problems of fresh manure. In addition, properly made compost doesn't burn plants. Many gardeners add lime or rock phosphate or whatever is needed to their garden soil just once, then maintain their soil for years thereafter by just adding an inch or two of compost each year.

I went through a stage in which I had compost piles, classical hot compost piles that you turn all the time. It was when I lived in a rented house in town in Corvallis. The landlord mowed the lawn and collected and piled the clippings. In addition, in fall, there were huge piles of leaves from deciduous trees available. So there were plenty of compost ingredients.

After I moved to a somewhat bigger house, made more garden beds, and got ducks, making compost didn't fit into the new situation. I didn't need a compost pile for kitchen wastes any more. I just threw them out on the hillside for the ducks to pick over. What the ducks didn't want attracted insects, sow bugs, and the like, and the ducks ate those too. I didn't need a compost pile for grass clippings, because I left them on the yard. I didn't need a compost pile for leaves, because I left them under the trees. Leaf litter contributes to fertility and creates a richer area for insects and worms. Ducks really enjoy billing through leafy surface litter and dining upon the insects and worms. I didn't need compost piles for garden waste and debris. I tossed the slug-munched or inferior tomatoes and greens over the fence to the ducks. Any soft debris that the ducks didn't like got piled upon a vacant garden bed area, which would turn into a new, already fertile, soft garden bed in a year or two. Any coarse woody debris went into semipermanent debris piles.

I didn't need compost piles for duck straw-manure bedding. I used some of that on the garden just straight to maintain soil fertility. The rest I spread in sheets about 6 inches deep in various shady places unsuitable for vegetables. This, too, made good forage for the ducks. Composting fungi don't heat up shallow layers of compost as they do bigger, aerated piles. But shallow piles are thin enough for the ducks to be able to bill through them. The hot, fast compost pile is a way of recycling plant nutrients by turning them into fungi. My slow, shallow, cold piles recycled plant nutrients into sow bugs, worms, slugs, and myriad other critters, which my ducks recycled into eggs. By using the manure on the garden straight or to make duck forage, I just moved it once and didn't have to turn it at all.

Coarse woody debris from the property goes into the semipermanent debris piles, where it creates niches and breeding spots for ground beetles and various other good guys such as mason bees.

I never really decided to quit making compost. It just kind of happened. All things considered, I'm glad. I have a weak back, and pitchforking the same ingredients several times was never my idea of fun.

The above litany represents the era when I was still growing vegetables in the backyard. These days, I no longer grow vegetables in the backyard. Instead, there are the couple of acres a few minutes' drive away. Once one is up to a garden of an acre or more, making compost by hand tends to be impractical except for a little to use as potting soil. You just can't make enough compost to much affect a garden that size. If you have manure, you use it straight. In short, the practicality of using compost as the mainstay of garden fertility depends upon the size of the garden you are trying to maintain and how good your back is. For the tiniest gardens, people tend not to compost because they can't afford the space. At gardens of an acre or more, composting tends to become impractical unless you also have livestock manure and a tractor with a front-end loader to move materials around and help you turn the pile. It's the gardens of intermediate size where composting is most valuable.

Some people use beds or bins of red worms to eat their kitchen waste instead of the fungi in hot compost piles (or the sow bugs, worms, slugs, and ducks in my cold piles). This is a nice solution for what to do with kitchen wastes where the kitchen waste amounts are modest and there are not huge amounts of other wastes to be composted.

A Debris Pile Addendum

About the semipermanent debris piles—these are burn piles that evolved. Coarse debris such as sticks, branches, tree trimmings, and blackberry vines go into one of two big debris piles. I have one at each end of the property. They started as burn piles. I even burned one once. But it's only legal to burn a burn pile around here in the rainy season, when it won't burn. It's too much of a fire hazard to burn a burn pile in the summer when it will. After the first pile, I still made burn piles, but I never quite got around to burning them. My piles grew to about 6 feet high, 6 feet wide, and 10 feet long. Then they seemed to reach some kind of equilibrium. I keep adding woody material to them each summer, but the piles never get any higher. Meanwhile, I generate all the mason bees needed, probably, to pollinate the entire neighborhood. And ground beetles thrive in the debris piles. Ground beetles eat symphylans, a major garden pest here. I think many predators of garden pests need exactly what I provided accidentally—a permanent debris pile—in order to thrive and breed and help create a well-rounded healthy ecology.

CHAPTER EIGHT

Potatoes

In Praise of Potatoes. Potatoes and Adventures in Resilience. Potatoes, Nutrition, Diets, and Dieting. Potatoes, Glycoalkaloids, and Solanum Sensitivity. A Potato for Every Purpose. Growing Potatoes—Themes and Variations. Water. Harvesting. Potato Yields. Storing Potatoes. Avoiding Potato Diseases. Saving Your Own Potato Seed and Maintaining Potato Varieties. Basic Potato Cooking Methods. Cooking White and Yellow Potatoes. Cooking Blue Potatoes.

In Praise of Potatoes

Many diet pundits these days malign potatoes. The attack is misguided. After water, the most important nutritional factor is calories. A garden that is going to get you through hard times has to produce calories, not just salads. In temperate regions there is no crop capable of yielding more calories per square foot than the potato. Protein is the second-most critical nutritional component. Potatoes have substantial levels of protein. Per unit of land, potatoes can yield amounts of protein greater than any other crop except legumes.

There is no crop that is as easy to grow on a small scale as potatoes, or that yields as many calories or as much protein per hour of work. Potatoes can be grown in areas with too little heat for grain crops. Potatoes can thrive and produce a crop with unseasonable early or late freezes, storms, and many kinds of horrid weather that destroys grains and many other crops.

Small grains require fine seedbeds, which means tractors or rototillers (or the equivalent in draft animals and equipment). Potatoes can be grown on rough ground. With nothing more than a shovel and a heavy hoe, and starting from noth-ing but lawn or weed patch or pasture, you can grow enough potatoes to provide all the calories and most or all of the protein your family needs for a large part of the year.

Growing potatoes requires little or noth-ing as store-bought inputs. Potatoes don't need very fertile soil. Merely tilling in a cover crop or pasture can grow great potatoes.

Potatoes are drought resistant. They can be grown without irrigation in many areas where most summer crops require irrigation.

To harvest and prepare most grains you need special threshing, drying, dehulling, or grinding equipment. Anyone who can build a fire or boil water can prepare potatoes.

Homegrown potatoes of the right varieties are spectacular in flavor compared to anything the supermarket can provide. In addition, commercial potatoes are one of the crops in which there is the greatest use of seriously nasty poisons. So if you care about avoiding pesticide residues in your food, growing your own organic potatoes should be a high priority.

For people in a wide range of temperate climates, potatoes are the easiest of all vegetable crops to store.

Potatoes are satisfying. In the kitchen and the diet they are versatile. With many possible varieties, flavors, and cooking methods, you can eat major amounts of potatoes every day without getting tired of them. And there is nothing like the sense of satisfaction and security you feel when cold weather hits and you stand in your garage gazing happily at a wall of shelves filled with bags of potatoes of several different kinds, all neatly labeled and tucked away for winter.

To the High Heavens I praise the potato, and recommend planting it, eating it, and honoring it.

Potatoes and Adventures in Resilience

Spring 2008. For storable staple crops Nate and I plant a cornbread corn patch, a polenta corn patch, beans, winter squash, drying squash, and lots of potatoes. There is a plague of birds. They pull up and eat all the corn as soon as the seedlings emerge. Farmers throughout the region lose their sweet corn plantings to birds and must replant. Nate replants, but the bird plague continues. He saves the replanted polenta patch by camping out in it with a shotgun. The cornbread and polenta patches are too far away from each other for Nate to protect both. We decide to sacrifice the cornbread and protect the polenta. Others throughout the region lose the second plantings of sweet corn and give up, just planting cover crops. Our potatoes emerge and grow vigorously and happily with no particular attention from us.

Meanwhile, summer doesn't come. It rains and stays cold for more than an extra month, slowing and delaying most warm-season crops throughout the region. Our corn, squash, and beans all lag. Our potatoes, however, are thriving. They

love cold, wet weather. Just looking at the vigorous plants is cheering. They had no fertilization other than our plowing under a grass-clover cover crop. The tilling was so shallow it was difficult to get the seed tubers more than just barely covered initially. Hilling up is late. The plants got no pampering. Yet they thrive.

A rabbit starts mowing down the bean plants. It doesn't bother the potato plants, which have poisonous tops.

After a slow start to summer, we then have a cooler-than-average remainder of the summer. Our corn, beans, squash, and tomatoes are further delayed. The potatoes are apparently delighted with the cooler summer. We rediscover what Irish and other European peasants learned generations ago during the erratic weather of the Little Ice Age. The very weather that delays or damages grains and many other crops is exactly the kind of weather that allows potatoes to thrive and produce especially well. So growing potatoes and a grain crop at the same time provides a balance that contributes resilience to weather extremes.

Our winter squash crop is late. Fortunately, fall freezes come late and we get a good crop. But our squash are still curing indoors in October and most of November. And our polenta corn is still on the cob, still drying out enough to shell. But Nate and I don't mind. We are too busy having fun with our potatoes. We have hundreds of pounds of potatoes tucked away in bags on the shelves in the garage, a few hundred pounds of 'Yukon Gold' as well as good yields of several new varieties. We taste and explore and boil and bake and make hash browns and eat potatoes day after day. We excitedly compare notes about each new variety. Our potatoes satisfy us fully—body, mind, soul, and sense of adventure.

Potatoes, Nutrition, Diets, and Dieting

Potatoes are an excellent source of carbohydrates, protein, and vitamin C. In pre-potato-famine Ireland, many peasants ate pretty close to an all-potato diet for major parts of the year. The average Irishman ate 13 pounds (5.9 kg) of potatoes per day during fall and early winter. Assuming these were largely boiling types, that amount of potatoes provides about 4,500 calories and 120 grams of protein. Women and children averaged about 9 pounds (4.1 kg) of potatoes, for 3,100 calories and 80 grams of protein per day. It is clear that, for physically active people, an all-potato diet can provide all the calories *and* all the protein they need. These amounts of potatoes also provide all the vitamin C a person needs. If you are doing enough physical labor to require a 3,000- to 5,000-calorie-per-day diet, potatoes can meet most of your nutritional needs.

But what about those of us who, in ordinary times, need to watch our weight? Like many others, I need to restrict the calories in my diet these days. Where do potatoes fit in the diets and gardens of people who need to practice calorie restraint?

Potatoes have about the same or lower caloric density as cooked grains such as rice, pasta, polenta, bread, winter squash, or sweet potatoes. A hundred grams of cooked brown rice, for example (slightly less than ¼ pound), has 119 calories. Bread has about 240–290 calories per 100 grams. A single piece of bread, depending upon the size of the slice and recipe, has 80–110 calories. A 1-cup portion of some typical unsugary cereals (Cheerios, Corn Flakes, Total, and Grape Nuts) has 100, 100, 133, and 400 calories, respectively. A hundred grams of baked potatoes, however, has a mere 93 calories. A hundred grams of potato boiled in the skin has even fewer—only 80 calories. The same amount of mashed potatoes (with milk added) is only 65 calories. Mashed potatoes with milk and fat added are still typically only 94 calories per 100 grams.

If we fry potatoes, however, we double the caloric content. In addition, butter has about 100 calories a tablespoon. My approach is to figure that French fries or hash browns need to be an occasional treat, not a staple. In my potato-variety growing and tasting, part of what I look for are varieties that taste great baked, boiled, mashed, or steamed, and when served plain or with just a little butter and salt and pepper.

Protein is the second most important nutritional parameter after calories. Potatoes have impressive levels of protein. A boiling variety with 2.1 grams of protein per 100 grams fresh weight, for example (which is 79.8 percent water), has 2.1 percent protein. That initially seems low compared with grains. However, that is comparing wet potatoes with dry grain. To get an appropriate comparison, we need to correct for the water. On a dry-weight basis, the boiling potato has 10.4 grams of protein per 100 grams dry weight, or 10.4 percent protein. Brown rice has 7.5 grams of protein per 100 grams and only 12 percent water. So brown rice is 9.6 percent protein on a dry-weight basis. Bread wheats have higher amounts of protein than potatoes, but by the time the absorption and biological value of the proteins are taken into account, the protein situations are comparable. Of plant foods, only legumes provide substantially more protein per unit of dry weight than potatoes.

However, if we are on a calorie-restricted diet, how good a protein source something is depends less on the absolute amount of protein and more on the balance between protein and calories. That is, how much protein can we get without also getting too many calories? More specifically, as an example, how much protein would be provided by 2,000 calories of potatoes or other staples?

If we ate nothing but potatoes, and had a 2,000 calorie/day diet, we would need to eat 5.8 pounds (2.63 kg) of boiling potatoes. That amount of potatoes would provide us with 52 grams of protein, an amount sufficient for some people but marginal for others, depending upon their weight, gender, level of physical activity, and other characteristics. The 2,000-calorie diet, however, comes close to meeting the protein needs for everyone. A 2,000-calorie diet of rice provides only 32 grams of protein, which is inadequate. A 2,000-calorie all-wheat (bread or pasta) diet provides 62 grams of protein. This number is not substantially more than the equivalent 52 grams/100 calorie number for potatoes. However, wheat needs to be penalized because its protein is absorbed less well than that of potatoes and rice. And wheat protein, like that of other grains, is short on lysine. Numbers I've found for absorption and quality considerations are variable, but are large enough so that 52 grams of potato protein could be expected to be biologically equivalent to more than 62 grams of wheat protein. In other words, when it comes to getting enough protein, the all-potato diet is actually better than an all-rice diet, an all-pasta diet, or even an all-bread diet.

The 2,000-calorie all-potato diet would also provide 421 milligrams of vitamin C, which is several times greater than the government's recommended daily allowance (RDA) for vitamin C. It would also provide 184 grams of calcium—a useful amount, but probably not all we need. The all-potato diet would be totally deficient in essential fatty acids, however. And it would be deficient in vitamin A (carotene) and some other vitamins and minerals. In addition, potatoes have very little dietary fiber. However, no all-one-food diet is an optimal diet. And examining a theoretical all-potato diet does show us that it's nutritionally reasonable to have potatoes as a large part of our diet if we can grow great potatoes and enjoy eating them.

Potatoes have a high glycemic index. That is, we digest potatoes very quickly, and eating them causes a fast release of sugar into the bloodstream. If you are diabetic or have carbohydrate sensitivity, that doesn't mean you should deny yourself potatoes. It *does* mean you should watch the amounts of potatoes you eat, the times of day you eat them, and what else you eat them with, just as you do with rice, bread, pasta, cereal, or any other high-carbohydrate food that has a high glycemic index. I'm not diabetic, but I do have carbohydrate sensitivity, especially in the morning. If I eat a huge bowl of mashed potatoes or a big baker for breakfast, for example, I simply go to sleep. Then, when I wake up, I feel shaky and sick and famished, and I have a fierce craving for food, especially sweet things. The food craving problems go on all day. What has happened is that the too-large amount of potato has caused a spike in my blood sugar, which causes me to be sleepy as well as to overproduce insulin. The spike in insulin drives blood sugar levels down fast and to below normal and leaves me with too little blood sugar a mere two or three hours after eating. Exactly the same thing happens if I eat too much rice or bread or anything with sugar in it (jam, honey, syrup) in the morning.

If I eat a modest portion of potatoes for breakfast, though, I'm fine. I have plenty of energy and no sugar jags. I can eat large amounts of potatoes without difficulty later in the day. However, some people need to watch their intake of high-glycemic-index foods at all times of day.

The high glycemic index of potatoes refers to what happens when you eat just potatoes. When you put fat on them, that slows down their digestion. Effectively, it reduces the glycemic index of the potatoes. And if the potatoes are part of an entire meal made up of lower-glycemic-index foods, that, too, reduces the effective glycemic index of the potatoes. If you are diabetic or have carbohydrate sensitivity, you need to take the high glycemic index of potatoes into account when you work potatoes into your diet.

Potatoes, Glycoalkaloids, and Solanum Sensitivity

Potatoes that are properly grown and stored are great food—for most of us. But some people can't eat potatoes. And improperly stored potatoes can actually be poisonous. Potatoes contain the glycoalkaloids α-solanine and α-chaconine. At lower levels these glycoalkaloids are present in all potatoes and contribute to their flavor and ability to discourage insects and herbivores as well as to resist viruses, fungi, and other pathogens. In larger amounts, glycoalkaloids make the potatoes bitter. Total glycoalkaloids above 20 milligrams per 100 grams can cause a burning sensation in the mouth and throat and are generally toxic. Toxic glycoalkaloid levels are found in wild potatoes but also in domestic potatoes that have been improperly handled or stored. Some people are especially sensitive to the glycoalkaloids in potatoes and/or other solanums (tomatoes, eggplant, peppers, and tobacco) and can experience difficulties or signs of glycoalkaloid poisoning even when eating potatoes with ordinary glycoalkaloid levels.

Symptoms of potato-glycoalkaloid poisoning include gastrointestinal symptoms such as nausea, vomiting, abdominal pain, and diarrhea as well as systemic symptoms such as headache, drowsiness, fatigue, skin oversensitivity, labored or difficult breathing, and itchy neck. In some people solanums appear to be able to cause or exacerbate joint pain and arthritis. Potato glycoalkaloids are cholinesterase inhibitors, so they interfere with nervous system function. Severe poisoning can include fever, rapid weak pulse, rapid breathing, hallucinations, delirium, coma, and death. However, severe glycoalkaloid poisoning is uncommon because high levels of glycoalkaloids are bitter enough to be unpalatable. Mild glycoalkaloid poisoning and solanum sensitivity on the other hand, are probably more common than is usually realized.

When potatoes are exposed to light during storage, the skins become green and synthesis of glycoalkaloids increases. Greening of the potato skin is independent of glycoalkaloid synthesis. So green potatoes are poisonous, though the glycoalkaloids are not green. The green is just ordinary chlorophyll. You can't remove the glycoalkaloids by peeling the skin of the potatoes. Nor should you chop off the green part of a potato thinking you can eat the rest. The green chlorophyll in the skin is an *indicator* of the toxins, not the toxins themselves. So don't eat potatoes that show green anywhere on the skin. Don't feed them to livestock, either. Livestock are also vulnerable to glycoalkaloid poisoning.

Glycoalkaloids are not destroyed by cooking. They taste bitter. So don't eat potatoes that are obviously bitter. Also, don't eat potato sprouts, which are also poisonous, as are potato leaves and stems.

Glycoalkaloid synthesis is also caused by harvesting potatoes immature, damaging them in harvest, improper temperature control in storage, wet conditions before harvest, or chilling or freezing. When in doubt as to whether potatoes might be toxic, taste the raw skin. If it tastes bitter or causes a burning sensation, don't eat the potatoes.

Raw potatoes are inedible for humans, pigs, poultry, and other monogastric animals. People sometimes talk about eating raw potatoes out of hand. Raw potatoes aren't poisonous to us. However, they aren't food, either. Raw potatoes have huge amounts of digestive-enzyme inhibitors that are destroyed by cooking. Raw potatoes can only be digested by ruminants. The digestive-enzyme inhibitors are consumed and destroyed by the bacteria of the rumen in ruminants. For people, pigs, or poultry, potatoes should be cooked. (For references on feeding potatoes to livestock, see note 8-4.)

Glycoalkaloid synthesis is fast enough under ordinary conditions of displaying potatoes for sale in farmer's markets or grocery store shelves as to be a major marketing problem. Conventional wisdom is to manage potato sales in such a way that no potato is exposed to more than a day of light. Potatoes that have been displayed at a farmer's market for a day need to be eaten or fed to livestock, not stored or taken to the next market. (See note 8-3.)

In summary, potatoes handled and stored properly are great food for most people—but not for everyone. And potatoes handled or stored improperly can be poisonous enough to be not very good for any of us.

A Potato for Every Purpose

Specific gravity of a potato is a measurement of the density of a potato variety compared with water, which is 1.000 by definition. The specific gravities of the commonly grown potato varieties run from about 1.055 to about 1.095. These specific gravities correspond to dry matter contents of about 16.5 percent to about 24 percent. The rest of the potato is water. So commercial potatoes run about 76–83.5 percent water. The high-specific-gravity potatoes have about 50 percent more food value (and calories). Stating the converse, the low-specific-gravity potato has 33 percent less food value (and calories). You could choose to grow just high-specific-gravity potatoes to get the most food per unit of work lifting potatoes and more efficient food storage. But you would end up with varieties that are best for baking and frying and none optimal for boiling. Low-specific-gravity potatoes of the right varieties can be boiled or steamed without falling apart. The usual red potatoes found in cooled bins in supermarkets are low-specific-gravity potatoes. Russet and other baking potatoes are higher-specific-gravity varieties. When baked, they have a so-called mealy texture. New potatoes are usually substantially lower in specific gravity than fully mature potatoes, even of the same variety.

If you love new potatoes, you will want some early potato varieties so as to have new potatoes as soon as possible. New potatoes can produce your calories during much of the summer. But you may need a later potato for the main storage crop—potatoes that mature when it is cool enough for you to store them. Early-maturing potatoes may sometimes allow you to avoid potato disease epidemics by maturing before most epidemics appear. Some early potatoes may be held in the ground for months until storage conditions are appropriate and the potatoes keep well. ('Yukon Gold' is one.) Mid-season and late-maturing varieties have a longer effective growing season, thus can produce the best yields.

Varieties can have skin colors of white, tan, yellow, blue, pink, red, and purple. Flesh colors can be white, yellow, blue, pink, red, or purple, and don't necessarily correlate with skin color. Many gourmet potatoes with excellent flavor have yellow flesh. But yellow flesh doesn't guarantee great flavor. Some white-fleshed potatoes are also very flavorful. Blue-fleshed potatoes can be spectacularly delicious if used and dressed in ways that complement their quite different flavor. Fingerlings are no more flavorful than the more flavorful full-sized potato varieties. They are much more work to harvest and to prepare in the kitchen, but are popular in the gourmet potato market.

For the resilient gardener, a major requirement in a potato variety is often storing ability. Some varieties don't store well, and some varieties have a short tuber dormancy period—that is, they sprout soon after going into storage.

My friend Merry Youle, who lives in Hawaii, prefers potatoes with a short tuber dormancy. That's because, in her climate, she can plant and grow potatoes at any time of year but can't store them well. So she needs a potato that sprouts promptly for planting the next crop.

To choose potato varieties to grow, first consider what potatoes grow well in your region. Look in your local or regional seed catalogs. Especially consider flavor. Many commercial varieties don't taste any better when homegrown than those in the grocery store. Many varieties do well only in certain places and are too prone to scab or other disease or insect problems in other areas. Look in local farmer's markets and taste the gourmet varieties that are being grown and sold locally to find varieties you might like to grow. Ask other local gardeners. It's useful to get all the catalogs of seed companies with good listings of potatoes. These catalogs are often the best source of information about varieties, and what one doesn't tell, some other often fills in.

Each year, Nate and I try some new potato varieties and discard those that don't measure up. We taste every variety we grow baked, as hash browns, mashed, boiled, and boil-steamed. Potato quality and flavor are intimately associated with cooking methods. There is no such thing as an all-purpose potato if you want true gourmet flavor and quality. Here are our current favorites. All these varieties yield well when grown organically, without irrigation, and under conditions of modest fertility. They all have spectacular flavor when cooked appropriately. All keep well. All make good-sized, clean potatoes. And all are sufficiently resistant to diseases under field conditions so that we are easily able to save our own seed potatoes for replanting.

For baking: 'Amey Russet' (white), 'Green Mountain' (white), 'German Butterball' (yellow), 'Azul Toro' (blue), and 'Negro y Azul' (blue) are spectacular. We would not want to be without any of these potatoes for baking. Each has a distinctive delicious flavor and aroma. And each has the classic lovely, mealy baked-potato texture.

For hash browns: Nate has evaluated all our spuds as hash browns. 'Yukon Gold' and 'Azul Toro' are the ones he likes best.

For mashing: 'Yukon Gold', 'German Butterball', 'Satina', 'Skagit Beet Red', 'October Blue', and 'Azul Toro' all make delicious mashed potatoes, each with a distinctively different flavor, except for the two blues, which taste similar mashed. 'Skagit Beet Red', intensely red inside and out, makes mashed potatoes that are intensely red. 'October Blue' and 'Azul Toro' mashed potatoes are intensely blue.

For whole (intact) boiled potatoes: 'Yukon Gold', 'Satina', 'October Blue', or 'Skagit Beet Red'.

For potato salad: 'Yellow Finn' was our favorite for potato salad up until I learned to boil-steam potatoes. We've subsequently retired the 'Yellow Finn' and instead use boil-steamed 'Yukon Gold' for potato salad. (I don't like waxy potatoes for anything except potato salad. And 'Yellow Finn' is so late, it isn't available until after potato-salad season is over.)

'All Blue' is OK baked or as mashed potatoes, but is pallid in both flavor and color compared with our three preferred blues. We have retired it. 'Island Sunshine' doesn't have much flavor baked, boiled, or mashed compared with our favorites. It is supposedly resistant to late blight, however. 'Negro y Azul' is the most powerfully flavored blue spud we have tasted. It is also the deepest blue. It is a full-size spud but has a fingerling shape, so it's like a giant fingerling. We love 'Negro y Azul' baked. But boiled, mashed, or fried, its flavor is so potent it is overwhelming.

'Yukon Gold' is very early. 'October Blue' is late and 'Negro y Azul' is very late. The rest are somewhere in between in terms of maturity. 'October Blue' is *by far* our best-yielding potato variety.

'Azul Toro', 'October Blue', 'Skagit Beet Red', and 'Negro y Azul' are potatoes bred by Tom Wagner, an independent potato and tomato breeder. He also grows and maintains 'Amey Russet'. (For contact information for Tom Wagner, see appendix B.) The other potato varieties are available from many sources.

Growing Potatoes—Themes and Variations

Potatoes are basically a cool-weather crop. They thrive best in places where the summer temperatures aren't too hot and the nights are cool. However, potatoes are flexible and yield well grown in all kinds of regions far beyond the ideal.

Soil

Potato land should be well drained. Soft loam is ideal. But just about any soil will do as long as it's soft enough for potatoes to form and expand properly. Even gardeners with heavy clay soils can still grow fine potatoes, however, by using one of the mulching approaches. Potatoes are often planted on new rough ground where sod or weeds have just been tilled under. It isn't ideal for potatoes, but you can get a good crop of spuds on such ground where you might not be able to get a good crop of anything else because of the lower fertility and weed-control problems.

Potatoes prefer a lower soil pH than legumes or most garden crops. The latter usually thrive best at a pH of 7–8. Potatoes prefer 6–6.8. When starting a new potato patch, most people either don't lime it, or lime it less than they would for a general garden plot. Plenty of potatoes are grown in ordinary garden soil, however. Scab is more of a problem at higher pH. Scab-resistant varieties may be essential when growing potatoes in ordinary garden soil.

Potato ground should be rotated. Never grow potatoes on ground that has had potatoes or close relatives on it in the last four years. "Close relatives" means other solanums, that is, members of the family Solanaceae, the nightshade family. The common garden solanums are potatoes, tomatoes, eggplants, peppers, and tobacco.

Potatoes don't need or want soil that is as nitrogen-rich as is needed for many garden crops. Too much nitrogen can give viney plants with fewer spuds, and the spuds may be more watery, less flavorful, and less storable.

Don't put fresh manure on potato ground. It leads to scab. Aged compost or thoroughly composted manure are great soil amendments to provide fertility for potatoes.

Nate and I fertilize our potatoes only by tilling in a cover crop. This is a traditional way to provide fertility for potatoes. We simply sow crimson clover in the fall. Enough grass comes up unsolicited so that we end up with a grass-clover cover crop. We mow or scythe the stand in spring, then till it in. (Unmowed, the cover crop doesn't incorporate into the soil very well. The mowing is essential.)

Many traditional farmers put potatoes on ground that has just grown corn or other fertility-demanding crop. The corn crop received manure, compost, or fertility imports. The following potato crop does fine on whatever fertility is left over from the corn. In our rotations, potatoes usually follow corn or squash.

Some sources say that you shouldn't put potatoes on ground that's just been in grass because the tubers can get riddled with wireworm tunnels. Wireworms are the larval stages of various species of click beetles. Some grassland or sod is infested with varieties that can affect potato tubers and some isn't. Plenty of people do go directly from sod to potatoes without wireworm problems, though. (We do. And we haven't had any wireworms.) In fact, potatoes are a traditional "sod-busting" crop, that is, the crop to plant the first year when you are transitioning land from pasture (or lawn or weeds) into cultivation.

When to Plant

Most potato varieties have some resistance to mild freezes. However, the seed tuber pieces and the growing potato stems can be killed by hard freezes. So seed tubers are usually planted deep enough to be below the level of light freezes and late enough so that hard freezes are over by the time the stems have emerged. When freezes kill stems, new stems can grow from beneath the freeze line; but this sets the plants back and is best avoided.

People usually make their first plantings of potatoes somewhat before the last expected freeze. Anywhere from about three weeks before until two months after the last expected freeze is potato-planting time in the northern tier of the United States.

In the South, you may need to get potatoes in as early as possible to avoid summer heat. Or you may fall-plant your potatoes. In some regions, both spring- and fall-planted crops are possible; in others, potatoes can be planted and grown essentially year-round. Your regional seed company catalogs and gardening books will give you the most common times for planting potatoes in your area.

Buying and Preparing Potato Seed Tubers

The "potato seed" we start our potato patches with is not actually seed, but tubers or pieces of tubers. These are either small potatoes or pieces of larger potatoes of the desired varieties.

Don't plant supermarket spuds. They are treated with sprout inhibitors and won't grow. I don't get seed potatoes from local farmers or from the farmer's market, even though these would grow. Instead, I buy certified seed, usually from one of the mail-order seed companies. This certification has nothing to do with organic certification. It does involve third-party certification, but the issue is whether the seed meets standards with respect to being free of disease. Many gardening books tell you to buy fresh certified seed tubers each year. That approach isn't suitable for those of us who care about resilience. In this chapter I assume you will be keeping your own seed potatoes once you have started growing any particular variety, and I include a detailed section on the subject.

For seed potatoes, ideally you want a piece of potato or a small potato that is about 1 to 4 ounces (that is, about the size of an egg) and that has two or three good sprouts or "eyes." (When we are stretching our seed supply we cut to one sprout per seed piece except where sprouts are too close together to cut apart without the critical part of the potato drying out. This tactic results in occasional gaps in the row but gives us bigger potatoes as well as lots more potatoes per pound of seed.) Sprouted potatoes are fine. Long sprouts, however, mean the tuber will be more difficult to plant without breaking the sprout. Potatoes with short, thick sprouts are ideal. Larger potatoes should be cut into smaller pieces for seed. If left whole, the big potato forms a huge wad of rotting slime right down there among your spuds. In addition, more than three sprouts can lead to too many stems and lots of small, crowded, poorly

growing spuds. Poorly grown spuds don't taste as good or store as well.

We cut big potatoes into pieces and plant them right away. Some people treat the cut pieces of seed potato with sulfur and some don't. We don't. Some people let the cut potato pieces sit indoors in a monolayer for a day or two so that the cuts scab over and some don't. We don't. Whether you actually need to let cut seed heal or treat it with sulfur is said to depend upon your region, soil type, soil pathogens present, and weather conditions. Freshly cut tubers can supposedly rot instead of growing, especially in wet soil. Until we run into problems, however, we do as little work and use as few interventions as possible. On a field scale, it's *much* easier to just cut tubers and plant them right away.

Fingerling potatoes have lots of eyes. Cut fingerling seed potatoes so that you have two to three eyes per piece, even though this will give you a smaller-size seed than you ideally want. It's tempting to use fingerlings whole or just cut them in half for seed. The result is a forest of stems and large numbers of very tiny, crowded, poorly grown, mostly unusable potatoes.

Use a sharp knife to cut the potatoes. Wash your hands and knife frequently when cutting seed potatoes, especially in between different batches, to prevent spreading diseases from a bad tuber to good ones. I do the cutting on layers of newspaper and change the newspapers between varieties or lots.

Don't plant any tubers that show any signs of rot, scab, scurf, or other diseases. Sort homegrown seed before planting and eliminate all those showing signs of disease or viruses.

How many pounds of seed potatoes do you need? Given good growing conditions, you can usually expect to get about ten times as many pounds of potatoes as the weight of seed tubers you plant. For fingerlings, the yield is about fifteen to twenty times the planting weight.

Planting, Weeding, and Hilling Up

Ideally, we want our seed tubers to end up about 8 to 12 inches deep in the ground. This is important, because most of the root system and the potatoes develop above the seed tuber. The tubers form at the ends of *stolons*—lateral underground runners that are initiated at each underground node of the potato stem. Much of the root system develops from adventitious roots, which are also initiated from the below ground nodes on the stem. So if the seed tuber is near the surface of the ground, there is little room for roots or potatoes. In addition, tubers near the surface will push out of the ground as they expand, become exposed to light, develop glycoalkaloids, and become inedible. So if we just planted our seed tubers 2 inches deep, we would get a low harvest of small potatoes, nearly all inedible. We want the seed tuber about 8 to 12 inches deep, with soft soil over it.

Some people do the obvious thing and just plant the seed tubers 8 to 12 inches deep right from the beginning. Most of us don't find that workable, however. Our tilling may not be deep enough. Also, in early spring in many regions, the ground is too cold that deep, and the seed would rot, or the plants would get a slow start. In some cases the soil is too heavy for sprouts to be able to bust through 8 to 12 inches of it. So most people plant the tubers shallow initially, then hill up additional soil over the row after the shoots emerge.

To "hill up" we hoe soil between the rows onto the potato rows. (Or we use a potato hilling attachment mounted on a tractor or rototiller or behind draft animals. Or we plow alongside the row in such a way as to throw more soil over the row. Or we use a rotary plow on a rototiller to till between rows and toss the soil up on the rows.) The hilling up is done various numbers of times and to various depths. The object is to end up with a row of potatoes that has a mound of soil over it that is 8 to 12 inches high over the seed tuber pieces, tapering to about 18 inches wide at the base. The hilling up creates a nice soft area for the roots and edible tubers of the potato plants and is also the major method of weed control. The major alternative to the theme of hilling up involves using mulch. Here are some examples of patterns that work.

Variation 1. Nate and I usually start by planting our seed tubers 2 inches deep. Our rows are 3½ feet apart. We need that much space to provide the soil for hilling up onto the rows. We make the trench with our furrowing plow. We cover the potatoes as well as hill up a couple of inches over the row using a rake or hoe. When the plants are about 6 inches high, we hill up again, carefully leaving the top 2 inches of each plant exposed. A few weeks later, when plants are 6 inches high again, we hill up a second time. We may hill up a third time. Or not. We finish all the hilling up before the plants start flowering. Most varieties initiate tubers before they start flowering.

Variation 2—the trench method. In this variant, you dig a trench, place the tubers in the bottom, cover them with a few inches of the removed soil, then backfill with the rest of the soil as the plants grow. You can mix compost or some mulch-type materials into the soil as you backfill if your soil needs extra softness, organic matter, fertility, or volume. This method is particularly useful if what you have is a lawn or pasture and just a shovel and hoe.

Variation 3—growing in mulch. Some people plant the tubers 2 inches deep, then, after plants are 6 inches high or so, they add mulch. More mulch is added once or twice more as the plants grow. That is, the potatoes are hilled up with mulch instead of with soil. You want to end up with at least 8 inches of mulch over the potato seed after the mulch has settled. Some people even place the tubers right on top of the soil surface and add mulch over them.

Generally, plants hilled with mulch are less productive than those hilled with soil, and the potatoes are smaller. (See note 8-7.) I think this is because a potato plant hilled up with mulch has most of its root system in a medium of low fertility. However, there are usually enough potatoes to make a successful potato patch anyway. In heavy clay soils or on rocky ground, especially with small plantings, mulching instead of hilling up is often the preferred method. Mulch also gives you cleaner potatoes that are easier to harvest.

Variation 4. John Jeavons describes how to grow potatoes intensively in double-dug beds in detail in *How to Grow More Vegetables.* You can also plant in ordinary single-dug raised beds. Just space the potatoes more generously than in the turbocharged Jeavons-style beds.

Water

The general advice given about watering potatoes is to apply water uniformly and regularly, and not more than the plants need. Potato plants need water most during the period when tubers are initiating, which is generally before flowering

starts. We are advised to keep the ground moist but not wet up until the time of flowering. After flowering starts, the plants don't need as much water.

It can be easy to overwater potatoes if you plant them in among other garden crops. Potato plants are better at scrounging water than most other garden plants. Overwatered tubers can be watery and less flavorful and keep less well. They may also be more vulnerable to fungal diseases.

Irregularly watered tubers may have hollow hearts or irregular shapes or even branches (from getting too much water late in the season, which promotes regrowth and expansion of the tubers). Dry tubers suddenly exposed to too much water can develop cracks. Hilling or mulching helps provide constant moderate moisture conditions for the tubers.

Many people who irrigate their potatoes stop watering at some point toward the end of the season. This encourages the plants to finish transferring all their nutrients to the tuber and to die down, and helps the tubers to harden their skins and cure in the soil. And drier soil is easier to lift tubers from and gives cleaner spuds. Also, the drier tubers can go directly into storage. Wetter tubers may need to be dried out first.

Nate and I grow potatoes without irrigation. Commercial potatoes in Willamette Valley are always irrigated. The flavor of the dryland-grown potatoes is much more intense, and the potatoes are considerably denser. We grow our potatoes in deep soil with enough clay content to retain water well. We give our potato plants 16 inches of space in the row instead of the more normal 12 inches, just out of the general principle that unirrigated plantings (that aren't mulched) should be given more space than equivalent irrigated ones. We don't yet know whether the extra space is necessary or optimal. (We plan to experiment with spacing.)

Harvesting

The first consideration in harvesting potatoes is to minimize their exposure to light. Other considerations are gentleness, timing, temperature, and humidity.

When to harvest. Potatoes are fully developed and ready to harvest two weeks after the vines are killed or die back naturally. Many varieties die back naturally. With long-season potatoes, people sometimes wait until the vines are killed by frost. Alternatively, after the potatoes are fully developed, you can just mow or cut the vines two weeks before you want to harvest. Storage potatoes should be allowed to sit in the ground for at least two weeks after the vines are dead before being harvested. During this period of in-ground curing, the potato skins toughen, which makes the tubers much easier to harvest, handle, and store without damage. Potato plants continue adding nutrients to the tubers throughout the growing period. Even during the period of vine die-down, the potato plants are transferring nutrients to the spuds. We let all our potato varieties die down naturally. I suspect that the best nutritional value, the most food, and the best flavor come from varieties that finish and die down naturally.

Ideally, lift your spuds on a cool, dry overcast day. If the potatoes are coming out of damp ground, let them sit on the ground a couple of hours to dry out before going into storage.

Lifting the spuds. If the soil is light enough and you have just a couple hundred row feet or less, you will probably lift your potatoes by digging beneath each plant by hand. With heavier soils or larger plantings of potatoes, you'll probably dig the potatoes with a garden fork. You put your fork into the ground near each potato plant and use it to pry up most of the soil under the plant. Then you collect the potatoes with a little hand work. Using a fork means cutting an occasional potato. Injured spuds should be set aside to eat immediately or be fed to livestock. The cuts do heal, but the spuds don't store as well as uninjured tubers. Injured spuds produce more heat in storage, and the injuries can give access to mold.

For larger-scale potato harvesting, there are tuber-lifting attachments designed for use with rototillers or tractors. Absent the specialized equipment, the classic approach with a tractor or draft animals is to run a plow down the side of the row close enough to the tubers to lift most of them but far enough away to avoid injuring too many. Then you finish the collecting and digging by hand.

Place the potatoes where you want them. Don't just throw them around. Potatoes bruise easily, especially the high-specific-gravity types. And bruised potatoes don't store well. Limit the number of potatoes in piles or boxes to keep the potatoes no more than about two feet deep.

We cull any potatoes with green parts as we harvest. It's easiest to eliminate such potatoes in bright daylight. In addition, when digging by hand, it is obvious which potatoes are too near the surface, and those can be inspected carefully for any green parts. Misshaped or damaged potatoes or those with scab or other skin flaws go into separate lots to be eaten soon (or fed to livestock). Green potatoes should be discarded or composted. Green areas don't show up on blue potatoes. So with blue varieties, it is especially important to examine and eliminate those near the surface of the ground in the field.

If potatoes are wet when harvested, you may need to leave them on the surface of the ground a few hours to dry out. If it's not dry outside, you may need to put potatoes in open ventilated boxes or other storage (in the dark) for a few days to let them dry out before placing them into long-term storage. Here in maritime Oregon, we try to lift all our potatoes before the winter rains arrive seriously enough to wet the ground down where the potatoes are. Muddy potatoes are more difficult to deal with. We don't harvest more potatoes than we can eat or sell up until about September. That's because in August we don't have good storage conditions for potatoes.

It's optimal to lift and store potatoes without washing them. Unwashed potatoes store best. However, if the potatoes are muddy or are too dirty to be attractive for market, they may need to be gently washed. This can be done by spraying them with a hose. They must then be allowed to dry before being put into storage.

Potato Yields

Commercial potato plantings in Willamette Valley average 36,000 pounds per acre. This translates into about 2.5 pounds per row foot and 250 pounds per 100-foot row. Yields of about half to about twice that are ordinary commercial yields, depending upon the region, potato variety, soil, and other factors. These yields mostly represent plants crowded in the rows and helped along with soluble chemicals and irrigation. However, they don't necessarily exceed the yields you'll obtain on rich garden soils. If you grow potatoes with more modest fertility or limited water, your yields might be somewhat lower. Yield figures are mostly for long-season varieties. Short-season varieties cannot be expected to yield as well as the best long-season varieties for your area.

Storing Potatoes

Potatoes like it cool and very moist. Commercial potato growers cure their potatoes for 5 to 10 days at 59°F–68°F (15°C–20°C) with a relative humidity of 90–95 percent. The curing period allows potato skins to toughen and harvest wounds to heal. Then they put the cured potatoes into long-term storage conditions that vary according to intended use:

1. Fresh market potatoes are stored at 39°F–45°F (4°C–7°C) in the dark at 98 percent relative humidity.
2. Processing potatoes are stored at 47°F–54°F (8°C–12°C) in the dark at 98 percent.
3. Seed potatoes are stored at 32°F–36°F (0°C–2°C) in diffuse light at 98 percent.

Potatoes of all kinds keep best the closer they are to freezing, as long as they don't actually freeze. However, when potatoes are stored near freezing, some of the starch converts to sugar. This gives the potatoes a sweetish flavor, which tastes weird and unappealing. And when fried, sugary potatoes burn. So eating potatoes are, ideally, stored at a higher temperature than seed potatoes.

Glycoalkaloids help the *seed* tubers avoid insect damage and tuber decay. In addition, sprouts that develop in diffuse light will be short, thick, and sturdy.

Under optimal storage conditions, potatoes of the best-storing varieties can keep up to ten months.

Most of us don't have two or three areas for storing different kinds of potatoes. We are happy enough to have one adequate storage area, and the eating and seed potatoes are placed in the same area. In addition, many of us don't bother with a special aboveground curing stage except what happens accidentally. Our early-season storage conditions aren't as cold as is ideal, and that serves as a curing stage. Furthermore, our long-term storage conditions have more to do with what is easily possible given our climate, rather than what is optimal. And we don't usually expect to keep eating potatoes for ten months. We eat them before then. We keep only our seed potatoes for up to ten months. For seed potatoes, some softening and sprouting doesn't matter.

Nate and I store paper grocery bags of potatoes in our garage. It's an attached, unheated garage, an excellent and traditional place for good-enough storage of potatoes in many climes. The warmth from the house keeps anything in the garage from freezing. The garage isn't very airtight, so the humidity is usually relatively high and the garage sufficiently ventilated. We tuck the potatoes away in paper grocery bags with the tops rolled down, and without holes. (Paper bags breathe to some extent.) There is some light in the garage even when the garage door isn't rolled open. And it sometimes is. If the paper bags were left open, the potatoes would green up and develop glycoalkaloids. They would also dry out. A large paper grocery bag will hold about

10 to 15 pounds of potatoes and still leave room enough to roll down the bag's top. This amount per bag also seems to result in an optimal moisture level under our conditions. When we put 15 to 20 pounds in each bag, the bags seem to be a bit soggy, and potatoes sprout earlier and more vigorously. We have also used cardboard boxes (without holes in them) to store potatoes, but the cardboard itself becomes visibly soggy, and the potatoes sprout earlier and tend to mold and rot. Boxes might be preferable under drier storage conditions. If you use cardboard boxes, be aware that, if there are any openings and there is light in the storage area, the potatoes around the openings will green up and develop glycoalkaloids.

I keep a maximum-minimum thermometer-hygrometer in the potato-storage area. In fall when the area tends to be at a higher temperature than is optimal for potatoes, I open the garage door early in the morning to cool the garage. I also open it occasionally whenever the relative humidity in the garage is getting a bit too low and it's raining outside. Given this approach, we can keep some varieties of potatoes in prime eating condition through April, and can keep seed potatoes through June (though they sprout, of course). Without much attention the garage mostly stays between 45°F and 55°F, and between 90 and 98 percent relative humidity.

Here in the mild maritime Northwest, potatoes were often stored in open boxes or crates on shelves in an insulated room in the (unheated) barn designed for the purpose. Such a potato room is dark and has ventilation ports that can be opened or closed as needed. The book *Root Cellaring: Natural Cold Storage of Fruits & Vegetables*, by Mike and Nancy Bubel, has many ideas about how people store their potatoes in different climates. Potatoes are often stored in clamps on the ground in milder areas. A clamp is a storage area made by hilling soil up over a pile of vegetables to insulate them from freezing weather. *Small-Scale Postharvest Handling Practices* gives diagrams and exact dimensions and details about field storage clamps, other simple structures for intermediate-scale storing of potatoes, and a way of storing potatoes in a layer 2 feet deep in a barn. Potatoes are stacked on structures that allow for ventilation. Ventilation is critical to prevent overheating. If stacked too deep, potatoes bruise.

We are usually advised to go through all our storage containers once a month to eliminate any rotten potatoes so they don't ruin all in the container. Nate and I don't do this. We rarely have any rotten potatoes. (People living elsewhere or who irrigate their potatoes could have more of a problem.) In addition, with our potatoes spread out in small lots of 10 to 15 pounds per bag, if we did have a rotten potato that affected the entire bag we wouldn't lose much. Last winter we went through our bags just once, in January. This winter we didn't go through the bags at all. We just ate our way through the eating spuds, some of which lasted through April. We didn't lose any bags from rot.

Potatoes don't like apples. Apples produce ethylene gas, which encourages potatoes to sprout. Also, apples stored with potatoes can pick up potato flavors, which make the apples taste unappealing. Many people make it a point to store their apples and potatoes separately. Many other people get away with storing apples and potatoes in the same area. It's probably a matter of ventilation.

Avoiding Potato Diseases

Diseases are much more of a problem with a crop propagated from vegetative tubers, as potatoes are, than with crops normally propagated by true seed. Diseases also tend to be a more significant problem in crops that are widely grown, as potatoes are. Late potato blight, *Phytophthora infestans*, the pandemic disease of the Irish Potato Famine, is an ever-present reality these days. Late blight regularly wipes out fields in Europe and North America in certain regions and years. Here in Willamette Valley, late blight is present virtually every year, affects some fields every year, and wipes out entire fields in some years. In addition, potatoes are vulnerable to early blight, scab, *Verticillium* wilt, bacterial rot, and other bacterial, fungal, and viral diseases. Here is a guide to avoiding or minimizing the impact of potato diseases.

1–3. The first three rules of potato growing are rotate, rotate, rotate. That is, never grow potatoes on ground that has grown potatoes or other solanums (tomatoes, peppers, eggplants, tobacco) in the previous four years.

4. Many potato diseases are transmitted by the plants and seed tubers. So start your potato patch with certified seed whenever possible, then learn how to save your own seed properly using the techniques described in the next section.

5. Don't leave cull potatoes in the field where they can serve as breeders or transmitters of disease.

6. Weed out all volunteer potato plants.

7. Till under crop residues at the end of the season.

8. Walk the potato rows regularly and immediately remove and destroy any plant that looks

different *in any way*. This "field roguing" is described in the next section.

9. Eliminate any potato variety that doesn't yield well. Many viral diseases are transmitted by the tubers and are invisible except for the fact that the plants don't yield well.

10. Practice first-order biodiversity. Sometimes (over the decades and human generations) the potato crop will falter or fail. So grow a repertoire of staple crops, not just potatoes.

11. Practice second-order biodiversity. A field full of a number of varieties of potatoes is likely to be more resistant to diseases than a field of just one variety. In addition, with many varieties, you have a better chance that some will be resistant to the next disease that comes along.

12. Disease-resistant varieties can help. Scab-resistant varieties are very useful. A lot of breeders are currently working on developing late-blight-resistant varieties. (Unfortunately, so far they have focused on commercial-style potatoes rather than specialty potatoes with outstanding flavors.)

13. Potatoes that mature early may mature a crop and die back before late blight or other diseases reach the field. So early potato varieties can be part of the strategy against diseases, even when the individual early varieties are not biologically resistant to the diseases in question.

14. Growing potatoes without irrigation can limit many pest and disease problems. Early and late blight are fungal diseases. They spread best in wet weather. Those who irrigate are advised not to irrigate at night where fungal diseases threaten.

15. Leave your tubers in the ground at least two weeks after the tops of the plants are dead and gone. That way, any tubers infected with late blight or bacterial rot will be likely to show themselves by rotting instead of being included in and destroying your stored potatoes.

Saving Your Own Potato Seed and Maintaining Potato Varieties

Many books and articles on growing potatoes will tell you to buy new certified potato seed every year. That pattern doesn't give you much resilience. In addition, many varieties that are the most delicious are not available commercially, or are available only in small amounts with prices too high to justify buying more than a starting quantity for further increase. Andean peasants created potatoes and maintained hundreds of varieties for thousands of years without benefit of any seed certification industry. Nearly all potato-growing peasants in the developing world today, of necessity, save their own seed. So can we.

What *is* certified seed, anyway? Certified seed is not guaranteed free of diseases, faster than a speeding bullet, or magical. The certification process starts with a tissue-culture laboratory that makes a tissue culture from the apical tip of the growing shoot from a potato of the desired variety. The growing tip has mechanisms to exclude viruses and is most likely to be free of diseases of all sorts. The tissue culture of the variety is then induced to form a plant, the plantling is grown to make mini-tubers of potato, and the mini-tubers are then field-grown under special conditions for a number of generations to increase the volume of stock and keep the increase of diseases as minimal as possible. Usually, certified seed fields are in cold climates and/or high altitudes where many diseases are less of a problem. Primarily, however, certified seed fields are rogued for plant diseases (by exactly the same process I will outline and which you can learn).

Here are guidelines for saving your own potato seed and maintaining potato varieties:

1. Follow all the guidelines in the previous section, "Avoiding Potato Diseases."
2. Inspect and rogue the growing plants in the field. That is, examine each plant for signs of disease and remove it before it can spread diseases or produce tubers. Some diseases show up best or only in the growing plant.
3. When harvesting, set each batch of tubers from each individual plant as a group next to where the plant grew and examine each individual plant's production. Choose seed tubers only from plants with average or above average yield of clean (disease-free) tubers. Sometimes poor yield is the only outward indicator of disease.

Diseases that show on the surfaces of tubers may show only on some tubers a plant produces, not all. Where some tubers of a plant are diseased, many of the others probably are also, but just not as seriously or obviously. So don't select seed tubers from a plant that has obviously diseased tubers, even if some individual tubers from the same plant look clean.

Nate and I save all the nicest tubers from the chosen seed-tuber plants, whatever their size. Tiny tubers are handy because they can be planted without cutting. However, tiny (later) tubers often carry more of a disease load than the biggest (earliest) tuber. Planting tiny spuds is easier, however.

Avoid the huge potato that is the only potato on a plant that had little yield otherwise. That is sometimes a sign of disease.

Avoid plants whose tubers are all tiny.

4. If any potato shows signs of rot, don't save any seed from that plant or from its immediate neighbors.
5. When we are uncertain as to which tubers are the best to save, we create different lots, which we plant separately. That way, we find out whether those occasional blemishes of a certain kind represent a disease that is going to matter.
6. After choosing the seed-tuber plants, we select the best, cleanest individual tubers, as described later.
7. Finally, diseases can affect the sprouting pattern of the tubers. So, before we cut seed, we do a final inspection of the sprouting seed tubers and eliminate any whose sprouting characteristics indicate disease.

Roguing the Growing Plants

First walk the rows under the right conditions of light and wind and identify and mark the plants that should be rogued. Don't touch the rogues. You can mark each rogue without touching it with a stake that has a piece of surveyor's tape tied on it. Second, dressed appropriately and armed with disposable or washable rubber gloves, plastic pails or bags, a shovel, and a trowel, walk the rows and remove the marked rogue plants. Remove both the tops and underground parts of the plants. Dig up and remove the seed tuber and tubers if they are developing and as much root system as you can get. Don't touch healthy plants while you are removing rogues. Third, get the rogue material out of your field and off your property. Fourth, change clothes, dispose of or wash rubber gloves, and wash your shovel and trowel thoroughly.

Roguing depends upon being able to see and notice a huge variety of fine details. For this you need good but diffuse light, no wind, and a mind that is alert. Early in the morning or anytime on the morning of an overcast, calm day is ideal. (I always rogue in the morning, as there is always some wind here in the afternoon.) Wait until after the dew has evaporated. Dew, full sun, or moving plants make it difficult or impossible to notice certain symptoms. Keep the sun behind you when you rogue. Do it when you're fresh, not after you've done weeding or other tasks. Identifying the rogues requires maximum attention to small details.

Do the first roguing early—within a week or two of when plants emerge. It's by far best to remove diseased plants early on, before insect activity spreads diseases. In addition, it's easiest to get all of a rogue plant out when it is small and before it starts developing tubers. However, not all diseases will show up early. So a second roguing should be done later. All roguing needs to be finished before potato rows grow over and adjacent plants grow together.

For viral diseases spread by insects, adjacent plants are likely to already be infected by the time you discover a diseased plant, particularly later in the season. So it may be best to remove the plants adjacent to the diseased plant as well as the diseased plant itself.

Identifying the Rogues

Here are the symptoms to look for that may indicate diseased plants. Affected areas may be limited to just part of the plant. Many diseases first appear on lower leaves, so it is important to inspect plants below the canopy:

1. Plants are smaller or stunted.
2. Distance between nodes may be shorter, giving plants a bushier appearance.
3. Stem tips die; branching may occur below dead tips.
4. There are wilted areas on one or more stems.
5. One stem is wilted. (Even if the other stems appear healthy, the entire plant is infected.)
6. Leaves are too small.
7. Leaves are wilted or crinkled on entire plant or part of the plant.
8. Leaves are rolled.
9. Leaf edges are bronze.
10. Leaves are a different color.
11. There are black or brown spots on leaves or sections of a plant.
12. Some leaves or part or all of the plant is blackened.
13. There are too many stems.
14. There are obvious signs of mold or fungus on part of the plant.
15. There are lesions of any kind on the plant.
16. Stems are too upright.
17. Stems are too sprawled.
18. There is anything whatsoever different about the plant compared with what is normal for the variety.

Tuber Screening

These tuber characteristics are indicators of disease.

1. Potatoes show one or more areas of rot.
2. Many tubers are misshapen or excessively knobby.
3. Potatoes show scab (raised or sunken scab-like scars on the skin).
4. Potatoes show black scurf. Black scurf looks like lumps of black dirt but doesn't rinse

off easily like dirt does. You can scrape it off with a fingernail. (The black lumps are actually the reproductive bodies of a fungal disease.)

5. Potatoes show silver scurf, which looks like a whitish overlay in patches or on areas of the potato skin.
6. Skins are too rough.
7. Skins are excessively russeted for the variety.
8. Skins show cracks, blemishes, discoloration, or defects of any kind that might be associated with disease.
9. Tubers show signs of mold.
10. Tubers have necrotic rings, that is, some layers of the potato are rotten, as indicated by discolored areas or streaks on the surface of the tubers or dark rings when the tuber is cut open.
11. The end or part of the tuber is decayed.
12. Tubers don't have the right shape for the variety or are irregular or misshapen.
13. Tubers are set too close to the plant for the variety. (These would represent a plant that has stolons that are unusually short.)
14. Tubers don't detach from stolons (except where this is typical for the variety).
15. Eyes are deep for the variety.
16. Tubers have many "dead eyes" (eyes with no sprout buds).
17. Tubers are different from what is typical of the variety in any way.

Final Inspection of Sprouting Seed Tubers
After you have your bags of seed tubers, examine them and screen them further before planting. Many diseases affect dormancy or sprouting characteristics. Here are some signs a seed potato may be diseased and should not be planted:

1. Premature sprouting in storage; tubers break dormancy too soon.
2. Slow sprouting.
3. Irregular sprouting. (For example, only one or two eyes sprout, or only the eyes on one spot on the tuber, not any others.)
4. Blank or dead eyes (eyes with no sprouts).
5. Hair sprouts, that is, thin stringlike sprouts instead of thick healthy-looking sprouts.
6. Sprouts are leaflike.
7. Sprouts have a different branching pattern.
8. Sprouts or tips of sprouts die. Sprouts may regrow and branch below broken, dead or diseased tips.
9. Anything different about sprouts or sprouting pattern.

Basic Potato Cooking Methods

If you want to fry potatoes or fix them in ways requiring large amounts of added fat, or that depend primarily on added fat or fatty ingredients for flavor, or that require lots of labor, consult other sources. My recipes are simple, low-labor recipes designed to bring out and feature the flavors of the potatoes themselves. I usually use the potatoes, dressed appropriately, as a one-bowl meal, or as the main featured course. When they do accompany meat, I usually give the potatoes at least equal billing. Since I am usually cooking for just one or two people these days, many of my recipes start with a cold baked or boiled potato or two. I never boil or bake just enough for one serving. I cook extras to use in dishes that start with cooked potatoes.

Wash and clean spuds with a vegetable brush and remove any damaged spots.

For baked potatoes, stab each spud with a knife a couple of times so it doesn't explode in the oven. Put the potatoes directly on a rack that is in the lower middle of the oven and bake the spuds at 380°F (193°C). (Don't wrap them in aluminum foil; that isn't baking and won't give you any delicious baked-potato flavor.) Bake until the potatoes are soft (easy to get a dull fork all the way through them). This takes about 40 to 90 minutes, depending upon size. For certain varieties like 'Green Mountain', I like a very thick crunchy crust, which requires an extra 15 to 30 minutes of baking time.

Boiled potatoes: I choose potatoes that are all about the same size so that they will all be cooked at the same time. I usually boil spuds whole. I start the potatoes in a pot of cold salted water (about 1 teaspoon of salt per gallon of water) and bring the covered pot of salt water just barely to a boil. Then I turn the heat down to a level that creates a slow simmer and cook the spuds until they are soft when poked with a fork.

The faster potatoes are cooked, the more they tend to fall apart. When I cook a huge pot of potatoes for both duck and people food, it takes half an hour before the water comes to a boil, and the potatoes stay more intact than when a smaller amount is brought to a boil faster. (I suspect that the reason some people find it useful to boil potatoes in open pots is that it slows the cooking down somewhat. One could presumably get a similar effect more efficiently by just turning the burner to a lower setting so the potatoes take longer to come to full temperature.)

For mashed potatoes, it doesn't matter if potatoes fall apart a bit. For potato salads, I use boil-steaming so that the potatoes will stay as intact as possible.

Steaming potatoes: Unless the potatoes are tiny, steaming usually involves cutting the potatoes into pieces first. I like to cook potatoes whole, and for whole 2–4 inch potatoes, it takes too long for them to steam. So instead, I boil-steam them.

Boil-steaming: I put a steamer basket into the pot and put in the cleaned spuds. Then I cover the spuds with salted water, bring the pot to a boil, and simmer the spuds for 10 minutes. Then, using a second steaming basket and a spatula to hold the spuds in place, I pour off all the excess water, leaving just enough for steaming. Then I cover the pot (completely) and put it back on the heat and steam the potatoes until they are soft (usually about 20 minutes for the size potatoes I usually use). Some of the potatoes may still crack, but even the cracked potatoes stay together well enough to eat out of hand or use for potato salad.

Chunky mashed potatoes: I like my mashed potatoes fixed in a chunky style that allows me to leave the skins on the potatoes. So I either boil potatoes or boil-steam them whole. Then I run a knife through the cooked spuds to break the skins into bite-sized pieces. Then I run a coarse potato masher through the spuds enough to break them into chunky mashed potatoes, and I add some of the hot cooking water to get the texture and moisture content I want. (Use *hot* water or milk to get the right texture for mashed potatoes.) I usually season the white or yellow mashed potatoes with butter, salt, and pepper. (Blue or red mashed potatoes get seasoned with butter, tamari sauce, and pepper.) I usually leave part of any batch of mashed potatoes unseasoned to use as leftovers for thickening soups or for combining with (salty) canned tuna or salmon.

Using leftover baked potatoes. I often eat leftover baked potatoes out of hand. I also use leftover baked potatoes in the same sorts of dishes as left-over boiled potatoes. They are drier than boiled potatoes, however. So I usually add extra water to compensate, and let the dish sit a while so the baked spuds can hydrate. The dryness of leftover baked potatoes can be a real advantage. They soak up sauces readily.

Cooking White and Yellow Potatoes

White-fleshed and yellow-fleshed potatoes have fairly delicate flavors that are easily overwhelmed. I use seasonings with a gentle hand. White and yellow potatoes are nicely complemented with salt, pepper, butter, olive oil, toasted sesame oil, curry powder, (quality) canned tuna, canned salmon, spaghetti sauce, hard-cooked eggs, mayonnaise, pickle relish, Dijon mustard, lemon or lime juice, lime or citrus oils, quality light vinegars (such as white balsamic, sherry, or light artisan vinegars), and sauerkraut, and with *small, careful* amounts of garlic, onions, or roasted garlic or onions. Appropriate varieties of white and yellow potatoes make nice potato salads.

White or yellow potatoes nicely complement the white meat of chicken or turkey as well as pork, ham, lamb, and fish (including tuna and salmon). White and yellow potatoes taste good with, but are somewhat overwhelmed by, the dark meat of chicken or turkey as well as beef, duck, or goose. I always choose white or yellow potatoes to go with whole roast chicken or turkey. Here are some of my ways of fixing white or yellow potatoes:

Deppe's Devilish Potato Salad
I dice leftover white- or yellow-fleshed baked potatoes and add them to a dressing made with mayonnaise, pickle relish, Grey Poupon Country Dijon mustard, Italian seasonings, and water. I add chopped up celery or some other crunchy vegetables. For the dressing, I use enough mustard to give a final effect halfway between standard potato salad and the yolk part of deviled eggs. I add enough water to dilute the dressing so that it will be just the right consistency after the potato has absorbed most of it. I let the potato salad sit in the refrigerator half an hour before eating it. Using leftover baked potatoes, which readily absorb liquids, makes it unnecessary to use hot potatoes in this recipe.

Semi-Sour Spuds
I often dice white or yellow leftover potatoes (baked, boiled, or boil-steamed), add water, salt (or tuna), pepper, and butter or olive oil, then zap in the microwave. (Sometimes I also add a couple of drops of toasted sesame oil.) Then I add a fine gourmet light vinegar such as white balsamic or sherry vinegar or an artisanal white, and mash a little of the potato to help make a sauce. I wait at least half an hour before eating, and eat warm, or zap just a little more to reheat.

Cream of Potato Soup
I turn any soup into a full main course by adding enough (salt-free) mashed potatoes or mashing whole leftover potatoes into the soup.

Mashed Potatoes and Tuna
I start with some unseasoned mashed potatoes, add a can of albacore tuna to the

bowl and some olive oil or butter. Then I zap the bowl in the microwave and I add a little lemon or lime juice or a gourmet-quality light vinegar such as white balsamic or sherry vinegar.

Zapped Potatoes

This involves fixing potatoes in an 8-inch Pyrex bowl in the microwave oven. I cut the potatoes in chunks and add a little cumin, curry powder, pepper, and oregano. I half-fill the bowl with water. (Some of the potato chunks are sticking above the water, while others are submerged.) I microwave on high for eight to sixteen minutes, until the potatoes are soft. Then I mash the potatoes with butter and add a little salt (or, alternatively, a can of tuna).

Roast Lamb (or Pork, or Chicken) with Onions and Potatoes Supreme

Follow the recipe in the next section for Roast Duck Supreme, but use white or yellow potatoes and a bone-in lamb-shoulder roast, leg of lamb, pork roast, or roasting chicken. Use seasonings appropriate for the meat on the potatoes and onions as well.

Cooking Blue Potatoes

I consider blue-fleshed potatoes to be an entirely different food from white-fleshed and yellow-fleshed potatoes. I used to think I didn't like the flavor of the blues. That is because I was trying to fix blues just like whites or yellows. Now that I've learned to use them, I love the blues.

Blue-fleshed potatoes have a *powerful* flavor

and a powerful, distinctive aftertaste. Blue potatoes combine well with larger amounts of seasonings and other powerful flavors. They go with salt, pepper, butter, tamari sauce, dark miso, and serious amounts of garlic, onions, or roasted garlic or onions. They are also wonderful with chili, salsa, steak sauces, and dark meat of chicken or turkey, as well as beef, duck, goose, smoked herring, and liver. Blue potatoes have a smoky, somewhat beefy flavor that can be brought out and featured by combining them with other smoky- or beefy-flavored things. Instead of using salt with blue spuds, I prefer to use more strongly flavored salty ingredients such as tamari sauce or dark aged Hatcho miso. (Soy sauce would be good too, if you can eat wheat.) Since blue potatoes overwhelm and dominate the white meat of chicken or turkey, I choose white or yellow potatoes to go with breast meat or whole roast chicken or turkey.

I consider 'Skagit Beet Red' an honorary blue potato when it comes to cooking. However, I often eat it mashed with butter, tamari sauce, seasonings, and ketchup or salsa or spaghetti sauce to bring out and emphasize its outrageously red color.

Don't boil blue potatoes with whites or yellows. Boil blues by themselves.

I never combine blue potatoes with whites or yellows in recipes. They don't go with the same things, and blue potatoes make all the potatoes taste like blues. The classic red, white, and blue potato salad is designed for maximum visual appeal, not for optimum flavor. Any potato salad with blue potatoes in it would taste better without them.

Here are some of my favorite blue-potato recipes:

Mock-Beefy Blue Potatoes Supreme

I dice leftover blue potatoes. I use some left-over smoky-style tea (Lapsang Souchong) saved from breakfast to reconstitute some aged dark Hatcho miso (Eden brand). I use a handheld blender to blend up the tea, miso, and some garlic. Then I bring the bowl with those ingredients to a boil in the microwave to take the edge off the garlic. Next I add the diced potatoes and butter (or other fat or oil). I mash a little of the potato to turn the fluid into a thick sauce, zap again to heat up the potatoes, then let everything sit for half an hour so the potato chunks absorb the flavors. I zap again to heat the dish before eating it. The resulting dish features pieces of delicious-looking brown-colored potato in a rich, thick brown sauce, and the dish tastes very beefy even though there is no meat in it. (The potatoes turn brown because the pigment in blue and red potatoes is pH-sensitive.)

Chili and Blue Potatoes

I dice some cooked blue potatoes into bite-sized pieces, fill the rest of the bowl with chili, and zap the bowl in the microwave to heat everything.

Smoked Herring and Blue Potatoes

This dish uses the herring and oil from a little 3-ounce can of smoked herring. The can of herring provides all the oil and salt. I macerate some garlic in water, then put it in a bowl and zap it in the microwave enough to boil the water and briefly cook the garlic. Then I add leftover diced blue potatoes, and zap the bowl again. Then I add the herring (with all the oil and water), break it into chunks, and mash some of the herring and some of the potatoes with a fork to make a thick gravy. I zap the bowl again to heat up the fish and help the potato absorb the herring oil and smoky fish flavor. I let the bowl sit at least twenty minutes, then reheat and eat.

Liver, Garlic, and Blue Potatoes

I start by dicing leftover cooked potatoes and adding water, pepper, and tamari sauce so the potatoes can hydrate and absorb flavors while I cook the meat. I chop the liver into bite-sized pieces, stir-fry it, then set the liver aside temporarily. Then I macerate a very generous amount of garlic in water and dump the water-garlic in the pan to deglaze the pan and briefly cook the garlic. Next I add the chunks of cooked blue potatoes and let them heat up. I mash enough of the potatoes to make a thick gravy, add back the liver, taste everything, and add more pepper and tamari sauce to taste. Then I let the dish sit in the pan for five minutes or so to let all the flavors meld. (I use just enough water so that I'll end up with a dish that is served on a plate, not a bowl, with the gravy clinging to all the ingredients, not running off.) The result is a rich, attractive brown gravy and brown potatoes with bits of liver.

Roast Duck (or Turkey Thighs or Drums or Beef) with Onions and Blue Potatoes Supreme

Whenever I roast a duck, some turkey thighs or drumsticks, or a beef shoulder or pot roast or chuck cut, I like to include blue potatoes.

I cut several big yellow onions in half, slice the halves into thin slices, and break them up into loose half-rings with my hands. Then I season the sliced onions with cumin, sage, and pepper and put half of the onions down in a layer on the roasting-pan rack. With beef, I season it with cumin, sage, and pepper too. With turkey thighs, I sometimes also season it, pulling back the skin, seasoning, then tucking the skin back over the meat. I don't eat the poultry skin, which, in this dish, isn't crisp.

On top of the seasoned onions goes the meat. Then a ring of whole blue spuds goes around the meat. (I choose the size of the potatoes according to the expected time for the meat to cook.) The rest of the seasoned onions go on top of the meat and potatoes. I cover everything with the roasting pan lid (which has a couple of open holes in it), put the pan in the lower middle of the oven, and turn the heat to about 380°F. The onions and meat roast. The potatoes seem to partly roast and partly steam. For a 6-pound (live weight) Ancona roasting duck (excess drake, actually, about 4 to 6 months old), it takes about 1½ hours. Properly cooked duck meat should be pink on the inside. With beef, the time depends upon the size of the cut of meat. Cook it until it is succulent and soft. For a big roast and lots of onions and potatoes it can be up to 3½ hours.

By the time the meat is cooked, the potatoes are also cooked, the onions are roasted, the pan under the rack has lovely fatty oniony seasoned drippings ready to mix with the onions, tamari sauce, and pepper and slather over the meat and potatoes, and the entire house is filled with the powerful blending, intertwining, almost erotic aromas of roasted onions, meat, and blue potatoes.

CHAPTER NINE

The Laying Flock

Backyard Poultry. Ducks versus Chickens. Poultry for Various Purposes: Choosing a Type and Breed. Laying Duck Breeds and Behavior. Feeding the Free-Range Laying Flock in Ordinary Times. Feeding Poultry in Hard Times. Ducks for Garden Pest Control. Duck Egg Cookery.

Backyard Poultry

My ducks can use parts of the yard that are too steep, too wet much of the year, or too heavily shaded for gardening. Their manure fertilizes the yard and garden. Here in maritime Oregon, it is much easier to grow grass and slugs than garden plants. Ducks are great at converting grass and slugs into eggs. And the quality of those eggs exceeds anything I can buy. Ducks are experts at yard and garden pest control. Poultry provide us with garden fertilizer and make good use of excess or second-grade garden produce. In addition, free-range eggs can supply us with long-chain omega-3 fatty acids, which aren't available from plant foods. Is it any wonder that so many gardeners love poultry? Gardening and poultry go together naturally.

My resilience is enhanced profoundly by having ducks, even, strangely enough, not counting the eggs. I'm a happier and more joyful person with ducks. My life is richer. If I find myself feeling discouraged or overwhelmed, I just go and sit with the ducks for a while. It seems to be impossible to stay depressed for very long when surrounded by a flock of foraging ducks.

Many people who want to produce their own eggs think of chickens automatically and never consider whether their needs might be better served by ducks. This is true even in the maritime Northwest, where ducks (but not chickens) can forage happily outdoors year-round. I encourage everyone who wants a home laying flock to start by fully considering the chicken versus duck issue.

This chapter isn't complete enough to serve as your sole source of information on keeping poultry. You should also read one or more general books.

Urban and Suburban Poultry

Even with only a small suburban or urban yard, you may be able to keep a few laying ducks or chickens. Check with your local animal control officer and with neighborhood association rules. Portland and Eugene, Oregon, for example, will let you keep three hens or ducks. Corvallis, Oregon, will let you keep a flock as long as you keep them on your own land. I now live outside the Corvallis city limits. However, a neighborhood association's rules apply. Our neighborhood association allows horses, cattle, sheep, and home poultry flocks, but not goats, pigs, or commercial poultry flocks.

For those interested in laying ducks, the definitive book is *Storey's Guide to Raising Ducks*, by Dave Holderread. For those who choose laying chickens, there are many possibilities (see note 9-2). In this chapter, I focus primarily on the interfaces between gardens, poultry, and resilience, and upon information not readily available elsewhere.

Ducks versus Chickens

The most ecologically well-adapted livestock for the maritime Northwest is the duck. The best-laying duck breeds lay better than the best-laying chicken breeds. Ducks can free-range year-round in our region. Ducks forage much more of their diets than chickens and eat a larger variety of natural foods common here. Ducks eat snails and slugs, and are better for yard and garden pest control. Ducks love our weather. (I should perhaps mention my biases. I've kept five breeds of chickens, two breeds of geese, and seven breeds of ducks. The ducks are my favorites, especially Ancona ducks, and at this point, I keep only a flock of thirty-two Ancona ducks. But I like chickens too.)

Many people who are allergic to chicken eggs can eat duck eggs. A few people are allergic to both. I have also run into occasional people who claim to have problems eating duck eggs who can eat chicken eggs, though this pattern seems to be rare. Ducks from the better-laying breeds and strains can lay well enough to earn their keep for years. Laying chickens are usually not producing economically beyond the second year.

Ducks are much easier to control than chickens. Ducks of laying breeds can be easily confined with a fence only 2 feet high (as long as they have food and water and their buddies with them). Most of the egg breeds of chickens can fly well enough to get over any fencing. Keeping them out of the garden or the eaves of the porch often requires wing-clipping every bird.

Ducks tend to lay eggs that are bigger than chicken eggs from a breed of equivalent size. Some dual-purpose duck breeds (such as Anconas) lay eggs that are very big for the size of the bird.

Ducks normally lay their eggs between 4:00 a.m. and 8:00 a.m. daily. This means they lay their eggs in the nests in their night pens instead of hiding a nest in the yard. You can pick up the duck eggs just once per day, at the same time that you let the ducks out to forage. Chickens have a twenty-six-hour laying cycle, meaning each hen lays a little later each day. So a flock of chickens is laying at all times of the day and night. When allowed to free-range, they sometimes come back to lay in their nests and sometimes don't. So recovering all the eggs can be problematic.

Chickens can help with pest control in yards, gardens, and pastures under certain circumstances. But chickens don't eat big slugs or snails, two of the most important garden pests in the Northwest. (Some chickens may eat small slugs or snails.) And the scratching of chickens tears up plantings and scatters manure and dirt over the rest. Ducks are considered the premier critter for pest control. All the laying breeds of ducks are big enough to eat even 8-inch banana slugs, and do so with enthusiasm, swallowing them the way a sword swallower does a sword.

Ducks are easy to herd. You can use one or two herding staffs, or you can just walk behind the ducks with your hands extended sideways, making scooping motions in the direction you want the ducks to go and saying, "Let's go, ducks."

"It's Great to Be a Ducky in the Rain (The Ducky Song)"

I made up this song for my ducklings but also for all ducks and children (of all ages) everywhere (me included). Sing it to the tune of the children's song that starts "If you're happy and you know it, clap your hands." Ducklings are very impressed by singing and whistling, and will be the most attentive and intense audience you will ever have in your life the first time you sing or whistle for them. Adult ducks like to be "tucked in" for the night with a few songs (in addition to their clean water and food).

It's great to be a ducky in the rain. Quack! Quack!
It's great to be a ducky in the rain. Quack! Quack!
In rain I'm always wetter, and it's better to be wetter.
It's great to be a ducky in the rain.

It's great to be a ducky in the sun. Quack! Quack!
A little sun will not harm anyone. Quack! Quack!
I'm really very lucky, to be a lucky ducky.
It's great to be a ducky in the sun.

It's great to be a ducky in the water.
   Quack! Quack!
In water I do just what duckies oughter.
   Quack! Quack!
I swim and dive and dash, and play
   and bathe and splash.
It's great to be a ducky in the water.

It's great to be a ducky in the hay. Quack! Quack!
I make a cozy nest and then I lay. Quack! Quack!
Then I have a lovely rest, tucked in my cozy nest.
It's great to be a ducky in the hay.

QUACK! QUACK! Quack! Quack! Quack!
Quack! Quack! Quack! Quack!
(Descending in scale and volume, a distinctive trill that ducks do.)

Note: When actually singing this song to baby ducklings, say "Wuk! Wuk!" instead of "Quack! Quack!" Quacks are alarm calls and can frighten or confuse babies.

In Asia, the free-range egg industry is based upon ducks that are kept in secure permanent quarters at night and herded to various separate foraging areas during the day. Since chickens can't be herded, the night pen or house usually needs to be in or adjacent to the foraging area. To rotate chicken forage, you move their house, which must be portable. To rotate duck forage, you just herd the ducks to a different spot during the day, leaving their permanent pen in its permanent spot.

The crowing of roosters is much louder than any noise ducks make. Neighbors are less likely to hear or object to the sounds of ducks.

In many areas free-range chicken eggs are only seasonal, but free-range duck eggs are year-round. Here in the maritime Northwest, the free-range duck is happy foraging outdoors the entire year, and ducks of appropriate breeds are good winter layers. Ducks delight in cold rain. Chickens are so miserable in cold rain and use so much energy keeping warm that they either don't lay or their egg production isn't economical. The duck is the only way to get economical, year-round, free-range egg production in the maritime Northwest and other areas with cold, wet winters. (In areas where the ground is frozen much of the winter, there is no way to get winter *free-range* egg production from any poultry.)

Ducks can forage a larger part of their diet than chickens. Chickens eat mostly grain and animal life, with greenery as a salad. Ducks eat grain and animal life but also considerably more greenery than chickens, including grass, as long as it is succulent and growing.

In addition, ducks can make excellent use of wetlands, waterways, lakes, and ponds.

Ducks are more resistant to disease than chickens. Ducklings are hardier than chicks. Ducklings are more heavily feathered and have a layer of subcutaneous fat. They are designed for cold, wet weather. Ducklings can be outdoors earlier in spring than chicks. If allowed to waterproof themselves properly, ducklings can be out foraging in their third week (see note 9-14). Chicks are normally kept indoors the first six to eight weeks.

Ducks, however, are much more vulnerable to four-footed predators than chickens, especially chickens with intact wings. Some people with marginal fencing or night housing can keep chickens but not ducks.

Chickens are much more readily available and usually cheaper. Day-old chicks of many breeds are often sold sexed, so you can get exactly as many of each sex as you want. Most laying breeds of ducks are much less available and are usually sold as straight-run only, meaning you don't know how many of what sex you're getting.

Ducks need bathing water. Chickens maintain their skin and feather condition via dust bathing. Some people find it much easier to provide a dry dust bath than a bathing pool. Books sometimes say ducks can be raised without bathing water. Although this is technically true, raising ducks that way isn't kind. Ducks keep their skin and feathers in condition by bathing in water and preening and coating their feathers with wax. All you need for a handful of ducks is a kiddy pool of water changed a couple of times a week. My ducks have a small pond I made by propping up a piece of pond liner on the hillside so I can open one side and drain it and hose it down easily. If you are unwilling to provide bathing water for ducks, I suggest you get chickens.

Chickens are a much better confinement animal than ducks. Ducks drink far more water, have a much looser, more liquidy poop, and need more space when confined than chickens. Some people need to confine their poultry and bring the garden produce and food to the birds. Chickens are usually the better choice for that situation.

In areas where winter is harsh and the ground is frozen or covered with snow for months, any poultry has to be confined. This fact can translate into chickens being the most workable option. If I lived in Minnesota or Wisconsin, or upstate New York, I think I would keep chickens instead of ducks.

The "chicken tractor" is a small portable house with no floor that is moved around to fresh ground every day or so. There are many books and articles about this style of poultry keeping. It is actually a confinement situation in which the birds get a little greenery but not actually very much animal material. It works best for commercial broiler chickens, which don't forage very actively or move far from the feeders anyway. Laying hens in chicken tractors produce eggs that are more a commercial-diet-based egg than a free-range one. However, chicken tractors are the only option many people have for their laying flock, and the chicken tractor, managed optimally, produces eggs that are better tasting, probably more nutritious, and certainly more ethical than those from commercial caged layers.

Chicken tractors work best with chickens. You can't just substitute ducks. Laying chickens roost on raised perches at night and will use nests stacked in a bank against the wall. So the chickens use three dimensions of the space in a small movable house. The "chicken tractor" usually has one wall of nests that can be accessed from the side without entering the pen and a built-in roost on one side or end. A chicken tractor for ducks is problematic. Ducks use only floor space, and so need much more floor space than chickens, even before taking into account that their manure is much wetter. They need extra floor space for nests and resting. They need much more water and bigger water containers and bathing water. By the time you have given the ducks a big enough pen to be comfortable for them, it won't be able to hold many birds in it, and it will not be very portable.

In America and Europe, chicken eggs are the standard. Most people don't know how to cook duck eggs. During the last two decades, I've developed cooking methods and recipes for an American style of duck egg cookery, which I present in the final section of this chapter. If you sell duck eggs, you will need to do some customer education.

Many people will enjoy trying both chickens and ducks. Generally, the two species should not be brooded together or housed in the same night quarters (unless they're in separate pens). They have different requirements. However, chickens and ducks can usually share their daytime foraging area.

Poultry for Various Purposes: Choosing a Type and Breed

Both ducks and chickens have types and breeds that represent different virtues and purposes. There are extreme egg-laying types, dual-purpose egg-meat types, and heavy meat types. The extreme-egg types, chickens or ducks, are small, scrawny, nervous birds that give us the most eggs when fed optimally and perfectly on commercial chow, and have the best efficiency at converting feed to eggs. The eggs are not particularly large. Extreme-egg types of ducks or chickens have little inclination to go broody. If they do go broody, they are unlikely to stay with the job long enough to hatch a clutch.

The classic extreme-egg type of chicken is the White Leghorn. The best chicken-egg production these days, however, is by hybrids of various extreme-egg kinds, who can give you about 200–280 eggs per bird in their first year. The best extreme-egg type of duck is the Holderread strain of Khaki Campbell (see note 9-5). Even though this is a pure breed, these ducks *average* 320–340 eggs in their first year of laying (in small flocks under good conditions).

Extreme-egg-type birds (chickens or ducks) have so little meat on them that most people do not butcher them; the meat of the excess young males or spent layers is wasted.

At the other extreme are big, heavy types of poultry bred primarily to produce a meaty carcass.

Most don't lay enough eggs to be kept as layers. In addition, the eggs they do lay are more costly to produce because the feed-to-egg conversion rate isn't as good as for smaller, skinnier birds. Some meat breeds have been bred to grow as fast as possible. These can produce a fryer or broiler carcass in seven or eight weeks (in a full confinement situation with commercial feeds). These types have fatty meat. Even if allowed free range, these birds aren't very active and don't go far enough from their feeders to make much use of the range. The Cornish Cross chicken and the Pekin and Aylesbury ducks represent this class.

Some heavy meat breeds grow more slowly, are more active foragers, and make great roasting birds at three to six months of age. This class isn't economical to produce commercially. But the meat is outstanding in flavor compared with the fast-growing breeds that are butchered young, and the meat is less fatty. Jersey Giant chickens and Rouen, Saxony, Appleyard, and Muscovy ducks are in the slow-growing, roasting-bird meat-poultry class.

For the home flock, I strongly favor the dual-purpose breeds of both chickens and ducks. The dual-purpose bird is a bigger bird with a meatier carcass than the extreme-egg types, but she isn't as big or meaty as the extreme-meat breeds. She doesn't lay as well as the extreme-egg types but can do almost as well. In addition, she lays bigger eggs than extreme-egg types, sometimes much bigger eggs. She is usually calm and sensible and more enjoyable to work with than the extreme-egg types. She does not go into a panic over every little thing nor try to run through fences when scared, endangering herself in the process. She often has more personality and more complex and

Heirloom and Endangered Poultry Breeds

Many of the best breeds of laying ducks are critically endangered breeds. Many dual-purpose and egg-type chicken breeds are also rare. Some of these breeds can work well for the home laying flock. The best dual-purpose laying duck, the Ancona, for example, is a critically endangered breed. I encourage everyone to join the American Livestock Breeds Conservancy and to consider combining the keeping of a laying flock with the preserving of a worthy but endangered poultry breed. Many rare breeds and their current preservation status are described on the American Livestock Breeds Conservancy Web site at www.albc-usa.org. ALBC produces four substantive publications annually (including a breeders directory) that alone are well worth the price of membership.

natural behavior than either the extreme-egg or extreme-meat types.

Excess males of dual-purpose breeds give a carcass with enough meat on them to be worth butchering and dressing, and the meat is less fatty than that of fast-growing meat-type fryers. If you consider both eggs and meat, dual-purpose breeds may be the most productive of all. Even many pastured-poultry producers with laying flocks are using dual-purpose breeds for layers. The classic example of the dual-purpose layer in America is the Rhode Island Red chicken. Joel Salatin, pastured-poultry producer extraordinaire, now uses Rhode Island Reds for his free-range egg production. He markets the spent layers as stewing birds.

Many females of dual-purpose breeds are perfectly competent to raise the next generation. Many a keeper of these breeds has had a lady disappear for a while, only to show up a few weeks later with a dozen babies in tow. I believe the kind of small flock that would most contribute to community resilience in the advent of a long-term mega-disaster is the small flock of dual-purpose birds that is capable of producing eggs, meat, and replacement birds, and that can rapidly spin off additional flocks for the community.

There is much information available on chicken breeds for the home laying flock, and there are dozens of reasonable choices. Robert Plamondon's *Success with Baby Chicks* has particularly realistic information on the subject. *Storey's Guide to Raising Chickens* also has good information on chicken breeds. Both give numbers on productivity and cover some aspects of the behavior of different breeds that can matter, information that is generally harder to come by than mere descriptions of breeds. Information about laying duck breeds is largely available only in Holderread's book. No information is available on the behavior of the different breeds of laying ducks with respect to free-ranging. I have developed that information by keeping flocks of different breeds in parallel with Anconas, my major breed. I present this information in the next section and in the chapter notes.

Laying Duck Breeds and Behavior

The best breeds for the home laying flock are the Holderread line of Khaki Campbells (see note 9-5), Welsh Harlequins, Indian Runners (of carefully chosen lines only), Magpies, and Anconas. The Holderread Campbells and Indian Runners are widely available. The rest are rare breeds. You can find pictures of all of them on the Internet. Campbells are basically brown. (Drakes have bronze or brown-gold heads.) Welsh Harlequins are cream, buff, white, and speckled. (The drakes have green heads.) Runners come in about every shade and color and pattern. Magpies are white with colored spots on the back and head. And Anconas are pinto-style white mixed with various colors in various broken patterns. Campbells and Harlequins lay white eggs. Some Runners, Magpies, and Anconas lay greenish or bluish eggs.

Campbells, Harlequins, and Runners are extreme-egg types. They are light, skinny birds with nervous dispositions. Holderread Campbells are the most productive of all poultry, with flock averages of 320–340 eggs per bird (in small flocks). Welsh Harlequins lay about 240–330 eggs per year. Runners have an exotic upright coke-bottle shape, and have been selected much more for beauty than for egg production in recent decades. To get Runners that lay 200 eggs per bird or better, you'll need to choose the specific line and source carefully. Some Runners lay green or blue eggs. All these breeds are excellent foragers.

For production of *big* eggs as well as for dual-purpose production of eggs and meat, I recommend Anconas. Anconas lay about 210–280 eggs per year, mostly jumbo and super-jumbo size. Some Anconas lay green or bluish green eggs. Anconas are calmer, more sensible, and easier to work with than the extreme-egg breeds. They are quite mellow and flexible about their dominance hierarchy. They have one, but nobody seems to take it very seriously. Nobody excludes anybody from anything because of it. There is enough meat on the cull Ancona drakes to make fine roasting birds. Anconas have the standard laying-duck shape, except that they have legs and feet that are oversized for the size of the bird. They rarely have any foot or leg problems. Anconas come in various colors with pinto-style white markings that allow you to identify each individual, even at a distance. The colors are black, blue, chocolate, lavender, and silver.

Anconas are the best foragers of all the medium-weight duck breeds. As individuals, they forage as well as even such light breeds as Campbells and Harlequins. Anconas have female flock leaders. Because of their female leaders, Ancona flocks forage better than Campbell or Harlequin flocks. Anconas have more complex flock behavior than other duck breeds, with a more sophisticated ability to communicate. (See note 9-12.)

Anconas are very alert and sensible about predators and make better watchdogs than the geese I used to have. They are especially smart about hawks. It is sometimes possible to keep Anconas where all other poultry get eliminated by hawks. (You must have brush or a deck or somewhere for the ducks to run under when hawks are about, though.) With a pure flock of Anconas, I can usually tell what the flock is doing just by sound. With a flock of mixed breeds, the vocalizations are more ambiguous, and I can't always tell what is going on without looking.

Ancona ladies are usually capable of hatching out a clutch of eggs and make good mothers.

I haven't any direct experience with Magpies. They are said to be excellent layers, however, laying 220–290 big eggs per year. They seem to be somewhere in between the light extreme-egg type and the dual-purpose Ancona.

Campbells, Harlequins, Runners, and Anconas can all be fed a free-choice diet without getting fat, and are so committed to foraging that they forage very actively even when fed free choice. They eat forage preferentially and just eat enough chow to fill in the gaps in the foraging situation. (Saxonies or Golden Cascades, in contrast, become fat when fed free choice. Fat ducks don't lay.)

Campbells, Harlequins, Runners, and Anconas will come home nicely at night and pen themselves (with proper management). Not all breeds do this. Saxonies, for example, have a tendency to fall asleep under a bush somewhere and miss pen-up. For additional information on breed behavior and on the behavior of various combinations of breeds in mixed flocks, see the chapter notes.

There are several other breeds of dual-purpose ducks available in America; namely, the Buff Orpington, Cayuga, Crested, and Swedish. These can give a decent amount of eggs but are not in the same league as the breeds I have recommended. Egg production of the Orpington is listed by Holderread as 150–220 per year. The rest are about 100–150. Many people enjoy keeping these breeds, however, and don't need more egg production.

Pekin, Aylesbury, Rouen, and Muscovy are heavy meat breeds. They don't lay well enough for a laying flock. Saxony and Silver Appleyard are also heavy meat breeds, but they lay well enough to be suitable for those who want primarily roasting ducks along with eggs as a by-product instead of the reverse. Feed conversion to eggs will not be good enough to warrant keeping Appleyards or Saxonies if you want to sell eggs.

Feeding the Free-Range Laying Flock in Ordinary Times

In this section I assume you have access to commercial feeds. I also assume you have a relatively small flock—anything from a handful to a hundred or so layers. (For bigger flocks, you will be milling your own feeds or having them custom-milled to your specification.) In the next section I'll talk about "hard times" poultry feeding—feeding poultry with little or no access to commercial feeds.

First, I suggest feeding free-range ducks commercial chicken chow, not commercial duck chow. Duck chow is a specialized product that costs more. The chicken chow usually turns over faster in the feed store, thus is fresher. Free-range birds with decent forage get enough vitamins and minerals so that the difference in the exact needs between ducks and chickens is not an issue. (Ducklings do need extra niacin, though. See note 9-14 for more on raising and feeding ducklings.)

However, *do not feed medicated chicken chow to ducks*. Some chicken medicines kill ducks. Also, *do not feed ducks chow with fish meal in it*. Fish meal gives duck eggs a fishy or off-flavor. I advise against using chows with animal by-products in them. (People, cattle, and sheep can get mad cow disease from animal by-products in poultry chow.)

Your basic duck or chicken book will have at least one chapter on feeding your adult flock and separate information on feeding babies. However, everything will be oriented toward the flock that is fully confined and that is fed the commercial chow as 100 percent of their diet. The usual advice is to feed adult laying birds a 16 percent protein laying chow (which has high calcium to support eggshell production). However, the chow has a fixed amount of energy and protein. When birds are running around outdoors their needs change from day to day depending upon the forage and the weather. In addition, free-range birds dilute the total calcium in their diet with their foraging and lay soft-shelled eggs. You can correct the latter problem by giving the birds oyster shell grit free choice. But it's more useful to take a completely different approach with free-range poultry. I'll describe the smorgasbord feeding pattern I use with my ducks. The same pattern is used by people with free-range chicken laying flocks.

In the smorgasbord approach, I give my ducks at least two different separate foods, free choice, in separate containers. One container has a commercial chicken starter or broiler chow (20–22 percent protein). This is the highest protein chow that is economical. The other container has grain. I use whole corn. (Some people use the high-protein chow and two different grains, all in separate containers.) My birds also have free-choice access to two different kinds of grit. One is oyster shell grit, which provides calcium as it wears down in the gizzard. The other is granite grit, which doesn't. (Some people use just oyster shell.)

In other words, the birds have a smorgasbord of two kinds of food, one as high-protein as practical, the other high-energy. The birds mix and match the food, depending upon the forage and the weather. On cold days they eat more corn. On mild winter days, when there are lots of large night crawlers on the surface of the ground, the ducks only eat a mouthful of chow or two and mostly just eat corn. With as many worms or slugs as they want, they can fulfill their protein needs by foraging and just need some corn for energy. Corn is a lot cheaper than commercial chow. So feeding birds smorgasbord-style is most economical. And I think the birds like having a choice as much as we do.

Many people have just adult laying hens or ducks without males and provide just oyster shell grit. However, I have several drakes in my flock of thirty-two. Male poultry should not be forced to over-eat calcium just to get the grit to grind their food. I also merge young ducks with the adult flock at about five weeks of age. Young poultry can be crippled if forced to eat too much calcium.

Corn is the most common grain used. Poultry like corn. Ducks like corn and feed wheat. They are not very enthusiastic about "twice-cleaned" oats (which have the hulls but no awls). I use whole corn for adult ducks. Cracked corn doesn't keep well and often comes from the mill with huge clumps of mold in it.

To introduce birds to a new kind or brand of feed or a different grain, the usual recommendation is to mix the old feed and the new in increasing proportions. I don't agree. At least, not for ducks. Ducks need several days to try out a new feed. They try just a bite the first day, then increasing amounts on subsequent days. (I suspect it's a behavior that helps free rangers avoid poisoning.) So to introduce a new food, I just put down a bucket of it, leaving the buckets of familiar feed. After a week or so, all the ducks have tasted, seriously tried, then become familiar with the new food. If they like it, they'll be eating it. Then I discontinue the other food. If you just switch foods or add new and old foods together, you may risk nearly starving the ducks for several days. Ducks try new foods readily. They just start cautiously. This way of introducing a new food also constitutes a way of asking the ducks what they think about the new food.

Occasionally ducks will stop eating a feed. This usually means something is wrong with the feed. Mills make mistakes with feeds much more often than you might imagine. If the ducks stop eating a feed (and are just eating their grain), take their word for it and try some other brand.

Feeding Poultry in Hard Times

How do you feed your flock if you run out of job or money, or if the economy or infrastructure collapses and you no longer have access to commercial poultry chow made from corn and soybeans?

The traditional way of feeding poultry involved grain. Poultry were always given some grain, even when they were given nothing else. Grain is not a complete diet for poultry. But if it is just a dozen birds who have acres of forage, all the table scraps and butchery waste from a large family, and the excess from a large garden and orchard, a little grain and some oyster shell may be all that is needed. Note, this is only true when the birds can forage almost all their protein by eating as many bugs or worms as they want.

Scale is everything. When I had just four birds, the scraps and garden excess went lots further than they did after I had 32. And each bird in the smaller flock had better forage. By the time you get to 100 birds, you generally are selling eggs and buying some feed, even if you have a farm and grow your own grain. A hundred years ago, farmers with a flock of 100 layers usually fed them homegrown grain, oyster shell, and "beef scrap," along with lots of forage. It was the flock of a dozen or so birds (or fewer) on a huge place that could be maintained easily without buying anything (assuming the farm grew its own grain). Those with their own grain and 100 birds were generally selling eggs and buying beef scrap. These days, we use the high-protein poultry chow instead of the beef scrap. The rest of the pattern is equivalent.

The less-than-optimally-fed flock generally isn't nearly as productive as it could be. However, it may not need to be optimally productive to still be well worth having. And the forage situation is everything. Free-ranged on extensive good range, ducks can pick up all or much of their protein and all their vitamins and minerals except calcium, and may do pretty well with just grain (or other high-energy food) and oyster shell. For example, Holderread's book gives the following production levels for Khaki Campbells with various different forage and management regimes: Campbell ducks given grain and free-ranged on pasture and a pond gave 75–150 eggs per year. Ducks given 16 percent laying pellets and pasture gave 175–225 eggs per year. Ducks given 16 percent laying pellets and pasture, and also a controlled light regime of sixteen hours per day, gave 275–325 eggs per year. It is no surprise that full-fed ducks with controlled lighting lay so well. Notice, however, that the ducks fed just grain and with natural lighting still gave a useful amount of eggs. However, also notice that these birds had a great forage situation with both extensive pastures and a pond. Four birds in a backyard can have equally great forage, though, especially if you deliberately enhance and manage part of the area for forage.

Any time you are feeding poultry a restricted diet instead of free choice, make sure you have enough containers or trough space so that every bird is getting her share. And watch the smaller birds. If the smaller birds have poor, rough-looking feathers and the bigger birds have shiny feathers, it means the bigger birds are getting most of the food.

If you are going through hardships and must underfeed birds, give them most or all their feed in the evening so they don't have to go to bed hungry. Penned up at night, they are helpless to do anything about being hungry. If they are hungry during the day, they can run around and work harder at foraging (and look forward to coming home to a nice dinner).

I grow corn for people to eat but not enough to use as poultry food. I buy generic dent corn for poultry food. However, there are two crops that I've found I can substitute for the corn (or grain): winter squash and potatoes. Sweet potatoes or yams should also work and be equivalent in food value to the winter squash.

Feeding Poultry Potatoes

My duck flock, when given free-choice cooked potatoes, don't eat any corn and eat only half as much commercial chow. In other words, they get all the energy they need from potatoes, and much of their protein as well. On mild winter days when there are lots of big night crawlers about, the ducks pretty much eat only potatoes, or only potatoes with just a couple bites of chow per duck. So as long as the potatoes last, my feed bill is reduced by about two-thirds, even with the birds still getting free-choice chicken chow.

The potatoes need to be cooked. Poultry, being monogastric animals, cannot digest raw potatoes any better than people can. I dump potatoes into my biggest kettle until it is two-thirds full, then swish the potatoes around in several changes of water till they are mostly clean. I discard any potatoes with green coloring as well as any floaters. The floaters are certain small potatoes that actually began developing, then were robbed of their carbohydrates to support development of the other potatoes on the plant. (Potato plants don't necessarily finish all the potatoes they initiate.) Floaters, like green potatoes, can have high glycoalkaloid content. I salt the water, bring it to a boil, and cook the spuds until they are soft. The first time in the season that I feed potatoes, I coarsely slice the layer on top in the bucket. By the time the ducks get down to the bottom layer, they are digging right into the whole spuds. (Ducks have serrations on the edges of their bills that can act a bit like tiny teeth.) Ducks love the potatoes so much that they simply ignore the (feed-grade commercial) corn until the potatoes are all gone. For the amount of water and potatoes I cook at once, it takes the pot about thirty minutes to come to a boil, then another forty-five minutes to cook the spuds. However, I usually have my own dinner from the pot, too, so the time involved isn't too burdensome. We grow hundreds of pounds of prime potatoes, so end up with useful amounts of undersized or second-grade potatoes. These make great poultry food. We plan to expand our potato growing in the future so as to grow a few hundred extra pounds of potatoes just for the ducks.

My birds still get and eat commercial chow free choice with their spuds. However, if I had fewer birds or a bigger yard (that is, better forage), I think I could feed just potatoes (and oyster shell) during potato season if I had to.

Feeding Poultry Winter Squash

Cooked winter squash, according to my ducks, are a good source of energy but don't provide significant protein. That is, when given free-choice squash, in addition to their chow and corn, the birds quit eating corn but eat the same amount of chow. I cook the squash. This is necessary for ducks. I don't know whether it would be necessary for chickens. I suspect that chickens could eat the raw squash better than ducks but that the food value wouldn't be as high. But I'm guessing. There are two kinds of squash I use for duck food.

Delicatas are small squash that weight 2 pounds or less each. Each plant produces 3 to 5 prime fruits and additional smaller skinny (thin-fleshed) cull fruits. The culls keep just as well as the prime fruit. I knock the stems off a couple of prime squash for my own dinner and about 6 to 8 of the undersized culls, and stick them each with a fork to release steam as they cook. Then I put them in my biggest pot and cover them with water. I use a steamer basket upside down weighted down with a rock on top of the squash to hold the squash under water. I cook the squash until they're nice and soft, about forty-five minutes after they come to a boil. (I take my dinner out a little earlier.) The cooked squash are so soft they fall into pieces as I dip them out of the cooking water using a large slotted spoon. The ducks eat the squash, skins, seeds, and all.

The other squash we use a lot for poultry chow is the big Oregon Homestead line of 'Sweet Meat' squash (described in the squash chapter). Each plant produces about three or four prime squash and another smaller squash or two that isn't as prime and that often isn't fully ripe. These are obvious because they are a darker color. They still keep for months, however, and make good duck food. And even these smaller culls are about 14 to 20 pounds each. I halve a squash, remove the seeds, and bake the squash just as for prime squash. (The seeds are too big for the ducks to swallow.) In winter, the heat from the oven merely replaces some of the heat from the furnace and is not waste. The ducks usually eat the whole squash, including the skin.

Delicata squash lose their quality by about January, so we feed the smaller subprime delicatas to the ducks but don't grow extra delicatas for them. 'Sweet Meat–Oregon Homestead' squash, even the undersized or immature fruits, keep well all spring. The prime fruits increase in quality the entire time, but even the culls keep well and don't lose quality. With all other squash varieties I have tried, immature or undersized or late fruits don't keep more than a month or two. So 'SM' is the best squash to grow for duck food. Ducklings love 'SM' squash. My current batch of ducklings is being raised mostly on 'SM' squash, 'October Blue' potatoes, duck eggs, forage, and just a little commercial chow. (See note 9-14.)

Oyster Shell

If you don't feed the birds oyster shell, they won't lay much more than the dozen or two eggs wild birds lay. So it might be a good idea to stockpile oyster shell.

In addition, if our oyster shell supply were to become limited, obviously we would feed all the eggshells back to the birds so as to simply recycle the calcium as much as possible.

Forage Improvement

It is easier to provide our birds with enough energy than enough protein. We can provide the energy with grains we grow ourselves or buy or trade for locally, and/or with squash or potatoes. The key to the protein is the fauna in forage. I over-sow my yard with white clover, which ducks like better than grass. I also deliberately create areas that breed worms and other small, delicious critters.

My main tactic is to spread 6- to 12-inch-thick swaths of straw-poo from the duck pen under trees and in other spots that don't grow good pasture or lawn. These shallow beds grow night crawlers, manure worms, sow bugs, and slugs, all very useful to ducks. Ducks bill through the beds and extract the protein. (Chickens scratch in such piles to remove the goodies.) The more sow bugs and slugs and earthworms I grow, the less high-protein chow I have to buy.

Windfall and subprime fruit can provide a lot of the energy ration in season. Mulberries were often planted in poultry yards. They drop fruit over a long period, and poultry love them. Dave Holderread planted a number of trees and bushes as poultry forage some decades ago. He tells me that mulberries turned out to be the most useful perennial forage he knows of for ducks.

I grow extra tomatoes just for the ducks. Big tomatoes are fine. I don't know whether the tomatoes have much importance nutritionally to the ducks, but they love them above all other garden produce.

Other Possibilities

Do not feed raw legumes to poultry, not even peas. Cooked beans of various kinds can be workable but usually aren't practical except as kitchen scraps. (Too much labor and too little yield to grow for animal feed.) I would expect sweet potatoes or yams to work as well as winter squash as a replacement for the grain (energy) part of the diet. But the squash don't have to be dug. I haven't tried sunflower seeds, since I can't grow them very well. If you can, buy a bag, and ask your chickens or ducks what they think about them.

In the Depression era, roadkills were supposedly often used to feed poultry and hogs. In areas with plenty of game, the best parts can be eaten by people and the less prime parts given to poultry. Butchery wastes were also traditionally given to poultry. Many flocks have been fed primarily on things like restaurant garbage or stale bakery produce. (These days, it is illegal to feed garbage to hogs if you sell meat, unless the garbage is cooked. I suspect that if you want to sell eggs, the same laws apply. Because I sell eggs, I no longer feed even table scraps to my flock.)

From first principles, I would expect wheat to be a better grain to use than corn if you need to feed your birds just grain. Wheat has more protein and less energy than corn. So in theory, we would not need to provide quite as much protein to balance out the ration if the grain we used was wheat instead of corn. Do not feed confined birds just grain or squash or even potatoes. These are not sufficient unless the birds can pick up enough protein, vitamins, and minerals from having high-quality forage.

Ducks for Garden Pest Control

That ducks are supreme for garden pest control is widely recognized and mentioned in many books and articles. Exactly how to use the ducks and still have a garden left afterwards never quite seems to be mentioned. This section is a summary of my experience.

When it comes to greenery, ducks eat virtually everything people do, and more besides. So if you just turn a flock of ducks into a garden, you won't have a garden for very long. Even if they don't eat the tomato plants or squash leaves today, they will eat them tomorrow or the next day. They will eat the tomato plants long before they bear any toma-

> ## Ducks in Rivers and Lakes
>
> If your property has a river or lake, how do you get your ducks home at night? For an answer I asked Dave Holderread, the author of *Raising the Home Duck Flock*. He says you *can* have a flock of free-range ducks who have complete access to a lake or river and keep them coming home. But you need to use every possible trick. First, don't give the ducks free access initially. They must be penned in a more restricted area for a while so that they are used to coming home at night. Second, they should be fed only at night and kept a little hungry during the day. Finally, use a bell, whistle, or gong at chow/pen-up time. And of course, don't turn ducks loose into raging rivers with currents too fierce to swim against. Not all water is duck water.

toes. They think corn plants are just big succulent grass that should be inside of ducks. They eat any grape leaves lower than about three feet. (Laying ducks can jump.) They even eat all the tops off the onions and garlic. And you can just forget it with lettuce, cabbage, kale, sorrel, or any salad plants. The only greens people eat that ducks don't eat are the very hottest varieties of mustard.

Ducks don't scratch in gardens like chickens. However, they have wetter and more projectile poop, so anything within about 8 inches of the ground can get pooped upon. They can also tromp on small tender seedlings. Chickens both tromp on young seedlings and scratch them up. But neither ducks nor chickens do the seedlings a whole lot of good. So using ducks in a garden while crops are growing is never a matter of just letting the ducks have full access unsupervised. It's a matter of management and timing.

1. Ducks provide considerable slug protection for a garden when penned or allowed to forage near but not in it. Slugs like duck poop better than anything in the garden and will actively desert the garden and seek the duck poop—and get eaten by the ducks. Some people talk of putting a duck run all the way around a garden, but this isn't necessary. Just a duck area within about 20 feet of the garden is good enough. Putting the duck area right next to the garden is handiest, though, because you can then just toss the cull produce over the fence.

2. Ducks have dependable priorities when foraging that we can use for garden pest control. When first allowed or herded into a new area, ducks will run all over and eat all the most valuable, mobile, high-protein items first—slugs, worms, sow bugs, etc. Then, only after they have picked off all the pests, do the ducks go for the salad. So turn the ducks into the garden while you're working in it, and just keep an eye on them and herd them out as soon as anybody starts on the salad course.

3. Sometimes I have a row of tender small seedlings in the garden where I want to use the ducks. These need to be protected from getting tromped on. I use bamboo stakes to make a crude barrier on one side of the seedlings. A bamboo-stake barrier about 5 inches high on one side of the row is enough to encourage the ducks to walk around instead of across the row. And sections of barrier are easy to move to where they are needed.

4. I don't let ducks into areas of a garden that have low-growing greens in them that I plan to eat soon and raw.

5. Ducks or chickens can be used to clean up a garden after the crops have been harvested.

6. I use 2-foot-wide hardware cloth to separate ducks from gardens or sections of garden. I like the hardware cloth because it is stiff enough to need minimal support and because I can step over it. It's adequate to hold ducks as long as they aren't separated from buddies and aren't starving or thirsty. The common 2 × 4 inch fencing isn't ideal, because it's just the right size to catch the head of a duck. Likewise with 2-inch chicken wire. (The 1-inch chicken wire is OK.) Combo cattle-poultry panels are useful for many purposes. Ducks can reach about a foot through them.

7. In a yard, you can often just turn the ducks out to forage freely as long as you have a perimeter fence to keep out stray dogs and other daytime predators. (To fence either a garden or poultry area these days, I would go with electric poultry net, which keeps out raccoons and many predators that can climb ordinary fences. See *Day Range Poultry* by Andy Lee and Pat Foreman.) Many ornamental plantings make good ornamentals partly because they are unpalatable to most creatures.

8. If your yard, pasture, or orchard is large, you can use water and shade to encourage ducks to rotate their attention, spread out their manure, or direct pest control to certain areas. Ducks will hang around more near a water bucket or kiddy pool with bathing water.

9. Ducks need shade on sunny days. So if you don't have trees, you may need something to provide shade.

10. Ducks won't forage in high grass where they can't see predators.

11. Ducks will usually not forage very far from

hawk protection. That is, they are reluctant to move out into areas with no bushes, trees with low branches, or other objects that can be ducked under or around in the event of a hawk attack. I prop up a 4 × 8 foot piece or two of plywood about 2 feet off the ground in areas I want the ducks to use that have no natural protection.

Duck Egg Cookery

Most people don't know how to cook duck eggs. Even some duck raisers and authors of duck books speak of leathery or hard whites or fishy or off flavors, or of using duck eggs for baking only, or of mixing them with chicken eggs—all signs of improper feeding of laying ducks or of cooking the eggs wrong. To have great duck egg dishes we need to start with prime duck eggs, then respect their uniqueness. To get prime duck eggs we avoid feed that contains fish meal or forage areas where ducks eat too much fish. To respect the uniqueness of duck eggs, we cook duck eggs like duck eggs, not like chicken eggs. Properly cooked free-range duck eggs taste just like free-range chicken eggs, only more so. Duck eggs are a little richer and have a more intense flavor.

Duck eggs need to be cooked more gently than chicken eggs. Anything you can do with a chicken egg, you can do just as well with a duck egg once you modify the cooking methods appropriately. However, there are some things that you can do much better with duck eggs than chicken eggs. I think egg-drop soup was invented by people who had laying ducks, not chickens. Chicken eggs don't have enough flavor to taste like much when dripped into a simmering soup. Only duck eggs have enough flavor to make a great egg-vegetable

hash. And the extra richness and succulence of the duck egg makes it supreme for hard-cooked eggs served plain with just a little salt and pepper.

Correcting recipes for egg size. Unless stated otherwise, large chicken eggs are the standard in cooking. If you use an equal number of jumbo or super-jumbo eggs, you'll have way too much egg, too much protein, and too much fluid in the recipe. Generally, I go by volume of eggs instead of number. A large chicken egg is equivalent to about 0.2 cups by volume.

Baking. Use duck eggs just like chicken eggs.

Meringues. Duck egg whites or whole eggs beat up as nicely and equivalently to their chicken egg counterparts. Duck eggs make fine meringues, sponge cakes, and angel food cakes.

Fried eggs. Use a heavy pan not much bigger than the layer the eggs form when broken into it. I start the cooking on medium-high but turn the burner to medium-low right after the eggs go into the pan. Cover the pan and take it off the heat during the last part of the cooking. The white should be tender and succulent. If your fried egg has a dry or leathery white, you've overcooked it. (Try a lower temperature, a shorter cooking time, a smaller pan, or covering the pan or taking it off the heat for a greater part of the cooking.)

Scrambled duck eggs. I use a heavy pan, which is covered and off the heat for the last part of the cooking. I scramble the eggs, adding a little salt, cayenne pepper, and oregano. (You can add milk if you want. I don't.) I start the cooking on medium-high and stir the eggs with a spatula a few times initially until they start chunking up. When I have mostly big chunks of egg dispersed in some remaining liquidy egg, I turn the heat to medium-low, cover the pan, and cook 2–3 minutes—until the eggs are lightly brown on the bottom. Then

I use a spatula to turn the eggs over in spatula-sized sections, then cover the pan, remove it from the heat, and leave it for 3–5 minutes to finish cooking the other side of the eggs. I end up with sort of hamburger-patty-like slabs of eggs. These make great leftovers, hot or cold, and make good sandwiches or finger food. If you want the eggs classically looser, go a bit further with turning the eggs in the pan initially, until there is not enough excess liquid egg to form the slabs. Then turn the eggs and finish the cooking with the pan covered and off the heat.

Hard-cooked duck eggs. One of the most delicious things to do with a duck egg is to simply hard-cook it and eat it with a little salt and pepper. It took me more than a decade to learn how to do that—that is, to hard-cook a duck egg properly and actually separate it from the shell afterward. Duck eggs have thicker shells than chicken eggs, and the membrane in between the shell and the egg holds more firmly to both than does the membrane of chicken eggs. Most ways of shelling chicken eggs don't work for duck eggs.

Duck eggs should be at least three weeks old for hard-cooking. Younger eggs don't shell out easily, no matter how you do it. (Chicken eggs need to be at least a week old.)

Any hard-cooked duck or chicken egg that has a dark ring between the yolk and white is overcooked. The dark ring represents precipitated sulfury compounds that don't taste good. It takes much less cooking to overcook a duck egg than a chicken egg. To cook duck eggs gently enough, I bring the eggs just barely to a boil, then remove the pot from the heat and allow the rest of the cooking to take place off the heat. I use unsalted water. Eggs and water can either be at room temperature or straight from the refrigerator. I cover the pot with just an open vent or crack to release steam and turn the burner on high. I watch the pot as the water comes close to a boil and take the pot off the heat when one area of the water (but not all the water) produces big bubbles and a rolling boil. When I remove the pot from the heat I close the vent or crack so the pot is covered completely. I time the off-heat cooking and drain the water off or dip out the eggs at the right time.

You need a large enough volume of water for the cooking off the heat to work. I usually cook 22–26 eggs at once in my biggest pot, in 1½ gallons of water. For this volume of water, the right amount of time for the cooking off the heat is 16 minutes. If I want just a few eggs (1–8), I use a 2-quart pot with 1½ quarts of water. For this volume, the right amount of cooking time off the heat is 20 minutes. (For amounts in between, you can extrapolate.)

(If you live at high altitudes, you may need to modify the recipe to provide a little more heat, since water boils at a lower temperature at higher altitudes. You might need to bring the water to a full boil and even let it boil for a minute or so. Experiment. For reference, I live near sea level.)

In order to get the shells off the duck eggs, avoid ever dumping the hot cooked eggs in cold water (with or without swishing to break the eggs). That works with chicken eggs but makes it impossible to remove the shells from duck eggs. Instead, either shell the duck eggs hot or let them air-cool naturally, after which they can be refrigerated cooked and in the shell and will still shell out fine.

To shell a hot hard-cooked duck egg, I use a flow of cool (not cold) tap water to chill the egg just enough to handle. I use more cool water on my fingers than on the egg. I usually eat a couple of each batch of hard-cooked eggs hot. I let the rest continue to cool slowly to room temperature on a tray. Then I refrigerate them and peel them as needed.

Here are some of my favorite duck-egg recipes:

Sausage Duck Eggs Supreme

This is a variant of scrambled eggs. I use a pound of good locally grown pastured-pork sausage and 2 cups of duck eggs. This is enough to make a slab about ½ inch thick in my heavy 12-inch frying pan. A thickness of up to about ¾ inch is easy to cook properly and to shape so that it makes the nice burgerlike slabs I like.

First I fry up the sausage. Then I add the unseasoned scrambled duck eggs, deglaze the pan into the wet eggs, and proceed as for scrambled eggs, ending up with slabs, as previously described. These sausage-egg slabs are great either hot or cold.

Taco-Burger Duck Eggs Supreme

Make just like Sausage Duck Eggs Supreme, except use a pound of grass-fed hamburger instead of the sausage. Work a tablespoon each of chili powder and cumin and a little salt and pepper into the meat before cooking.

Lamb-Burger Duck Eggs Supreme

Make just like Taco-Burger Duck Eggs Supreme, but use grass-fed ground lamb, and as seasonings to work into the meat, use a tablespoon each of cumin, curry powder, chili powder, and a little salt, pepper, and cinnamon. (This "Moroccan" spice combination goes well with all lamb dishes.)

Curried Lamb-Burger Duck Eggs Supreme

Season the meat with 2 tablespoons curry powder, salt, and pepper and proceed as for the other "Supremes."

Zapped Egg and Rice (Potato, Polenta) Bowl

Put 1–2 cups of cooked potatoes, polenta, grits, rice, or any other cooked grain in a bowl, cover it, and zap it in the microwave long enough to get it thoroughly hot. Then make a little pocket in the rice and break in the duck egg. (I use a fork to break up the yolk a little.) Sprinkle some pepper on everything, recover, and zap the bowl for two minutes or so, just enough to cook the egg. Then run a fork through the egg to separate the egg into chunks and mix everything together. Add salt or wheat-free tamari sauce, butter, or other oil, and sometimes a few drops of toasted sesame oil, to taste. Sometimes I add a little gourmet light vinegar or lemon juice.

If I want to serve a number of people, I put a suitable amount of cooked potatoes or grain in an 8-inch Pyrex bowl, cover it with a lid, and zap it long enough to heat it. Then I make several depressions in the heated carbs around the edge of the bowl, and proceed as before, cooking just long enough to cook the eggs.

Duck Egg Hash

This is basically just stir-fried vegetables, with or without meat, scrambled with duck eggs. If there is meat, stir-fry and brown it first. Then add a little water to deglaze the pan and stir-fry the vegetables. With ground meat, I work seasonings into the meat and also add some to the longest-cooking vegetables. After the vegetables are cooked, I add back the meat, add the scrambled eggs, and proceed as for scrambled eggs, except I stir the cooking eggs so as to end up with loose vegetables and browned meat chunks all lightly coated with cooked egg, not slabs. I sometimes add a little ketchup to the cooked hash. Sometimes my hash is taco-flavored, or Moroccan-spiced, or curry-flavored, using seasonings as described with various versions of "Duck Eggs Supreme."

Egg-Drop Soup

Egg-drop soup is one of the joys of having duck eggs. You can turn even a can of commercial soup into something really special with a duck egg or two. Heat up the soup. Then stir the liquid so it is swirling and gently drip in the egg(s). Drip the white of each egg in first, then the yolk, stirring so as to get attractive separate white and gold strings in the soup. The egg cooks within about thirty seconds in the hot soup. I add the egg just before I'm ready to serve the soup. For a big bowl of soup for one person, one egg is all you need. (If you turn the whole soup into a soup-flavored custard you've added too many eggs.)

Egg Bits

I scramble two jumbo or super-jumbo eggs in a small bowl, cover with a paper plate, and zap in the microwave for two minutes.

The egg puffs up into a uniform foam that cooks into a solid spongelike disk. Remove the disk from the bowl promptly to prevent overcooking and slice it into bits. I use these bits in soups, salads, and stews. Sometimes I add ¼ teaspoon of tamari sauce first to get a kind of protein-bit flavor. The texture of the cooked foam and the fact that it cooks perfectly without overcooking depends upon the small volume. Scaling up doesn't work. The egg bits have a bland, neutral taste, and don't particularly taste like eggs. So I use them for adding nutrition to dishes where I don't want the flavor of eggs.

Duck Egg Herring Paté

Duck-egg herring paté is delicious as a spread for crackers, in sandwiches, or as a main course. I use a little 3½-ounce can of Brunswick kippered seafood snacks (salted herring) with the juice, one hard-cooked duck egg, and a touch of some alliums (finely diced garlic, scallions, shallots, or onions). I mash the eggs and herring with a fork, mix them together, and add the alliums to taste.

Duck-Egg-Yolk Salad Dressing and Sauces

The yolk of a properly hard-cooked duck egg is so rich and tender that it disperses readily in fluid and can be used as the basis for delicious salad dressings or dipping sauces. The yolk replaces any oil that you would otherwise have used in the dressing or sauce. I strip off the white and mash the yolk of the hard-cooked egg with a fork. Running a fork over the egg yolk once gives a series of thin slices. Then I use a spoon to mash and disperse the yolk slices into a little water and add the paste to the rest of the ingredients. Use the dressing the same day you make it. (Once you have completely dispersed a duck-egg yolk like this and exposed it so thoroughly to air, the omega-3 fatty acids oxidize rapidly.) Here are a couple of examples of dressings or sauces:

Duck-Egg-Yolk Russian Dressing

Fork-mash the duck egg yolk and disperse it into a smooth paste with water. Mix in Heinz ketchup, balsamic vinegar, a little sugar, pepper, and Italian seasonings (or oregano). Then add a bit more water to get the desired consistency.

Duck-Egg-Yolk Steak Dipping Sauce

Just mash a yolk from a hard-cooked duck egg into a little water to make a paste, then add your favorite steak sauce. I use, for example, about half Heinz 57 sauce and half Texas Original BBQ sauce. The one egg yolk gets mashed into about three times its volume of sauce. Then I slice the steak into portions and add all the hot juice that flows out into the sauce as well.

CHAPTER TEN

Squash and Pumpkins

Why You Can't Buy a Prime Winter Squash. Three Squash Species, Three Curing and Use Patterns. Seven Superb, Gourmet-Quality, Long-Keeping Winter Squash Varieties. Fall Squash—Delicious Delicatas and 'Small Sugar'. Summer Squash. Following in Buffalo Bird Woman's Footsteps—Adventures with Drying Squash. A Modern Squash-Drying Rack. Growing Squash and Pumpkins. Harvesting, Storing, and Curing. The Perfect Pumpkin Pie. Hoarding Seeds of Squash and Pumpkins. Saving Seeds of Squash and Pumpkins.

Why You Can't Buy a Prime Winter Squash

Bad squash, like bad coins, tend to drive out the good. Wherever bad coins circulate, people keep back the good ones and spend the bad. Soon only bad coins are circulating. The grower who picks squash too early is the first to market. He beats out those who grow their squash to full maturity by weeks. Customers see those first displays of squashly beauty in the fall and celebrate the season by buying one. Then they try to eat it. Then they remember why they don't usually buy squash. So year after year, the customer is discouraged from buying squash, and year after year, the fact that squash can be a spectacular, gourmet-quality food remains largely a secret.

Squash in the supermarkets and even those in the farmer's markets are often not of the best varieties. However, even the good early varieties are picked immature. Then they are sold uncured. *Cucurbita maxima* (the most common "winter squash") varieties should have a full month of curing before going to market. Farmers are not set up to do that, and customers don't know that they should, and it isn't worth the effort anyway if the squash isn't full grown. If we want prime winter squash, we must select premier gourmet varieties, then grow and cure them ourselves.

Three Squash Species, Three Curing and Use Patterns

There are three major squash species grown and used in the United States and Canada: *Cucurbita maxima*, *C. pepo*, and *C. moschata*. (A fourth, *Cucurbita mixta*, isn't widely grown, as it requires too much heat for most people in the United States to grow and has poor flesh. In Mexico, however, there are many mixta varieties, which are grown primarily for their edible seeds. I won't cover *C. mixta* in this chapter.)

Squash varieties of the *Cucurbita maxima* species need a full month of storage indoors to cure into prime quality. Many max varieties will keep several months. Some varieties actually become sweeter and develop more intense flavors for six months or more of storage. 'Sweet Meat— Oregon Homestead' is actually sweeter and more flavorful at six months than when harvested and is still only getting better. Some varieties, such as 'Sweet Meat–Oregon Homestead' and 'Blue Hubbard', are very large and are especially nice for those who want to use prime winter squash as a major part of the homestead food supply. There are also prime smaller varieties such as 'Buttercup', for those who just want a meal at a time for a person or two. The better-keeping max varieties can provide prime squash through March and even beyond. The very largest varieties of orange pumpkins, which are not culinary quality, are also maxes.

Cucurbita maxima varieties include 'All Gold', 'Amish Pie Pumpkin', 'Atlantic Giant', 'Autumn Pride', 'Banana' (all), 'Big Max', 'Big Moon', 'Black Forest', 'Blue Ballet', 'Buttercup' (all), 'Flat White Boer', 'Gold Nugget', 'Hokkaido' (all), 'Hubbard' (all), 'Jarrahdale', 'Kindred', 'Kuri' (all), 'Marina di Chioggia', 'Mooregold', 'Queensland Blue', 'Rouge Vif d'Etampes' (a.k.a. Cinderella), 'Sibley', and 'Turban' (all).

The species *Cucurbita pepo* includes nearly all our summer squash as well as most of the small and medium-sized Halloween pumpkins that are not culinary quality, many ornamental pumpkins, naked-seeded pumpkins, and many gourds. It also includes a few winter squash varieties of prime eating quality such as the delicatas and the classic 'Small Sugar Pie' (a.k.a. 'New England Pie Pumpkin'). All the pepos of prime culinary quality are small.

The pepos require only about seven to fourteen days of curing. So we can eat the little prime pepos while we are waiting for our maxes to cure. Ideally, we eat up the pepos before the end of December. Even those that are among the better keepers are not prime beyond that time. The pepos are prime right after the curing period

and deteriorate from there, with the flesh getting stringier, and the sugar and flavor going downhill. The better-storing pepos such as the delicatas are prime for two months only, and good for no more than three. The prime pepos such as delicatas and 'Small Sugar' have flavors that are distinct enough from those of the maxes so as to constitute an entirely different vegetable.

Cucurbita pepo varieties include 'Acorn' (all), 'Baby Bear', 'Baby Boo', 'Baby Pam', 'Cocozelle' (all), 'Connecticut Field', 'Crookneck' (all), 'Delicata' (all delicatas, including 'Cornell Bush', 'Delicata JSS', 'Honeyboat', 'Sugar Loaf', 'Sweet Dumpling', and 'Zeppelin'), 'Half Moon', 'Jack Be Little', 'Lady Godiva', 'Lebanese', 'Long Pie', 'New England Pie', 'Omaha', 'Ronde de Nice', 'Scallop' (all varieties), 'Small Sugar', 'Snack R Jack', 'Spaghetti' (all), 'Straightneck' (all), 'Styrian', 'Vegetable Marrow' (all), 'Winter Luxury Pie', 'Zapallito del Tronco', 'Zucchini' (all), as well as various ornamental gourds (many, but not all, varieties).

Cucurbita moschata includes the butternut and "cheese" pumpkins such as 'Waltham Butternut' and 'Long Island Cheese'. They generally prefer warmer growing conditions than pepos or maxes. Grown here in the maritime Northwest or, apparently, in New England, they don't make fruit that are up to the quality of the best maxes or pepos. Some, such as 'Tahitian Melon Squash', can be superb, grown in warmer places with much more heat and a longer season than we have in Oregon. (I tasted one that was greenhouse-grown.) The moschatas require seven to fourteen days of curing. Some moschata varieties keep even longer than the maxes. Some moschatas are also highly resistant to disease and to vine borers, so they are especially useful in southern growing regions.

Butternuts have a smooth skin that is easier to chop off than the skin of the maxes or pepos. So they are often used when one wants raw, de-skinned squash pieces to sauté or use in soups. It is still a pain to chop the skin off, only less of a pain than with pepos or maxes. In addition, when you boil or steam cut squash pieces they become very bland-flavored. When I want squash in a soup, I instead use mashed baked squash of pepo or max varieties.

I won't talk further about the moschatas in this chapter. Oregon is just not moschata country. However, if you live in the South, you should check your local seed-company catalogs for good moschata varieties and include them in your repertoire. Amy Goldman's book *The Compleat Squash* is an excellent resource for investigating the culinary quality of virtually any variety of squash you might be thinking about, including the moschatas and mixtas.

Cucurbita moschata varieties include 'Butternut' (all), 'Cheese' (all), 'Chirimen', African 'Choctaw', 'Courge Longue de Nice', 'Fairytale', 'Futtsu' (all), 'Golden Cushaw', 'Kentucky Field', 'Kikuza', 'Musque de Provence', 'Orange Cushaw', 'Orange Striped Cushaw', 'Ponca', 'Seminole', 'Tahitian Melon Squash', and 'Tromboncino (a.k.a. 'Zucchetta Rampicante'). The 'Tromboncino' is, unlike the moschatas, usually used as a summer squash.

Each of the three squash species has distinctive seeds, leaf types, stems, and stem attachments to fruits that make the three species easy to identify once you have seen a few varieties of each. *Seed to Seed* by Suzanne Ashworth has a much more complete list of the varieties included within each species (and includes *Cucurbita mixta* varieties as well).

Seven Superb, Gourmet-Quality, Long-Keeping Winter Squash Varieties

Big, long-storing max squash are ideal for the primary homestead squash food supply. It is much easier to harvest, or open and clean one 20-pound squash than twenty 1-pound squashes. In addition, the small squash are mostly skin and seeds. The bigger squash has a much higher proportion of flesh. For the main food supply, I prefer a squash as big as possible, up to about 22 pounds, which is the largest size I can bake in the oven. Baked mashed squash freezes well, so having a small family is no reason to forgo growing the big squash that do the most efficient job of providing us with serious amounts of food.

'Sweet Meat–Oregon Homestead'
Nate and I grow 'Sweet Meat–Oregon Homestead' as our major winter squash. This is a 16 to 24 pound slate-blue-gray, disk-shaped squash with very sweet, rich-flavored flesh that is unsurpassed in quality. The flesh is up to 3½ inches thick. The seed cavity is tiny. Given the size of fruit and thickness and dryness of the meat, this squash is by far the best one for producing serious amounts of truly gourmet-quality food with minimal labor. (A 'Sweet Meat–Oregon Homestead' will give you about three times as much food as a 'Blue Hubbard' of equal size.) The baked squash freezes well. I ordinarily bake a squash, eat a meal of it, make a couple of pies from it, then freeze the rest. The next time I want squash, I open another and repeat. By late spring, I've processed all the squash and have a year's supply frozen. Baked mashed 'Sweet Meat' squash is the main vegetable I freeze.

'Sweet Meat' squash is an Oregon heirloom with huge seeds and a capability of germinating in cold mud and growing vigorously in cool weather. The plants have big vines that run 20 feet in all directions. However, the commercial 'Sweet Meat' has deteriorated and no longer has thick flesh, big seeds, or an ability to excel in typical Oregon spring weather. I searched for years to find a line that was still not too badly deteriorated, then reselected it for the original virtues. The results, after a few years and more than a ton of squash, is 'Sweet Meat–Oregon Homestead' (see note 10-2).

With all other varieties of squash I have grown, the immature or undersized late fruits on the vine don't keep well. However, even the immature and subprime fruits of 'Sweet Meat' keep well. They don't continue to sweeten as prime fruits do. But they don't deteriorate either. When properly harvested and stored, nearly every 'Sweet Meat' will keep without losing quality until the following summer or even longer. The fact that even the culls of 'Sweet Meat' keep well matters. Those culls are one of the major foods for my duck flock in winter and spring.

Using 'Sweet Meet'. Eat no 'Sweet Meat' before its time. I follow the old Oregon tradition, and open the first of the 'Sweet Meats' for Thanksgiving. I open the squash with a big bowie knife and a rubber mallet so as to get exact halves. Many people open them with a hatchet. (The thick, leathery skin plus thick flesh are a bit much for an ordinary kitchen knife.)

One traditional way of fixing 'Sweet Meat' is to cut it into 3-inch squares—which are 2 to 3½ inches deep, depending upon just where they were on the fruit—then bake the squares, flesh side up. Prepared this way, the outside of the flesh dries and caramelizes and is like candy, with an inner core of soft, sweet squash. Such chunks of 'Sweet

Meat' are often taken to potlucks and served, hot or cold, as finger food.

My usual approach, however, is to bake a 'Sweet Meat' by cutting it in half, removing the seeds, and placing the two halves cut side down on a baking sheet and baking at 350°F until the squash is soft all the way through. (I use a rack position midway in the oven.) I don't scrape or clean the fruit's inside surface before cooking; I just remove the seeds. The coarser flesh near the seed cavity helps protect the rest from drying out and is easier to remove when cooked. The squash partly bakes and partly steams. The halves generally take 1½ to 2½ hours. After the squash is soft all the way through when poked with a fork, I remove the baking sheet with the squash, chop off what is wanted for the immediate meal, and set the rest aside to cool.

I usually mash 'Sweet Meat' with a little salt and butter, though it also tastes great just plain. Adding sugar is overkill and would make the squash overly sweet. In fact, sometimes I take

Boiling or Steaming Cut Squash

Don't. Boiling or steaming cut squash or squash chunks is how to turn a delicious, gourmet-quality, perfectly cured, prime winter squash into watery pulp little better than commercial canned pumpkin. If you're going to go to the trouble of growing good winter squash, go to the trouble to prepare it properly—that is, by baking or, in the case of smaller squashes, by pricking them and boiling them whole. Smaller squash or pumpkins can also be pricked and baked whole.

the opposite approach and make Lemony 'Sweet Meat' or Limey 'Sweet Meat', in which I add butter, salt, and a little fresh-squeezed lemon or lime juice for a delightful sweet-and-sour effect. Sometimes I use a pint of frozen 'Sweet Meat' as the basis for a sweet-and-sour stir-fry or a hot-and-sweet-and-sour soup. This variety is also the squash I usually use for pies.

'Sunshine F_1'

I usually don't grow hybrid varieties, as they aren't compatible with my desire to save my own seeds. In addition, the best hybrid squash generally don't have the flavor and quality of the best open-pollinated lines. 'Sunshine F_1', a brilliant red, disc-shaped squash bred by Rob Johnston of Johnny's Selected Seeds, is an exception. It weighs about 3 to 5 pounds and is a little moister than 'Sweet Meat'. The flesh is just as fine-textured, however, and almost as sweet. The flavor is somewhat different but equally delicious. 'Sunshine' is the only red squash I've ever had that is top-quality. ('Rouge Vif d'Etampes', for example, is equally scarlet but is coarse in texture, watery, and lacking in flavor. 'Delicious' isn't especially delicious; neither is 'Boston Marrow'.) The flesh thickness of 'Sunshine' is comparable to the better squash of its size. 'Sunshines' keep until January when harvested and cured as I describe, only improving in quality the entire time. (They deteriorate rapidly thereafter.) 'Sunshine' fruits have a medium-thick leathery skin that is easy to cut open without resorting to heroic tactics. The plant is early and is a vigorous half-bush type. It can produce prime squash here in Oregon even in cool summers or on limited water.

We like the max part of our squash patch to have plenty of 'Sunshines' as well as 'Sweet Meats'. The

'Sweet Meat' is a full-season squash that produces the most food the most efficiently in most years. But sometimes circumstances don't cooperate, and we don't really have a full season. In those years, the 'Sweet Meats' may not fully mature. 'Sunshine' gives us those spectacular flashes of red in the pumpkin patch at harvest each year, but is also what we depend upon to produce gourmet-quality squash even from a late planting or when the season is truncated or things go wrong. 'Sweet Meat' makes superb squash only when it's well grown. 'Sunshine', on the other hand, seems to make superb squash even when poorly grown.

One year Nate grew a dryland garden here in maritime Oregon, where it doesn't rain all summer. He bucket-irrigated each squash plant twice—that is, gave each plant two buckets of water twice during the season, for a total of 20 gallons per plant. The buckets were 5-gallon buckets with small pinholes in them that fed the water out slowly. Most squash plants of most varieties were so stunted using this growing system that they produced nothing. The 'Sweet Meat' and the 'Sunshine', however, both produced decent amounts of good-looking fruits, in spite of the water limitation. The 'Sweet Meat' fruits, though, were subprime and inferior. We fed them all to the ducks and Nate's cow and pig. The 'Sunshines' were prime. The other winter squash that produced prime fruit under these conditions was 'Katy Stokes' Sugar Meat'. ('Sweet Meat'–finished pork, by the way, is spectacularly delicious. The meat is actually sweet, and the distinctive flavor and aroma of the squash is unmistakable.)

In 2009, when Nate and I got such a late start on our newly leased land, we planted fewer 'Sweet Meats' and more 'Sunshines'. We weren't sure we would have enough time for the 'Sweet Meats' to fully mature. That proved to be a good choice. On top of the late start, we had a cool summer. The 'Sweet Meats' that year were good compared with most squash but not nearly what they can be—not prime. The 'Sunshines', though, were as spectacular as ever.

'Katy Stokes' Sugar Meat'

Oregonian Katy Stokes maintained her own line of 'Sweet Meat', and each year as she ate the squash, she saved seed from the very sweetest fruit. I believe 'Katy Stokes' Sugar Meat' represents a cross between 'Sweet Meat' and a smaller blue squash, which Katy Stokes then stabilized. 'Sugar Meat' plants are vigorous vines. The fruits are less than half the size of 'Sweet Meat', running 5–12 pounds. The flesh is as thick as other varieties its size and is, if anything, sweeter even than 'Sweet Meat'. The flavor of 'Sugar Meat' is excellent, much better than that of most squash, and right up there in that elite league with 'Sweet Meat', 'Buttercup', and 'Sunshine'. I prefer the more multidimensional flavor of well-grown 'Sweet Meat', as well as its size and thickness of flesh— in a good year. However, 'Sugar Meat' squash are *considerably* better than 'Sweet Meat' in a bad year. In the year of Nate's dryland garden experiment, with the squash limited to 20 gallons of water per plant for the season, 'Katy Stokes' Sugar Meat' (along with 'Sunshine') produced prime food, while the 'Sweet Meats' were used only for savory dishes and duck food.

'Katy Stokes' Sugar Meat' was initially introduced by Nichols Garden Nursery under the name 'Katy's Sweet Sweet Meat'. It is becoming popular in markets around here as 'Sweet Meat', which causes confusion. (Modifiers tend to get lost in marketing.) Nichols, with Katy's concurrence, has subsequently changed the name to 'Katy Stokes' Sugar Meat'. 'Katy Stokes' Sugar Meat' is a completely new, unique variety, with a different size and flavor from 'Sweet Meat', and with its own special virtues. Market growers as well as gardeners should take note.

'Buttercup–Burgess'

This squash is an all-time classic heirloom squash. It is a blocky, dark green squash of 3 to 5 pounds with a button at the end. 'Buttercup' is a vigorous, productive vine. It's generally better quality than most of the variant Buttercup varieties that have been bred and introduced since.

Hubbards

There are many Hubbard varieties that are especially popular in New England, with 'Blue Hubbard' the one most mentioned with respect to quality. The name 'Hubbard' seems to represent a shape—fat in the middle and pointy at the two ends—more than a genetic ancestry. Traditional Hubbard varieties were big squash, with some varieties going to 50 pounds or more. The classic 'Blue Hubbard' has flesh about 1 to 1½ inches thick and a rich, distinctive flavor. There are now also many smaller Hubbard varieties.

In my Oregon garden, 'Sweet Meat–Oregon Homestead' far outperforms any of a half dozen Hubbard varieties I have tried, for quantity of flesh per weight of fruit, sweetness, flavor, fine-grained texture, and keeping ability. I also prefer the thick, leathery skin of the 'Sweet Meat' to the hard shell of the Hubbard. The 'Sweet Meat' skin is thick enough to give good protection to the fruit but can still be eaten by livestock such as pigs and milk cows. My ducks clean up all the bits of cooked 'Sweet Meat' skin with its bits of squash clinging. They can't make as good use of squash with a hard shell. The hard-shelled Hubbards have some advantages, however. Sometimes a deer gets in the field near the end of the season and takes bites out of some of the 'Sweet Meats'. The bites usually heal, but mold often starts there, so the bitten fruits need to be eaten within two months. Deer don't seem to bother the Hubbards. Sometimes a gopher or other rodent burrows into a 'Sweet Meat' from below, leaving not much more than an empty skin to harvest. I have never had that problem with a Hubbard.

To open a hard-shelled squash such as the Hubbards, I don't cut them. I take them outside and drop them on the driveway from about waist height. Usually they break cleanly into two halves, lightly held together by flesh and pulp. If the squash doesn't break, drop it from higher up. I bake and use Hubbards just like 'Sweet Meats', except they bake faster because the flesh is thinner.

Hubbards may be slate blue, deep green, orange, and even black, which can help round out the color palette in the squash display.

'Sibley' is a slate-blue, banana-shaped or tear drop-shaped squash of up to about 30 pounds. It has a leathery skin. The flavor of 'Sibley' is delicious and is distinctively different from that of 'Sweet Meat', 'Sunshine', the Hubbards, and most other squash. The plants are vines.

'Flat White Boer' is a very flattened, big, disk-shaped squash of up to 30 pounds that grows on a viney plant. It has fine-grained yellow flesh of excellent texture and flavor, and the flavor is distinctively different from all the squash already mentioned. The flesh is also moister than those already mentioned and is very thick, about 3 inches or more; the seed cavity is tiny. I know of

no other white squash or pumpkin that is worth growing if you actually want to eat it. 'Thelma Sanders Sweet Potato' and 'Cream of the Crop' are white acorns (pepos) that are fine-grained and have thick flesh for the size of the fruit, but they have very little flavor. The white pumpkin 'Lumina' has thin, coarse, awful-tasting flesh. 'Manteca White' (a max) is coarse in texture with less flavor and sugar than the squash that make my seven-squash short list.

(The 'Guatemalan Blue Banana', a hard-shelled banana squash with pointed ends that I once loved, doesn't appear to exist anymore. Nothing now being sold or distributed by that name resembles what I once grew. Only the name has been preserved, not the variety. Alas, that I did not hoard or save the seeds when I had the chance.)

Fall Squash—Delicious Delicatas and 'Small Sugar'

When it comes to *C. pepo* species, acorn varieties have to be mentioned because they are so popular in markets. None of them, though, approach the quality of the delicatas. Most people who like acorns put lots of sugar or syrup on them. If you are one of those people, try some delicatas, or any of the seven max squash in the preceding section and skip the artificial sweeteners.

Delicatas. The sweetest and most spectacularly flavorful pepo squash are the delicata varieties. They are small squash, ranging from about ½ to 2 pounds. My favorites are the tan delicata varieties 'Sugar Loaf–Hessel' and 'Honeyboat' (see note 10-3). These are the sweetest and have the richest and most complex flavor as well as the driest flesh. Other good delicata varieties include 'Delicata

JSS', 'Zeppelin Delicata', 'Cornell Bush Delicata', and 'Sweet Dumpling'. The 'Sweet Dumpling' is dumpling-shaped; the rest are shaped like short, fat zucchinis. 'Sugar Loaf–Hessel' and some 'Cornell Bush' plants give shorter, fatter fruits than the others.

Except for 'Cornell Bush', a PVP (plant variety protected, that is, a proprietary variety), the delicata varieties all have a vining growth habit. 'Cornell Bush' is said to be resistant to powdery mildew, but that resistance amounts to only about one week in our fields. Disease resistance is usually to particular disease lines, and which line is usually present can vary by region. So the powdery-mildew resistance of 'Cornell Bush' may matter more elsewhere. I've found the 'Cornell Bush' as commercially available now to be somewhat variable in quality and not quite as good as it was immediately after its release a few years ago. (The fact that 'Cornell Bush' is a PVP is usually not listed in seed catalogs. I consider this situation inappropriate. I think when we buy seed, we have a right to assume we are buying full rights to it unless told otherwise.)

Delicatas can be baked, and taste spectacular baked if you get one with thick enough flesh and can bake it without scorching it. I bake only the biggest of the delicatas. I halve them lengthwise, remove the seeds, and bake them cut side down, as described for 'Sweet Meat'.

My usual way to fix delicatas, however, is to prick each whole fruit to release steam, put them in a pot of water, hold them submerged with an upside-down steamer basket weighted down with a rock, and boil them until they are soft. This method works as well for thinner-fleshed fruits as for perfect ones. In addition, it cuts the prep

Microwaving Squash

Small squash such as delicatas can be halved, turned face down, and cooked in a microwave oven. But it doesn't save any time. The squash cooks to soft in ten to fifteen minutes. However, they don't taste like much. The prime flavor develops only after the cooked squash have sat at least an additional half hour, at which point the squash must be reheated.

time to almost nothing, since it is so much easier to cut open and remove the seeds from a cooked delicata.

I normally dress a delicata only with butter and salt. Occasionally, I make Lemon Squash by dressing with butter, salt, and lemon juice.

The other particularly noteworthy *C. pepo* squash I like is 'New England Pie', a.k.a. 'Small Sugar Pie'. This little orange pumpkin is only about 4 to 6 pounds at best (with many fruits being smaller). The vine doesn't grow all that vigorously, and the fruit matures and turns orange only late in the season, and only if encouraged. "Come along there, li'l pun'kin babies, you can do it, you can do it, I know you can." That is what I tend to say when I'm not at all sure they can. But they do. Takes 'em the full season, though.

'Small Sugar' is not sweet by squash standards. It's only sweet compared to other pumpkins, that is, ornamental or livestock-feed pumpkins. 'Small Sugar' has a fine texture. But again, only by pumpkin standards. Its texture is not fine compared with the *C. maxima* squash I featured, or the delicatas. However, 'Small Sugar' has a unique flavor. The flavor is totally different from that of all other squash or pumpkins and is wonderful in pies. That distinctive flavor and the fact that 'Small Sugar' is not so sweet means that 'Small Sugar' is a better general-purpose culinary vegetable than the sweeter squashes.

Baked mashed flesh of 'Small Sugar' is my favorite fall squash or pumpkin for soups and stews. I also love to season the mashed flesh with butter, salt, and cumin and serve it mashed-potato style, with meat and gravy layered on top. Or I put down a layer of the squash in a Pyrex pie plate, then a layer of cheese, then bake the dish long enough to melt the cheese. Another of my favorites is a layer of squash with chili on top. All these dishes work because 'Small Sugar' has a distinctive great flavor but is not very sweet.

The last three years that I have tried to grow 'Small Sugar', seed from three different sources proved to be either crossed up or didn't have the characteristic flavor of 'Small Sugar'. Some were sweet, a step in the wrong direction for my purposes. So I think the commercial trade is in the process of losing or destroying the variety. I'm hopeful that the variety isn't lost yet, however, and intend to try again next year with seed from companies who have been doing their own seed production of the variety.

Under my conditions, 'Small Sugar' requires two weeks of curing, then is really prime for about six weeks only. After that the characteristic 'Small Sugar' flavor disappears pretty rapidly and has pretty well vanished by week thirteen. Also by then the flesh is getting stringy, and some of the flesh thickness is lost as the flesh near the seed cavity turns into strings. When people say 'Small Sugar' keeps three months, they are talking about how long it lasts without molding or rotting. But if you want prime flavor, cure the Small Sugars over two weeks, then use them within the next six weeks. Trust me.

'Winter Luxury Pie' and 'Long Pie' (a.k.a. 'Nantucket Pie') are widely praised as pie pumpkins by other knowledgeable growers. These are fine-grained in texture, and productive when grown here, but have very little flavor. It may be a matter of climate.

Summer Squash

Summer squash are squash that are harvested immature and used in the stage in which they are still young and tender. Examples are various zucchini varieties, pattypan varieties, and crooknecks and straightnecks. Summer squash are most commonly sliced and sautéed or added to stir-fries. Bigger ones that are still tender are sometimes halved, stuffed, and baked. Some people like their zucchini to be "mild," that is, essentially tasteless. For many years, I didn't grow summer squash, because tasteless food doesn't thrill me. However, there are varieties of summer squash that are delicious.

My favorite commercially available summer squash is 'Costata Romanesca'. It's a pale green zucchini-shaped squash with ribs that can grow up to 4 feet long. This variety has a nice flavor, a texture that remains firm even after stir-frying, and it is good even when picked at the size of a pound or two. (Many summer squash varieties have to be picked at a size of just a couple of ounces to have much taste, which involves lots of picking per amount of food. Not my thing.) I also like 'Golden Bush' and 'Gold Rush F_1'. So far I haven't found a green zucchini with enough flavor to be worth growing. (I know one exists, because

I bought it in a store once. But I don't know the variety. I know many green zucchini varieties it isn't, alas.) The heirloom 'Early Crookneck' has a powerful flavor, but one I don't happen to like. But many people love it. 'Zephyr F₁' has a delicious flavor as well as a firm, crisp texture. So if you, too, have been unthrilled by the ordinary green zucchinis, give some of these other summer squash varieties a try.

Summer squash are usually bush plants. It is much easier to pick bush squash plants than vines. As with green beans, to keep the plants productive, you must keep them picked.

In Nate's dryland garden experiment, 'Costata Romanesca' and 'Early Crookneck' did better with minimal water than other summer squash.

Immature squash of winter squash varieties can be picked when young and tender and used as summer squash. However, most big, viney winter squash varieties don't flower and refruit very prolifically, so they are not nearly as productive when used as summer squash as the varieties we usually grow for that purpose. In addition, to get optimum yield and quality in winter squash, we usually want to allow the plants to put all their resources into developing their prime, sweet mature fruits.

Following in Buffalo Bird Woman's Footsteps— Adventures with Drying Squash

For Buffalo Bird Woman, the Hidatsa Indian featured in *Buffalo Bird Woman's Garden*, it was dry slices of immature squash that were the main squash staple, not fully mature squash. I love growing squash. And Buffalo Bird Woman had a production system for dried squash that looked very efficient as well as fun. So I studied the text and pictures in the book for hours.

Buffalo Bird Woman and other Hidatsa and Mandan Indian women harvested their squash when they were about fist-sized. (We don't know what varieties they were using. Their squash varied in color and shape, and they may not have been pure varieties.) At this stage, the squash skin was still tender and the seeds immature enough to be palatable. That is, the squash were being harvested at the summer squash stage. It was slices of summer squash, including the seed cavities and immature seeds, that were dried.

The picked squash were cut into slices about ⅜-inch thick. The ends were set aside. The rest of the slices were skewered onto sharpened willow sticks through the soft pulp in the middle of the seed cavities, and the slices were then separated along the stick to allow airflow between them. Each stick with its squash was then placed on a raised drying rack in the sun. The squash took several days to dry completely. If rain threatened, the entire frame with all the sticks of squash was covered with hides.

After the squash was dried, a second, thinner willow stick with a piece of string attached was threaded through the holes of the squash on each stick. (This is while the slices were still on the first stick. The holes around the stick expand as the squash dries.) Then the squash was efficiently transferred from the stick to the needle-stick to the string. Each string of squash was tied into a circle and then hung indoors or hidden with corn and other dry staples in buried food caches.

When Buffalo Bird Woman made a stew, she threw ground corn, beans, meat and fat, and an entire string of dried squash into the pot and boiled it until the corn and beans were done. At this point, the squash had softened and fallen off the string and broken up, and the string (still tied in a circle) was removed.

When I read all this, of course I had to try dried squash. But what about varieties? I didn't have whatever variety Buffalo Bird Woman was using, if it even was a pure variety. Would different varieties taste different? Would I like the flavor of dried squash of any variety? Would I like it well enough to do the work of drying? And could dried squash be produced in Oregon? I decided to start backward. What did dried squash taste like? Would I like it? These were questions I could answer by just drying some squash in a dehydrator and skipping the issue of Oregon's weather. If I didn't like dried squash, I wouldn't need to figure out how to produce it.

What varieties should I try? Where should I start? Oftentimes when I ask this kind of question, I factor in a huge dose of cheerful optimism. What would be the best possible answer? What answer would make growing and drying squash most practical? I look for that answer first.

The best option, I decided, would be if I could produce great dried squash from varieties I already grow for other reasons. The large, viny varieties of prime winter squash I grow mostly wouldn't be suitable, though, I thought. Those plants need the full energy of the plant and the full growing season to produce and sweeten their big winter squash. Their quality and productivity would be sabotaged if I asked them to also crank out lots of immature fruits. What would be optimal is if standard summer squash varieties could produce good dried squash using the bigger summer squash that are past their prime for use as summer squash. Summer squash plants are mostly bushes that are in the business of cranking out huge amounts of immature fruits. Summer squash also have a tendency to "get away from you," that is, to grow, seemingly overnight, from tiny fruits into squash that are too big to be really useful as high-quality summer squash. What would be most wonderful and practical would be if these bigger "escapee" summer squashes were delicious dried. Bigger squash would also give more food for each motion of picking or slicing. Of summer squash, my favorite variety, as mentioned above, is 'Costata Romanesca'. So I started there.

I started out making ⅜-inch slices, as Buffalo Bird Woman did, but dried them in a dehydrator at 125°F. Dried 'Costata Romanesca' quickly proved to be powerfully delicious. The flavor of the dried squash was unique and distinctive, and so wonderful I would have been happy to grow the variety for dried squash alone. (The flavor was much more powerful and quite different from the flavor of 'Costata Romanesca' as a summer squash.) I was inspired to check out some other varieties.

The next squash I tried was 'Dark Green Zucchini'. It produced dried squash that tasted like, well, nothing. It had virtually no flavor. Many other varieties also produced bland dried squash that were, as far as I was concerned, not worth the effort. Variety was everything. Some varieties produced spectacularly delicious, rich, flavorful dried squash, squash that tasted so delicious in soups and stews that I rapidly expanded from a small round dehydrator to a big Excalibur, primarily just to produce dried squash. Here's a summary of the drying quality of selected varieties:

1. Most of the green zucchini varieties, including 'Seneca F_1', 'Dark Green', 'Spineless Beauty', and 'Nimba', produce

bland, virtually tasteless dried squash. One very dark green zuke variety whose label was lost produced a dried flavor that was actually foul.

2. 'Costata Romanesca', 'White Egyptian', and 'Magda F_1' produce very delicious dried squash that taste similar to each other. Of these, 'Costata Romanesca' is best for drying for size reasons, and because it actually has a higher dry matter content to start with. So you get more food for your processing work.

3. 'Golden Zucchini', 'Golden Bush Zucchini', and 'Gold Rush F_1' produce delicious dry squash of a completely different flavor class than 'Costata Romanesca'.

4. I tried drying many winter squash too, just to check out the flavors. Some had foul flavors. 'Sweet Meat', 'Sunshine F_1', 'Black Hubbard', and 'Chicago Hubbard' are all delicious dried and give a third, completely different flavor.

5. My initial supposition, that it would be impractical to dry winter squash, turned out to be only generally true. There are useful exceptions. 'Sweet Meat' sometimes produces a late flush of immature fruits that can be dried. And if you treat a few of your 'Sunshine F_1' bushes as summer squash and keep them harvested, they will act like summer squash and crank out flush after flush of fruit great for drying.

6. I dried one medium green-colored zucchini I bought in a store that was spectacularly delicious dried. It made a dried-squash flavor that was yet again different from the three other flavors I've found. It also had a powerful, rich flavor when stir-fried. I have been unable to locate its variety name.

However, that experience did prove to me that there is at least one green zucchini in the world with a rich flavor when stir-fried and a great flavor dried.

7. There are many other summer squashes and zucchinis that have shapes or sizes that don't lend themselves to drying. 'Yellow Crookneck' and 'Sunray F_1', a yellow straightneck, are summer squash that develop a hard skin and unpalatable seeds by the time they are at the right stage for drying, for example. The scallop shape doesn't lend itself to making slices, and the scallop varieties generally develop tough skins and/or unpalatable seeds before they are at a good size for drying.

The best stage for drying most squash is when the squash is 1 to 4 pounds, depending upon the variety. 'Costata Romanesca' is a variety that, if allowed to mature fully, produces squash that are up to 3 feet long. It is an especially nice summer squash, with good flavor and a firm texture (even after cooking), and it is tasty as a summer squash when harvested at up to about a pound in size. The skin is tender and the seeds are immature enough to be palatable up to about 3 or 4 pounds. In fact, the little 1-pound squash are not the most flavorful when dried. It is the bigger squash, 1 pound and up, that taste best dried. Even 4-pound Romanescas can be sliced and dried. However, squash in the 1- to 3-pound range yield a larger amount of dry squash per pound of fresh squash. 'Romanesca' skin stays tender until the squash are very big, however, and it is tenderness of the skin and maturity of the seeds that determines when a squash is too big to dry. This varies with the variety. If the seeds develop far enough so that the seed coats are tough and unpalatable, you can still halve the fruit, remove the seeds, and slice and dry the flesh. (But you can't dry such pieces on sticks.) Once the skin has begun to toughen, the fruit is too big for drying, even deseeded.

'Costata Romanesca' stays tender-skinned so long because it is planning to be a 3-foot-long squash. So a 'Romanesca' squash that is 4 pounds is still a baby with a tender skin and edible immature seeds. The slices are about 3 to 5 inches across, representing a significant amount of food for each slicing motion. Most summer squash varieties don't get nearly so big. When the final squash size is 4 pounds for many varieties, they are at or near full size and have tough skins and inedible seeds. When the squash is intending to be a small squash, you don't have much leeway after the summer-squash stage in which to catch fruits of the right size for drying. You can dry smaller fruits, fruits in the summer-squash stage, but that is counterproductive and inefficient. You don't get much dried food for picking and drying dozens of small zucchinis. And they must be dried in a dehydrator; they aren't wide enough and don't have big enough seed cavities to work well on sticks. Furthermore, the tiny fruits have less flavor dried than the bigger ones. In addition, the thing that is most practical for gardeners is having something to do with the summer squash that escape from the prime summer squash stage.

I would suggest you start off drying squash first with 'Costata Romanesca' and with a big gold zucchini such as 'Golden Bush Zucchini' or 'Gold Rush F_1'. That will give you two very different, delicious flavors. Second, I recommend you just try drying whatever summer squash you like that are of the right shapes and sizes for it and see if you end up with something delicious.

I dried my first squash in a little round dehydrator. It was inadequate for anything but experiments. I next tried drying on sticks like Buffalo Bird Woman. Buffalo Bird Woman used willow sticks whose dimensions she specified exactly. (It matters. Thicker sticks break the squash slices and they fall off. Thinner sticks cut through the squash slices under the weight of the squash, and the slices fall off.) I approximated with dowels. With a little experimenting, I settled on a ½"× 4' dowel as the ideal modern squash stick. (In actuality, ½-inch dowels are slightly thinner than a real ½-inch diameter. Home Depot carries 4-foot dowel lengths.) My first version of a drying rack involved just pounding some nails into two wood beams that were supports for the second-floor deck, and that happened to be the right distance apart to support squash-sticks. I left the squash slices outdoors for several days. Even though it was August and as dry as any of our August weather ever gets, the squash didn't dry. We have moist, cool nights even in August, with heavy dew on the ground each morning. The squash made progress on drying during the afternoons, then re-hydrated each night and morning.

So next I tried putting the squash sticks outdoors and bringing them indoors each night. That actually did work. But it was a pain. I could only move one squash-stick at a time, so that meant a trip between the house and the deck for every squash stick every night and morning; and it took at least three or four days to do the drying. It just wasn't my sort of thing.

Meanwhile, by this time, inspired by the flavor of dried-squash soup and stew, I had splurged and bought a nine-tray Excalibur dehydrator. This dehydrator allowed me to get into serious squash drying. I developed four basic styles when drying squash using a dehydrator.

Big rounds. In the first style, I slice the squash ⅜ inch thick, just as for stick drying, but put the slices on the dehydrator trays instead and set the thermostat at 125°F. It usually takes about a day to dry the slices. The slices don't stick to the trays and don't have to be turned over. However, to save drying time, I usually turn the trays around about two-thirds of the way through the drying. I dry until the slices are brittle. Then I transfer them (quickly, while still hot) to plastic bags. (They absorb moisture from the air rapidly.)

Chips. I got the idea of making chips from the Excalibur company's book on dehydration, *Preserve It Naturally II: The Complete Guide To Food Dehydration.* For chips I cut the squash into slices about 3⁄16 inch thick. When the shape of the fruit is round, as with 'Sunshine' and 'Sweet Meat', I halve each fruit lengthwise first, then slice the halves. Otherwise it's hard to get even enough chips by hand. The 3⁄16-inch thickness gives a chip that is just the right thickness to eat out of hand, and thick enough to use as a dipper. The *C. pepo* squash make better chips to use with bean dip or salsa, as they aren't very sweet. 'Sunshine' and 'Sweet Meat' chips are a little too sweet for that role, and are most delicious eaten plain. 'Sunshine' is our favorite squash for making sweet chips. We now devote a few 'Sunshine' plants completely to providing squash for chips. We keep them picked and cranking out young fruits just like summer squash plants. (The rest of the 'Sunshine' plants we leave alone to produce prime winter squash.)

Chip-sliced squash take about half a day to dry in the Excalibur, and don't have to be turned. Squash chips are very hygroscopic (absorb moisture quickly), so I take them out of their plastic bag only a handful at a time. If I dump out a whole bowlful, the last to be eaten will be soft instead of crunchy.

Slivers. I cut the squash into quarters or appropriate pieces lengthways, then push the pieces through a salad shooter and aim the flow of slices at an Excalibur dehydrator tray placed over a large cutting board. I move the salad shooter around to get a more or less even pile of slices about ½" thick that covers the entire tray. Then I rearrange a little by hand. I can fit about a pound of slices per Excalibur tray. I dry the trays for several hours, then rustle up and rearrange the bits on each tray by hand when they have partially dried. Making the slivers and drying them is more work than drying ⅜-inch rounds. Their big advantage is they re-hydrate faster—more like 15 minutes in a soup instead of 45.

Squash powder. You can make squash powder by putting dry (brittle) squash rounds in a blender or coffee grinder and letting the blades chew them up. (This was another idea suggested by the Excalibur dehydration book.) The squash powder makes great soups and stews.

I put my dried squash rounds or chips in food-grade plastic bags and put the bags in heavy plastic buckets with lids. (Insects sometimes eat through plastic bags.) The dried slivers I press into glass jars, not minding if they break up further. Squash powder also goes into glass jars.

Dried squash seems to keep indefinitely without losing quality in any obvious way. (That represents a storage life greater than that of beans, which do lose quality obviously if kept more than about a year.) I have had batches of soup based mostly upon dried squash that was six years old, and it was as tasty and delicious as ever. Undoubtedly, though, vitamin losses do occur with drying and long-term storing.

A Modern Squash-Drying Rack

After a few years of drying squash in an Excalibur dehydrator, I started wanting much more dried squash. I began to covet Buffalo Bird Woman her drying rack with dozens of sticks of drying squash. By this time, Nate and I had joined forces, and he had tasted enough dried-squash-based soups and stews to be eager to help make more of them possible. We wanted lots more dried squash. So we conferred. The result was a simple, portable squash drying rack that can be used indoors or out. The rack could be placed in an appropriate plastic tunnel to make a solar drying situation with drawstring-closed vents that could be closed at night. If we had a woodstove, we could put it next to that. The entire rack full of squash could be moved from outdoors to indoors easily at night. And the rack could even be used indoors in front of a fan. We didn't know quite how we would be using the rack. We wanted many options.

Our rack is a simple frame made from four pieces of 2 × 2 inch lumber cut down into the appropriate sizes, four right-angle corner braces, some screws and some nails. Our rack is an upright rectangular frame 6 feet high and a bit under 4 feet wide, with rows of nails down the two vertical sides to support the squash sticks. The rack is supported in an upright position simply by leaning the top crosspiece against something, or it can be propped into an *A* shape with a forked stick. For details, see photo insert and note 10-4.

A couple of details turned out to be missing from the account of squash drying in *Buffalo Bird*

Woman's Garden. First, it is necessary to oil the dowels initially. Otherwise the squash slices dry onto the sticks more or less permanently, and the sticks have to be scraped or scoured before they can be reused. So I make a squash stick by whittling one end of a 4' × ½" dowel into a gentle 3-inch point, and then I saturate the entire length of the dowel with olive oil, leave it overnight, then wipe away the excess. The stick only needs to be oiled once.

Second, it is useful to jiggle or rearrange the squash slices partway through the drying process to loosen them from the stick. After that, the slices dry loose and are easy to remove.

In my first effort to use my new drying rack, I decided, as usual, to be maximally optimistic. What would be the most convenient for me if it worked? I decided to try just drying the squash indoors in front of a fan. In summer, I have a heavy fan positioned so as to blow air from windows in the rest of the house through the kitchen door and out the kitchen windows at night. (It's almost always quite cool at night. Just opening windows at night and closing them in the morning is the traditional Oregonian concept of air conditioning.) If the squash rack were in the dining room near that fan, I thought, I could simply swing the fan around to dry squash during the day when the windows are closed. And the squash rack would be just a few feet away from the kitchen where I wash and slice the squash.

So I simply propped the squash rack up in front of the fan right there in the dining room. I did not really expect this scheme to work. That first batch of squash dried pretty well in about four days, though. That is about as good as Buffalo Bird Woman was doing outdoors with full sun. A big fan is a powerful tool. My squash dried to a stage that was leathery, and just short of brittle.

That isn't good enough for chips, but it's fine for rounds.

Sometimes I "finish" th ⬛⬛⬛⬛⬛⬛ sh in my Excalibur. For chips ⬛⬛⬛⬛⬛⬛ dered squash, I need dried-to-brittle squash. It's easy to finish the dried squash in the Excalibur, because the slices have dried into all kinds of shapes and aren't flat any more. So I remove two-thirds of the Excalibur trays, make a big pile of dried squash on each of the three remaining trays, and finish the squash to brittle dryness in just a few hours (without any turning of squash or trays).

My squash rack can hold up to eight squash sticks placed at 6 inches apart. For the sizes of squash I dry, those that are about 1 to 3 pounds per squash, three squash will fit on each stick. So a full load is about twenty-four squash, or about 48 pounds of squash per full rack at an average of 2 pounds per squash.

Dried squash are (very) roughly 5 percent dry matter, so 48 pounds of fresh squash consolidate down to roughly 2.4 pounds of dried squash. Dried squash is concentrated food. The bulk of our dry squash these days is rounds dried on the rack. The main use is for soups and stews.

Growing Squash and Pumpkins

Squash and pumpkins like rich soil, moderate amounts of water, and plenty of sun and warmth. They are capable of growing in pure compost, in fact. However, they aren't as heavy feeders as corn. Most varieties do well enough with ordinary garden soil.

Squash succumb to the slightest freeze. So we plant squash or pumpkins after all danger of frost is past and the soil has warmed up. A traditional way to plant a few hills of squash is to work a shovelful of manure or compost into each hill, then plant (or thin to) two or three plants around each hill. Nate and I don't fertilize the hills specially, and have just one plant per hill. We space smaller plants at 4 feet apart in the rows, with our standard 3½' spacing between rows. With big viney types, we space rows at 7 feet apart, and put the hills at 6 to 8 feet apart within in the row. Our method of planting squash (with a 3-tube planter) is described in chapter 5.

Many people these days start their squash and pumpkins from transplants rather than direct-seeding. I think this practice is partly responsible for ruining the big squash varieties. Plants of big viney varieties have big vigorous taproots that head for the center of the earth as soon as the seed germinates. When the seed is started in a pot, the taproot runs out of pot while the top of the seedling has barely broken the surface of the soil. The root is invariably damaged or broken off during transplanting. The result is that the slowest-germinating, slowest-growing plants from each lot of seeds are the only ones that have an intact root system after transplanting. When you save seed from the "best" plants of a vigorous, big-vined variety after starting the plants in pots, you are actually automatically selecting for the plants that germinated or grew most slowly—that is, the wimpiest plants, not the best. Big viney plants started from transplants will never have a root system as vigorous as those started from direct-seeding. I recommend direct-seeding all big viney varieties.

When the variety is a bush or half-bush type, the seedling's root system is a bush or half-bush form also. So while bush and half-bush varieties can be direct-seeded, they also lend themselves to starting in pots and transplanting. Most summer squash varieties are bush or half-bush types. The bushing pattern is associated with prolific flowering and refruiting, which is just what we want in summer squash. For summer squash, starting seeds in pots in a greenhouse or under lights indoors can mean a summer-squash season that starts a month earlier.

Squash and pumpkins like full sun. Any shade will slow their maturity time. So plant in full sun if you have it. Plant in partial shade only if your region and the variety give you maturity time to spare, or you have sun so fierce that most plants prefer some protection from it. Part of American gardening lore is the idea of interplanting corn, beans, and squash. However, in most areas of the country, squash do better with full sun, not shaded by corn. And big, powerful, viney squash will grow right up the corn and knock it over. Buffalo Bird Woman seems to have grown corn and squash together only in the sense that they were in blocks in the same garden. They weren't interplanted.

Big viney squash plants can often root at the nodes, thus gaining additional resources to support the plant and fruits. You can get the best out of a big viney squash plant by throwing a couple of shovelsful of soil up on the roving vines at nodes here and there to help the plants form these auxiliary root systems. The rooting at the nodes is one reason why it is counterproductive to put big squash at the edge of a garden and let them spread into the lawn. The vines can't root in sod. Big viney squash here do better with overhead irrigation than drip, because with drip irrigation and no summer rain, most of the surface of the ground is too dry for rooting at the nodes.

The basic strategy for controlling weeds in

If You're Short on Bees

These days, because of colony collapse disorder or pesticide use of neighbors, some people have so few bees that squash flowers don't get pollinated. A few summer squash varieties are parthenocarpic, that is, don't require fertilization to make fruit. But most squash or pumpkins don't set fruit without fertilization. With no bees, you will have to fill in. Just pollinate the flowers yourself, using methods similar to those I describe in the section on seed saving. However, you don't have to tape buds or flowers. All you need to do is transfer pollen from male flowers to female flowers in the morning when the male flowers are releasing their pollen. You have to transfer pollen between flowers of the same species. Pollinate pepo flowers with pepo pollen, for example. Unless you are saving seed, it doesn't matter whether the flowers are from the same or different plants or the same or different varieties, as long as they are the same species.

squash is to weed very well early in the season, then forget about weeding later after the vines run out into the space between the rows. At that point, if you have spaced the squash appropriately for each variety, you have a pretty solid squash or pumpkin patch that shades out and suppresses most weeds. Weeds that start from seed at that point will just be plowed under when you turn the squash patch under in fall, before they have time to make seeds.

Till in squash or pumpkin residues each fall and rotate your squash patch to new ground that has not been growing cucurbits as a preventive measure against pests and disease. If your pumpkin patch is relatively isolated from others, your pest and disease problems may be minimal. About the only problem we have is a few cucumber beetles and powdery mildew in fall. The powdery mildew here is regular enough so that it usually kills all the plants, but ordinarily only after they have already matured all the squash and the first freeze is already near. For diagnosing diseases and pest damage, see Gail Damerow's *The Perfect Pumpkin*. Regional seed catalogs will usually give you information about the specific pests and diseases that matter in your area.

Harvesting, Storing, and Curing

I don't harvest squash until the vines die down, or the stems on the squash are too dry or dead to be actively transferring nutrients to the squash, or until frost threatens, whichever comes first. Some years my squash season ends when the vines have all succumbed to powdery mildew. Sometimes I harvest the last of the squash just ahead of the first predicted freeze. Exposure to even a light freeze harms the storage life of the squash. Exposure to a serious freeze ruins the squash.

When we harvest, we don't want to break the fruit off at the stem, because if we do, the moist, juicy stem scar is vulnerable to mold and storage life drops. Instead, we cut or break the stem in between the fruit and vine so that there is a stub of stem on the fruit. Some varieties snap off easily; most, however, must be cut. Garden shears are the easiest way to do it. Most people will tell you to cut so that you end up with a 1- to 2-inch stub of stem on each fruit. I cut the stems to about

3 to 5 inches long initially, then trim them to the final length of 1 to 2 inches after the fruits have been indoors drying out a few days. If the stem is shorter than 3 to 5 inches, I cut the vine on each side of the stem. Most varieties of squash should not be lifted or handled by the stem, because the fruit will break off. However, some varieties do have sturdy enough attachments to allow handling by the stems. There are always occasional fruits whose stems got knocked off in the field. Eat those first.

Books and articles about squash frequently speak in terms of an outdoor curing period. For example, after describing cutting the squash and leaving stem stubs, the Johnny's Selected Seeds catalog says: "Cure in the field to dry and toughen skins by exposing fruits to sun for 5–7 days or so, covering in the evening if frost is likely. An indoor method of curing is to expose squash to 80°F–90°F (27°C–32°C) with ventilation for 3–5 days." The "covering in the evening" assumes that you have cut the squash and consolidated them in a spot at the edge of the field (ready for loading into a cart or truck).

What people actually do with respect to curing, though, has more to do with their region and the year's particular weather. Here in maritime Oregon, in squash-harvesting season, it is often raining. And when I am harvesting because a freeze is threatening, I want the squash safely out of the field. I don't have any workable way of covering the amount of squash we harvest. I also don't have any place that has temperatures of 80°F–90°F for indoor curing, either. My home is usually 60°F–68°F that time of year. That has to do for both people and squash. So the squash are always brought home at once and welcomed in with the people. There is a curing period, that is, a period after harvest in which the squash are allowed to sit and after-ripen before being eaten. But the curing temperature and conditions are the same as the rest of the storage. In other words, my idea of "curing" just amounts to not eating the fruit until it has been stored a certain amount of time.

I handle my squash *gently*. I never drop or toss them. I *place* them. I place big, heavy squash such as 'Sweet Meat' in a monolayer in the cart or truck, and I use old towels or sheets or rags between them to help cushion them for the ride home. I harvest the smaller squash such as the delicatas and 'Sunshines' into stacking crates, stacking them up and filling the crates. It doesn't seem to hurt most small squashes to be in a crate buried under a foot of other small squash. I place squash in the crate so the cut stems or any pointy ends don't jab into anybody.

People often suggest washing the squash with water with some bleach in it. I don't do that. We all come in from the field dirty. My house is dirty. What's a little dirt among friends? Once home with my squash, I distribute them everywhere. Every room, every empty table, every bookshelf is improved by a diversity of squashes of many shapes and colors. Two walls of a back room lined with industrial-weight shelves take some of the bigger squash. Other big squash are lined up on the floor next to the wall all around the living room and fill every empty corner and replace every doorstop. Any area against the wall where you don't actually walk should be lined with big squash along the floor. Furthermore, if you put tarps in the corners out of the way, you can make foot-high piles of delicatas there. With this atti-tude, it's pretty easy to store a ton or two of squash indoors without much difficulty, even without the

shelves. I place each big squash so that whatever spot it sat on in the field is now exposed to the air. The stacked crates of smaller squashes form a wall of squash.

After my squash have been inside for about three to five days, I turn each big squash so that a different part of the squash touches the floor and the first spot gets a chance to dry out. I also trim the stems with sheers to the final length of 1 to 2 inches. And I rearrange the small squash in their crates and stir up the piles of delicatas on the tarps on the floor.

Ideal temperature for storing squash beyond the initial curing stage is supposedly 50°F–55°F with a relative humidity of 50–70 percent. My household conditions of 60°F–68°F and 40–70 percent are supposedly not ideal, but they're close enough. And perhaps they are ideal. My squash store as long as or longer than anyone else's. The squash seem to like my methods.

The best squash flavor doesn't develop until the squash has been fully cured or stored the right amount of time before being eaten. Generally, *C. pepo* varieties need to sit in my house for two weeks after harvest before they are prime. Most *C. maxima* varieties should sit at least a month. 'Sweet Meat' is best with at least two months. The squash can be eaten earlier, but they aren't as sweet as they could be, and don't have as much flavor or as much complexity to the flavor, or as much aroma. *C. moschata* varieties are said to need two weeks to cure, but I haven't checked that out personally. It is clear that the curing time is temperature dependent. When my elderly mother was alive, I kept the upstairs part of the house warmer, and the upstairs squash cured and were ready to eat faster. It took the pepos only about a week, and the 'Sweet Meats' just a month.

When a squash tastes somewhat starchy instead of sweet, it is usually a curing problem. The squash was probably eaten before its time. When a squash isn't starchy but has thinner flesh, less flavor, or less sweetness than expected, it is generally because it was picked immature or was poorly grown.

The Perfect Pumpkin Pie

Recipes for pumpkin pie generally assume you are using poor-quality, watery boiled squash or pumpkin, most likely the bland stuff from cans. Such pies are based more upon the flavor of milk, cream, sugar, and spices than upon the squash or pumpkin, which is only a minor ingredient. I wanted to learn to make a pie from 'Sweet Meat' squash, which has considerable sugar of its own and its own rich flavor. I wanted as much squash as possible in the pie and as little as possible of other ingredients. I did not want to use evaporated or condensed milk, which have objectionable flavors and large amounts of cow's milk protein. My pie would need less added sugar than most, because 'Sweet Meats' have so much sugar, and the pie would be mostly squash. I also wanted the pie to emphasize things I grow myself, that is, squash and eggs, and de-emphasize things I don't grow, that is, dairy products and sugar. I particularly wanted my pie to minimize dairy protein, which gives me problems. If possible, I would design the pie to get the protein needed from eggs, not milk. I even experimented with soy milk powder. It didn't work. Soy milk may be white and have protein in it, but it tastes nothing whatsoever like milk. The perfect pumpkin pie must have some dairy in it. Delightfully enough, dairy *protein*

turns out to be unnecessary. I use heavy whipping cream, which has only traces of milk protein. This makes pies I can eat substantial amounts of for several days straight without getting a stuffy nose or other allergic reactions. Of course, using cream runs the calories up. But it adds flavor and richness to the pie, and I can deal with extra calories more easily than not being able to breathe.

I believe desserts should be serious food. I don't usually eat desserts. When I do eat a dessert, though, I often pig out cheerfully, eat only the dessert, and call it dinner. That helps take care of the calorie issue, if the dessert is serious enough food to justify substituting it for dinner. So when I design a dessert, I'm willing for it to be rich and full of calories, as long as those calories are not empty calories. Using these principles, I included as many eggs as possible in the Perfect Pumpkin Pie, maximized the amount of squash, and limited the sugar and cream to what is necessary to give the spectacularly delicious pie I wanted. Most of the year, I view my Perfect Pumpkin Pie as a glorious but somewhat indulgent way of having eggs and squash for dinner. Only on holidays do I eat the Perfect Pumpkin Pie *and* a full meal. That takes care of the calorie issue. (Some people would suggest that it's OK to have such a rich dessert only if you restrict the portion size, but when I'm in the same house with a Perfect Pumpkin Pie, that isn't going to happen. I need other approaches. Like restricting everything else.) My recipe will work with any richly flavorful prime gourmet winter squash or pumpkin such as those I recommend. (At least, all those big enough to provide substantial amounts of flesh.)

I found I could not produce a great squash or pumpkin pie with a commercial pumpkin-pie spice mix. Most have either too much clove seasoning or none at all, and the spices tend to be stale. So I developed my own pumpkin-pie spice mix. It is a 16:4:4:1 ratio of cinnamon to ginger, nutmeg, and cloves. Spices in little jars are often stale, even on the store shelf. I always buy bulk, sniffing before buying. Also, use real vanilla powder, not an extract. The vanilla powder* has a much richer and more complex flavor. (Bob's Red Mill sells it: www.bobsredmill.com.) Store the spice mix and the vanilla in the freezer. Even frozen, neither retains its full potency beyond a year. Use real brown sugar. (Real brown sugar has just one ingredient—brown sugar.) A light or medium-dark brown sugar is best. (Very dark brown sugar has too much molasses flavor, which overwhelms the flavor of the squash.)

The brown sugar in the recipe must be balanced with the sweetness of the individual squash. I use just 1 cup for two big pies for fully prime, fully cured 'Sweet Meat' squash. For less prime or less cured 'Sweet Meats' I use 1½ to 2 cups. For prime, full-cured Hubbards I would suggest first trying 2 cups. With a little practice, you will learn to taste the mashed squash or pumpkin and figure out exactly how much sugar you'll need for that individual fruit.

Use mashed baked squash. It can be freshly baked, baked a day to several days before and refrigerated for making into pies later, or thawed from your frozen stash (of baked squash/pumpkin).

If you can eat wheat and enjoy making crusts, you can use whatever pie-crust recipe you like. However, being unable to eat wheat, I find crusts problematic and just too much work. I make my pies completely crustless. Most of the labor of making the pies is in the crust, and the crust is high in fat and calories. If you love pumpkin pie but find yourself making it rarely, give my crustless

> ### The Perfect Pumpkin Pie Filling—
> ### Ingredients (for two big pies):
>
> 6 cups baked mashed 'Sweet Meat' or other prime squash or pumpkin
>
> 2–2¼ cups eggs (I use duck eggs, but chicken eggs are fine.)
>
> 2 cups heavy whipping cream
>
> 1–3 cups brown sugar, packed down, depending upon the sweetness of the individual fruit
>
> 2 Tbs. Carol's Perfect Pumpkin Pie Spice Mix (16:4:4:1 cinnamon, ginger, nutmeg, cloves)
>
> 1 tsp. real vanilla powder
>
> ¼ tsp. salt

version a try, even if you can eat wheat. My crustless pie looks just like a pie and is solid enough to cut and serve as wedges. In order to bake a crustless pie and not have the filling burn, I use heavy Pyrex pie plates, cook the pies more carefully and gently, and pre-warm the filling to lukewarm by setting the bowl with the filling inside another bowl of hot water for a while. (My pie plates, the biggest I could find, have internal dimensions of 8 inches across at the bottom, 9¾ inches across at the top. If yours are smaller you'll want to adjust the recipe.)

Directions. Measure and combine the mashed squash, spice mix, vanilla, sugar, and salt in a large stainless steel bowl. Add the eggs. I use a hand mixer to beat the eggs (on top of the squash mix) for a few seconds, then add the cream and blend everything into a smooth batter. Any strings from the squash end up wrapped around the mixing blades and are thus automatically removed.

Pre-warm the batter by placing the bowl with the mixed ingredients inside another bowl or pan filled with hot water to bring the batter to lukewarm. (This shortens cooking time, and the edges and center of the pie cook more evenly.) When the batter is warm to the touch, pour it into the two pie plates.

I put the pies on the second rack from the bottom in an oven preheated to 350°F. It takes about 45 to 55 minutes to bake the pies. (This cooks the pies more gently than the standard bottom-rack position.) My perfect pies have much more squash and eggs and less fluid than most, and have completely different cooking characteristics than ordinary pumpkin pies. When my perfect pie is done, it puffs up into a convex shape as if it thinks it's a rising cake, and it has a thin, light golden-tan crust over the entire pie, including the middle. The crust is actually dry to the touch. (If the edges are puffed up but not the middle, it isn't done yet.)

Remove the pies from the oven and put them on a rack to cool. During cooling, the pie surface sinks down to become ordinary concave pie shape and the delicate crust disappears. Now, here comes the hard part. *Cover the pies and refrigerate them for a day*. It takes a day in the refrigerator for the full flavor to develop.

We usually eat the Perfect Pumpkin Pies plain. But for Thanksgiving and Christmas, I also make whipped cream. I use 3 tablespoons of sugar per cup of heavy whipping cream.

Hoarding Seeds of Squash and Pumpkins

In chapter 4 I introduced the idea of hoarding seeds, that is, putting away a long-term, ideally frozen stash of seed of every variety you care about, whether you save seed of the variety or not. I didn't start out with that policy. I started out, as most seed savers do, simply saving seeds of certain varieties and not others. Since I was actively breeding both pepos and maxes, I had to do lots of seed saving for my breeding projects. I figured I didn't have to also save seed of the squash varieties that are widely available commercially. As should be graphically apparent from the rest of this chapter, that turned out to be a big mistake. No matter how widely used and available a variety is, we really cannot count upon the commercial supply. I did not actually need to save seed of every variety initially, however. It would have been sufficient if I had simply hoarded some of the good "store-bought" seed of each variety I cared about. Then I could have used the hoard to start saving my own seed of a variety when something went wrong with the commercial lines.

To hoard squash seed we have bought, we often need to dry it additionally. Refer to the section in chapter 4 for the basics of drying bought seed for freezing or storage in airtight containers. Omitted from that account was how to evaluate squash seed to see whether and when it is dry enough. The way to do this is to shell out some seeds and examine the seed shells and the meats separately. When the seed is dry enough, the shell is brittle, and the meat is also. The meat snaps clean when you bend it instead of bending. Very often, small seed such as is typical of pepos is easy to dry, but people often don't dry the big seeds from the larger-seeded max varieties well enough. What happens with the latter is that it is easy to dry them to where the shell or whole seed is dry enough to snap, but the meat isn't. The moisture content is too high. In addition, the moisture from the meat re-hydrates the shell in storage, often enough so that the seed molds if stored at room temperature. So to evaluate the dryness of squash seed, always shell some and test the meats.

Saving Seeds of Squash and Pumpkins

Saving our own seeds is the ultimate act of gardening resilience. It's also a lot of fun. We can produce seed of much higher quality than what we can usually buy. In addition, by doing selection properly, we can improve each variety and shape it so that it better fits our growing conditions, tastes, and purposes. We can enjoy a glorious bounty of seed. We can over-sow cheerfully, saving ourselves considerable work in the process. We can have seed enough to share, seed enough to give away, and in some cases, even seed enough to sell. Buffalo Bird Woman normally traded a single string of seed ears of corn for a tanned buffalo robe. Seed is *valuable*. Knowing how to save seed is one of the most valuable of gardening skills. Good seed is the ultimate high-value garden crop.

There are four basic aspects to seed saving. One is just the physical processing of the seed. Many people think of this as the primary aspect. It isn't. Learning to clean squash and dry squash seed just gets you some seed that will grow some something or other. The squash or pumpkins that result may be nothing like the plant the seed fruit came from; the fruits may not even be edible. *The primary aspect to seed saving is controlling pollination* so that the seed you save is pure seed of the variety you want.

If I just go save seed from a random squash of, say, 'Sugar Loaf–Hessel', from my squash patch, that seed will not be pure SL–H in most cases.

SL–H is a member of the species *C. pepo*. It can be fertilized by pollen from any other plant that is of the same species, that is, any other *C. pepo*. Nate and I grow several different *C. pepo* varieties and have breeding projects involving pepos. Bees buzz all over the entire patch. Each flower gets visited by bees repeatedly—dozens of times, in fact. (Flowers do not release their pollen or nectar all at once, and bees are competing with other bees for every little bit.) Some of those bee visits are likely to be by bees that recently visited one of our other pepo varieties. In addition, bees do not honor human property lines. They can also visit the squash patches of neighbors. The fruit and seed that represent crosses with other varieties looks exactly the same as the pure seed.

So, to ensure pure seed of SL–H, we need do one of two things. One option is to grow no other pepo except SL–H. This is generally necessary when we want to produce lots of seed, as for commercial sale. For this to work, we must also be far enough from neighbors who are growing

Saving Seeds from Hybrids

Remember that hybrids don't breed true. In most cases you can save seed from them, but that seed doesn't reproduce the characteristics of the hybrid. Instead, each offspring is different, and is a mix of the characteristics of the two original parents. However, you can, in most cases, save seed from a hybrid as the first step in breeding a similar open-pollinated variety. I describe "dehybridizing" hybrids in my previous book, *Breed Your Own Vegetable Varieties*.

other pepos. (For how far, see "isolation distances" in note 10-5.) If we are far enough from squash-growing neighbors, this means we can grow one pepo, one max, and one moschata without any fear of cross-pollination between the varieties. Only varieties within the same species cross. If I want to sell squash seed and have a relatively isolated garden, I could grow, for example, 'Sugar Loaf–Hessel', 'Sweet Meat–Oregon Homestead', and 'Waltham Butternut' without any fear of their crossing, so as to produce and sell pure seeds of all three and have three different squash to eat.

If I grow SL–H as my only pepo, and my garden is sufficiently isolated from all others, there are still some potential problems. If there is one off-type plant in the lot, its pollen can end up in the seeds of lots of fruits. And you often can't tell an off-type plant until it's too late, after the fruits have matured, for example. That off type might not even be the right variety. It could be a volunteer from prior years, or could have been planted by a squirrel. When I do field-scale seed saving, I plant only where there have been no squash planted recently, and I plant seeds into exact positions so as to be able to identify the gardening contributions of squirrels. (Squirrels often bury excess seeds. Gardeners often leave cull squash and pumpkins out, to the delight of squirrels. Squirrels prefer to bury seeds where it is easy to dig—gardens and compost piles. One winter I fed the squirrels sunflower seeds and cull 'Sweet Meat' squash. That spring every garden and compost pile in the neighborhood sprouted volunteer sunflowers and SM squash. I no longer feed squirrels.) Finally, while I can evaluate and select fruits on the best plants in the patch for seed saving, most have been pollinated by pollen from many different plants, and some of the

Getting Your Starting Seed

Whenever I am planning to either hoard or save seed, I start with the genetically best seed I can get. Where the variety is a standard commercial one, it can be useful to buy a packet from several different seed companies. They may all be buying from the same commercial grower. But often they aren't, and some lines can be considerably better than others.

pollen parents might be the worst in the patch. Selection based upon just the female parent is useful, but isn't as effective as selection based upon both parents.

Most squash-loving gardeners don't want to be limited to just three varieties, one of each species. We want a glorious cornucopia of colors, sizes, shapes, and flavors. In addition, many gardeners have neighbors who also grow squash. And most gardeners don't need seed from a field of one variety; they just need enough seed for personal use. So most gardeners forget about isolation distances for squash and instead resort to hand-pollinating. We tape certain squash buds and flowers closed to cut the promiscuous bees out of the equation, and we perform pollination services ourselves in a more continent and controlled fashion. If we hand-pollinate, we can both grow and seed save on as many different varieties as we want of each species. The hand-pollination approach has the advantage that, if there is an off type in our patch that we don't recognize until after the fruits have matured, it is no disaster. We just refrain from seed saving from the fruits on that plant. We also consult our records and eliminate any hand-pollinated fruits that involved pollen from the off-type parent. We get much more powerful selection when we can select for both the best male and female parents.

Hand-Pollinating Squash and Pumpkins

Squash and pumpkin plants have separate male and female flowers on each plant. Any female flower can be fertilized by pollen from its own male flowers as well as from the male flowers from all other varieties that are of the same species. You can tell the female flowers or flower buds because they have a baby squash on the stem under the flower (see photo insert).

Find male and female flower buds in late afternoon or early evening the day before they are due to open. You can tell these "ripe and almost ready" buds by size and the fact that they are starting to color up. Tape them shut. (You don't tape earlier, because the buds would grow enough to rip holes in the bud as it expanded against the confining tape.) I use strapping tape. Masking tape doesn't work as well since it's wet here in the morning. Ideally, you would like two male buds for every female bud we plan to pollinate. It takes all the pollen from two males to fertilize all the ova and give us the most seed. Using two males also makes it more likely that the pollination will "take," that is, set a fruit instead of aborting. It's useful to put a stake with a marker near taped buds so you can find them again easily.

Then you come back the next morning. The big buds we taped would have opened into flowers by then if left unmolested, but the tape prevents that. At some point in the morning, depending upon temperature and moisture, the pollen in the male buds starts "dehiscing," that is, shedding. (The pollen turns bright yellow, fluffy, and loose, and comes off easily.) Dehiscence occurs slightly later in sealed buds than in open, untaped flowers. So just notice when bees start working the patch, and check out a taped male bud or two to see if they are ready. (It can be as early as 6:00 a.m. here on warmer, drier days, as late as 10:00 a.m. on cool days when I watered recently.) If you wait too long, the pollen drops from the anthers and can't be easily recovered and used.

Pluck a couple of taped male flowers, take them over near the taped female flower you want to pollinate, and rip the tape (and the end of the petals) off the male flowers and strip off the petals so that each becomes a paintbrush topped with pollen (see photo insert). Then rip the tape (with the end of the petals) off a female flower, and holding a male flower by its stem, gently daub pollen onto all three parts of the female flower's stigma. Repeat with the second male flower. Retape the female flower (with fresh tape, now somewhat lower down on the petals). Keep an eye out for bees and work fast once you open the taped flowers. Bees are not above diving right into a flower just as soon as you take the tape off. Record both the female and male parent on a piece of surveyor's tape you loop gently around the vine near the stem of the pollinated female flower. (I number all the plants in the patch with a number based upon row number and position in the row.) When the fruit is ready for harvest, tie the surveyor's tape around the fruit stem. Hand-pollinations take best when they are on the first few flowers of the season, and on the first flower or two of any particular vine. In addition, these flowers produce the biggest, most mature fruits, which give the biggest, most vigorous seed. In addition, fruits, including hand-pollinated fruits, often abort in very hot or overly dry weather. Later-season hand-pollinations are likely to take only if I strip off all the fruits on the vine that are already developing. On any vine upon which I want a hand-pollination, I strip off all open-pollinated flowers or fruits until I have made the hand-pollination. On those first few flowers on each vine early in the season, in good weather, nearly all my hand-pollinations take. A month later, when each vine has set multiple fruits, close to none of my hand-pollinations take, unless I strip off all preexisting fruit. (Then about two-thirds take.)

Selection

There is actually no such thing as "maintaining" a variety. Every plant picks up mutations every generation. Most of these mutations cause the plant to be more like a wild plant and less desirable as a domestic plant. If we simply save seed without doing any plant breeding, the variety rapidly deteriorates into something much less desirable. Varieties are not very stable. We must breed actively in order to retain their excellent characteristics. That is, to be good seed savers, we must be plant breeders, deliberately selecting what germplasm to perpetuate. The core plant breeding method of seed saving is selection. That is, we select our best plants and save their seed. But what is "best"? This is a question that deserves considerable thought in every situation, and gets down to the core of what we want from a garden in general as well as from any particular variety, what we believe in, and who we are. Most seed savers select rather randomly, often completely by accident selecting for characteristics that are the exact opposite of what they want.

I earlier gave an example as to how starting big-vine squash and pumpkin varieties in pots and transplanting can lead to selecting for slow germination and wimpy growth. Another frequent counterproductive situation is to plant too early, so that all the fastest-germinating seeds that germinate and grow well in cool weather get eliminated by a late freeze. The subsequent patch will consist of plants whose seed took longer to germinate and came up safely after the freeze.

If one plant has the biggest fruits, seed savers often erroneously choose that plant or the biggest of those fruits for seed saving. But that approach can result in selecting for a variety whose flesh is more watery. (It's easier to make water than food. The bigger-fruited plant may have been producing the same amount of real food but just putting more water into the fruits.) I think there is really no substitute for evaluating the culinary quality of each fruit before we accept it as parent to the seeds we save. This is impossible for commercial seed production but is easy to do in our gardens and kitchens. Generally, we should evaluate all the production of a plant, not just a single fruit. Sometimes a plant makes just one big fruit. We shouldn't select that fruit unless just one big fruit per plant is what we want.

I like vigorous plants that start well from direct-seeding early in the season. I grow organically. I use no seed treatments. I use no sprays of any kind, even organic ones. In addition, I need plants that can do well under ordinary field levels of fertility, such as can be maintained by using legume cover crops. So I plant that way in order to be able to select for plants that do well under those conditions. I always plant excess seed, at least three seeds for every plant I keep. In cases where I am selecting most actively for germination and cold-growth ability, I may plant a dozen seeds for every plant I keep.

Commercial seed producers run machines through entire fields harvesting the seed in the field. This method of harvesting automatically selects for plants that have bigger seed cavities and more seeds but thinner flesh. It also automatically selects for smaller seeds; the fruits with more but smaller seeds will contribute a larger fraction of the plants in the next generation. The original 'Sweet Meat', with its thick, very dry flesh, tiny seed cavity, and huge seeds, has only about 250–350 seeds in a 20-pound fruit (as does my line, 'Sweet Meat–Oregon Homestead'). Is it any surprise that the commercial industry ended up with a variety with a seed cavity two or three times as big, with much thinner fruit and smaller seeds? That is what they were selecting for.

Seed savers sometimes say they only want to maintain preexisting varieties such as heirlooms, not to do plant breeding or create anything new. However, *competent* seed saving requires plant breeding. In addition, some varieties are always lost through time, or become unworkable as the plant diseases or human needs and standards evolve. Our ancestors were creators of culture, not just passive transmitters. They created new songs and new learning and new technology as well as transmitted the old traditions. They both created and transmitted crop varieties. We should too.

The essence of selection is to save seeds from the best. Obviously, we do not want to save seed from the worst plant we have. If some or all of its being worst is heritable, we would be selecting for a variety that would be inferior to what we started with. We want, if possible, to be improving a variety. So we want to choose our seed fruits from our best plants. But what is "best"? Clearly, the biggest fruit in the patch isn't best if it is the only fruit the plant produced. We want plants that are generally productive and that produce fruit of the right size that is true to type. Furthermore,

half the genes come from the pollen parent, the "father" squash plant. We would like that plant to be best too. But that is just a start.

Many of the characteristics we care about with squash and pumpkins aren't apparent until the end of the season or even until after fruits are harvested and opened and tasted. So I usually do several hand-pollinations of several fruits when I want to save seed, recording both the female and male parent on the piece of surveyor's tape I use to mark each hand-pollination. (Again, as stated before, I number all the plants in the patch with a number based upon row number and position in the row.) Then I evaluate all the plants toward the end of the season, noticing and noting any that weren't as productive or weren't what they should be. I also notice any significant differences in powdery mildew resistance (which we always have here late in the season), or anything else noteworthy. I record the plant number with a permanent marker near the stem of each fruit before I harvest. Then I open and taste fruits from relevant plants (those representing plants for which I have hand-pollinations) before making the final seed-saving decision, to make sure they have the appropriate thickness of flesh, flesh quality, and flavor. So a good parent plant must produce a good number of fruits of the right size and shape and type, be vigorous, and be relatively disease free for the variety, and its fruit must have all the culinary characteristics it should have. I usually make several hand-pollinations using different plants, then save seed only from the fruits that had the good female as well as male parents.

Selection is considerably less obvious than one might think. At its best, it reflects our concept of the essential nature of the variety as well as our own values and our own essential nature. I cover various aspects, surprises, and subtleties of selection in much greater detail in my book, *Breed Your Own Vegetable Varieties: The Gardener's and Farmer's Guide to Plant Breeding and Seed Saving.*

Another issue in seed saving is numbers. How many plants should we save seed from? Clearly, if we save seed from just one fruit of one plant, that isn't enough. Something could go wrong with that one hand-pollination. (Occasionally bees bite into taped flowers late in the season, for example.) In addition, if one parent carried an objectionable mutation, all our seed would be affected. We are usually told to save seed from twenty to one-hundred or more plants, depending upon the species. Twenty is the more relevant number for squash. (See note 10-8.) However, nobody I know does this for squash unless they are selling seed. Especially not with big-vine types. I don't either, usually. Though I do the equivalent. Basically, I cheat.

There is a trade-off between the total numbers of fruits we keep seed of and our ability to evaluate properly which the best parent plants are. I think it is more important to evaluate and choose the parent plants as well as possible rather than save seed from a larger number of plants and fruits. I'm pretty happy if I get about five fruits representing mostly different male and female parents (say seven to ten different parent plants). However, the next year, instead of using my new seed, I may grow up more of my old seed and get another five good fruits representing a different seven to ten parents. And the following year, I might start with that original seed and get another few good hand-pollinations from the best plants of that year. There is no rule that says you have to do your entire round of seed saving all in one year.

For plenty of varieties, I only grow half a dozen plants per year. I hand-pollinate whichever happen to be ready when I'm doing hand-pollinations. If one or more fruits turns out to be a hand-pollination of a good mother with pollen from a good father, I save the seed. If not, I don't. I just plant another five the next year. Over a few years, I end up having saved seed for the next cycle from five fruits with somewhat more than five parents. And that is generally good enough, especially if I have a permanent stash of earlier seed I can go back to if it isn't good enough. (For those worried about inbreeding or genetic bottlenecking, see note 10-9.) This approach allows saving seed from many varieties without doing a lot of work.

I don't normally combine seed from different hand-pollinations. Every fruit is a separate lot, and I keep all the lots separate. When I plant the seed, I also record the exact lot. That way, if there are any problems, they become apparent. And if one lot is giving me especially nice results, it gets identified.

Seed Processing

The biggest, heaviest seed on a plant comes from the biggest, most mature (earliest) fruits. I harvest as outlined in the section on harvesting and curing. Then comes the after-ripening period. That is, the seed continues to mature and become heavier as it sits quietly in the curing fruit. I let all seed fruits after-ripen for at least a month, even the pepos. If the fruit is less than optimally mature, I give it as long an after-ripening period as possible short of the fruit rotting or molding. (It isn't practical for large commercial seed producers to store fruit so as to after-ripen seed. This is one reason why it is so easy to hand-produce seed that is much better in quality than commercial seed.)

There are two basic ways to process squash seeds. Most of the time I process the seed from a single squash at a time. I open the squash, remove the seeds and put the halves in the oven, then process the seed. Usually, while the seeds are still attached in clumps I eliminate any areas of immature seeds. Then I loosen the seeds into a bowl of water and rub them with my hands. Usually, they float. (So does the pulp. So I prefer to exclude as much pulp as possible from the beginning.) I scoop the seeds with my hands into a second bowl of water and repeat the process. Sometimes I pour the water and seeds through a strainer and rub the seeds around against the strainer and run tap water through them. Mixing and matching and repeating produces clean seeds.

Next comes the drying. I spread the seeds in a monolayer on a dehydrator tray and set the temperature at 95°F. Now I proceed a bit differently for small seeds and big ones. With small seeds, I dry for about eight hours to one day. After the seeds have been drying a few hours, I come back and rustle them up with my hands so that they won't stick to the tray when dry. Then I examine the seeds for dryness as already described. If they are dry enough, I seal them into Ziploc bags. (Brands matter. Many cheaper brands are thinner plastic.) Or I put them into a ½-pint jar and freeze them.

If the seeds are large, especially if they are huge, such as for 'Sweet Meat–Oregon Homestead', some Hubbard varieties, and 'Amish Pie Pumpkin', the surface of the seeds may crack if they are dried too fast. For these, after a few hours of drying and the rustling-up step, I turn the dehydrator off or take the tray out for a day. Then I return the seeds to the dehydrator and finish the drying. For the biggest seeds of the biggest varieties, the second stage of drying may take a day or more. It is especially important to break open big seeds and evaluate the meats for dryness, as described earlier in this chapter.

If you don't have a dehydrator you can dry seeds in a strainer. I have dried large amounts on a screen in front of a fan. You can't usually get seeds dry enough to seal into airtight containers or freeze that way, however, unless you have very low relative humidity, such as in a desert environment. (You can store such seeds in paper envelopes. But for long-term storage, you need drier seeds.) However, you may be able to finish off seeds in front of a wood stove or space heater if you want optimal dryness and don't have a dehydrator. (Some people dry seeds with silica gel. It's a huge pain, though, and not appropriate for larger amounts of seeds.)

The second way to process seeds is more suitable when we have lots of fruits of one lot we are processing at once. We dump the pulp into a bucket or container of water, work the seeds free of pulp, and then leave the mess to ferment a little. The seeds start off floating along with the pulp. After the seeds sink, drain off the rest of the mess, wash the seeds several times, and get them into the dehydrator right away to dry as already described. It generally takes one to three days for the seeds to sink. You have to watch them and catch them promptly.

Fermentation processing does a better job of eliminating diseases and destroying germination inhibitors than does merely hand-washing the seed. Hand-washed seed often doesn't germinate well in indoor germination tests, even though it germinates very vigorously outdoors.

CHAPTER ELEVEN

Beans

The Big Bean Picture. Cooking Beans for Maximum Flavor and Minimum Toot. Selecting Our Own Friendly Microbial Members of the Grand Alliance. Hold the Water. Bush Beans versus Pole Beans for Dry Seed. Interplanting Corn and Beans. Bean Strategies. Uncommon Common Beans. Fava Beans. Cowpeas. Runner Beans. Popbeans. Tepary Beans. Why You Can't Recognize Bean Crosses; Seed Saving, Isolation Distances, and Numbers. Harvesting and Threshing Beans. Turbo-Winnowing. How Many Beans?

The Big Bean Picture

Dry beans, peas, lentils, and other grain legumes represent the richest source of protein we can find in the plant world. Legumes are also excellent sources of carbohydrates, so are good calorie as well as protein staples. Beans as calorie or carbohydrate sources have the added advantage of having a low glycemic index. That means they are good food for diabetics and for those who are carbohydrate sensitive. Beans are also an excellent source of fiber.

Beans are easier to harvest and thresh than all other grains except corn and easier to use than all grains, including corn. We don't have to dehull, grind, or bake them into bread. We just need to soak them whole and boil them.

Saving bean seeds is the very essence of seed saving. As I put it in *Breed Your Own Vegetable Varieties*:

One wall of my living room is lined with shelves full of jars of my own seed. No wall decoration could provide more beauty, comfort, and security. Nothing else is

such a good conversation piece. Here is a touchstone, a shrine to what is essential. Here are memories of past seasons and accomplishments, and dreams for those to come. Here is a symbol that this is, indeed, hearth and home and homestead. Here is hope for the future.

It is myriad jars of *beans* of many different types that I display in the living room. Home is where the beans are.

Legumes come in a huge bounty of varieties and species. Depending upon the species and exact variety, we may use the dry beans, fresh green shelly beans, bean pods, and sometimes also shoots, flowers, tendrils, leaves, or roots. We also use legumes of many kinds as cover crops and green manure crops, and for animal forage, pasture, and hay.

Among the common bean (*Phaseolus vulgaris*) varieties, for example, we might grow 'Kentucky Wonder' or 'Roma' for green beans, 'Vermont Cranberry' for shelly beans, and 'Black Coco' or 'Jacob's Cattle' for dry soup beans. Shelly beans are green beans shelled out after the bean has become full size but before it begins to dry and harden.

The ideal variety for green beans grows pods and then delays in growing the seeds, giving us several days' leeway in picking the pods for use as green "snap" beans. The ideal variety for shelly beans produces pods and green seeds quickly but then delays somewhat before the seeds begin drying down, giving us a few days to catch the pod in the shelly stage. The ideal dry bean doesn't delay unnecessarily but runs straight through from pod stage to dry beans as quickly as possible (making it very difficult to get a good mess of green beans or shelly beans unless the planting is quite large). Many varieties have mixed characteristics and mixed uses. And flavors at various stages also matter. The heirloom pole variety 'Kentucky Wonder', for example, is usually planted for green beans but is often also used for dry beans. The green beans and the dry beans are both richly flavorful.

Here is the equivalent situation for peas (*Pisum sativum*): There are varieties used primarily or exclusively for dry or "soup" peas. These usually have tough, unpalatable, stringy pods. Then there are edible-podded peas such as 'Oregon Sugar Pod II', 'Oregon Giant Sugar' and 'Sugar Snap'. Then there are varieties we use primarily as shelling peas, such as 'Maestro' or 'Tall Telephone' or 'Green Arrow'. We can also grow pea shoots for greens or eat the young leaves.

Peas, fava beans, garbanzos, and lentils are cool-weather crops. They can tolerate freezes and grow well in cool weather. The rest of the species are warm-season legumes. Space doesn't permit giving growing information about every species.

The second edition of *Seed to Seed* lists twenty-five different legume species and gives growing information for each. In this chapter I focus primarily on legumes as a dry grain crop for long-term storage and use rather than as green pods or shellies. Information about growing green beans or green peas or edible-podded peas is widely available. In this chapter, I'll discuss only the particular bean varieties and species I grow and use regularly, and how they fit into our repertoire. Your goal will be to develop your own beany repertoire.

Cooking Beans for Maximum Flavor and Minimum Toot

Not eating beans can lead to digestive system upset. If you don't eat beans for a long time, then suddenly eat a huge amount of beans, you are likely to have gas, at the least, and possibly indigestion, bloating, and other signs of digestive system tribulation. Where you went wrong, however, wasn't in eating the beans. It was in *not* eating beans for so long. That is the way I look at it.

Our digestive systems adapt to bean eating. Whether this is because of changes in our systems themselves or changes in their ecology (such as the amounts and types of bacteria present), I have been unable to find out. However, I do know four things. First, we do adapt. If we eat beans regularly, we don't have the kind of digestive upset from beans as do those who eat them only occasionally. Second, it seems to go somewhat by species. Being used to common beans, for example, doesn't completely cover eating a huge amount of lentils after not eating lentils for a while, or vice versa. Third, when I haven't had a particular species for a while, I find it best to start by eating a small amount mixed with other foods rather than making the bean the main course. A small bowl of bean soup with a complete meal, for example, is a better reintroduction than a full meal of bean soup.

Finally, for the species that require long soaking, I generally soak the beans longer and "better" than most people do. Practically speaking, I soak beans for cooking exactly the same way as I presoak beans for planting. It is a longer soaking with more stirring and changes of water, which is especially designed to keep the beans fully oxygenated while they are germinating. Somewhere along the line, I adapted this method for soaking my cooking beans, noticing that it gave the best flavor of cooked beans. Only years later did I notice that, whenever I ate a can of beans or anybody else's cooked beans, I always got at least a little bit of bloating and gas, even when I was thoroughly used to eating the relevant species. I believe the standard method of soaking beans simply doesn't do an optimal job and that optimal soaking profoundly affects the digestibility of the beans.

There are two kinds of grain legumes—those that need long soaking before cooking and those than don't. It goes by species. Peas (*Pisum sativum*), lentils (*Lens culinaris*), cowpeas (*Vigna unguiculata*), and peanuts (*Arachis hypogaea*) don't require soaking. Every other grain legume commonly grown in North America does. Among those that require at least eight hours of soaking before cooking are common beans (*Phaseolus vulgaris*), garbanzos (a.k.a. chickpeas) (*Cicer arietinum*), soybeans (*Glycine max*), tepary beans (*P. acutifolius*), runner beans (*P. coccineus*), and lima beans (*P. lunatus*).

There is an interesting exception to the generalizations about the species that need soaking. So-called popbean varieties can cook completely and become delicious with just a few minutes of dry roasting, parching, frying, or microwaving. These include the *P. vulgaris* popbeans called *nuñas* as well as my own garbanzo variety, 'Hannan Popbean', which I describe later. The *nuñas* are not daylength-adapted for North America. 'Hannan Popbean' is. The *nuñas* as well as the 'Hannan Popbean' all have a flavor when popped that is like that of a roasted nut rather than like boiled beans.

For the beans that require soaking before cooking, most books will tell you that there are two methods. I disagree. There is only one method if you want to digest the beans easily. That "quick" method of starting with dry beans, then adding boiling water and letting them sit for half an hour, then boiling them—forget it. That method ruins the flavor and results in beans that are very hard on the digestive system. My method of cooking beans starts with a variant of the long-soaking method.

To cook beans, people usually start by picking them over if they need it. That is, they spread the beans on a tray, examine them carefully, and remove any moldy beans or pieces of rock. My beans usually don't need picking over, because I cut rather than pull plants when I harvest the beans. I also remove any unripe plants before harvest rather than letting immature beans get mixed into a lot. So I usually just dump the beans in a pot and wash them by swishing them in tap water and pouring it off a few times. (With lentils, cowpeas, or peas I just wash them as described and then cook the beans or peas in about three times as much water as the beans, skipping the soaking step. For all other beans, I soak first.) Next I fill the pot with cold tap water and leave it at least half an hour. This helps hydrate the skins so they are less likely to split when the temperature is higher. After about half an hour, I drain the water, then refill with cold tap water and some boiling water from a kettle I keep simmering for the purpose. That is, the beans will now be soaking in luke-warm water. The water is in huge excess, generally at least a couple of gallons of water for about a quart or two of beans.

The next issue is one of air. Basically, I'm just soaking the beans as if I were going to germinate them. To do that, I need to stir the beans. Otherwise, the awakening beans will use up the oxygen in the water and begin to suffocate and die, especially those at the bottom of the container. So I stir the beans once in a while. Every couple of hours, say, as I wander through the kitchen. Also, every four or five hours, on average, I drain the water and replace it with fresh. I usually time things so I can tend the beans for at least four or five hours before leaving them untended a while (such as overnight).

It takes most varieties of most species at least twelve hours to soak fully, that is, to imbibe as much water as they are capable of and become ready to germinate. It can take some garbanzo, runner beans, or fava varieties as much as thirty-six hours of soaking. When fully soaked and ready to cook, the beans should all be fully plumped out. If the ones in the bottom of the pot are small and unplump, you didn't stir or change the water enough. Old or poorly grown beans may imbibe water irregularly, in which case it isn't possible to get an optimally cooked batch of beans from them.

When the beans are ready to cook, I pour off the water, rinse them in a change of water, and

Store-Bought Beans

Commercial dry beans are often old or poor-quality seed. In fact, I have generally found those little 1- or 2-pound bags of beans in the supermarket to be old enough or poorly enough grown to be impossible to prepare properly. Often they just don't imbibe water well enough. However, around here, as a result of the larger Hispanic population, most supermarkets now carry 10- and 20-pound bags of pinto beans, and these are usually acceptable quality. The little bags of beans in the supermarkets still tend to be as bad as ever. Co-ops may carry bulk beans. Bob's Red Mill carries many bean varieties.

Choose beans that have few splits. Split beans don't cook optimally, and many splits indicates that the entire crop was grown, harvested, or threshed suboptimally. Whenever I'm buying beans I also evaluate how many beans are moldy or discolored. If there are many, that represents lots of time it will take sorting through the beans. In addition, it often indicates poorly grown or poorly harvested beans that will not soak uniformly enough to make a good batch. I also inspect the beans for any wheat grains. Beans are often combined with the same equipment used for wheat, which sometimes leads to contamination of one grain with others.

add water to at least a couple inches above the soaked beans. Then I add the tiniest pinch of salt (about 1/16 tsp. or less), the seasonings, and a teaspoon or two of vegetable oil. The oil is just to keep the beans from foaming and boiling over. I add more fat later on in cooking.

As seasonings, one of my favorite combinations for two quarts of dry pinto, black, or other dark, full-flavored beans is 1 Tbs. curry powder + 1 Tbs. ground cumin + 1 Tbs. chili powder + 1 Tbs. ground sage + ⅛ tsp. cinnamon. And often garlic or onions. After the beans have become soft, I add salt or tamari sauce to taste and fat of some sort. Meat drippings if I have them. About ¼ pound of butter sometimes. Then the final trick is to add something a little acidic after taking the beans off the heat. A little lemon or lime juice in each bowl, for example. Or some vinegar in the pot. Tomato paste or ketchup also works well in many a pot of bean soup. Sometimes I thicken the bean broth by blending some of the beans with a hand blender right in the pot.

I eat most of my beans just cooked and seasoned simply and eaten straight. I don't usually make them into dishes such as baked beans, because these involve adding so much sugar. With potatoes and very prime, sweet winter squash, I already have enough high-glycemic-index foods in my repertoire, and like to keep beans in their pristine, low-glycemic-index purity in my cooking repertoire.

There are many spice combinations that give delicious end results. Oregano and thyme are other spices I often use with beans. For white or golden beans I frequently use primarily curry powder. However, I have never used exactly the same combination of seasonings twice. In all cases, though, my beans are cooked basically the same way. They are cooked essentially unsalted, but with a touch of oil to prevent foaming or boiling over. Then I add a generous amount of fat or oil of some kind as well as salt or something salty

Unfried Refried Beans

A second major way I use beans is as cooked purées. I just purée some of the cooked beans and freeze them in 1-pint plastic boxes to use as unfried refried beans, or as a thickening component or the basis for a sauce for stir-fries, soups, or stews. For "unfried refried beans" I just thaw a brick of the seasoned bean purée and heat it in the microwave oven to use as the main protein course. I often mix light bean purées into white or yellow mashed potatoes and black or dark bean purées into mashed blue potatoes. Both combinations complement with respect to flavor and visual appeal.

after cooking. Finally, I add a little of something sour to balance out and bring out the complexity of the flavors. Then I let everything sit in the pot a while so that the beans can absorb the salt and fat flavors.

You don't add salt, vinegar, or tomato paste to your cooking beans earlier, because these prevent beans from softening. Don't add cold water or other cold ingredients once the beans have started cooking, either, as the beans won't cook properly and become soft afterwards. If you need to add additional water, bring it to a boil separately, then add it to the beans. I don't add butter earlier, because I use grass-fed Kerry-Gold butter, and it has significant omega-3s in it, which I don't want to ruin by long boiling. Sometimes I use fancy delicious olive oil as the fat, again adding it only after the cooking so as to preserve the flavor. The mystical effect of lemon or lime juice is ruined by cooking. In fact, it's best to add the citrus juice to the individual bowl just before serving.

Soybeans contain a lot of oil. Most varieties are intended to be grist for the agribusiness processed food industry and are not very palatable. However, 'Black Jet' soybean is a good culinary variety. I don't add fat to 'Black Jet', except for the little bit in the beginning to prevent foaming during cooking. There is already so much oil in 'Black Jet' that it tastes best without adding any extra.

Those little packages that contain many different varieties of soup beans are delightful visually, but they are inferior as food. Different varieties of beans take different amounts of time to soak as well as to cook. If you mix two different kinds of beans together, you cannot usually soak one optimally without oversoaking or undersoaking the other. In addition, the cooking times will not match. One will have to be overcooked. In addition, if you use beans in ways that bring out their flavors, you will season differently for each bean variety. Cook each of your bean varieties separately and optimally.

Beans keep well, but not indefinitely. Old beans are no treat for the taste buds or the digestive system. I like to use most of my beans within a year of harvest, and all of them within about a year and a half of harvest. Fresher beans soak as well as cook faster and have the best flavor.

Selecting Our Own Friendly Microbial Members of the Grand Alliance

A huge advantage of legumes is that they are able to form associations with nitrogen-fixing bacteria. In soils that haven't grown the relevant legume species in recent years, it can be useful to inoculate seeds with commercial inoculants. These are mixtures of appropriate bacteria (plus filler) for particular species. There are general mixes available that usually cover garden peas, common beans, and some specific others. Nate and I often find ourselves having to buy inoculants specifically for favas, chickpeas, or cowpeas, or getting specific mixes that cover those. For many years, with a long-term organic garden, I didn't inoculate, because when I tested it, using them or not seemed to make no difference. Now, however, with a new garden that was a long-time grass pasture with few legumes, we have gone back to inoculating and testing.

The nitrogen-fixing microbes don't grow well in high-nitrogen soil. So we usually avoid fertilizing much prior to a legume crop, especially with anything rich in nitrogen.

Generally, to inoculate beans we put them in a container with a bit of water in them to dampen the surface of the beans, then dump the inoculant in and stir everything until the beans are coated black with inoculant. This is more effective than dumping inoculant in the furrow.

All the microbes in the legume inoculants are generic for the entire country. They seem to all be coming from one company. That the nitrogen-fixing microbes are applicable for use anywhere in the country is widely assumed, but I don't believe it. I think once we have looked closely enough, we will find that particular strains of microorganisms perform best in particular regions. So I have started selecting for my own microbes. That is, for each planting of a particular species, Nate and I collect soil and root debris from under the best, most productive plants at the end of the year, and we use that material to inoculate some of the furrows in the next year's planting of that species. (We've just started doing this, so the results aren't in yet.) What we are hoping is to select for beneficial nitrogen-fixing bacteria, mycorrhizal fungi, and anything else in the soil or in or on the roots, known or unknown, that might be helping our plants perform. That is, we are trying to select for the best-performing associated friendly microorganisms as well as the best legume varieties.

Of course, the soil and debris we collect may carry disease microorganisms. But our tactics of taking soil and debris only from the most productive plants and inoculating it into only some of the next year's planting trenches serves as a precaution. In addition, we always inspect legume plants several times during the season, starting when the seedlings are just a few inches high, and we rogue out any that show any signs of disease.

I encourage everyone to do some similar experimenting to see whether we organic gardeners and farmers can select our own farm-specific or region-specific beneficial microorganisms for legume and other crop varieties of all sorts. Nitrogen-fixing bacteria can minimize our legume crop's need for nitrogen inputs in fertilizer. Mycorrhizal fungi facilitate the uptake of other nutrients as well, and so also allow plants to thrive with fewer inputs. We would expect to be able to see the effects of friendly beneficial microbes best when growing our legumes with low or moderate rather than high levels of fertility. Those are the conditions we should use when attempting to select deliberately for such organisms.

I challenge and invite all organic gardeners and farmers everywhere to join me in deliberately recruiting and selecting our own lines of friendly microbial allies to join us in the Grand Alliance.

Hold the Water

It's best to plant legumes being grown for dry beans in an area where you can hold the water off after the plants start to dry down. So it is best to put the dry bush beans in a separate patch or at one end of the garden. Once pods start to dry down, if they are rained or watered upon, the pods tend to re-hydrate, the beans re-hydrate some as well, and the skins of the beans split. The pods and beans may even mold.

The common bean is particularly vulnerable to being ruined by rain or water in the drying-down stage. Cowpea, runner bean, and garbanzo bean pods seem to be able to shed a good bit more water without rehydrating inconveniently. Here in maritime Oregon, the most practical common bean varieties are early varieties that finish drying down completely in August and can be harvested before the fall rains. We water our summer-grown bush drying beans up until the first few pods begin to dry down. Then we let the plants finish maturing the crop with the water left in the ground.

If your problem is drought or needing to irrigate, consider adding teparies, garbanzos, and cowpeas to your repertoire. These are reputed to be more drought-tolerant species than common beans.

Bush Beans versus Pole Beans for Dry Seed

Nate and I grow almost entirely bush bean varieties for our dry seed. These generally mature their seed more or less all at once, which facilitates harvesting before the rains. To harvest our bush dry beans we just cut the plants and put them on a tarp indoors until we get around to threshing.

With pole beans, the beans mature over a longer period. In addition, you have a support of some sort, such as poles, a fence, or corn plants. This means that you have to hand-pick the individual dry beans as the pods dry. Furthermore, if you grow pole beans on corn plants, as we do, you'll need a big, late-maturing type of corn, which must be watered, at least in our region. This means we need to hand-pick dry bean pods from the corn patch before every irrigation. All in all, we prefer to grow green beans on our corn, and grow primarily bush beans of various kinds for dry seed. One exception is that we do like pole varieties of runner beans as dry beans. For these, the beans are so big that it is worth the extra time it takes to hand-pick the individual pods.

Interplanting Corn and Beans

Pole bean varieties give the most yield and the richest flavors of any green beans. I love the jungle like feel of a patch of tall corn draped with bean vines dripping with beans. I sometimes deliberately enhance the jungle feel by planting a few 'Heavenly Blue' morning glories in among them, where their big blue flowers add a dramatic touch. (Their annual vines create no weed problems.) A few tall-growing nasturtiums in the corn patch add to the cheer and complexity. I love to pick green beans standing comfortably within the pleasant, cool shade of the corn patch on a hot summer afternoon. I love eating beans (and spicy nasturtium leaves and flowers) from the corn patch all summer, then having the additional boon of the corn harvest at the end of the season. And what could possibly be more all-American than growing beans on corn?

One approach is to grow green beans of any variety we like on the sunny three edges of the corn patch, but not in the middle. An alternative approach we use is to sow 'Withner White Cornfield Bean', a very shade-tolerant common bean variety, throughout the patch.

It is often said that most beans are shade tolerant. That is true if what you want is vines, not beans. Most bean varieties don't flower very prolifically in shade. To grow most ordinary varieties of pole beans on corn, we use only the outside corn plants on the south, east, and west sides of the patch.

Buffalo Bird Woman grew several bean varieties. All were bush beans grown separately from the corn. Her corn varieties were mostly small with multiple stalks rather than tall, single-stalked varieties. Many American Indians grew pole beans on corn, however. Often, for example, three corn plants were grown per hill, with hills 6 feet or more apart, and each three-plant cluster would have a pole bean plant or two twining around and among the corn plants. These pole beans did not need to be particularly shade tolerant, as they received nearly full sun. The corn provided support. So did the beans, in their own way. Beans growing on corn don't stick to just one plant. The bean grows up a single stalk for a while, then the growing shoot gets bored and leaves the cornstalk it is on and quests around and finds and grows up a neighboring stalk for a while. The result is that a bean plant or two in each hill of corn ties the corn plants together and helps keep them from lodging (falling over) in the wind.

European settlers usually grew their corn in fields of rows and fertilized with manure to allow the higher plant density and associated higher yields. In many cases, they grew pole beans only on the outermost plants in the patch, and this strategy, too, does not require a shade-tolerant bean. The word "cornfield" in a bean variety's name simply means that someone, somewhere, once grew the variety on corn. It doesn't always mean it is a shade-tolerant bean that can be grown in the middle of the patch.

I did an experiment once in which I grew five different varieties of pole beans on a friend's patch of 'Bloody Butcher' dent corn. The corn was about 12 feet high, and was spaced with only about 12 inches between plants, much too tight for a corn of that size. The ground deep in the patch was in nearly full shade. I planted each bean variety on three different (east-west) rows starting from the east edge and continuing deep into the patch. Alas, I misplaced my notes. I remember only that one variety was 'Withner White Cornfield Bean' and another was 'Genuine Cornfield Bean'. The 'Genuine' has a small brown and gray striped seed. It did not like Oregon. It didn't perform well even on the edge of the patch, giving low numbers of beans, and only very late in the season. The other three varieties, whose names I don't recall, did fine on the edge of the patch but yielded next to nothing from the interior plants.

'Withner White Cornfield Bean', which at that time was (quite confusingly) called 'True Cornfield bean', had an entirely different attitude. It yielded well even in the nearly full shade of the overly dense planting of corn. Furthermore, its leaves expanded to giant proportions in the deep shade. I measured leaves that were a foot across. Alan Kapuler had long offered 'True Cornfield' through Peace Seeds, but I felt the variety was overlooked because that name was so similar to the better-known 'Genuine Cornfield Bean'. So we changed the name of 'True' to 'Withner

White Cornfield Bean', in honor of the family that had preserved it and passed it along to Alan Kapuler.

'Withner White Cornfield Bean' is now our main green bean. It is very shade tolerant. I have even interplanted it among tomatoes and have harvested both tomatoes and beans from one support system. 'Withner' is flat-podded and light green and has a delicious, distinctive taste. It is stringless at the green bean eating stage. It requires just a couple of minutes of boiling to be fully cooked. Its shape and fast-cooking tendency recommend it for stir-frying. The seed is small and white and a little curved. The plants grow to about 10 feet high. That works pretty well even in 8-foot corn, as the beans run along the rows as well as climbing the plants.

To grow pole beans on corn:

1. Match corn and bean varieties. Don't put a bean that grows 20 feet on a corn plant that grows only 4 feet. It is OK to grow beans that are about 4 feet higher than the corn, however, since beans do use up some of their length skipping from corn plant to corn plant within the row.

2. You have to match irrigation needs and maturities of the corn and bean varieties. In areas where beans must be irrigated, you need a full-season corn that is going to also want to be irrigated. (With a short-season corn, we need to hold the water off the corn so it can dry down, but the beans need regular watering.)

3. If you use ordinary spacing for the corn, don't plant a bean plant on every corn plant. Instead you should plant one bean for every two or three corn plants.

Nate and I often want the pole beans as much as or more than the corn. We grow early varieties of corn as our main corn staples. The late, full-season corns we grow are actually being grown as much for bean poles as for the corn itself. So we often plant the corn with 50 percent more space between plants than we would otherwise. (That is, we'll thin corn that is going to grow to 8 to 10 feet tall to 18 inches in the row instead of to 12 to 14 inches). Then we plant a bean for every corn plant. That is, we end up alternating corn and bean plants in the row.

4. Give the corn a head start. Sow the corn first, let it grow to about 4 inches high, then sow the beans. Otherwise, the beans will overgrow and shade out the corn.

5. I always presoak bean seed before interplanting it with established corn. By the time the corn is established well enough so that it is time to plant the beans, the corn is deeply enough rooted so that, when we water appropriately for the corn, the top few inches of soil don't stay wet enough to germinate the beans. Presoaking the bean seed allows us to water the corn patch as is appropriate for the corn. The presoaked bean seeds already have all the water they need to germinate and put roots down deep into moist soil.

6. We plant the shade-tolerant 'Withner White Cornfield Bean' either on the edges or throughout a corn patch. We plant other varieties only around the edges.

7. The key to a good yield of green beans is to keep the beans picked. Once a bean plant starts producing seeds inside the pods, it concentrates its energy on finishing the seeds and quits producing green beans.

8. Even one maturing pod is enough to cut short a pole bean plant's production of green beans. For this reason, when I do seed saving on a green bean variety, I leave a section alone and unpicked for seed, and eat off the rest of the patch. I don't try to eat off and save seed from the same plants.

9. Pole varieties of lima beans, cowpeas, and runner beans also work well on corn.

10. Peas can also be planted in corn. They don't twine up the corn as beans do. However, we can grow little patches of a dozen plants between generously spaced corn plants. Alternately, we can plant wide rows of peas in alternate aisles in the corn patch. With a little extra effort we can tend the patch and pick from the remaining aisles. The peas in each clump or wide row partly support each other, and the clumps or rows are supported by the adjacent corn.

11. Beans don't contribute any nitrogen to the adjacent corn plants. Legume cover crops release the nitrogen they accumulate only after they are turned under and decompose. Growing legumes, though, do compete less for nitrogen with the corn than would another corn plant. This is valuable, because corn is especially nitrogen-demanding.

12. People often hope that interplantings might give as much of both crops (the corn and the beans) as either planted in a pure stand, but on only half the space. I have never seen it work that way. If it did, it would suggest that you are giving your pure plantings more space than is optimally efficient. However, in my experience, you can get a near full crop of corn (for the space) by giving the corn 50 percent more space than you would in a pure corn planting, then can get a generous crop of beans besides. Those corn plants given 50 percent more space often make bigger and more ears than corn with tighter spacing, even with the beans growing in the extra space. So the 50 percent reduction in the number of corn plants in a patch of a fixed size doesn't translate into a 50 percent lower

corn yield, but instead to say, perhaps 20 percent less (as a guess). My ideas about yields are only crude impressions, however. Yield is not the main reason I grow beans on corn, and I have never done a serious comparison.

Bean Strategies

Flavor comes first in our bean patch. Mild-flavored varieties have the virtue that they can add nutritional value to many dishes without much affecting the flavor. These are appreciated most by those who use their beans mostly as baked beans, or in soups or stews with meat or cheese. These cooking styles depend upon the ability of beans to absorb other flavors rather than on the flavor of the beans themselves. I prefer to grow richly flavorful beans that make a wonderful main course by themselves, beans that are great with just a little salt and pepper and fat, beans that can leave me feeling happy and fully satisfied when cooked and eaten simply and without needing to be combined into dishes including sugar or molasses, meat, or cheese. So we grow only varieties that have rich, delicious, distinctive flavors. That's our first principle.

Our second general bean strategy is that we prefer to grow staple crops that can be grown without irrigation. For us, that means growing cool-season legumes either as overwintering crops or in early spring. The cool-season legumes are fava beans, garbanzo beans, lentils, and peas. Of these, favas and garbanzos are part of our repertoire. Peas grown for dry peas in Willamette Valley get too many pea weevils to be palatable. However, we grow edible-podded peas, both overwintered and as succession plantings throughout the summer.

Lentils are a possibility we have yet to explore.

Our final bean strategy: we prefer to grow one variety of each of many different species rather than many varieties of one species. So, for example, instead of growing five different *P. vulgaris* dry bean varieties, we grow just one. Or none, because we sometimes reserve the *P. vulgaris* niche for pole green bean varieties. Then we also grow one cowpea, one tepary, a fava, and a garbanzo. We're also breeding our own runner bean line. We plan to try soybeans, lentils, and limas also. Of these, we can cook the cowpea without soaking, and the garbanzo, which is a popbean, just by popping. The rest take long soaking. Four of the species are cool-weather types; the rest are warm-weather types. This approach gives us a variety of beans, growing at different times of year, as well as plenty of flavors and cooking niches. It's also a strategy that makes for maximum resilience to diseases and weather.

Uncommon Common Beans

I've grown a lot of different common bean (*Phaseolus vulgaris*) varieties for dry beans. The ones that work best here are those that mature early enough to dry down a crop in August before the fall rains. *P. vulgaris* varieties are especially likely to be ruined if rained upon after they have started drying down, as I described in the "Hold the Water" section.

Here are some varieties that are early and very productive here, but that I don't grow because they have a bland flavor: 'Jacob's Cattle' (a.k.a. 'Trout'), 'Soldier', 'Speckled Bays' (a.k.a. 'Taylor Dwarf Horticultural'), 'Vermont Cranberry', and 'Brown Swedish'. 'Speckled Bays' and 'Vermont

Cranberry' are far better as shellies, in my opinion, than as dry beans.

'Hutterite' is a yellowish green bean that is on the late side here. Its big virtue is that it disintegrates in cooking to make a purée. However, the purée is utterly bland. In addition, the thin-skinned beans split much more easily in response to exposure to a little rain than do *P. vulgaris* varieties with normal seed coats. If I want a bean purée, I use a blender on a bean with actual flavor, and skip the 'Hutterite'.

'Flageolet', a small greenish white bean that is considered primarily a shelling bean, also makes delicious dry beans. They actually taste a good bit like green beans, even as a dry bean. They are a bit late to finish in August here, though.

'Black Turtle' and 'Red Mexican' are too late to finish in August here. The true 'Navy' or 'Navy Pea' bean that was a major commercial bean when I was a kid seems to be lost. It had a wonderful, unique flavor. The commercial beans sold under that name these days are flavorless. Apparently breeders "improved" the bean agronomically but forgot all about flavor.

The two real winners in my *P. vulgaris* dry bean repertoire are 'Black Coco' and 'Gaucho'. Both are very early—early enough to dry down in August. 'Black Coco' is a good-sized roundish bean that is black raw and rich chocolate brown with a brown broth when boiled. It is as early and as productive as any bean I have grown. The flavor is wonderful. The bean is widely adapted.

'Gaucho' is a small gold bean that is also as early and productive as anything I have grown. It, too, has a delicious rich flavor. It appears to be lost commercially. We're doing a seed increase to reintroduce it.

The other main *P. vulgaris* varieties we grow are the two pole bean varieties 'Kentucky Wonder' and 'Withner White Cornfield' Bean. I have already described 'Withner' in the section on interplanting corn and beans.

'Kentucky Wonder' has a rich, powerful flavor as a green bean. It takes about eight or ten minutes to cook when boiled. A handful of 'Kentucky Wonder' green beans in a soup flavors the entire soup. 'Kentucky Wonder' is also a good shelly and dry bean, but we use it just as a green bean. We grow it on the outer rows of corn. True 'Kentucky Wonder' has brown seeds, not tan or white seeds. The so-called 'Kentucky Wonder White-Seeded' has little flavor.

Interestingly, when some people say a green bean tastes great, they mean it is "mild," that is, what I would call "bland." These people like 'Blue Lake', which is beautiful and holds its color when canned, but has little flavor. 'Oregon Giant' and 'Cascade Giant' are striped beans that are also bland.

Common beans are largely self-pollinating. In some areas, common beans don't outcross much, and people can plant many different varieties in one garden with just a few feet of isolation, save seed of them all, and keep all the varieties pure. In other areas, common beans do outcross enough so that they require some isolation distance. In Oregon State University fields not far from my home, bean breeders don't have to worry about beans crossing. But I once grew a dozen varieties with 5 feet between varieties, and all of them crossed up. This is probably because university and extension people use conventional methods, including herbicides and insecticides, and their fields don't have the insect variety and numbers that exist in established organic gardens and fields.

Fava Beans (*Vicia fava*)

Some varieties of fava beans overwinter here in the maritime Northwest. Others don't. In New England and the Upper Midwest and Far West and Canada, spring planting of favas will be the ordinary approach. Favas set pods only in relatively cool weather. So they aren't the obvious choice for the South or Southwest.

Overwintering fava beans here can be subject to a disease that makes unpalatable black blotches on the seeds. Some varieties are affected more than others. Not irrigating the beans at all and avoiding irrigation drift from irrigated crops matters a lot. Those with mild but drier winters have an easier time overwintering their favas. We usually plant our overwintering favas in mid-October so as to avoid aphid-transmitted diseases. I generally watch for the hard freeze that kills the aphids, then jump-start my favas by presoaking the seed indoors as described in prior chapters.

All the small-seeded cover-crop favas typically grown around here (including, in my opinion, 'Sweet Lorane') are relatively unpalatable as dry beans. So is 'Windsor'. The big-seeded types are usually grown for shellies. I know of only one variety that is delicious when grown for dry seed—'Iant's Yellow', which was bred by Mushroom (a.k.a. Alan Kapuler) after a single yellow-beaned plant showed up in some material obtained from Ianto Evans. Mushroom named the bean to honor Ianto's work collecting, distributing, and promoting fava beans in the maritime Northwest. Ianto himself bred some fine varieties, such as 'Aprovecho Select', the tastiest green shelling fava I've had. Unfortunately, people didn't realize that different fava varieties need serious isolation from other favas to be maintained as pure strains, and 'Aprovecho' exists in name only these days.

'Iant's Yellow' is delicious as a dry bean. Like all favas, it requires more soaking than most beans before cooking (1 to 1½ days as I recall). 'Iant's Yellow' is gold-tan on the outside and yellowish inside and has a black hilum (eye). It is a medium-sized bean. It has more disease resistance than most favas and overwinters well in mild climates like ours. The flavor and texture as a dry bean is spectacular. The skin on the cooked beans is pleasantly chewy instead of unpalatable and tough, as is common with most fava bean varieties. 'Iant's Yellow' isn't particularly good as a green shell bean, however. The shellies aren't very big and have little flavor.

Fava beans outcross enthusiastically, being dependent upon bees for a part of the pollination process. (They don't need bees to transfer pollen, but they do need them to jostle the flowers just right.) The "small-seeded" cover-crop types and large-seeded types will cross readily with one another. If you want to save pure seed of a fava variety, you will probably need to grow just one variety at a time unless you have a large farm and can locate different patches far enough apart. "Far enough apart" is about a mile, strictly speaking. However, for how to evaluate when, how, and how much you can get away with cheating about such isolation distances, see my prior book *Breed Your Own Vegetable Varieties*.

Cowpeas (*Vigna unguiculata*)

Also known as "Southern peas" or "crowder peas," cowpeas are a traditional bean of the American South. However, a few varieties can and should be grown more widely. Cowpeas have up to 30 percent protein, are drought tolerant, don't need to be soaked before cooking, and are resistant to being ruined by rain once they start to dry down. If you have summer rain, it may be easier for you to get good cowpea crops than good common bean crops. Most northerners are familiar with cowpeas as commercial black-eyed peas, or as the garden varieties grown for pods, sometimes called "yard-long beans." Black-eyed peas can be used as shellies or as dry beans. Dry black-eyed beans are somewhat coarse in texture but have a powerful, delicious, meaty flavor.

Many years ago I did trials on a number of different lady pea varieties. Lady peas are a type of cowpea that has a tiny cream-colored seed with a very fine-grained texture and a delicious flavor. They take about forty minutes to cook and do not need soaking. However, all the lines I tried were too late to finish in August. Except for one plant in one line. . . .

That single special plant was about three weeks earlier as well as having a more determinate bush habit than its siblings. Yet it had about the same yield. I saved the seed of the special plant separately from the others, and grew the seed out for several years, each year selecting for earliness and the more determinate bush form. The result is a new variety I have named 'Fast Lady Northern Southern Pea'. Nate and I expect to introduce 'Fast Lady' in fall of 2010 through Fertile Valley Seeds.

'Fast Lady' has brilliant, beautiful yellow flowers and long pods it holds up above the bush. Given the tiny seed and the high productivity, we are planning to experiment with using 'Fast Lady' for a summer cover crop. The green pods are also tasty, and the green beans make good shelled beans. The shoots and young leaves also make an acceptable potherb, but as with pea shoots, I'm happy to have an occasional batch and don't consider them a prime green. I think 'Fast Lady' is the earliest lady pea. It may be the earliest and most northern-adapted cowpea variety. Since we grow everything organically, 'Fast Lady' is also well adapted for organic production.

We plant our 'Fast Lady' seed at about 2 inches apart in the row and don't thin at all. So, depending upon germination rate, our spacing is 2 to 4 inches. We hold the water after the first pods start to dry down. Dry 'Fast Lady' seed is especially easy to thresh.

My favorite way of fixing 'Fast Lady' is to boil the beans for forty minutes with some onions and, when they are tender, just add salt, pepper, and butter, and enjoy.

Runner Beans (*Phaseolus coccineus*)

Runner bean varieties outcross enthusiastically, and we are breeding our own line of pole dry runner bean, so we don't grow any standard runner bean varieties at the moment. However, 'Scarlet Runner' and 'Blackcoat Runner' both make spectacularly delicious, huge dry beans with rich flavors. These are pole varieties, so you have to pick the dry beans gradually as they mature. 'Blackcoat' is shade tolerant and can be grown in corn. It is also pretty resistant to being ruined by water when it starts to dry down. (I don't know whether this is also true of 'Scarlet Runner' or other runner beans.) We find it more practical to hand-pick pods of runner beans for dry beans than other species because the pods and beans are so big. The scarlet flowers of both 'Scarlet

Runner' and 'Blackcoat Runner' look delightful in the corn patch. Neither is great for green pods. 'Scarlet Emperor' and other varieties are generally grown for green pods, but we don't like the flavor of runner bean pods very much, and prefer growing runners for dry beans.

It is often stated that runner beans are somewhat more cool tolerant than other beans, and that is true. However, if you plant them earlier than common beans, you get fewer and smaller beans. If I plant in early May, for example, the plants grow happily; however, all the first and biggest sprays of flowers fail to set pods because the weather is too cool for pollen to be released. For the best yield and bigger beans, I plant in late May or early June, at the same time or a bit later than we plant common beans. That way all those first huge sprays of big flowers actually set correspondingly big pods with big seeds.

I have tried "bush" runner bean varieties such as 'Jerusalem Runner' for dry beans. They don't work for us. They are short-vined types rather than bushes. The heavy pods with their big seeds invariably drag on the ground and get munched by insects or ruined by mold. The bush runner beans really need support. And they are too bushy and low-growing to grow well on corn. So for runner beans, we stick with the fully vining varieties, even for dry beans.

Popbeans

Garbanzo beans, also known as chickpeas (*Cicer arietinum*) are a cool-weather and drought-tolerant bean. I described my adventures in discovering and beginning to select true popbean varieties of garbanzos in *Breed Your Own*

Vegetable Varieties. After much experimenting, I focused upon one particular USDA landrace accession that was uniform for bean color and popping characteristics. It was wildly variable for everything else, however. Some plants contained mostly one big seed per pod, others two or three smaller seeds. Plant size and form varied from 6 inches across to 3 feet across. Maturity time varied all the way from late July to so late in the season that the plants were only starting to form pods in October. The landrace material showed good resistance to the soilborne pathogens such as *Pythium* and *Fusarium*, so germinated reliably when not treated with fungicides and grown organically. (Most garb varieties do not.) Many plants also showed some resistance to various aphid-carried mosaic, leaf roll, and enation diseases of legumes, which are endemic in Willamette Valley. But many plants weren't resistant. Some plants had such a sprawling habit that the branches were mostly lying on the ground; others were so upright they were like trees; and there was everything in between. Given the wide range of maturities, there were a few plants that were early enough to finish without irrigation, but most of the planting needed irrigation. And some of the plants needed to be hand-harvested virtually every week for several months. All the seeds popped nicely, but they had to be size-sorted before popping. Seeds of different sizes require different amounts of cooking for popping.

I selected for the single big seed per pod, because I envisioned a popbean snack food to be eaten out of hand. Each year I eliminated all plants that showed any signs of diseases until I got material that is uniformly resistant to everything an organically managed field in Willamette Valley can throw at a garbanzo. I also selected for high productivity, a medium-erect plant type, and a maturity time that allows the beans to finish *without irrigation* in late July or early August from an early spring (March or April) planting. The result is the 'Hannan Popbean', which I expect to release in fall of 2010. 'Hannan' is planted later than the earliest pea planting but earlier than beans. It is resistant to all the soilborne as well as aphid-transmitted diseases common in our area. It is highly adapted to growing organically. And it produces uniform, big plants with big seeds, and with mostly one seed per pod. When grown optimally, a single plant can yield as many as 200 or more seeds. And it can be grown in Willamette Valley completely without irrigation, drying down as the soil dries out in late spring and early summer.

My favorite way to eat Hannans is popped and out of hand as a snack. They taste like a delicious roasted nut. I usually just pop a handful in a microwave oven. I warm the oven up first by zapping a cup of water for a couple of minutes. Then I put about ⅓ cup of popbeans down in a ring around the edge of the bottom of a paper plate and cover with another paper plate. I then zap the beans on high for 45 seconds. You can hear occasional soft sizzling pops, but not much. You have to mostly go by time. Most beans will split open and expand by about 30 percent. (See photo of popped and unpopped Hannans.) All will expand some and become soft and completely cooked and edible. I don't use any fat. Popbeans have to be thoroughly dry to pop properly. I run mine through a dehydrator as for saving seed in order to get them dry enough to pop properly.

Alternately, you can pop Hannans in a skillet as I describe in the corn chapter for parching corn. This allows popping bigger amounts at once.

(With beans, we call it "popping," but it is actually parching. Parching is done with dry seeds; you don't use oil.) Use a heavy skillet, and preheat it before you add the beans. Stir the beans while you toast them. It takes them about five minutes to pop. The beans jump around a little in the skillet but don't jump out. Don't overcook them. They produce a rich roasted-nut aroma as they pop. If they smell burned, they are.

You can also soak Hannans and eat them like any other richly flavored boiled bean. Or you can pop them, then cook them without soaking.

'Hannan' popbeans are roundish and either mottled black and brown or solid black. When the pods dry completely before the plants are harvested, the beans are black and brown mottled. If you harvest when most of the pods are dry but some are still green, the green pods, after they dry, will give black seeds. Both colors have the same delicious flavor, pop nicely, and germinate well.

In my experience, garbanzos outcross readily. I grow popbeans at least half a mile from all other garbanzo varieties for both saving seed and for the edible crop. It is particularly important to isolate popbeans, because crosses are not visible on the seed, but will destroy the popping ability of the bean.

The pods of garbs shed water better than those of many beans, and are less vulnerable to rehydrating or molding if subjected to an inconvenient rain. Garbs are also highly drought tolerant.

Garbanzo bean plants have an acidic exudate on the surface of the leaves and pods. It's composed of malic and other organic acids. In India, people put cloths under the plants at night and wring them out into water in the morning to make a lemonade-like drink. I once got something very like severe sunburn on my hands and feet by harvesting mature but not dry plants with bare hands and wearing open sandals.

Tepary Beans (*Phaseolus acutifolius*)

Teparies are a species of bean used by Native Americans in the American Southwest. They are much more drought resistant than common beans. Most don't do well here or in other more northerly areas. However, one day when I was visiting my friend Mushroom, he announced that he had planted all the tepary varieties he could find, and one actually did well in our region. 'Black Mitla' is more widely adapted and less daylength sensitive than most tepary varieties. In addition, 'Black Mitla' has the most powerful flavor of any bean I have ever eaten. It is very delicious. The seeds are small enough and the plants productive enough so that we plan to try 'Black Mitla' both as a summer cover crop as well as an unirrigated crop next year.

Tepary beans can carry bean common mosaic virus without showing much effect from it themselves. Other bean species are generally more obviously affected. So tepary beans can spread BCMV to other varieties. We grow our tepary patch a bit apart from other beans.

'Black Mitla' is a short-vined type rather than a real bush. We plant and thin to about 4 inches apart in the rows. The vines grow out to form a thick, intertwined mat about 2½ feet across and a foot high centered on the planting row. This works OK, though, because the pods are small and are held up in the vines rather than dragging on the ground. To harvest, we just roll the dry mat up, clipping the stems as we go. We set the mat aside indoors and thresh the beans out (by stomping the mat on a tarp) when we get around to it.

Why You Can't Recognize Bean Crosses; Seed-Saving, Isolation, Distances, and Numbers

Many people think that beans cross much less than they do, and thus don't isolate them as well as they should. They are misled by the situation with corn, where in some (but not all) cases crosses actually show up on the kernels that have received the stray pollen from a different variety. Most externally visible characteristics of a bean seed are determined by the mother plant, however, not by the genes in the individual seed. For starters, the seed coat itself (including the hilum, or eye) is made by the mother plant, not the individual seeds. So if you deliberately cross flowers of a white-seeded plant by using pollen from a black-seeded plant, the crossed seeds will be white, just like those of the pure white variety.

Let's suppose you cross a bean with round pods and oblong-roundish seeds with pollen from a plant that has flat pods and large, flattish seeds. The seed that represents the crosses will still be roundish. As best I have been able to figure out, the seed shape is determined by the pod characteristics of the mother plant instead of some kind of shape program in the seed. So again, the mother plant, which determines what kind of pod to make, is the one that controls what shape the seed will have. The genes in the seed itself have nothing to do with it. So when the seed is the result of an accidental cross to another variety, there is nothing to tell the seed saver that there is a problem.

When you grow out the crossed seed in the next generation, you may or may not see a difference in plant type or seed color or shape, depending upon what genes in the cross were dominant. So your cross may not even show up in this first generation. The generation after that, however, the F_2 plants, will be segregating various characteristics. So some plants will produce different seeds from others. (Each individual plant always produces just one pod shape and seed type and color.)

Some bean species, such as common bean, are relative inbreeders. That is, the flowers are so constructed that most of the time the flower is fertilized by its own pollen. Bees may get involved but aren't required. Some flowers, such as favas, need bees to physically jostle the flowers, even though the bees often cause self-pollination rather than outcrosses. However, species that need bees generally outcross more than those that don't. In my experience, all the species can outcross to some extent under organic growing cultivation in the Northwest, where there are myriad pollinators, and where cool, mild conditions allow stigmas and pollen to live a long time.

In my previous book, *Breed Your Own Vegetable Varieties,* I tell tales of growing a dozen or so *P. vulgaris* varieties in rows separated only by about 5 feet and getting all possible crosses. (In all cases, the crosses were invisible on the beans involved, and only showed up one or two generations later.) In addition, I recount believing official USDA and university information on the isolation needed for garbanzos—none, supposedly; they were strict inbreeders, supposedly; self-pollinating before the flowers opened, supposedly. Well, I got crosses in all possible directions among a couple dozen garb varieties, even those that were in the rows spaced farthest apart (about 100 feet). And those tiny little bees that looked like midget bumblebees sure did like the garbs. After I figured out what those little bees were up to, I had to discard five years of work and go back to the beginning in order to breed the 'Hannan Popbean'.

The problem is, university workers who come up with the numbers for outcrossing are generally using chemical agriculture methods. They don't have the pollinator pressure that exists in any healthy, long-term organic growing situation. In my fields, I figure that there are species of beans that everyone knows cross readily and species that cross anyway, at least to some extent, whether everyone knows it or not. Call me a cynic when it comes to "inbreeding" legume species. If I want two beans to cross so as to start a new variety, I do not even bother doing a hand-pollination. I simply interplant the two. I'll always get some crosses.

Most people isolate their beans by too little distance. However, it's also the case that most people with a large garden can grow more than one type of bean and keep them relatively pure. In some areas, some species may not have the pollinator activity to cross much. But wherever bees are working the flowers, there is always a potential for crossing. Even with that potential, however, most gardeners can successfully grow and save seed of two or more varieties of a species by putting them on opposite sides of the garden with other crops in between. If you alternate blocks of *P. vulgaris* varieties with another species, that can help. You may still have some outcrosses. However, absolute purity may not be an issue for you if you are just producing seed for yourself rather than selling it. If you grow 'Hannan Popbean', though, grow only that variety of garbanzo bean. A popbean crossed to another garb doesn't show up in that generation but is no longer a popbean inside. It can give you a broken tooth by not becoming soft when popped.

You can establish how much isolation you need by growing a variety with purplish plants and a variety of the same species with green plants, then saving seed from the green-plant variety. You will not see anything different about the crossed seeds. However, if you plant those seeds and get some pink plants, each pink plant represents a purple-green hybrid.

Nate and I grow only one variety of each species that we grow for seed, because we want to be able to sell seed, and in some cases, we are the only source or the ultimate source of foundation seed for the variety. If you aren't the only source, absolute purity matters less. If you aren't selling seed at all, you can afford to be much more casual. You can, for example, put a little of your starting seed in the freezer for backup, then grow as many varieties as you like, giving them the best isolation from each other you can, but not getting too hung up about it if it isn't very much. If and when you start getting obvious segregation from crosses, you can go back to your pure seed, having learned much more about what you can get away with. A cross isn't the end of the world, either. That's how new varieties start. You might like something that develops from a cross far more than the original varieties.

Mushroom often grows alternating rows of *P. vulgaris* pole beans and *P. coccineus* pole beans. This undoubtedly results in fewer crosses than if different varieties of one species were adjacent. However, 'Shroom does get some crosses, which he mostly either notices and rogues out, or uses to develop new varieties. Mushroom tends to notice everything. If you notice everything you can get away with more.

Except for popbeans, if you are growing beans just to eat rather than to save for seed, you don't have to isolate them at all, and can grow as many varieties as you want of each species. One prac-

tical approach is to grow just one variety of a species you are doing seed saving for that year and save enough seed for several years. Then you can grow multiple varieties of each species in the years in which you aren't seed-saving for that species.

In some cases, you can recognize the F_1 plants that result from a cross. When this is the case, you can simply cull the hybrids and keep your bean varieties pure, even if they cross occasionally. For example, if we were not planning to sell seeds, we could cheerfully grow 'Black Coco' bush drying bean and 'Withner White Cornfield' bean, both *P. vulgaris* species, at the same time, and even adjacent to each other. In a cross, tall generally is dominant to short, and the purple plants of 'Black Coco' will produce pink plants when crossed to a green-plant type such as 'Withner'. So I would be able to recognize off-type F_1 hybrids, which would be tall, pink plants. The hybrids would show up in a block of either parent.

I encourage everyone to consider our approach of growing beans from a wide variety of species so as to both enhance the biodiversity of the garden as well as to avoid the issue of isolation. In most of North America, we can grow one variety each of garbs, favas, soybeans, teparies, common beans, runner beans, cowpeas, lima beans, peas, and lentils—that is, ten different legume species. Such an approach not only eliminates the isolation problem, but the diversity of species enhances our garden's resilience with respect to both diseases and weather. (Remember that plants and bees are unimpressed with property lines. If you have neighbors with gardens very close to yours, you may also have to take their plantings into account.)

How many plants should we save seed from? Even though most beans do outcross, they are all still mainly self-pollinating inbreeders. Even those that outcross with greater enthusiasm, such as favas and runner beans, are still happy inbreeding. Highly inbred lines and genetic bottlenecking are not really a problem. This means that you could save seed from just one viable bean plant if you needed to. In practice, people prefer to save seed from at least twenty plants. Each plant is slightly different, so most bean varieties are mixes of slightly different, mostly inbred lines. When we save seed from just one seed, we keep just one rather than a greater number of the lines. However, many a variety has been rescued by planting a single seed.

Selection is the key to maintaining good bean varieties. The process isn't as obvious as is often thought. See the discussion of selection in the squash chapter.

I rogue all legume plantings about three times during the season starting when the seeds are a few inches high, removing any plant that shows signs of mosaic patterns or curled leaves, or that shows yellowing, or that is different from what it should be. If the plant is much affected, I usually remove its neighbors too. This roguing is partly to limit diseases in my plantings but also to select for varieties that are resistant to the diseases that matter in my region.

The basic rule of selection is to keep seeds from the plants that perform best in the ways that matter. We want varieties that do well grown organically, and under conditions of modest inputs and modest levels of fertility. So when I try out or maintain varieties, I always grow them in that way. For 'Withner White Cornfield Bean', in addition, I grow the plants on corn and keep beans only from plants that produce well deep within the shady interior of the corn patch. Any

old pole bean can grow on the edge of the patch in the sun.

Harvesting and Threshing Beans

For saving seed of pole beans, I hand-pick the dry pods before every irrigation and toss them in a large plastic tray. Then I either thresh them on a tarp as for bush beans, or hand-shell them, depending upon the amount and variety. It's much more laborious, either way, than harvesting and threshing bush dry beans. That's why our main dry beans are bush types.

We can get the highest quality of dry bush bean seed by holding the irrigation off the bean plants and letting the plants and pods dry out completely, then harvesting before there is any rain. However, that depends upon not having any rain in August, and upon the beans being early enough to dry down in August before the rainy season begins.

In areas of the country where rains during summer are normal, as well as with late varieties here, we usually must harvest before the plants are dried down completely. A common approach is to wait until half the pods are completely dry. At that point, most of the rest of the pods will be starting to dry, and the smallest and latest pods will still be green. Then you cut the plants and stack them in a shallow pile on a tarp somewhere where it is dry, and let the plants finish drying. With bigger piles you may need to turn the plants every few days.

Before I harvest beans, I walk the rows and mark any plant that was especially glorious. If it had twice as many beans as everyone else, I will want to save its beans separately in case it represents a new better subline. On the other hand, it might represent an accidental outcross or undesirable mutation with respect to eating quality. Either way, planting it as a separate subline is useful. I also mark the plant's position in such a way that I can collect root material and soil from under the plant, so as to possibly be selecting any desirable microorganisms that might be involved, as already described. If the bean does better because it is better able to form friendships with particular microbes, I want to save both the beans and the microbes.

Next, I remove all the plants that gave less than average yield. We process that seed separately just for food, not for planting. By keeping planting seed only from plants with average or above average yield each year, I select for plants that do well in my region and under my growing conditions. In addition, it provides an additional selection against any diseases that aren't obvious. Diseases usually affect yield.

I always cut the plants at the base rather than pulling them. It is much easier and faster to harvest by pulling the plants. But it just isn't worth it in the long run. Pulled plants add a lot of dirt, clods of soil, and stones to the "cleaned" seed. The dirt will come away in winnowing, but some of the clods of soil and stones will be just the right size to end up in the cleaned beans. The result is beans that you have to laboriously pick over before you can cook up a batch. I hate the picking over so much that I tend not to use beans that have to be picked over. So I cut the bean plants instead of pulling them and leave the dirt and rocks where they belong, in the field.

Some varieties of some species shatter. That is, the pods may break open and drop seeds in the field. With varieties that shatter, you may need to harvest whenever the oldest pods start to shatter, even if many pods are only partly dry. A good trick for harvesting seeds that shatter around here is to harvest in the morning when the plants are a little moist from dew. Moist pods don't shatter.

When it comes to threshing the beans out of the pods, we want the pods to shatter easily. I always thresh my beans in the middle to late afternoon of a warm, dry day. The seeds at that time will be much easier to break out of the pods than if I try to thresh on a damp day. If I try to thresh in the early morning, when it is most comfortable to do the work, it is counterproductive. It is much more work, and much more of the seed is lost.

Books talk about there being several ways to thresh beans, including beating them with a flail. I don't know anyone who does it that way. Most varieties hold on to their beans too determinedly for flails to work very well without extraordinary effort. Banging bean plants inside a barrel is also often mentioned. However, that is only useful for small amounts, and for varieties that release their seeds easiest. What I do, as does everyone else I know who raises substantial amounts and threshes them by hand, is to tromp on the beans on a tarp.

I choose a dry afternoon so the pods will shatter as easily as possible. The plants and pods should all be completely dry. It doesn't hurt to leave dry bean plants around on a tarp as long as they are somewhere dry. (Mine often sit for months until I get around to threshing them after the summer crops are all harvested.) I put on a pair of clean shoes with soles that have only small grooves in them, so they won't trap beans in them or deliver debris to the batch. I put a second smaller tarp out for the threshing and move subpiles of beans to the threshing tarp. (A thick layer doesn't work too well. I like a layer just a few plants thick.) I stomp the beans free of the plants mostly using a rolling motion of my foot, and working on each section of beans methodically.

Once a batch has been stomped free of the pods, I gather up the corners of the tarp and give it several sharp shakes so the beans settle to the bottom of the tarp-bowl. The stems and bigger pieces of debris end up on the surface. I lift the whole empty plants and much of the pod and leaf debris off the surface, leaving a mix of concentrated beans with smaller pod and leaf debris and dust. I dump the beans in a waiting container, move another batch of dry plants to the threshing tarp, and repeat the process until I have all the beans threshed. At this point, the material in the tarp is only about one-third beans by volume. The rest is small pieces of pods, leaves, and dust.

Turbo-Winnowing

Winnowing, the final step of cleaning grain, refers to separating it from dust, chaff, and debris. I used to use screens of various sizes to remove stems and large debris, then winnow with a fan. However, I've found it is much easier and faster to remove the large debris by gathering and thumping the tarp as I described. In addition, over the years, I've got much better at winnowing and can now clean beans using just one, very fast step of fan-winnowing. I call my method "turbo-winnowing."

Traditionally, people winnowed beans by tossing the dirty beans in a basket in the wind so the chaff and debris could blow away. That depends upon the wind being steady, not variable. I prefer to choose a relatively unwindy day and use a fan. I use just an ordinary square window

fan (outdoors). I put the fan on a card table, as close to the edge of the table as possible. Then I put a large plastic tray that measures about 3' × 1½' × 5" on the ground next to the table to catch the beans. (Kitchen trays aren't big enough with large enough sides to work as catching trays. The beans bounce. I use a big plastic box of the sort that is used to store stuff under beds.) I set the fan on high and pour the stream of beans and debris through the wind from the fan into the catching tray. Place the tray wherever it needs to be so that the beans fall into the tray and the debris is blown beyond.

Here are the nuances that I have learned over the years that turned ordinary winnowing into turbo-winnowing:

1. I don't pour from a jar or bowl, which gives a thick stream of beans less uniformly affected by the stream of air. Instead, I pour from a 3½-gallon *square* bucket, so that the beans pour as a thin uniform sheet about 10 inches across as they pass through the airstream of the fan. Pouring from a round-edged container requires pouring much more slowly, and usually involves multiple passes. Pouring from the square bucket, I can completely clean 3 gallons of beans and debris in one pass in about 15 seconds or less.

2. The airstream from a fan is a bit complex. The center core is a steady stream going in one direction. But around the edges of that central stream are whirlpools, backdrafts, and turbulence. So when I pour the beans, I pour with the edge of my square bucket down inside the upper part of the airstream, below the area of turbulence.

3. Raising the fan up on a card table and putting the catching tray on the ground means that, after the airstream acts on the beans and debris, they have a drop of about three feet before being caught. This long drop gives far better separation than just putting the fan and tray on the ground. The drop gives the beans and debris more time to separate based upon their differing trajectories.

4. The size of the pouring container isn't critical. What is critical is that it be square rather than round. A 3½-gallon pouring bucket is ideal for me, though, as it holds as many beans as I can lift and deal with easily. The 3½-gallon square bucket is a common size for foods; used ones are often available from food co-ops or restaurants. I also use these buckets for storing bigger lots of cleaned corn or beans.

5. I adjust the position of the pouring bucket so that the stream of clean beans falls just inside the catching tray and the debris, dust, and light, underweight beans all fall outside or blow away.

6. I use the same winnowing method for nearly all grains and seeds. However, with tiny seeds such as brassicas, I may winnow onto a tarp with folds arranged perpendicular to the flow from the fan. With tiny seeds, it can be unpredictable where the good seed will land relative to the light, underweight seed and debris of various kinds.

7. I haven't used any of my screens for screening seeds in years, in spite of cleaning about 400 pounds or more of seed per year. Turbo-winnowing makes owning and using seed-cleaning screens unnecessary.

How Many Beans?

In my experience, 10 to 15 pounds of beans per 100 row feet is a good yield, and 20 pounds is possible with only the most productive varieties and everything going unusually perfectly.

When it comes to beans, using the threshing and turbo-winnowing method I described, it's pretty easy to thresh and clean several hundred pounds of beans and other grains by hand. How long the threshing takes varies a lot, depending upon variety. The winnowing takes insignificant time using turbo-winnowing. (One could use the principles of turbo-winnowing with natural wind, but it would require choosing the time and wind conditions just right.) The major labor in winnowing is just setting up the tray, card table, pouring bucket, and fan, and rounding up containers for the cleaned grain. I can grow and clean a couple hundred pounds of beans a year and still have it be fun and still have plenty of energy left for the several hundred pounds of corn I also like to grow.

CHAPTER TWELVE

Corn

Corn and Nutrition. In Defense of Corn. Drying Sweet Corn. Types of Grain Corn—Flints, Flours, and Dents. Rediscovering Corn. Breaking the Cooking Code. Flint Corn Varieties and Uses. Fast-Cooking Polenta. Carol's Universal Skillet Bread. The Dedicated Cornbread Skillet. Parching Corn. Flour Corn Varieties and Uses. Semi-Universal Pancakes. Semi-Universal Sponge Cake. 'Magic Manna'. Savory Corn Gravy. Saving Seed of Corn—Isolation Tricks and Tactics. Avoiding Inbreeding Depression. Selection. Growing, Harvesting, and Storing the Corn Crop. Yields. Guerrilla Gardening.

Corn and Nutrition

One reason I garden is because it is a way of grounding myself, of putting down roots. When I grow corn, I put down very deep roots. Human beings and corn have been creating each other, affecting each other, depending upon each other, and evolving together for thousands of years. To grow corn is to become an active part of that process.

Growing corn is also just outrageous amounts of fun. Picking the ears and shucking them always turns into a celebration. Even shelling corn is fun. Nate cranks the hand sheller while I feed the ears in. We break out into unexplainable laughter at various points as we work. It's so easy, so fast, so glorious to see whole ears turn into piles of cobs and grain. And it's just so much fun.

Wherever corn grows well, it is the premier grain for producing calories. Corn is far easier to grow and thresh than other grains, including grain legumes, on a backyard or small-farm scale. Corn is often criticized nutritionally, however. And one or two of the criticisms are at least somewhat relevant.

First, corn is often criticized for its supposedly low protein content of 9 percent, as measured in modern hybrids. I can't say I worry overly much about this. Rice has an even lower protein content, and nobody criticizes rice for it. It is simply recognized that an all-rice diet provides some things, and not others, and that when rice provides most of the calories, some extra protein from legumes, meat, fish, or animal products needs to be part of the diet. Likewise for corn.

However, the 9 percent figure is typical for modern hybrid corn varieties, which generally have a lower protein content than traditional Indian corns. When open-pollinated corns are evaluated, they may have 12 percent or more protein, depending upon the variety. Selecting for high yield often seems to lower protein content. We have no protein data for most open-pollinated varieties. However, even were the protein levels in the corns I grow as low as those in the agribusiness hybrids, I still wouldn't worry about it. I don't eat only corn. I also eat legumes, potatoes, meat, fish, and eggs as well as lots of vegetables. I depend upon corn primarily to be a concentrated, storable form of carbohydrates, of calories. Even if corn contained no protein at all, I would still grow it happily.

The limiting amino acid in corn and other grass grains is lysine. Legumes usually are limiting in the amino acid methionine. When grains and legumes are eaten together, they balance each other so that the amino acid ratio comes much closer to exactly the ratio our bodies need. This is of considerable importance to vegans or to people who are too poor to have meat, milk, eggs, or fish in their diets. To non-vegans, or those who do eat even modest amounts of animal products, overall protein levels as well as lysine content are not a problem.

A second potential limitation with corn is that the calcium in corn isn't very bioavailable. This can matter profoundly for those who are eating a diet that is pretty close to all-corn. Indians in Mexico and in the American Southwest often *nixtamalize* their corn. That is, they boil it in food-grade lime, then wash and knead and hand-rub the seed coats off the corn to get hominy *(posole)*. This hominy can be cooked in soups or stews. It can also be wet-ground into dough and made into tortillas or tamales. An advantage of this process is that the nixtamalization makes both the calcium and the niacin in the corn more bioavailable. A second advantage is that you can use corn varieties with tough or foul-flavored seed coats, ending up with delicious corn after the outermost seed coat (the pericarp) has been removed. A disadvantage, though, is that if you have a corn variety with delicious flavor in the pericarps or delicate edible pericarps, you lose those flavors and the fiber the pericarps represent. Fiber is also nutritionally valuable.

The final major potential dietary limitation of corn is that it has a low niacin content, and the niacin it does contain is not very bioavailable. Niacin (a.k.a. nicotinic acid, nicotinamide, or vitamin B_3) is a vitamin our bodies can make, given enough of the amino acid tryptophan, one of the amino acids in meat and animal products. However, in the American South, slaves were sometimes fed little more than corn mush. Pellagra, the disease of niacin deficiency, was widespread. Poor free people in the South often also had diets poor enough to cause pellagra. Pellagra is a serious disease characterized by the "four Ds"—diarrhea, dermatitis, dementia, and—ultimately, if uncorrected—death. Pellagra was widespread in the American South up until 1941, when laws were passed requiring vitamin fortifying of breads, cereals, and milk. Pellagra then virtually vanished. In the United States, pellagra is now usually found only among those with nutrient absorption problems or a genetic inability to synthesize niacin from tryptophan. However, when we eat primarily our own home-grown staples, we need a diet varied enough to include enough niacin.

Niacin is widely available in green leafy vegetables, yeast, legumes, other grains, and in meat and animal products and fish. We are likely to get pellagra only if we are eating all corn and no green leafy vegetables, and no meat or animal products. In the 1700s as corn spread throughout the world, however, a wave of pellagra also spread. Poor people often did have almost nothing but corn to eat. Most grains have more niacin and/or more bioavailable niacin than corn. (Sorghum is the other grain that, when eaten as nearly 100 percent of the diet, is also associated with pellagra.)

I don't worry about either the calcium or niacin content or bioavailability of corn. However, I don't ask corn (or anything else) to be all and do all that I need nutritionally. I would have plenty of calcium and niacin in my diet, even if corn provided none at all.

So I don't nixtamalize my corn. For me, the question is not: How can I have a diet that is all corn and still survive as well as possible on it? (For that question, the answer *is* nixtamalization.) Instead, the question relevant to me is: How can I have a delicious diet that includes many things, in which corn (the grain I can produce most easily) plays one role and provides many foods of kinds I like to eat—and that don't take much work?

Like other grains, when ground fine and baked into bread, corn has a high glycemic index. So if diabetes or carbohydrate sensitivity is an issue for you, review what I said in the potato chapter about how to incorporate high-glycemic-index foods into your diet. We generally grind polenta very coarse compared to the grind we use for bread making, which undoubtedly gives it a lower glycemic index.

Some varieties of corn, when made into cornbread, taste best without added sugar. Others really seem to need a little sugar to bring out the flavors. For those with diabetes or carbohydrate sensitivity, adding even a little sugar to a staple is a major issue. In general, flint corns lend themselves to being made into products without sugar. Parching corn requires no sugar. Many flour corn colors or varieties taste best with a little sugar, but there are some exceptions.

Nixtamalizing corn is labor intensive. And when you're done, you have hominy, not bread. One of the main things I need from my corn crop is real bread. To get from fresh hominy to bread requires wet-grinding into a dough, then pressing into tortillas and frying, one tortilla at a time—another high-labor, low-yield process. I would rather bake a couple of huge chunks of bread that can last several days. Or parch true parching corn in about a minute and eat it out of hand as a tasty snack. Or make polenta. Or cakes. Or use my flour-corn ears to make a rich-flavored savory brown gravy to thicken soups and stews or stir-fries. All these latter approaches take just a few minutes of work. These are the approaches to corn and corn cookery I'll discuss in this chapter.

An additional reason why I'm disinclined to nixtamalize is that I want the corn fiber in my diet. I want to eat the seed coats, or pericarps. So instead of focusing upon cooking approaches that discard the pericarps, I have instead investigated and rediscovered—as well as bred my own—corn varieties with delicate palatable textures and delicious flavors in the pericarps.

In Defense of Corn

Corn gets bashed by some these days for the ways in which agribusiness grows, mutilates, and transforms it, using much energy and creating much pollution in the process. This has no bearing on whether we should grow delicious, traditional corn varieties in our backyards and eat them as whole-grain products we make in our own kitchens. When we grow and eat our own corn, we *don't* mutilate it, transform it into junk food, waste energy, or pollute massively in the process.

Corn also gets bashed these days because it requires more fertility than most other crops. It also, however, produces a much higher yield than all crops except potatoes. Would it be more virtuous to cultivate three times the area of wheat with the same total cost in fertility instead of one-third as much land in corn in order to get the same amount of grain? I don't think so. If I put manure on the land and grow corn right after the manure, then squash and other crops the following year, then beans or potatoes, does the fact that I plant the corn first make the corn evil? If I forgo corn and plant squash after the manure, would that make the squash evil? Manuring is one of the most natural and ecologically sound means of maintaining soil fertility. *Something* has to follow the manure. Ideally, that something takes maximum advantage of the extra fertility available in the first year after manuring, and isn't harmed by following manure (as potatoes are). Corn is the ideal crop to follow manure.

As previously mentioned, corn gets bashed for having a low protein content. However, some corns contain 12 percent or more protein, whereas some wheats have 10 percent or less, and rice has even less protein than even low-protein corns or wheats. Nobody bashes the low-protein wheats, though. In fact we *need* lower-protein wheats to make noodles and other kinds of pasta. And rice seems to get a free ride in the approval department, whatever its limitations. Methinks I detect a bit of cultural bias operating here. Corn and potatoes, the most magnificent crops of America's indigenous farmers, are still being discriminated against for not being Old World crops, at least when it comes to prestige. In addition, when corn gives you twice the yield of wheat, it is generally giving you as much or more protein *per acre* than the wheat, plus all the extra energy as well. Which matters more? Protein content of the grain or total protein produced per acre? And how much does protein content matter if you eat eggs and meat and beans, and need corn mostly as a delicious storable carbohydrate?

Corn also gets bashed these days simply because we grow so much of it. That is, we are told that growing corn is evil simply because we and so many others have found it so productive and so worthwhile. The fact that corn is so widely grown is a situation I do take into consideration. That situation has disease and resilience implications I incorporate into my larger-scale agricultural patterns. However, I'm not willing to refrain from growing everything that is the easiest to grow and the most productive just because others like growing such things too. Instead, I look for diversity within the crop, view the crop as just one among many that I raise, and take deliberate measures to limit known problems. I grow open-pollinated flint and flour corns. The total crop of flint and flour corns in this country is tiny. In addition, I deliberately select for a corn's ability to grow with moderate levels of fertility. The overall bottom line, however, is preserving a pattern of agricultural biodiversity. Nate and I grow a mix of corn, potatoes, winter squash, drying squash, beans, duck eggs, tomatoes, kale, and many other things.

Corn is one of the most magnificent breeding accomplishments of humankind. Corn is deservedly a premier member of the Grand Alliance.

Drying Sweet Corn

This chapter is about the kinds of corn that are good for cornbread, polenta, parching, corn gravy, cake, and johnnycake. Sweet corn *doesn't* make good cornbread, polenta, etc. Sweet-corn polenta, for example, has a weird, unappetizing flavor and is watery, whatever variety of sweet corn you use. Dried sweet corn ground into meal for cornbread doesn't taste very good, either, and doesn't hold together to make good bread. (Some people talk about using dry black or red sweet corn in cornbreads, but these people are using mostly wheat flour in their cornbread. Those who use red/black sweet corn in polenta mix it about 1:4 with non-sweet corn.)

Sweet corn is a staple for some families during the green corn (corn-on-the-cob) season. However, information about growing and using sweet corn is widely available. So in this chapter I focus upon dry mature field corn as a long-storing staple crop.

If you grow sweet corn, however, you can dry it in the green stage to turn it into an additional staple. I used to do this back before I became so involved in growing and breeding flour and flint corns, and back before I decided I actually preferred sweet corn raw rather than cooked. I grew the sweet corn, harvested the green ears of corn, and boiled the corn-on-the-cob a few minutes. Then I ate some ears hot, put some in the refrigerator to eat cold, and chopped slabs of kernels off the rest and dried the slabs in a dehydrator. It takes the dried sweet-corn slabs about forty-five minutes to re-hydrate in a soup or stew. The reconstituted kernels taste very similar to fresh sweet corn kernels.

The Indian approach to dried green corn was to roast the whole ears of green corn, then finish drying the whole cobs, then shell the whole kernels off the ears for storage. This approach works well and was used for drying green field corn as well as green sweet corn. It works only with varieties that have relatively narrow cobs that dry out readily. Dried cooked green corn was always a minor staple compared to the dry mature corn crop. If the corn crop fails late in the season,

however, you might be glad if you have processed at least some green corn from the field before the disaster.

Sweet corn was little used by American Indians. Even those who did use it grew just a little of it, and used it only in a limited way. Dry mature field corn is a staple crop that required much less labor to produce than cooked dried green sweet corn kernels. In addition, some varieties of flour corns and dent corns are also sweet in the green ear stage. 'Tuscarora' flour corn and 'Hickory King' dent corn are reputed to make especially fine roasting ears, for example. Growing one of these varieties might make growing sweet corn redundant, even if you want a sweet-flavored corn-on-the-cob.

Types of Grain Corn— Flints, Flours, and Dents

There are three basic types of "field" or grain corn, that is, corn intended to be used as mature dry kernels: flint corn, flour corn, and dent corn. (Sweet corn and popcorn are special types of flint corn. Popcorn makes a nice snack but doesn't yield well enough to make it a major staple and so is not discussed here.)

The illustration shows cross-sections through a kernel of each type. All three types have a germ, which is the embryo of the seed; two outer layers, called the pericarp and aleurone; and an endosperm. The pericarp is the paper like outermost layer on the corn kernel. It may be clear or opaque, or colored red or bronze or brown. The second layer, the aleurone, may or may not also be colored. (This is where the genes responsible for blue or lavender color act when they are present.) The endosperm is the rest of the corn kernel

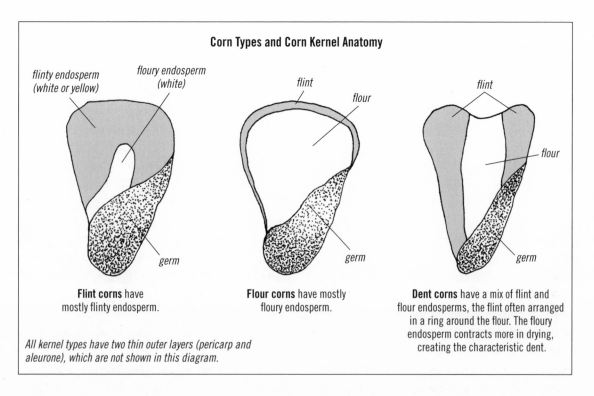

Corn Types and Corn Kernel Anatomy

flinty endosperm (white or yellow)

floury endosperm (white)

flint

flour

flint

flour

germ

germ

germ

Flint corns have mostly flinty endosperm.

Flour corns have mostly floury endosperm.

Dent corns have a mix of flint and flour endosperms, the flint often arranged in a ring around the flour. The floury endosperm contracts more in drying, creating the characteristic dent.

All kernel types have two thin outer layers (pericarp and aleurone), which are not shown in this diagram.

other than the two outer layers and the germ, and constitutes the store of food for the embryo. Modern corn processing "bolts," that is, blows or screens away the pericarps. It also degerms the kernels to get rid of the oil to make a long-storing product that won't go rancid. Supermarket cornmeal is ground-up endosperm only.

Corn kernels have two different kinds of endosperm, the floury and the flinty. The amounts of each differ in the different types of corn. Flint corns have mostly hard, flinty, glasslike endosperm and a little soft floury endosperm. Flour corns have mostly soft, floury endosperm and very little flinty endosperm. Dent corns, originally bred from crosses between flour and flint corns, have intermediate amounts of both kinds of endosperm. In dent varieties, the flint endosperm is wrapped in a column around the floury

endosperm. Floury endosperm contracts more as the corn dries, so dent kernels end up with dents in their tops.

Floury endosperm is always white. Flinty endosperm may be white or yellow. Commercial hybrids may have white or yellow flinty endosperms, but most commercially grown corn has a yellow endosperm and clear pericarps and aleurones, thus appears yellow. Yellow corn is preferred for animal feed because it supplies carotenoids, some of which can be converted to vitamin A. In addition, carotenoids give an attractive deeper orange color to egg yolks when corn is used as a main ingredient in poultry feed.

Flour corns were common among Indians of the American Southwest. However, there are also northern-adapted varieties such as those created and used by the Mandans in the upper Midwest and the classical 'Tuscarora' used by the Tuscarora Indians in New England and New York. Flour corns are easy to grind. Hit flour corn kernels with even a crude hand-crank Corona mill and they simply disintegrate into a relatively fine flour. With an impact mill, a true flour corn gives you a flour that is almost as fine as store-bought wheat flour. With a Corona mill—or even with a simple, cheap whirling-blade coffee grinder—you can make flour-corn flour finer than anything that can be ground out of flint corns using any method. You can use true flour-corn flour to make fine-grained breads, pancakes, and even real cakes such as angel food or sponge cakes—cakes with a texture indistinguishable from that of cakes made with wheat flour. And all true parching corns are flour corns, so can be used either to parch into a tasty snack or to grind and make bread, pancakes, or cakes. Some flour corns also make great gravy. Parching corn can be prepared with just a fire. Corn gravy takes just a few minutes to cook. These are very easy, low-labor cooking methods.

Insects love flour corn. They choose it preferentially and grow faster on it than on flint or dent varieties. Flour corn also molds more readily than flint or dent corns, though specific varieties matter. I suspect many flour corns have a higher protein content than flint corns. Commercial high-protein ("quality" or "opaque-2") corn is a flour corn. The opaque-2 gene is responsible for the higher protein and lysine content. Whether any or all of the traditional open-pollinated flour corns are opaque-2 types, I don't know.

Flint corn varieties were the predominant Indian varieties that were used in New England and other cold climates. They generally don't require as much heat as flour corns. (There are exceptions, though.) Flint corns are much harder to grind than flour corns. And even when ground as fine as possible in an electric impact mill, flint cornmeals have a gritty texture. Flint corns are resistant to being rained upon or even frozen when drying down. For this reason, while I may plant either early flint or early flour corns, when it comes to a late corn, I prefer flints. Flints can dry down and be harvested in the rainy season. Flour corns are likely to mold instead of drying down once the Oregon rainy season is underway. Long-season flint corns are also my favorite bean poles when I'm interplanting corn and beans in the field.

Midwestern dents are hybrids or stabilized crosses between flour and flint types. Their main virtue is their high yield. Agronomically, they have most of the best characteristics of both flour and flint corns. For culinary uses, they have all the limitations and mostly none of the virtues of either. They don't make good polenta or johnnycakes as do good flint corns. They aren't good for parching or corn gravy. They don't make a fine flour that can make dense, fine-grained breads or cakes, as can flour corns. Modern hybrid dent corn is pretty tasteless stuff, even when used as fresh-ground whole grain. But dents are not inherently flavorless. The classic open-pollinated variety 'Reid's Yellow Dent' makes a delicious wet-batter cornbread, for example. (It's best with a little sugar in the batter.) 'Oaxacan Green Dent' and 'Bloody Butcher' are said to make tasty cornbreads. 'Hickory King' white dent is renowned for roasting ears. I won't discuss dents further, since they don't fit well into my favorite cooking styles. The Corn Belt and the American Southeast are traditional dent corn territories, however. If you live in these regions, you should try some of the traditional open-pollinated regional dents. All corn varieties, including dents, will work with my Universal Skillet Bread recipe. 'Reid's Yellow Dent' is a very productive, mid- to full-season corn and is widely adapted. It makes large ears with two-ranked rows. (See note 12-1 for sources of seed for dent corns.)

You can buy 'Reid's Yellow Dent' cornmeal from Paul's Grains. Morgan's Mills sells cornmeal made from 'Rhode Island Whitecap'. Anson Mills sells cornmeal and grits made from traditional southern corn varieties (see note 12-3).

You can figure out what basic type of corn a given variety is by cutting open a few kernels with wire clippers to evaluate the proportions of flinty and floury endosperm. As I describe in the next sections, knowing the basic type of corn will tell you a lot about what it is good for and how to cook it. Variety names are not necessarily indicative, however. Most multicolored ornamental "flint" corn varieties, for example, are actually mixed and crossed-up in type and have cooking characteristics more like a dent than a true flint.

Native Americans mostly used corn varieties that were relatively pure for kernel type. They were usually pure flour corns or pure flint corns, though there were also a few dents and a few of mixed type. These days, many open-pollinated, "Indian," or ornamental corns are mixed in color. Native Americans largely used pure-color varieties, however. After I worked with pure-color varieties for a while, I saw why. The mixed-color corns have a variety of flavors that tend to add up to a kind of muddy flavor when they are prepared by grinding whole. In most cases, to get good

flavor in products made with corn as the only grain, you need pure-color varieties.

People sometimes choose only corn varieties that have yellow flint endosperms because of the nutritional virtues of the carotenoids. That approach eliminates all the flour corns, which have little endosperm, parching corns (whose endosperms are always white), fine-grained breads, corn gravy, real cakes and cookies, and more than half the repertoire of flavors. It would also eliminate the cream-colored flint corns, my favorite for sandwich bread. It would probably also eliminate all the highest-protein and highest-lysine varieties. Buffalo Bird Woman grew five main kinds of corn—a hard white, a hard yellow, a soft white, a soft yellow, and a soft red—all with different maturity times, flavors, and uses. I consider that approach a better model. In a healthful and varied diet, corn doesn't need to be the sole source of carotenoids or of anything else.

Rediscovering Corn

Amazingly, we have mostly lost the knowledge it takes to convert whole corn into delicious food in our kitchens. Even where we still have the traditional, delicious, people-food-quality corn varieties, we no longer have the cooking methods and recipes that go with these varieties. And where we have the recipes, generally, nothing is said about the corn varieties. Recipes came from particular parts of the country and assumed "their" corn. They do not work with just any corn. Most European settlers mixed corn with wheat or rye and used European baking styles that depend upon the cooking characteristics and gluten content of the wheat or rye, not the cooking characteristics of the corn. These are corn-flavored wheat breads, not cornbread. They are little help if you are gluten- or wheat-intolerant or can easily grow corn but not wheat.

An added problem is that the cornmeal we can buy these days is really not worth the effort of baking into anything. It is made from one of a number of hybrid dent corn varieties bred for high yield. These varieties are grown for animal feed and for dismantling in factories and reassembling into processed foods. They are not especially tasty when simply ground into whole-grain meal or flour and cooked using simple home methods. In essence, modern hybrid corn varieties are for animals and factories, and when we buy commercial cornmeal or corn flour we are getting what amounts to a culinarily inferior by-product of the animal-feed and food-processing industries.

I spent more than a decade testing and cooking hundreds of different varieties of corn in different ways. I ended up with a very simple generalization. . . .

Breaking the Cooking Code

Here is the simple generalization: *The flinty endosperm part of the corn kernel cooks well by boiling. The floury endosperm cooks well by baking.*

True flint corn varieties, varieties that are mostly flinty endosperm, cook best with methods involving boiling. So flint corns can make great polenta, which is basically just boiled corn mush with a college diploma, and served with a glass of wine. True flint corns make good johnnycake, which is simply boiled mush that is then briefly fry-steamed. Flint corns also make good puddings. It* is harder to bake flint corns into breads. However, it can be done by using a few tricks.

True flour corns have almost exclusively floury endosperm, and can be baked into fine-textured bread (again, with a few tricks), pancakes, and even angel food or sponge cake or crackers. They can be used to make gravy. They can be made into baked products every bit as fine in texture as those made from wheat flour. However, the floury endosperm just doesn't seem to cook when boiled. You can boil flour cornmeal or flour forever and it still has a somewhat uncooked flavor. Flour corns do not make good polenta, johnnycakes, or pudding. Certain colors and varieties of true flour corns, however, are those we designate as "parching corns," whose kernels, when roasted briefly at high heat, cook completely, develop delicious flavors, and make a great snack.

"Corn flour," as I use the term, is not available commercially at all, as far as I know. It can be made only from a true flour corn. "Corn flour" as sold commercially is just a finer grind of the standard hybrid dent corns that are used for animal feeds and coarser cornmeal. It can't be used to make good gravy, cakes, or fine-textured breads.

Dent corns have too much flour in them to taste fully cooked when boiled into polenta or made into johnnycakes or pudding. And they have too much flint in them to make a fine-textured baked bread or cakes or gravy. You can, however, make a classic wet-batter cornbread from dent corns (or flour or flint corns). I think this is because a wet-batter bread steams initially, then bakes during the final part of the cooking. (You can make a wet-batter cornbread from any corn using my Universal Skillet Bread recipe.)

Dent corns are also used in commercial polentas, but in these, the flinty part of the endosperm is usually mechanically separated and sold alone. Such polentas are yet one more tasteless, nutritionally stripped travesty of the agricorn industry. Italians make polenta from dent corns as well as flints that have a lot of flour in them, and they do make whole-grain polenta meals (sometimes), using special varieties of corn for it. But Italians don't just boil their polenta. They boil and stir it forever (forty-five minutes or more), then pour it in a pan in a thin layer and bake it forever more. That is, once again, to cook dents, you need both boiling and baking.

Just because a corn is a flint doesn't mean it makes great-*tasting* polenta. Additional characteristics besides the basic cooking properties are involved. Nor does any flour corn make great-*tasting* cakes. Again, other characteristics and flavors are involved. Likewise, while one can make my skillet bread with any flour, flint, or dent corn, each variety has a different flavor. Some, like the commercial dents, don't taste like much. Others are delicious.

Flint Corn Varieties and Uses

To make a good polenta or johnnycake from whole-grain flint cornmeal, the pericarp (seed coat) of the variety must be tender and palatable and needs to either be flavorless or have flavors that are delicious when boiled. Here are some flint corn varieties that will make good (quick-cooking) polenta and johnnycakes: 'Rhode Island Whitecap', 'Narragansett Indian Flint', 'Longfellow Flint', 'Abenaki Flint' (a.k.a. 'Roy's Calais Flint' or 'Abenaki Calais Flint'), and the three sister varieties I've bred myself—'Cascade Creamcap', 'Cascade Maple-Gold Polenta', and 'Cascade Ruby-Gold'.

'Narragansett Indian Flint' is a full-season flint corn originally grown by the Narragansett Indians in the Mid-Atlantic region of the East Coast. It is an 8-row flint, that is, it has a medium-thin cob with 8 rows of big kernels, and dries down very fast. Ears are either cream-colored or red. The red pigmentation on red kernels is located in the pericarp, the outer skin of the corn seed, which is maternal tissue. That is, it is genes in the mother plant that make the pericarp of the seeds, just like they make the cobs, leaves, stalks, and roots of the corn plant. And all the kernels on the ear have the same mother. So entire ears are either cream or red (or some shade of pink). You don't see individual kernels showing red.

'Rhode Island Whitecap' is a colonial selection of the original 'Narragansett Indian Flint'. (The ears are cream colored and glassy, not white. "White" flints are never white the way flour corn whites are white.) 'Narragansett' and 'Rhode Island Whitecap' like the moderate maritime climate of coastal Pennsylvania and Rhode Island. They are somewhat late to be grown commercially in New England reliably, but should be workable on a homestead scale given the resilience of flints at the end of the season, especially if you plant early. They are said to make 8-foot plants and 8-inch ears in their home turf. Here in Willamette Valley they make 10- to 12-foot plants and ears up to 10 inches. However, it generally takes until September or October, fully into the rainy season. This isn't much of a problem on the hand-harvesting scale, however. Flint corns are pretty impervious to rain while drying down. They don't mold easily. They can even be rained upon, then frozen solid, then thawed, and still go on to finish drying down a perfectly good corn crop. These characteristics make the late flint varieties much more practical than the late flour or dent corns, and make the late flints especially nice varieties to grow pole beans on. You can buy 'Rhode Island Whitecap' cornmeal (or whole, uncleaned corn, if you call and ask) from Morgan's Mill.

'Longfellow Flint' is a gold 8-row flint that is even a bit later than 'Narragansett' or 'Rhode Island Whitecap', but it yields better than either, has bigger ears, and is more broadly adapted. It has a tan-bronze pericarp overlying a deep gold endosperm. Here in Willamette Valley, 'Longfellow' can produce three *big* ears per plant, while, of course, also doing a good job of holding up the pole beans. Ears can be up to about 12 inches. (The ear lengths I give represent grain-bearing length only; total length can be much bigger.)

'Abenaki Indian Flint', a.k.a. 'Roy's Calais' or 'Abenaki Calais', is a very early New England 8-row flint that was rediscovered and introduced by Tom Stearns of High Mowing Seeds. It is sold by High Mowing Seeds and Fedco. It is only a few days later than 'Painted Mountain' flour corn, the modern open-pollinated standard for earliness. 'Abenaki' is early enough to dry down in August here. It yields well and has big ears for such an early corn, up to about 9 inches. It has a mix of pale yellow and red ears. The pericarps on the yellow ears are clear or opaque, and the endosperms are light yellow. There is a double-row pattern on the ears. That is, there are 4 double rows on each ear, with gaps between the doublets. The gaps between rows and the pale yellow color of the yellow ears make the corn less than ideal as an ornamental variety. But if you want an early, high-yielding flint corn that is delicious to eat, it is wonderful. 'Abenaki' is also very cold hardy and resilient. According to the Fedco catalog, 'Abenaki' was the only corn variety that gave a

mature crop in New England in 1816, the infamous Year without a Summer (see chapter 3).

'Abenaki' grown here in Willamette Valley doesn't have very good husk coverage, however. I lose a substantial part of the crop to birds, who find it to easy to open and eat the green grain out of the top of the ears. Once a bird opens an ear, nightly dews saturate the ears, and aphids, aphid goo, and mold generally make the rest of the ear inedible. I also find the gaps between the rows and the pale yellow color unappealing.

So I used 'Abenaki' as one parent to develop the 'Cascade' series of early flint varieties. I crossed and genetically folded 'Abenaki' together with 'Byron' flint, another early flint that has good husk coverage, a deeper gold endosperm, and a tan-bronze pericarp. Every time I have seen that pericarp color it has been delicious. So I grew the tiny handful of 'Byron' seed I had obtained from a member of the Seed Savers Exchange in alternate rows with 'Abenaki', even though I had never tasted 'Byron'. 'Byron' was a bit later than 'Abenaki', and had a "pencil" (very small-diameter) cob. That meant that even "large" ears had very little grain on them for the work of shucking and shelling. Worse yet, the cobs break into pieces when the ears are put through a hand-crank sheller. The other debris blows away readily when the grain is fan-winnowed. The pieces of cob don't. They have to be laboriously picked out by hand. The pencil cob makes 'Byron' unworkable for me.

In my mind's eye, however, there was the prospect of one or more new varieties that would combine all the best characteristics of 'Abenaki' and 'Byron', and lack their flaws. The 'Abenaki', by the way, had occasional white kernel contaminants—very valuable contaminants from my point of view. I had also long wanted an early white flint that could substitute for 'Rhode Island Whitecap'. So initially, as I gently folded together the genomes of 'Abenaki' and 'Byron', I deliberately selected in favor of white to increase its gene frequency enough in the breeding population so I could select out a good, vigorous early white flint in addition to other varieties with the Abenaki-Byron genetic background.

I had an idea in mind: a new breeding concept I call "sister lines." The idea was to breed ease of seed saving into the varieties right from the beginning, and end up with a number of different closely related lines with different flavors and uses that could all be grown in side-by-side patches without needing isolation from each other. The different lines would all differ from each other only by a gene or two and share one genetic background otherwise. The one or two genetic differences are so chosen that they dramatically alter flavor or cooking characteristics or some other essential property, giving all the advantages of growing several different varieties. The overall genetic situation is designed so that minor contamination or crossing between the sister varieties doesn't matter.

The Cascade series are very early flint corns that are sister lines derived from folding together 'Abenaki' and 'Byron', then selecting and stabilizing three different varieties from that breeding population. 'Cascade Creamcap' is a very early culinary equivalent of 'Rhode Island Whitecap'. (It has the same flavor and cooking characteristics as RIW. However, it does not have any RIW parentage.) The ears are cream colored. 'Cascade Maple-Gold Polenta' makes the very best gold polenta. It has a tan-bronze pericarp and a deep gold interior, a combination that tastes even more

spectacular in actuality than it did in my imagination. 'Cascade Ruby Gold' gives solid ears of several colors: red, red-brown, gold, maple-gold, and yellow. I'm still selecting to get rid of the pale yellow that was characteristic of 'Abenaki'. I want a variety that gives red ears, red-brown ears, maple-gold ears, gold ears, and bright, deep yellow ears. Then one sorts the ears by colors. The red and red-brown ears make very delicious cornbread. The two have two different flavors. The ears look similar in artificial or poor light. To sort them, you need sunlight. All the colors in the 'Cascade' palette make great fast-cooking polenta, but the maple-gold is the most spectacular. I designed and bred it specifically for its flavor as polenta. The gold and yellow ears make a mild cornbread. They are necessary in the genetic mix to maintain the overall vigor. In addition, they are needed if you want to use the 'Cascade' series as ornamental corn.

If you want mostly cornbread and just a little polenta, you can grow just 'Cascade Creamcap' for white cornbread, and 'Cascade Ruby-Gold' for all the other colors of cornbread plus a little polenta. For lots of polenta, plant 'Cascade Maple-Gold Polenta'.

The Cascade series are as early as or earlier than 'Abenaki'. They mostly have the medium-thin cob size and thickness of 'Abenaki', and ears are the same length or a little bigger. They have 8 to 12 rows of kernels. To dry down optimally, thickness of the cob seems to matter much more than number of rows or double-row form. I think there are genetic programs for cob thickness and grain size, but not row number. So when I have an ear with 'Abenaki' cob thickness and 'Byron' size grain, I end up with 12 rows; when I have 'Abenaki' cob thickness with 'Abenaki' size grain I get 8 rows. I am allowing both in the Cascade series. Both seem to dry down equally well. Occasional ears have the pencil-cob size typical of 'Byron'. I select against the pencil cob, but am leaving a small percentage of that characteristic in the variety in case anyone wants it in the future. (If I leave a little of it in there, someone who wants a pencil-cob version of my varieties could just select for them within my varieties.) The Cascade series have solid ears with no gaps between rows, though I have left a little of the double-row characteristic in the varieties as well . . . again, just in case someone wants it. I don't select at all based upon plant or husk color, and all varieties have a mix of red, purplish, and green husk and plant colors. I don't eliminate any characteristics arbitrarily. Let diversity live. I do select for yield in the context of organic growing conditions and for performance under conditions of modest rather than high fertility. The varieties of the Cascade series are early enough to dry down in August here, minimizing the need for irrigation and finishing the corn off before the rainy season.

If you grow all three Cascade varieties, you not only have three wonderful culinary varieties, you also have a good ornamental corn with solid ears in multiple colors. The Cascade series is bred specifically for flavor, and is early, productive, designed for organic production, and makes ears that are very beautiful. To grow all three Cascade varieties, I just plant them all in one long, narrow, rectangular field with rows running lengthwise for ease of tilling. Then I make two lines across the field and put the Maple-Gold at one end, the Ruby-Gold at the other end, and the Creamcap in the middle. I put the Maple-Gold at the upwind end. I harvest the 10 to 20 feet where the varieties meet in the field separately for food. It's full of crosses. I select seed ears for the next year's crops from the central part of each variety's section. The seed ears will have occasional crosses too. But a little miscegenation *between these particular varieties* doesn't matter. They are all pristine pure-flint types. The Maple-Gold and Ruby-Gold still have a little white in them anyway. (I'm still selecting it out, but it doesn't hurt anything.) I further screen the Creamcap seed ears by inspecting them and picking out any yellow kernels before I shell the seed ears. Any yellow kernels represent crosses with one of the other varieties, both of which have yellow/gold endosperms. You can also grow any two of the Cascade series side by side and just eat the edges where the varieties meet and save seed from the middle.

If you grow 'Abenaki' or any of the Cascade series, you can also plant a late corn such as a sweet corn without contamination problems, as they will pollinate at different times.

Both 'Abenaki' and the 'Cascade' series are easy to keep free of contamination from genetically modified (GM) and other corns. They are too early to cross with the GM feed corns or most other corns unless you have planted them very late. So in most cases, you can raise these particular flint corns for both eating and a pure seed crop, even if you have neighbors who are growing corn. If your neighbors are growing 'Painted Mountain', or 'Magic Manna', however, there is a problem. 'Painted Mountain' and 'Magic Manna' pollinate at approximately the same time as these flint varieties. It is not the end of the world, however, even if your neighbor plants 'Painted Mountain' or 'Magic Manna'. 'Painted Mountain' and 'Magic Manna' are flour corns. When a flint corn ovum is pollinated by pollen from a flour corn, the kernel that develops is distinctly chalky and opaque instead of glassy like flint corn kernels.

Red Corn Genetics and Selection

The fact that most Indian red-corn varieties (and my red corns) are mixes of red and non-red ears rather than pure red is no accident. It's best that way. The gene responsible for the red has a genetic load, that is, when homozygous (pure, present in two doses), the plant is small, the ears are small, and the yield is low. So to get good yields of big red ears, it's best to have heterozygous red varieties, varieties that have one dose of red in most red ears and that thus give varieties that produce two different ear colors. There will be some small, very dark red (almost black) ears in these varieties that represent homozygous (two doses of) red color. To save seed of a heterozygous red variety, eat the deep red-black and most of the non-red ears. Save the best and biggest red ears (the best heterozygous reds) as well as the very best whites (or yellows, in yellow lines). I like to plant about 80 percent red ears. The grain for planting should be mostly (heterozygous) red if you want as many red ears as possible but also want good yield and ear size. Plant less red if you want more of the other color. (Even if you plant 100 percent heterozygous red, you'll get only 50 percent red ears in the next generation. So you need to plant mostly red each year to get lots of red ears. And you need to actively select in favor of red each generation.)

The red gene, being maternally inherited, is tricky to select for. It is co-dominant, that is, it shows up in one dose. However, the color is expressed in the pericarp, the outermost skin of the corn kernel, which is maternal tissue. So it is the genotype of the mother that determines the pericarp color, not that of the seed. By comparison, the gene for blue color is expressed in the aleurone, which is tissue made by the seed embryo itself. So if you cross a pure white female corn plant with pollen from a pure blue male plant, the ears and kernels will be lighter blue or speckled blue and white. And the same will be true in the reciprocal cross, the cross of a female blue plant with pollen from a male white plant. However, if you cross a female pure white plant with pollen from a pure red plant, the ears will be white. If you cross a female pure red plant with pollen from a white line, the ears will be all red. But the F_1 seed is genetically heterozygous red, whichever way you do the cross. And that seed will give you all red ears in the next generation.

All this means that, when you look at a non-red kernel, it may be genetically red and may not be, and likewise for a red kernel. The seed's color just tells you what its mother was, not what it is. The results of crosses and genetic manipulations show up a generation later with maternally inherited characteristics. So producing pure red varieties is not only counterproductive, it isn't especially easy.

That is, flour corn crosses show up on flint corn ears. For just a few hundred pounds of flint corn ears, it is easy to inspect the ears and pick off an occasional floury kernel as long as there aren't too many of them. These early flint corns should be absolutely the easiest corns to do seed saving on as well as the easiest corns to keep free of GMO contamination.

All of these eight flint varieties I've described have single stalks with two or three big ears instead of plants with large ear-bearing tillers that end up as bushes with lots of little ears. Flints can have either pattern. Many northern Indian flints have bushy plants with lots of tiny ears and tiny grain. I stick with the single-stalk flints with big ears and big grain. It is much easier to harvest, shuck, and shell two or three bigger ears than four or five small ones. All eight flint varieties are also fairly resistant to lodging (falling over), especially if you hill them up.

Flint corn cornbreads taste best without sugar. (Most flour corn cornbreads taste better with sugar.) For my cornbread staple, I prefer the flint corns, as they are delicious, and I just don't want any added sugar in any of my staple foods. I use sugar occasionally, but only in special treats, not in foods that are my staples. (See the section on sugar in chapter 4.)

For sources of seed for these flint corns, see note 12-4.

My favorite flint corn staples are polenta, white cornbread, red cornbread, and red-brown cornbread—the latter three made using my Universal Skillet Bread Recipe, and with no sugar.

My favorite corn for polenta is 'Cascade Maple-Gold Polenta', which I bred specifically for spectacularly flavored polenta. 'Longfellow Flint' also makes especially delicious polenta. All the colors and varieties of flints I have mentioned make good polenta—not so glorious as 'Cascade Maple-Gold Polenta' or 'Longfellow', but still better than any corn I have ever bought for polenta, even whole-grain imported Italian types, supposedly from special polenta corns.

Skillet bread tastes quite different when made from cream, yellow, red, or red-brown ears of flint corn. I prefer cream, red, and red-brown flint skillet bread as my staple breads. Each has a distinctive flavor. I like to eat skillet bread plain, or as sandwich bread. It's great with cheese. (Goat or sheep or water buffalo cheese, which don't give me allergy problems.) I also tear cream skillet bread into chunks and put spaghetti sauce or other pasta sauces or stir-fried vegetables on it. In other words, it makes a good equivalent of noodles.

'Cascade Creamcap', 'Rhode Island Whitecap', and the cream ears of 'Narragansett' all taste similar when made into cream skillet bread. (Similar enough so that I rather doubt I could tell the corn breads apart side by side, though I haven't tried it.)

I also love red skillet bread made with red ears of all the flint varieties I've mentioned that give red ears. The red ears have a unique and powerful flavor when baked. I always sort out the red ears to use them preferentially for cornbread. The red ears don't taste any different from the yellow when used as polenta. The red color gives its unique flavor only in response to baking, not boiling. Cornbread made from the red ears has a powerful and delicious flavor that goes well with meat or cheese. I often mix red and yellow kernels 1:2, as the red has enough flavor even after being so diluted, and it is a way of using up the yellow.

The yellow ears of 'Abenaki' and the gold ears of 'Cascade Maple-Gold Polenta' or 'Cascade Ruby-Gold' have a mild flavor when made into cornbread. There is too much flavor to be as good in the uses for which I prefer cream ears. And there is too little flavor to stand alone (when baked) as a major flavor. I have eaten plenty of yellow cornbread, though, as a by-product of getting red. It's still tasty food. Just not my favorite among the wonderful choices I now have available to me. I generally use the 'Cascade Maple-Gold Polenta' for polenta, the cream flint ears for cream skillet bread, the red flint ears for red skillet bread, the red-brown flint ears for red-brown skillet bread, and the gold and yellow ears only after I run out of the others.

I don't make johnnycakes these days. Basically, the johnnycake is a very briefly boiled thick mush that is fried on a griddle or in a frying pan. That involves a lot of fat. And it only gives one meal for the labor. When I make polenta or cornbread, I make enough for several days at a time. (For directions on making johnnycakes, see note 12-5.)

Fast-Cooking Polenta

Conventional directions for making polenta usually involve boiling and stirring the mush for 45 minutes, then baking it. Even after 45 minutes of boiling, it doesn't taste cooked. The baking is required. The eight flint corns I have listed all make great *fast-cooking polenta*, polenta that can be cooked with just a 7-minute boil-stir phase, and that then finishes cooking completely when it just sits in the covered pot. It takes the right flint varieties, however. And no multicolored "ornamental" flints need apply; these are not pure enough flint types. (If you have a flint variety with mostly but not totally pristine flint character, it may work all right in my recipe, if you just increase the amount of water to up to 4 cups per cup of flour. Full dent or flour corn types may require 5 to 6 cups of water or more to make a mush and will not taste cooked however long you cook and stir them. They require the long boiling

and baking. The couple of Italian polentas I have tried are not fast-cooking.)

When I described my discovery, that some flint corns can make great polenta with such little work and no baking, to my friend Rose Marie Nichols McGee (the co-owner of Nichols Garden Nursery and a gourmet cook), she immediately invited me and my corn to come over for dinner and prove it. I brought over some corn ground just right to make polenta as well as a batch fixed the day before and hardened into a solid brick in a bread-loaf pan. I made the fresh polenta as described here, boiling and stirring a measured seven minutes, then setting the polenta aside to finish cooking, off the heat, in a covered pot.

Meanwhile, Rose Marie had been getting ideas about the leftover solid cooked polenta. She sliced it into ½-inch-thick slabs, sprinkled a few herbs on it, and baked it for a few minutes per side. On one batch she sprinkled cheese too. A few minutes later we had delicious, crusty slabs of polenta as finger-food appetizers. Both were delicious. And the crusts didn't involve frying! She then made a stir-fry of vegetables to top the fresh cooked polenta. Delicious!

I often eat polenta plain with a little pepper. (It already has salt and butter in it.) Or I make polenta and eggs with leftover polenta, as described in the section on duck egg cookery. Or I stir-fry vegetables (with or without meat), remove the vegetables temporarily, add a little water to deglaze the pan, then stir in and heat up leftover polenta. Then I add the vegetables back for delicious Stir-Fried Vegetable Polenta. I also love to put spaghetti sauce on polenta. Virtually anything you can do with leftover rice, you can also do with polenta.

Leftover polenta also makes a great dessert.

You can heat some up (in the microwave) and add brown sugar or jam or maple syrup and/or milk, cream, or butter. My favorite polenta dessert is Maple-Gold Polenta made with 'Cascade Maple-Gold Polenta' corn. For this I use leftover polenta, extra butter, and pure grade-B maple syrup (which is much darker and more flavorful than grade A). My variety 'Cascade Maple-Gold Polenta' is named both for the color of the pericarp and endosperm of the corn (maple-brown overlying rich, deep gold) as well as for this particular dessert, for which it is the perfect variety.

To grind polenta meal, I simply grind the corn in my hand-crank Corona mill. (See the section in chapter 4 on mills and milling.) My electric impact mill makes a meal that is too fine for polenta. Polenta meal should be coarse to give it the most appealing cooked texture. I run the corn through the Corona mill initially on a setting just coarse enough to crack the corn. Then I run the cracked corn through a second time with the burrs set as fine as practical and examine the resulting flour, then open up the space between the burrs until the biggest corn bits are about 2 millimeters long. This is as coarse a texture as one can have and still have the bigger bits cook all the way through with my recipe.

One cup of whole ground corn grinds into about 1¼ cups of polenta meal. I always make at least 2 cups of cornmeal into polenta at once. You need this amount or more, since the final cooking depends upon the heat retained by the pot and the volume of food.

Quick-Cooking Polenta

2 cups of coarse-ground meal from a true flint corn of pristine flint type

6 cups of water
4 Tbs. butter or other fat or oil
½ tsp. salt

Toss the butter and salt into the pot with the water and bring it to a boil. Then add the cornmeal in three batches, whisking each in. After the water returns to a boil, turn the heat down to medium-low and simmer the cooking mush for 7 minutes, stirring with a spatula the entire time. Then cover the pot, remove it from the heat, and let it sit quietly to finish cooking by itself. After 45 minutes, come back and give the polenta a final stir to stir in some of the water that will have separated a little bit. I like to eat some of the polenta hot and ladle the rest into bread-loaf pans, which I cover and refrigerate when cooled.

Carol's Universal Skillet Bread

It took me more than a decade to develop a recipe for making cornbread that tastes great, that holds together well enough to make sandwiches, that doesn't require any other grains, and that doesn't need xanthan gum or other artificial binders. Here's the primary trick: To hold the corn together, you add boiling water to part of the cornmeal to make it into a sticky semicooked paste. Then you add most of the other ingredients to form a thick, gooey "prebatter." You add the rest of the cornmeal (containing the baking powder) last. Both the sticky, cooked paste and the eggs help hold the bread together well enough so that no other grains, milk, or artificial binders are needed.

I got the basic concept of adding boiling

Skillet Bread Ingredients

(For 2 large loaves of flint corn skillet bread, 6 cups of cornmeal total) (See modifications at the end of the recipe for flour and dent cornmeals as well as how to establish amounts for different varieties.)

3 cups (half of the) cornmeal, placed in a large stainless steel bowl and whisked to break up any lumps

4 cups of water (in a pot)

12 Tbs. butter or other fat (2 Tbs. per cup cornmeal), also added to the pot

3/4 tsp. salt, also added to the pot

2 cups eggs (standing by, to make the pre-batter)

Dry ingredients:

3 cups (the rest of the) cornmeal, in a separate bowl, and

2 Tbs. Rumford baking powder (whisked together with the cornmeal)

For directions, see text (page 266).

For **flour corn skillet bread**, use 1/3 of the flour in the pre-batter and cut the water to 3 cups. For **dent corn skillet bread**, use a pattern between that of full flour and full flint types, depending upon how floury or flinty the particular variety is. For buckwheat and teff flours, see note 12-7. You may need to modify amounts of water and/or proportion of flour or meal in the pre-batter depending upon the specific variety and even the moisture content of the lot. Basically, if your bread is too dry it needs more water. If it is too moist it needs less. If your bread falls apart, you need a larger proportion of the meal or flour in the pre-batter step so there will be more paste to hold the bread together. If your bread is gooey, you need a lesser proportion of the flour or meal in the pre-batter step.

---

water and using the resulting paste from some very old southern white cornbread recipes as well as from an old Scottish recipe for oat cakes. I raised the proportion of paste and added the stainless steel bowl and one-minute waiting step as adjustments that result in a better-cooked paste, thus enhancing the bread's ability to hold together. I also grind my corns in the Whispermill, which gives the finest meal possible; this also helps make bread that holds together well. (One cup of corn makes about 1¼ cups of fine meal.) To my knowledge, this is the only cornbread recipe that produces

cornbread that holds together well enough to make sandwiches. The flour-corn cornbreads hold together even better than the flints; however, both can be used to make sandwiches.

The ingredients for skillet bread in the sidebar are for skillet bread made from true flint corns of very pure flint type. For these, I use half the cornmeal to make the sticky pre-batter paste, and use 2/3 as much water (by volume) as cornmeal. For pure flour corns, I use only 1/3 of the flour to make the pre-batter, and I cut the water to half as much water as corn flour. The pattern

The Dedicated Cornbread Skillet

I have two cast iron skillets that I use for nothing except cornbread. These are ordinary skillets, not the skillets sometimes called "cornbread pans" that have lots of divisions. I bought such a skillet, but it was too small, and oiling and cleaning all those separate sections is too much of a pain. I use my cast iron skillets only for cornbread partly because I don't want fish or hamburger flavors in my bread or cakes. (One does not ever wash cast iron with soap. Anything fatty contributes to the permanent cure on the pan and somewhat to the flavor for a while. Soap is fatty.) The other main reason I dedicate my cornbread pans to cornbread is because that way I never have to clean them, not even in water. The standard way of cleaning cast iron pans is to wash them in water only, then heat them gently to drive out the water, then re-oil them. Here's what I do instead.

When I take the cornbread out of the oven, I turn each skillet upside down over a cooling rack so the cornbread loaves fall out. Then I set the pans down and pour a dollop of corn or other vegetable oil into the hot pan and wipe it around with a paper towel. (I'm careful not to touch the skillets with my bare hands while doing this, as they are still very hot.) Then at some point later, after the skillets have cooled, I remove the excess oil with a paper towel, removing any crumbs in the process, and giving myself pristine oiled pans. (I leave only the oil that won't come off. I remove *all* the excess.)

I store my cast iron skillets upside down on a shelf. They should be stored open to the air. Storing upside down prevents dust from settling in the pans. When it's time for some more cornbread, I just pop the pans in the oven to heat them. They are already oiled as much as is needed. I not only don't ever wash my cast iron skillets with soap, I never even wash them with water.

---

for dent corns is somewhere in between. (For buckwheat or teff skillet bread, see note 12-7.) Most flour corn and dent corn varieties taste best with some sugar, about 1 tablespoon per cup of flour. Southern-style white cornbread is made without sugar.

For flint corn skillet bread, I start off by putting half the cornmeal into a large stainless steel bowl, one that's big enough to mix everything together. (The stainless steel matters, since this half of the cornmeal needs to cook into a sticky paste when the boiling water is added. A heavier bowl absorbs more heat and cools the ingredients.) The other half of the cornmeal goes into a smaller bowl along with the baking powder. I whisk both lots of cornmeal to break up any clumps in the dry ingredients and mix in the baking powder. Of course I use duck eggs in the recipe, but chicken eggs will work fine.

I set the oven rack on the lowest possible position and preheat the oven to 450°F. (I start preheating the cast iron skillets at the same time as I turn the heat on to boil the water.) Before I make the pre-batter, I take the cast iron skillets out of the oven. (The skillets are not heated to full temperature, which would cause the oil to smoke and burn. If the batter boils and bubbles when put into the skillets, they are too hot.)

The amounts given are enough for two large cast iron skillets, which will produce two large round loaves. My skillets are 8½ inches and 9 inches across, measured as internal dimensions at the base. (Everything around my house is individual.) The traditional preheating of the skillets gives a nice crust as well as shortens the cooking time and thus makes it easier to bake a cornbread that cooks all the way through and doesn't burn.

First toss the salt and butter or fat or oil into a pot with 4 cups of water and turn the heat on to bring it to a boil. Meanwhile, into the preheated oven go the two cast iron skillets. Bring the water-salt-butter to a boil and dump it into 3 cups of cornmeal. Then whisk it around quickly as it cooks and thickens into almost a solid mass. Leave the steaming meal for a minute to let it cook further. Then add the eggs, whisk to scramble them, and incorporate them fully, creating the pre-batter. Remove the cast iron skillets from the hot oven.

Dump the dry ingredients into the pre-batter, whisk them together very rapidly (in about two seconds), and immediately pour or scrape (with the aid of a spatula) half the batter into each of the two skillets. Place the batter-filled skillets in the 450°F oven.

I check the bread at 25 minutes. Sometimes I take it out then. Sometimes it takes an extra 5 minutes. When the bread is done, there is a nice golden brown crust on top, and the bread has pulled away from the sides of the skillet.

Turn the loaves out on a cooling rack and let them cool for at least half an hour. (The bread tastes good warm but doesn't taste good hot. I think it is still cooking and developing its flavors as it comes out of the oven.) I let the bread cool completely, cut one end off each loaf to eat, and put the rest of each loaf in a big Ziploc bag. (The whole rounds don't quite fit.) One bag goes into the refrigerator. The other stays at room temperature and is eaten over the next three days. When the first loaf is gone, the other comes out of the frig. The bread will keep without molding for only about three or four days, since it contains no preservatives.

To make sandwiches, I usually cut the loaf in ½-inch slices that are about 1½ inches wide, the thickness of the loaf, and I make sandwiches that are long rectangles instead of squares. These hold together better than squares and are easier to get my mouth around.

Parching Corn

My first experience with parching corn was in the living room of my friend and colleague, the irrepressible renegade germplasm collector, plant breeder, and seedsman Dr. Alan Kapuler, otherwise known as "Mushroom." That particular year Mushroom had grown seven different Hopi flour corns. When fall came, 'Shroom had ears of the varieties stacked all over his living room. Everyone who visited the Kapulers got handed a bag of corn and a container to shell into while they were visiting. By late fall, all the bags of ears had been turned into buckets of kernels, and Mushroom was trying to figure out how to use them. So he tried just toasting the different kinds of corn in a dry cast iron frying pan and feeding them (or trying to feed them) to his family.

"Here, try this one," Mushroom said, carrying a

skillet full of toasted corn over to the sofa where I was lounging in front of the woodstove. "Some of the varieties aren't so good fixed this way. In fact," he said laughing ruefully, "some of them are really awful. But my family actually *likes* this one."

I stared at the toasted kernels with more reservation than enthusiasm. I was thinking about "corn nuts," those hard, tooth-threatening entities one sometimes finds in little bags in the grocery store, and whose major flavors are rancid oil and too much salt. I took about three kernels from the pan, put them in my mouth, and bit down cautiously. The kernels crumbled at the first pressure. I munched a bit, and the corn seemed to turn sweet in my mouth, then suddenly developed a delicious, unique flavor. It was nothing like corn nuts or anything else I had ever eaten.

"Not bad," I said as I took a real handful. As I munched some more, the uniqueness of the experience finally sunk in. "In fact," I said, amazed, "this is actually *good*!" 'Shroom laughed. I helped myself to another handful. Every kernel was soft. I munched happily.

"I wonder if I could fix these in the microwave?" I said. 'Shroom shrugged. There are no microwaves in the Kapuler household, and none need apply.

"Here," he said, reaching into a bucket of corn and handing me a handful. "Take some home and give it a try."

When I got home, I put twelve kernels in a 2-inch Pyrex custard cup, covered it with a paper plate, put it in the center of the microwave turntable, set the oven for a minute on high, and pressed start. In about 30 seconds there was a very loud pop, then a cascade of pops. By 45 seconds, the popping seemed mostly over, so I turned the oven

off and took a look at what I had. In the custard cup were a dozen kernels of corn, still brightly colored in stripes of red and white. Now slightly larger than before, each one bore a distinctive split in the seed coat where the white interior showed through. I put a few kernels in my mouth and started munching. They were soft and sweet, and the flavor was spectacular. I looked at the remaining few grains of corn, and it was a moment of total stillness.

This stuff was delicious. Furthermore, it didn't require any oil at all. ("Parching" means to heat over dry heat, without oil.) All you need is a microwave oven or a skillet and a burner or a fire. Furthermore, my custard-cup parching method meant that I could evaluate corn varieties as parching corns with just a few grains of each variety.

I quickly dived into my corn seed collection and began testing everything. Different varieties had different cooking times, and all tasted awful burned. Many varieties popped or partially popped in an inedible fashion, with hard, uncooked, unpalatable sections. Some parched and became like commercial corn nuts, hard and only marginally edible, with no sweetness or special delicious flavor. I soon figured out that all "true parching corns" were flour corns. All flour corns would parch. Some parched faster and more uniformly than others. However, only a few varieties were sweet and delicious when parched. But I only had a couple dozen varieties of flour corn. Clearly that was not enough.

In the following days, I called the seed companies that had good collections of flour corns and asked for samples of all they had. I also called Mark Millard, at that time in charge of the USDA corn collection. No one knew which varieties would parch, but everyone was eager to contribute varieties and find out. Soon I had about two hundred flour corns to try, and my kitchen exuded exotic odors and loud pops for several days. When the popping died down, there were some surprisingly simple generalizations. Black and blue varieties were so awful I normally had to spit out the test samples. White flour corns are tasteless. Yellow flour corns have a yucky, foul-flavored aftertaste. The corns that were delicious when parched were all either red or lavender or magenta or purple, or striped or spotted with those colors. (A few black-looking varieties tasted good, but these were actually double-dose reds, not true blacks.) The best parching corns also had relatively small bits of woody material where the kernel attaches to the cob. And all good parching corns had excellent flour-corn-type kernels, with no dentish or flintish kernels.

Two of the best parching corns were two of the Hopi flour corns that Mushroom had been growing, one a magenta-colored corn, the other red and white striped. He had grown them a couple of years and sorted them into various lots, partly based upon beauty. However, in this case, beauty was counterproductive. The shiniest, most attractive ears were shiny because they had more flint character. The thin layer of flint around the kernels made them shinier, but inferior as parching corns. Knowing Mushroom, I went back and said, "Hey, I'll betcha you kept all the other lots too, the ones you selected against." He laughed. "Of *course*. You know me, I never throw away a seed." He gave me the other lots. I tested them using my custard-cup test and identified the lots that were the best parching types. That gave us one year of selection for parching quality in those two corns. With the coopera-tion of Seeds of Change, I arranged for growers in isolated valleys to grow out the two corns so Seeds of Change could introduce them. I did the selections myself, cob by cob, giving us a second round of selection specifically for parching quality. (I bartered my genetic services for a share of the crop, which took care of breakfasts for a good while. A handful of parched corn and a cup of tea make a great breakfast.) Seeds of Change and Peace Seeds introduced our parching-selected lines of these corns as 'Parching Magenta' and 'Parching Red Supai'.

Meanwhile, I had made similar arrangements with two other growers and Tessa Gowan, then of Abundant Life Seed Foundation. The result was growouts and introductions of two more great parching corns, one of which is still available—'Parching Lavender Mandan' (a.k.a. 'Mandan Clay Red'). (I obtained this from the USDA/ARS collection; it is accession number PI 213730.) Abundant Life Seed Foundation no longer exists. Tessa Gowan and Shane Murphy now have a small seed company called Seed Dreams, which sells 'Parching Lavender Mandan'. 'Parching Lavender Mandan' is early enough and cold-weather tolerant enough to grow in Port Townsend, Washington.

In addition, Native Seeds/SEARCH was already selling two corns that are great parching corns. One was 'Hopi Chinmark', another red-striped corn. The other was 'Hopi Pink', which, by the way, was not the same as anyone else's 'Hopi Pink'. It had red marks and spots and was more delicious parched. Craig Dremann of Redwood City Seeds also had a good parching corn, 'Aztec Red', which is actually lavender colored and has the biggest kernels. It is a very late Mexican corn that is too late for me to grow, however.

Some lines of 'Mandan Red' flour corn are also good parching corns. (Avoid those lines that have a lot of black kernels.)

Most pink, lavender, or purple flour corn varieties parch. Most don't have flavors as delicious as the varieties I have already named. There seem to be three basic flavor classes of parching corn depending upon whether the corns are based on red (pericarp), pink-purple-magenta (aleurone), or red and white striped (pericarp).

Parching corns are all good flour corns and make great bread. They were my introduction to flour corns. For several years, it was 'Parching Magenta', parched or as bread that was my main corn staple. 'Parching Magenta' has the best quality as a parched corn if you parch it by microwaving. However, 'Parching Red Supai' is better if you parch in a skillet, because it is more resistant to burning. These days, however, I use the red ears of 'Magic Manna' for my parching corn.

Mixed-color ornamental flour corns do *not* taste good when parched because of the foul flavors associated with parched black and yellow kernels. So 'Mandan Bride' and 'Painted Mountain', for example, which parch like all flour corns, do *not* taste good when eaten as parched corn. Parching quality alone doesn't make a good parching corn. It has to also taste good.

Sometime after my work with identifying and introducing parching corns, a friend of mine traveled to the mountains in Guatemala where people still use parching corns and have many parching corn varieties. He brought me samples of about a dozen. All were lavender, purple, magenta, or red, or had stripes or spots of those colors.

I often spend a lot of time figuring out and rediscovering things that many people in other times or places have known for centuries.

Eating Parching Corn

If you just crunch the parched kernels a couple of times and swallow them, you don't experience much sweetness or flavor. The starches in the kernels actually begin to digest into sugars when acted upon by the enzymes in saliva. So chew the corn a while. Munch a few kernels into a paste. Add a few more kernels and munch them while swallowing just a little of the paste. Keep adding more kernels to your mouth a few at a time and swallowing the paste a little at a time.

Parched corn tastes great all by itself. You don't need oil or salt. It also tastes great with a few nuts, peanuts, or sunflower seeds mixed in. I especially like it accompanied with aged cheese.

I have bought a few samples of parched corn from a couple of seed companies. They were oiled, which isn't parched corn as far as I am concerned. And they didn't taste all that good. They didn't have all that good a parching type or flavor. If you want to try parched corn before growing it, get an extra packet of one of the varieties I recommend and parch it yourself.

Parched corn will keep about three months at room temperature without losing much quality. (It's cooked, but the oils are in the germ, which isn't exposed to air.) This makes it an especially nice travel and camping food. Even five months after parching, parched corn is edible, though it tastes a bit stale at that point.

Microwave Parching

I prefer to microwave my parching corn. It's easy. I put something in the microwave I can zap for a couple minutes to heat up the oven. Then I put about ¼ to ⅓ cup of kernels in a single-layer ring in the bottom of a paper plate, cover with another paper plate, and zap on high. I set the oven for 3 minutes, but don't leave the corn for that long. (If I did, it would both lose its great flavor and burn, and it tastes awful burned.) Instead, I judge by the popping, just as one does with popcorn. It usually takes slightly over a minute. After the pops have mostly (but not entirely) died down, it is the time to take the corn out. A rich, delicious odor permeates the room as the corn comes close to being done. Get the corn out of the microwave within about 3 seconds of smelling that aroma. An occasional unparched kernel doesn't matter, since flour corns are soft anyway and actually taste pretty good raw. Unlike popcorn, kernels of parching corn that have cracked skins usually parch.

The moisture content of the corn matters for parching, though it is more flexible than for popcorn. I run my parching corn through the dehydrator just as for saving seed to get it to the right moisture content. Also, the total amount of corn matters. Less or more than the ¼ to ⅓ cup inside the double paper plates parches less well. And in my test situation with a custard cup covered with a paper plate, a dozen kernels parch, but not one or two or fifty. And covering with a glass lid doesn't work. It probably absorbs too many microwaves.

Skillet Parching

Use a heavy, cast iron skillet for parching. Do not use oil. Place the skillet over medium heat and preheat it. Add the corn and stir it with a spatula while toasting it. Stop when the pops begin to die down. The parching takes about a minute.

Campfire Parching

I haven't tried this myself; I've merely read of it. Buffalo Bird Woman, in *Buffalo Bird Woman's*

Garden, tells of the first meeting between her Hidatsa people and the Mandans, who were master plant breeders and gardeners. A Hidatsa scouting party, warriors all, stood on one side of a river looking at a Mandan camp on the other side. Both groups were safe from each other for the moment because of the river. But there was tension. No one knew quite what to expect from the others.

The Mandans responded quickly. They broke ears of parching corn in half, stuck them on the ends of arrows, toasted the ears on a fire, and shot them across the river. The Hidatsa had never seen corn before. But the magnificent aroma told them just what to do with it. When the Hidatsa found their way across the river in the morning, it was with peace in their hearts, and the thought of learning about corn in their minds. Hidatsa and Mandan tribes became close allies.

Flour Corn Varieties and Uses

The flour corn varieties taste quite different from the flints or dents. A white flint corn's flavor is nothing like that of a white flour corn's flavor. As with the flints, the colors have the major effect on flavor and establish the basic flavor class. So lavender, red, striped, white, blue, and yellow all give dramatically different flavor classes. And these flavors are quite different from those of the corresponding colors of flint corns.

'Parching Magenta' is a mid-early to mid-season corn that makes 6-inch ears with 12 to 14 rows of small kernels. It is simultaneously genetically lavender and pink. It's from Hopi strains selected by Alan Kapuler and myself for flour type and parching. It grows 5 feet tall and has ear-bearing

Semi-Universal Pancakes

Make these with flour-corn flour, teff, oat, buckwheat, rice, or other fine flour, but not with flint or dent corn flours. (This recipe makes great teff or buckwheat pancakes. Great enough so that I generally buy and keep some teff and buckwheat flour just for pancakes.) The trick to this recipe is to add enough water to get the batter to the right consistency, then mix in the baking powder as the last step and pour the batter into the (heavy) hot frying pan before the leavening action of the baking powder changes the texture too much to pour, or before the bubbles all dissipate.

Dry ingredients:
1 cup flour
1 Tbs. sugar (optional)
⅛ tsp. salt

1 egg
2 Tbs. melted butter or other fat or oil
1 tsp. Rumford baking powder
water, however much it takes to give a batter of the right consistency (about ⅛ cup for corn flour)

Preheat the burner. Use a heavy frying pan or skillet.

Mix together the flour, sugar, and salt. Dump the egg on top, scramble it with a fork, then mix it into part of the flour on one side of the bowl. (The egg doesn't wet all the flour.) Add the melted butter and mix that in to the rest of the dry flour (on the other side of the bowl).

Now add a bit of water, enough to make a very thick batter, mixing everything together. Then add more water, bit by bit, a tablespoon at a time, until the batter is almost thin enough to ribbon off the fork, but not quite. The batter sort of plops off and sort of ribbons. (I like a thick batter that makes pancakes about ½ inch thick.) Heat up the frying pan over medium-high heat before you do the final step, the addition of baking powder. I like to grease the hot skillet with butter just before I pour in the batter.

Add the baking powder, mix it quickly into the top of the batter, then into all the batter. Quickly pour the batter into the skillet in three or four cakes. To make thick pancakes, you have to be patient, especially when cooking the first side. Wait until the cakes are a uniform light brown before turning them. (There is no special behavior of bubbles to indicate when it is time to turn the cakes, as there is with wheat-flour pancakes. You have to peek underneath the cakes with a spatula before turning them.) Turn the cakes and cook the other side briefly. When they are approaching light brown, take the pan off the heat and give the cakes another two or three minutes to finish cooking (and drying out) off the heat.

---

tillers. I've grown hundreds of pounds of this corn, and I used it as my staple parching and flour corn for a number of years. The flour seems somewhat sweetish, even without any added sugar—

too much so to make non-sweet breads. I always preferred to use it for sweet breads.

'Magic Manna', my own flour corn, I describe in the next section.

Semi-Universal Sponge Cake

For this recipe you can use flour-corn flour, teff, oats, buckwheat, rice, or any other fine flour, but not flint or dent corn flour. Sponge cake is similar to angel food cake but includes the egg yolks. Sponge cake is mostly eggs with some sugar and a little flour. It doesn't have the fat of other cakes or most other desserts. It is serious food. The flour affects the flavor, but doesn't matter much with respect to texture, as flour is a minor ingredient. It is the eggs that hold the cake together. The leavening depends upon air that is incorporated by beating the eggs and yolks together and stabilizing the beaten foams. You will need to use a modern angel-food cake pan to have a good uniform texture on this cake—a pan with the cylinder in the center and a removable bottom. The pans are used ungreased, which helps the cake climb up and hang onto the sides of the pan. Then the pan is turned upside-down while the cake cools, thus avoiding compressing the light texture. This recipe is for two cakes; the cake pans are 9½ inches across at the top. I use a hand mixer to beat the egg whites and yolks.

4 cups eggs, separated into yolks and whites
½ tsp. cream of tartar
¼ tsp. salt
2 cups sugar

Dry ingredients (whisk together)
2 cups flour-corn flour
4 tsp. vanilla powder
1 tsp. nutmeg

Beat the whites part way. Add the cream of tartar and salt. Beat to a soft peak. Then beat in half the sugar in three additions. (These additions and this order of addition is part of the process of stabilizing the egg-white foam well enough to serve as the leavening.)

In a separate bowl, beat the yolks. Add the other half of the sugar in three additions.

Whisk the dry ingredients into the yolk-sugar mix, fold in the beaten egg whites, then divide the batter between the two pans. Use a preheated 325°F oven, with a rack position second from the top. Bake about 50 minutes. The cakes are done when they have mostly pulled away from the edges and the top is elastic to the touch. Cool upside down for 1½ hours or more before eating.

'Parching Red Supai' is a full-season corn that grows to about 7 feet and produces 10-inch ears with 12 to 16 rows of red or orange and white striped kernels. The ears are produced on the main stalk only. 'Parching Red Supai' is late enough here so that it finishes in the rainy season, which is problematic. It is much more produc-tive than 'Parching Magenta'. If you have more summer heat than I do, or a longer season, or less problem with dew and rain, give it a try. 'Parching Red Supai' makes an excellent savory (non-sweet) bread when made without sugar.

'Parching Lavender Mandan' (a.k.a. 'Mandan Clay Red') isn't red in color at all. It's lavender. It

Sweet Breads

Just use my Universal Skillet Bread recipe and to the pot containing the boiling water, salt, and butter or fat, also add 1 to 3 tsp. sugar per cup of cornmeal or flour. Most flour corns taste best with sugar. Most flint corns taste best without.

is an early corn that grows 4 feet tall and makes 6-inch ears with 8 to 12 rows of big lavender kernels. It appears to be more tolerant of cold or wet conditions and more resistant to molding than the Hopi flour corns I have grown.

'Hopi Chinmark' is a full-season corn with 10-inch ears of 12 to 14 rows of red or orange and white striped kernels. 'Hopi Pink' grows to about 6 feet and produces 12-inch ears with 14 to 18 rows of red, white, and pink kernels. These two varieties are available only from Native Seeds/SEARCH. (Other 'Hopi Pink' lines I've seen are not the same.) Native Seeds/SEARCH collects these from Native American growers on the Hopi reservation. I haven't ever grown them.

'Aztec Red' is a 10-foot Mexican variety with 12-inch ears with huge lavender kernels. It is very late (140 days or more). The main stalk tassels out way before the ears silk out; the ears are pollinated by tassels on the tillers. So you need to give the plants enough room to develop good tillers. It bears ears only on the main stalk. If I had the summer heat and a long enough season, I would give it a try.

'Mandan Red' flour corn is a medium-early corn that makes 6-inch ears on short bushy plants. It is better adapted to the upper Midwest than most of the Hopi corns.

'Tuscarora' is a very famous full-season white flour corn of the Tuscarora Indians. (It isn't a parching corn.) I have never quite got around to growing 'Tuscarora', though I have tried my recipes out with it. I think 'Tuscarora' must be more broadly adapted and mold resistant than most flour corns, because it is grown by Native Americans in New York as well as by Shane Murphy in California (the California branch of Seed Dreams), and it originated in the Southeast. The corn is said to have been brought from the Southeast to the Northeast with the Tuscarora Indians when they migrated. 'Tuscarora' is sometimes called 'Iroquois' or 'Six Nations', after the confederation of tribes to which the Tuscarora Indians belonged. It is an 8-row corn, but has bigger ears and bigger kernels than the flour corns I usually grow. It is famous for making good roasting ears and being a good corn for growing beans on. It makes a one-stalk plant instead of a bushy little plant with lots of tillers like so many flour corns. (Like other whites, it doesn't have any especially great flavor parched.) Breads and pancakes made with 'Tuscarora' flour (and a little sugar) have a distinctive pancakelike flavor very similar to pancakes made with wheat flour.

Black or blue flour corns such as 'Hopi Blue' are widely available, and 'Hopi Blue' is apparently widely adapted. It's a tall, full-season corn. I've bought and made flour from it, but not grown it. I find the blue corns make skillet bread I like for the first serving. But then I usually don't eat the rest of the loaf. The blues have powerful flavors that I seem to like more as an occasional thing than as a staple.

'Mandan Bride' is a multicolored flour corn that was long popular as an early ornamental corn. It is relatively productive for such an early corn.

However, it makes short, fat ears that don't dry down very easily around here. When ground into flour, 'Mandan Bride' has a muddy, unappetizing flavor. People don't normally eat it. It is not a good parching corn, either. Too many black, yellow, and white kernels.

'Painted Mountain' has replaced 'Mandan Bride' in my region as an early ornamental flour corn. It is a bit earlier and more productive. The ears are about the same weight, but they are longer and thinner and dry down faster and better. Like other multicolored flour corns, if you just grind it into flour it gives you a muddy, unappetizing flavor. And it tastes terrible as a parching corn because of all the black, yellow, and white kernels.

For sources of flour corn varieties, see note 12-8.

'Magic Manna'

'Magic Manna' is a culinary flour corn variety I built upon the genetic base of 'Painted Mountain'. 'Painted Mountain' is a variety that is the result of decades of breeding work by Dave Christiensen, who took many varieties of corn and folded them together to make a particularly early, productive, cold-hardy, drought-tolerant multicolored flour corn. 'Painted Mountain' has ears that are typically 8 inches long and 8-rowed. It has short plants with many ear-bearing tillers. At least usually. 'Painted Mountain' is far less vulnerable to molding in the ear than the other flour corns I have grown. It's early enough to dry down in August here. Best yet, for all practical purposes, Dave Christiensen selected, above all, for resilience. (He lives in Montana.) It's kind of hard to fail with 'Painted Mountain'. Even when the soil is so infertile and the planting is so late that

the plants only grow a foot high, they simply say, "Well, we can't afford tillers this year." So they skip the tillers entirely and make a good solid 6-inch ear on each of those little foot-high single stalks. I like that attitude. Usually, the plants make ear-bearing tillers, with the ears quite low to the ground. Bushy corn plants that make more ears rather than fewer, bigger ones aren't my favorite corn-plant style. But 'Painted Mountain' has so many virtues that I am willing to live with the bush style. The ears on 'Painted Mountain' are borne quite low. If you hill the plants up, the ears can seem to be coming right out of the ground. This helps the ear-bearing tillers resist lodging, especially if they are hilled up.

The main thing I have against 'Painted Mountain' is that I can't eat it. It doesn't work with any of the low-labor cooking styles I like to use. It doesn't make good parching corn, and it makes muddy-flavored flour. I know lots of people who grow 'Painted Mountain', but they sell it for ornamental use. Only Dave Christiensen himself seems to actually eat it. He nixtamalizes it. By the time 'Painted Mountain' became available, however, I had grown or tasted enough flour corns that it was obvious to me that the major flavor classes were associated with the color pigments; I knew what every color tasted like when parched, and what many of them tasted like when baked. I thought that, if I pulled some pure color lines out of 'Painted Mountain', I could create good culinary varieties that would fit into my cooking methods. Basically, I wanted the great flavors I could get from pure-color flour corns. But I wanted the greater earliness, better yield, greater mold resistance, and superior resilience of Dave Christiensen's 'Painted Mountain'.

I started out with ten pounds of 'Painted

Mountain' and laboriously picked out kernels of certain colors. I picked out red, lavender, yellow, white, and tan-pericarp-over-white kernels. I used the pure white in rows in between the other colors to give a little semi-isolation to each color. As before, I was guessing that the tan pericarp would represent something extra-delicious. I was interested in the red (over white) and the lavender (over white) because those configurations give good parching corns. The first patches of separate colors I grew were far from pure, and required untold hours of hand-sorting, an additional year of growing, and untold hours more of hand-sorting to create enough pure-color corn to try as flour. Everything was complicated by the fact that the interior colors are hidden by red pericarps. Red pericarps only taste wonderful as parching corn over white aleurones and endosperms. And with a red pericarp, you can't see the color of the aleurone or endosperm. In addition, pericarp colors are maternally inherited, which means that, while the red is dominant, it is often invisible, and a red kernel may or may not carry any genes for red.

When I had enough pure-color material to cook up batches of bread, I quickly found out:

1. The yellow made bread with a distinctive flavor that tasted good in the first meal, but which I was disinclined to finish. The leftovers tended to sit in the refrigerator until they molded. Like blue-flour corns, I didn't like the yellow flour corn well enough to grow it as a staple.
2. The lavender ears were smaller than the others, and the plants weren't as productive.
3. The lavender ears were heavily contaminated with black, as was the adjacent white

block. Lavender appears to be a genetically modified black, where the black is dominant and the genetic modifier gene that turns the black to lavender is a recessive.

4. The white flour when used in sweet breads had a pancakelike flavor.
5. The tan-pericarp (ivory) ears gave me a delicious flour.
6. So did the red ears.
7. The red ears (but not the other colors) were wonderful as parching corn.
8. A couple of years into the project, brown-pericarp ears appeared. The flour from the brown ears is delicious and isn't sweet.

After I thought about it a bit, I realized that I could design a single corn variety that had one genetic background, except for pericarp color, and that this would give me four different colors of ears, all solid ears, and a number of different flavors. I dropped the lavender and yellow, which wouldn't fit the design. To get the right flavors and make the genetics work, I needed to have a variety that had uniformly white endosperms and white aleurones and varied only for pericarp color, with the pericarp color being red, brown, ivory, or clear.

I've kept the numbers of plants up and selected so as to retain all the good agronomical characteristics of 'Painted Mountain'. Agronomically, 'Magic Manna' is just like 'Painted Mountain'. However, 'Magic Manna' produces solid-colored ears instead of multicolored ears—four different colors of solid ears that, after further investigation, turned out to have the following uses:

1. There are red ears that have pericarps that are red or various shades of pink. These

Savory Corn Gravy

When I started getting a few brown ears in my 'Magic Manna', they looked so much like kernels of delicious gravy that I, of course, immediately tried using them for that. I just ran the brown kernels through the Whispermill to get very fine flour. Then I used them to make hamburger gravy or to thicken stir-fries instead of commercial cornstarch. The gravy made with the brown ears is delicious. Apparently, that's what they had in mind all along.

I didn't have much brown corn, so I immediately tried making corn gravy with ivory, white, and red ears from 'Magic Manna'. The other colors had a somewhat sweetish flavor that just didn't work. (They might work to thicken sweet and sour recipes. I haven't tried that.)

To make savory corn gravy, I use about twice as much 'Brown Manna' corn flour as I would cornstarch. For example, to make Savory Hamburger Corn Gravy, I use a pound of grass-fed burger, a pound of onions sliced thin, a slurry made with ½ cup 'Magic Brown Manna' flour, and ½ cup water, and an additional cup of water. I season the hamburger and onions, fry the burger, remove it, fry the onions, then add a cup of water to deglaze and cool the pan and onions. Then I add the flour slurry and bring it to a boil and let it simmer until it thickens and tastes cooked. Then I add back the burger. These proportions give a thick gravy that is just enough to coat the meat and vegetables. I don't serve the gravy on potatoes or anything else. I serve it solo, with the corn gravy itself being the carbohydrate.

make great parching corn. They also make flour that produces great-tasting sweet breads and cakes with a distinctive flavor.

2. The brown ears have brown-orange pericarps. You need to sort in sunlight to tell them from red ears. These don't make good parching corn. (The kernels parch fine but don't taste especially good when parched.) The brown flour makes good savory breads (without sugar) go great with cheese or meat. 'Magic Brown Manna' flour also makes wonderful brown gravy.

3. The ivory ears make a flavorful flour for sweet breads. With a little sugar, they have a distinctive pancakelike flavor. They aren't good for parching.

4. There are also pure white ears. These make a blander flour that also has a pancake-like flavor when a little sugar is added to the batter. There is overlap between white and ivory, so for eating-grade corn, I lump the two and call it "ivory-white." I call the sweet bread I make from 'Magic Ivory-White Manna' flour "pancake cornbread," and sometimes eat it as a dessert dipped in maple syrup.

So I get parching corn, sweet breads and pancakes of two flavors, savory bread, and brown gravy—all from one corn patch. Welcome to 'Magic Manna'. I hope to introduce 'Magic Manna' in December of 2010 or 2011.

Saving Seed of Corn—
Isolation Tricks and Tactics

The kinds of corn varieties I'm talking about in this chapter are rare. Many must be harvested and shelled by hand. The seed is usually expensive. Generally, to grow them, you buy a little seed, then save seed yourself from then on. So growing the corn and seed saving go together. When you grow the corns, you will be simultaneously growing a food crop and a pure-variety seed crop. To grow a good corn seed crop you need to do three things: isolate your corn from other varieties that might cross-pollinate and contaminate it, avoid inbreeding depression, and practice selection.

Corn is a wind-pollinated plant. To grow pure corn varieties, we have to arrange things so that our corn will be pollinated by other plants of the same variety, not the varieties of neighbors. One approach often described is hand-pollinating, which involves bagging ears before they silk out, bagging tassels, then transferring pollen by hand. I find that approach completely unworkable on the scale I need. I depend upon natural open pollination.

Pollen from a neighbor's corn patch can land on silks on ears in your patch and give you crosses. Likewise, if you grow two different varieties, they will cross, and soon neither one will be pure. You can see crosses right on the ear in some cases, but not others. You can see crosses of field corns on sweet corn ears, because the crossed corn kernels will be full and fat instead of wrinkled. (You can't see crosses of sweet on field corn ears.) You can see crosses of yellow corns on white ears (but not the reverse). There will be individual yellow kernels wherever a stray pollen grain carrying yellow did the pollination on the white ear. You

can *usually* see crosses of blue corns onto white or yellow ears by the lighter bluish or blue-speckled kernels or greenish or green-speckled kernels. Not every crossed kernel shows up. But most do. (Heterozygous light blue aleurone over yellow endosperm gives a green or green-speckled kernel.) You can see crosses of flour corns onto flints, but not usually the reverse. The crossed kernels will look chalky instead of glassy like the rest of the kernels on the flint ear. You can't reliably see the crosses of dents onto flours or flints. You usually can't see the aleurone or endosperm colors underneath the red pericarps in red corns, so you can't identify these crosses reliably.

One approach to keeping our corn pure is to grow only one variety and to live a mile or more from any neighbors who grow corn. Most of us don't have that option. And most of us want more than one kind of corn.

My favorite second approach is to grow sibling varieties, varieties so designed or historically related that a little miscegenation between varieties doesn't matter. But so far that is only relevant for the Cascade series and for the late flint corn pair 'Rhode Island Whitecap' and 'Narragansett', which, practically speaking, are also sibling varieties to each other. (Growing note: Plant the 'Rhode Island Whitecap' upwind of 'Narragansett'.)

A regular tactic I use is to grow very early corn that, when planted at the early end of the window, will be pollinating before any corns that neighbors are likely to be growing. This is a good approach with 'Abenaki', the Cascade flints, and 'Magic Manna'. If anyone nearby plans to plant an early corn when I ask around, I get mine going even earlier by presoaking the seed before planting.

I usually scout the neighborhood regularly if there are other people growing corn, to see whether their corns are pollinating at the same time mine are. If, for example, someone's early sweet corn is pollinating toward the end of the early pollinating window on my early flour corn, and the pollination periods overlap, I can eliminate crosses simply by keeping only the first ear on each of my plants as the first cut for seed ears. These ears were all pollinated before my neighbor's early corn started to pollinate. The second or third ears on each of my plants would be the ones with crosses, if there are any.

One can grow two or three different corns that pollinate at different times. For example, I can plant an early flour corn and a late flint or sweet corn. If planted at the same time, these will pollinate at different times. Alternatively, I can plant two early corns, but plant one much later than the other. One can even plant three corns and keep the pollination windows separate, though it is trickier. I can, for example, plant an early, a midseason, and a late corn. Or I can plant one early corn and a late corn early in the season and another early corn six weeks later. However, the corns pollinating in the midseason and late slots are vulnerable to contamination from neighbors' corn. I find juggling three pollination windows a bit complex and somewhat unpredictable. (If the early one is inadvertently planted in a less fertile section of the field, it can end up overlapping with the midseason corn, for example.) I usually stick to two pollination niches. I like to grow 'Magic Manna' in the early window so it dries down in August. Harvesting flour corns in the rainy season is a chancy proposition. Then I grow a late flint in the late window. And I make collaborative arrangements with a friend to co-grow the Cascade series on a separate farm.

Another tactic is to swamp out stray pollen. I pick seed ears from the middle of my corn patch and eat the ones at the edges. The edge plants are more likely to have crosses from other people's pollen. Stray foreign pollen grains in the middle of the patch are far outnumbered by the thousands of pollen grains from my own patch.

I sometimes depend upon recognizing crosses rather than totally preventing them. For example, 'Rhode Island Whitecap' pollinates late, in the same window as commercial silage and fodder corn, which are frequently genetically modified (GM) corns. None grow near my garden. However, there can be corn pollen in the air from fields located a mile or more away. But these commercial silage corns are all yellow corns. Any stray pollen from a yellow GM corn is going to show up on 'Rhode Island Whitecap' as a distinctive yellow kernel in the background of cream kernels and can be picked out and discarded.

Walk the fields each season and eliminate off-type plants before they start to pollinate. A plant that is dramatically different, especially dramatically bigger, is frequently a hybrid that resulted from a stray pollen grain from a different variety.

Finally, when you screen ears and choose those for planting seed, always evaluate grain type. Crosses of corns of a different type often do show up when you examine the entire ear, even if they don't show up definitely on the individual kernels.

Usually, the corn you obtain as your starting material isn't perfect to begin with. It has occasional crosses and screwups in it. With attentive selecting and roguing, you can remove the bad effects of those screwups. If you remove more screwups than you create each year, that is good enough. You don't have to be perfect.

Avoiding Inbreeding Depression

Corn is very subject to inbreeding depression. Here's an illustration: Suppose you grow up a hundred plants and save grain each year from the plant that yields best. What kind of yield will you have in five years? Answer: Your corn variety will be so weak, wimpy, and low-yielding that you will be lucky to be able to keep it going at all. Its yield will stink compared with what you started with, even though you selected for the highest yield each year. Welcome to the concept of *inbreeding depression*. In corn, inbreeding usually produces smaller, weaker plants, smaller ears, and lower yields. To have good, vigorous lines of open-pollinated corn, we need the varieties to be somewhat heterogeneous genetically. (The exact mechanism of inbreeding depression and hybrid vigor isn't known.) To maintain that genetic heterogeneity in a corn variety, we usually need to save seed from large numbers of plants each year. A hundred is a number often given. I'm more comfortable with two-hundred or more good ears from different plants for the seed crop each year.

Selection

Review the sections on selection in the chapters on beans and squash, as many of the same principles and subtleties apply. With an open-pollinated corn, though, in many cases we are selecting based upon just the mother plant. A selection based upon the best plants for both parents would be better but usually isn't practical. Nevertheless, even selection based upon one parent is powerful, given time.

The basic selection method is to grow the crop under the conditions that we want the crop to perform under. Nate and I always grow our corn crops organically, and with relatively modest levels of fertility compared to what is typical for corn.

Varieties tend to deteriorate if "left alone" and just "maintained." You have to actively select for, that is, continue to breed for, the characteristics you want in order to improve them or even in order to merely maintain them in a variety. One of the characteristics we care about most for our corn varieties is ability to germinate vigorously under field conditions. In maritime Oregon, germinating in spring requires being able to germinate in cool wet weather. *Whenever possible, always plant excess seed.* To "select" we have to be able to choose the best, which we can do only if we have enough plants so that we do not need to keep every plant. I prefer to plant dense enough so that I have about two to four seedlings for every plant I keep. If I plant just enough seed so that I end up keeping every plant that emerges, I can't select for early seedling growth or yield under my conditions. I thin to final desired spacing. Part of the thinning is based upon spacing. But much of it is based upon plant size and vigor.

It is important to avoid thinning too early. I like to let the corn get at least four inches high before thinning. People frequently thin when the plants are only about two inches high, thinking that they are selecting for early or vigorous germination. This is counterproductive in several ways. First, the earliest plants to emerge are usually disproportionately those whose seed was planted a bit more shallowly than the rest. These may be more poorly rooted and more vulnerable to drying out than the plants from seed that was planted a bit deeper and that emerged a bit later.

Second, for about the first two inches of growth, the corn plant is depending upon the food supply established by the mother plant rather than upon its own genetic capabilities. Often, the biggest seeds germinate first. Which seed is biggest has to do with the size of the ear and the position of the seed on the ear, none of which reflects much upon the genes in the germling itself. I have seen mutants completely lacking chlorophyll that grew just as fast as the rest of the seedlings up until they were about 2 inches high. Lacking chlorophyll, such mutant seedlings are yellow and are incapable of photosynthesis. They grow that far and that well because of the food reserves established in the seed by the mother plant. After reaching about 2 inches high, such mutants stop growing quite suddenly and soon die. If we thin too early, we are not evaluating the genetic capabilities of the seedling.

Finally, germinating corn seeds have a choice as to how much of their energy to put into roots versus shoots. Modern hybrid sweet corn varieties usually send out a shoot only slightly after the root, and put about as much of their early efforts into both. Most Indian corn varieties put out a root well before the shoot and spend much more energy on the root. The root may become a big system 4 inches or more deep before the shoot reaches even an inch. (I've established this by germinating many different varieties on paper towels.) I prefer the pattern in which the root takes priority. It means that the corn seedling establishes itself thoroughly underground and uses up most of its reserves before the shoot emerges. When the shoot emerges, the seedling is most vulnerable to being pulled up seed and all by birds or having its top removed by slugs and other critters. With a big root system estab-

lished before the shoot emerges, the shoot grows rapidly and stays at the vulnerable stage only very briefly. And it may be so thoroughly well rooted that birds can't pull it up, or get very little nutrition from the mostly used up seed if they do. If I select for early emergence, I may be selecting for a variety that puts a larger part of its reserve of energy into making a shoot, the opposite of what I want.

I always walk the field and rogue out any off type plants before they release pollen. Even the best maintained and produced seed can always have an occasional seed in it that represents a contaminating cross in the prior generation.

Selection is always based upon desires. Do I want the highest total yield? Do I want the biggest ears? At what cost?

I usually harvest the first/earliest/biggest ear on each plant first. Seed kept from those ears represents an automatic selection for earliness in both parents. Seed saved from later ears can be pollinated by later corn plants, so isn't as powerful a selection for earliness. I usually select heavily for large ear size rather than total yield. Lots of little ears involve much more harvesting, shucking, and shelling work than a few big ears.

After removing the biggest/earliest ears, I usually mark late plants, plants that haven't yet ripened their first ear. These will be culled into the food supply. If I include their ears in the first cut of seed ears and choose the biggest ears, I can accidentally select for a later variety that produces bigger ears. I don't want a later variety that produces bigger ears. I want ears that are as big as possible on a variety that has the maturity I want.

I do a second cut that includes all the ears that mature a bit later except for those on the marked late plants. I usually take the biggest and best seed ears from the earliest ears as well as some of the grain from the second cut. That way I select in the first lot for ear size and earliness, and I select for total yield and increase the numbers of plants represented with the second cut.

I examine every prospective seed ear for overall type as well as any off-color kernels. I pick these out. They are easy to see on the ear before the corn is shelled. Sometimes a flint corn will show gradations of flour-corn characteristics on some kernels, or vice versa. This represents contaminating crosses in earlier generations that are segregating out. In such cases I eliminate the entire ear, not just the kernels that show the contamination the most.

If I have fewer than a hundred ears from different plants in any given year, I combine that year's corn with the corn from the prior growout of the same variety to keep the numbers up. One needs to have more than a hundred seed-grade ears for each round of selection. However, one doesn't necessarily need to do an entire round of selection in the course of one year. (Nowadays, I grow enough corn so that hundreds of good ears per year isn't a problem. But I've also grown plenty of smaller corn patches in my backyard.)

Growing, Harvesting, and Storing the Corn Crop

I've discussed seeding big seeds such as corn in prior chapters. I've also discussed the advantages of presoaking seed in certain situations. And in the fertility chapter, I discussed some of the traditional low-input approaches to fertilizing corn. (Put down manure before corn, then grow squash or other crops the second year, and legumes or potatoes in the third, for example.) In the bean chapter, I discussed turbo-winnowing for bean (or corn) seed. In chapter 4, I described how to dry corn or other big seeds well enough to seal in glass or plastic jars and store in a freezer (or run them through a freezer for a few weeks to kill insect eggs, a technique especially useful for flour corns). That is most of what you need to grow corn. But here are a few additional details:

1. Plant these field corns in blocks, not in long lines. A single row of corn will have mostly empty ears because there isn't enough pollen in the air for good ear fill. I consider 10 rows about the minimum, and 15 is better. Usually, the ears on the row that is upwind during the time of day for pollination will have mostly empty ears. (Modern sweet corn hybrids pollinate more profusely and with better synchrony than open-pollinated corn varieties.)

2. It's sometimes useful to control weeds by hilling plants up, especially with corn that has ear-bearing tillers. Hilling up helps prevent lodging.

3. I hold the water off after the ears start to dry down.

4. Varieties that have ears on the tillers often have to be harvested in several pickings, not just one. This can be helpful with all open-pollinated varieties.

5. Hand-shuck the ears within a few hours of picking. Some varieties, such as 'Reid's Yellow Dent', can be shucked on the plant with the aid of corn husking pegs, which are hooks mounted on straps or gloves. (Lehman's catalog carries them.) The varieties I grow don't work with corn husking pegs. Some varieties are easiest to shuck as you pick them. Not the ones I grow.

6. In the Midwest, corn can dry out well

enough so that the kernels can be ready to remove from the ears right out of the field. Not so here or in other damp climates. The ears need to dry out further indoors. I dry the flint corns by just putting the ears in mesh stacking boxes in the living room, about 20 to 30 pounds per crate (as much as I usually want to lift or carry). With the flour corn ears, I always turn a fan on the boxes for a couple of days after harvest to help avoid molding. (The bottom box in each stack needs to be an empty. If it contains corn, the corn molds.) People in New England or the Midwest often talk about corn cribs for storing whole-ear corn outside. Around here, such a corn crib would turn into one big corn-crib-shaped mass of mold.

7. If you try to hand-shell kernels off the ears, and the germs or bases of the kernels stay attached to the ear, the ear isn't yet dry enough to shell.

8. In the Willamette Valley, field corn isn't a commercial crop because it can't be combined. (A combine is a machine that removes the kernels from the ears and plants in the field.) Corn can't be combined here because the ears don't dry down well enough in the field. Corn can be combined in eastern Oregon. The Willamette Valley pioneers hand-picked their ears and let them finish drying inside, just like I do. Even in regions where combining is possible, these specialty or Indian corns often don't combine well. They and the machines have not been designed with each other in mind. Bushy corns with lots of tillers like 'Painted Mountain', 'Magic Manna', 'Parching Lavender Mandan', 'Parching Magenta', and 'Mandan Red Flour' can't be combined. 'Abenaki', the Cascade flints, 'Narragansett', 'Rhode Island Whitecap', and 'Longfellow' are single-stalk types and can be combined if you live in a region where combining commercial corn is possible.

9. Corn stores better on the ear than as loose grain (exposed to the air). Flour corn ears get insects in them if you leave them around unprotected very long, however. I always process the flour corn first, then the flints. I dry all seed corn kernels in the dehydrator. I store my seed-grade corn in the freezer, as described in chapter 4. I shell flour corn within a couple months of picking it and keep the kernels covered up and away from insects. I shell the flint corns when I get around to it, often months later. I don't run the food-grade corn through the dehydrator. I just store it in ½-gallon glass jars or in 3 ½-gallon plastic pails with covers for protection against insects as well as any rodent that happens by. A single mouse in corn even for a week or two while you set out traps can ruin a lot of corn. It will eat just the germs and discard the rest.

10. You can hand-shell modest amounts of corn as follows: Break the ears in half and, wearing gloves, rub and press ears against one another to remove the corn kernels. There are little metal corn shelling rings with inward-pointing teeth you can use, which may or may not help, depending upon the variety. Sometimes I use a nail file to flip out a kernel or row of kernels to get a reluctant ear going. Some varieties are much easier to hand-shell than others. The Hopi and Mandan flour corns are generally easy to shell. (Especially 'Parching Magenta', where I selected specifically for shelling ease, partly shelling a bit off every one of the several hundred ears that became the foundation for the variety and keeping only those that shelled easily. Likewise with 'Parching Red Supai'.) 'Longfellow' is hard enough to shell so

that I quit growing it for that reason back before I had a hand-crank sheller.

11. Hand-crank corn shellers are well worth the couple hundred dollars they cost once you start wanting to shell a hundred or more pounds of corn per year. You can buy them from Lehman's. The cob separator doesn't work for the kinds and sizes of ears I usually have. It jams constantly. It's easiest to just remove the cob separator. This means that you end up with the grain and bare cobs together, but it's easy and fast to remove the cobs by hand. Nate figured this out. I put up with jamming for years without its ever occurring to me, somehow. The shelling goes about three or four times faster without the cob separator. Old used farmstead shellers are considerably bigger and probably better than the small sheller from Lehman's. If you have a chance to buy one, grab it fast.

12. It's usually easiest to rototill under corn-stalks that are standing rather than cut and lying loose. Lots of people spend a lot of time cutting cornstalks down with a machete when it is unnecessary and actually counterproductive. If you do need to cut the stalks, a brush hook is more efficient than a machete. (Some traditional dent corns have stalks that are almost like trees.)

Yields

Modern hybrid dent corns grown in the Corn Belt can give those interested in records up to about 300 bushels per acre, but they require so much in inputs for those yields that it isn't practical. The practical yields are up to about 200 bushels per acre. That yield is for corn that is good for feeding animals and factories, not corn that is delicious gourmet people-food. It also demands the heavy application of chemical fertilizers, hybrid corns spaced 8 inches apart on rows 18 inches apart, and the specialized tractors and equipment required to till such tight rows (or herbicides). In other words, it's a number irrelevant for our purposes.

'Reid's Yellow Dent', a traditional high-yielding, open-pollinated dent grown in the Corn Belt, can give you about 100 bushels per acre or a bit more when grown organically. This is a good standard for comparison. Pioneer farmers in the Corn Belt frequently got about 100 bushels per acre or slightly more of good *full-season*, traditional open-pollinated dent varieties. Corn runs about 55 pounds per bushel over a wide range of kinds of corn. At a row spacing of 3½ feet, an acre of corn is about 11,000 row feet over pretty much all practical shapes of corn fields. So a reference yield of 100 bushels/acre translates into about 6 gallons (about 40 pounds) of corn per 100 row feet.

I wouldn't expect to get 6 gallons/100 feet in the cool Willamette Valley, even with 'Reid's Yellow Dent'. I haven't measured yields, but my guess is I would get a bit less with 'Longfellow', a little less yet with 'Narragansett' or 'Rhode Island Whitecap', and less yet for all early corns.

For early corns such as 'Painted Mountain', 'Magic Manna', 'Abenaki', and the three Cascade sisters, I use a different standard. These corns are so early they finish in August, thus saving nearly all the watering work. In addition, that permits planting a second crop, or starting an overwintering crop, or establishing a good cover crop. I use 3 gallons/100 row feet (about 20 pounds) as the standard for such early corns. I think those six corn varieties, of those I have grown, can come close to that standard.

Guerrilla Gardening

If you care about organic gardening and farming—if you envision a more sustainable agriculture and future—there is special reason to grow, breed, eat, and save seed from your own open-pollinated corn varieties. Every food crop variety is associated with certain growing methods and agricultural and cultural patterns. The varieties, methods, and patterns go together, support each other, and make each other possible. Modern commercial hybrid corn varieties are bred for optimum yield when grown in densely planted monocultures and given massive amounts of soluble fertilizers. That the fertilizer runoff pollutes groundwater and waterways is not considered. Neither is the fact that monocultures are highly vulnerable to pests and disease.

In addition, factory-farmed corn varieties have been stripped of their natural deliciousness and converted into something that is fit only for animal feed and the maws of factories. If you just grind some modern hybrid corn and make it into whole-grain cornbread, the flavor and culinary experience isn't worth the effort. You need a multimillion-dollar factory (and lots of sugar and salt and fat) to make modern hybrid corn taste edible. Furthermore, genetically modified modern corn varieties represent the bulk of the corn being grown in the United States today. GM varieties are legally restricted so as to prevent farmers from saving their own seed. For no other crop has agribusiness so completely taken over and subverted the essential nature of the plant, casually destroying flavor, nutritional value, human independence, and the environment in the process.

Embedded in those commercial corn varieties are the assumptions of their creators—that more is always better, that monocultures are best, that pollution, biodiversity, sustainability, and flavor don't matter, and that people should be eating only highly processed, refined foods. When you grow or eat corn varieties bred and grown by commercial agribusiness, you propagate its values along with its varieties. Corn is the core of modern agribusiness, the most important food crop in North America. In no other crop are the values of modern commercial agribusiness as thoroughly embedded. There is nothing we can do that is so ultimately subversive—there is no act of gardening that is so profound a rebellion, there is no act of eating that is so potent a blow for food quality and food system sanity—as to take back the corn crop in our own backyards, and to grow, breed, eat, and save seed of corn based upon an entirely different set of values.

Chapter Notes and References

Chapter 1. Gardening and Resilience

1-1. Some books of general relevance to this book and this chapter include:

Diamond, Jared. *Collapse: How Societies Choose to Fail or Succeed*. New York: Viking, 2005.

Diamond, Jared. *Guns, Germs, and Steel: The Fates of Human Societies*. New York: Norton, 1997.

Kunstler, James Howard. *The Long Emergency: Surviving the Converging Catastrophes of the Twenty-first Century*. New York: The Atlantic Monthly Press, 2005.

Krafel, Paul. *Seeing Nature: Deliberate Encounters with the Visible World*. White River Junction, VT: Chelsea Green Publishing Company, 1999.

1-2. (Hard Times . . .) This story featuring Confucius is a classic Taoist tale that appears in both *Chuang Tzu* and *Lieh Tzu*, two major Taoist classics. *Chuang Tzu* and *Lieh Tzu* are each available in several English translations. I drew on multiple translations of both sources for this version of the story.

1-3. (How Much Land . . .) McGee, Rose Marie Nichols, and Maggie Stuckey. *The Bountiful Container: A Container Garden of Vegetables, Herbs, Fruits, and Edible Flowers*. New York: Workman 2001. The definitive book on growing serious amounts of food in containers.

Chapter 2. The Plant-Gardener Covenant

2-1. (The Grand Alliance) The basic idea that it is an association of people, plants, and animals (rather than just humans) that has spread over the planet seems to be general, though not usually stated so explicitly. Also generally recognized these days is the idea that humans and various plants and animals have (to variable extents) domesticated each other (rather than humans acting unilaterally) and have co-evolved together. So is the idea that certain species (the classical example being dogs) essentially volunteered to domesticate themselves and might have had more to do with it than we did. That there is a domestication relationship between humans and entire landscapes is a recent idea presented by Kareiva, et al.

Kareiva, Peter, Sean Watts, Robert McDonald, and Tim Boucher. "Domesticated Nature: Shaping Landscapes and Ecosystems for Human Welfare." *Science* 316 (29 June 2007), pp. 1866–69.

Evolution was once thought to be very slow, with not much human evolution happening since people began doing agriculture, which they appeared to begin only in the last 10,000 to 15,000 years. We now realize that even peoples once considered nonagricultural were in fact practicing selection and breeding and shaping the "wild" plants in their environments. Northwest Indians, for example, selected and planted "wild" camas. The co-evolution of humans and domesticated plants and animals likely extended back tens of thousands of years before what we consider the earliest formal agriculture. That's plenty of time for evolution, even by the old standard that considered evolution a slow process.

Most biologists no longer believe evolution to be a necessarily slow process. Instead, the overall slow-appearing rate of evolution actually seems to reflect the average of long periods in which not much happens "punctuated" by periods of fast, sometimes extremely fast, evolutionary change. Profound evolutionary change sometimes happens in just a few generations. For a case study of the latter as well as an excellent and readable exposition of our modern understanding of evolution in general, see Jonathan Weiner's *The Beak of the Finch: A Story of Evolution in Our Time*. New York: Vintage, 1995.

2-2. Here are some books that are good sources of information about heirloom and other open-pollinated varieties:

> Facciola, Stephen. *Cornucopia II: A Sourcebook of Edible Plants*. Vista, CA: Kampong Publications, 1998.
>
> Guillet, Dominique. *The Seeds of Kokopelli: A Manual for the Production of Seeds in the Family Garden*. Mount Shasta, CA: Kokopelli Seed Foundation, 2002. (www.kokopelli-seed -foundation.com)
>
> Seed Savers Exchange. *Garden Seed Inventory*. 6th ed. Decorah, IA: Seed Saver Publications, 2005.
>
> Watson, Benjamin. *Taylor's Guide to Heirloom Vegetables*. New York: Houghton Mifflin, 1996.
>
> Weaver, William Woys. *Heirloom Vegetable Gardening: A Master Gardener's Guide to Planting, Growing, Seed Saving, and Cultural History*. New York: Holt, 1997.

2-3. (Experiment) Deppe, Carol. *Breed Your Own Vegetable Varieties: The Gardener's and Farmer's Guide to Plant Breeding and Seed Saving*. White River Junction, VT: Chelsea Green Publishing Company, 2000.

2-4. (Think Small) The basic idea that using a shovel is better than using a backhoe when you're at the shovel level of understanding I owe to Frank Morton (Shoulder to Shoulder Farm), founder of Wild Garden Seeds.

2-5. (Slow Down) Oregon's Willamette Valley, marked by Eugene at its southern boundary and Portland and the Columbia River at its north, is the main agricultural valley of Oregon and the home of most of its population. With summers hardly ever too hot and winters only occasionally below freezing, framed to

the East by the rugged peaks of the Cascades and to the West by the deep green Coastal Mountains, and with deep loam soils crisscrossed by streams and rivers, Willamette Valley is indeed a magnificent, bountiful, gentle, generous land.

2-6. (Save . . . Seeds) The two books I usually recommend for seed saving are (with unavoidable bias in the latter case):

> Ashworth, Suzanne. *Seed to Seed: Seed Saving Techniques for the Vegetable Gardener*. Decorah, IA: Seed Saver Publications, 1991.
>
> Deppe, Carol. *Breed Your Own Vegetable Varieties: The Gardener's and Farmer's Guide to Plant Breeding and Seed Saving*. White River Junction, VT: Chelsea Green Publishing, 2000.

Chapter 3. Wild Weather

3-1. Sources of information on climate and climate change I drew upon to create the synthesis in this chapter included:

> Cook, Edward R., Connie A. Woodhouse, C. Mark Eakin, David M. Meko, and David W. Stahle. "Long-Term Aridity Changes in the Western United States." *Science* 308 (5 Nov, 2004): 1015–18.
>
> Diamond, Jared. *Collapse: How Societies Choose to Fail or Succeed*. New York: Viking, 2005.
>
> Diamond, Jared. *Guns, Germs, and Steel: The Fates of Human Societies*. New York: Norton, 1997.
>
> Fagan, Brian. *The Great Warming: Climate Change and the Rise and Fall of Civilizations*. New York: Bloomsbury Press, 2008.
>
> Fagan, Brian. *The Little Ice Age: How Climate Made History—1300–1850*. New York: Basic Books, 2002.
>
> Gedalof, Ze'ev, David L. Peterson, and Nathan J. Mantua. "Columbia River Flow and Drought Since 1750." *Journal of the American Water Resources Association* (*JAWRA*) 40 no. 6 (2004): 1579–92. (Available free on the Internet.)

Macdougall, Doug. *Frozen Earth: The Once and Future Story of Ice Ages.* Berkeley: University of California Press, 2004.

Macdougall, J. D. *A Short History of Planet Earth: Mountains, Mammals, Fire, and Ice.* New York: Wiley, 1996.

Overton, Mark. *Agricultural Revolution in England: The Transformation of the Agrarian Economy 1500–1850.* Cambridge Studies in Historical Geography 23. Cambridge: Cambridge University Press, 1996.

Seager, Richard, Mingfang Ting, Isaac Held, Yochanan Kushnir, Jian Lu, Gabriel Vecchi, Huei-Ping Huang, Nili Harnik, Ants Leetmaa, Ngar-Cheung Lau, Cuihua Li, Jennifer Velez, and Naomi Naik. "Model Projections of an Imminent Transition to a More Arid Climate in Southwestern North America." *Science* 316 (25 May 2007): 1181–84.

Stommel, Henry, and Elizabeth Stommel. *Volcano Weather: 1816—The Story of the Year without a Summer.* Newport, RI: Seven Seas Press, 1983.

3-2. (Global Warming . . .) The article by Cook, et al. (note 3-1) compiled and reconstructed annual climate records from tree ring and other data for much of North America over the last 1,200 years. A notable result was that the period corresponding to the Medieval Warm period, a generally lovely period for Europe, was marked by overall greater aridity and frequent multiyear droughts in Western North America. If global warming overall translates into greater aridity and worse and longer droughts in the North American West, water may be a more important consideration than temperature when considering global warming in this region.

3-3. Most climate models seem to suggest that, in a period of global warming, droughts equivalent to or worse than those associated with the Dust Bowl era

might become common in the American Southwest. (See Seager, note 3-1.) When considering greater aridity and more multiyear droughts, it is clear that lands that are marginal for agriculture now because of aridity or droughts would be impossible for agriculture in a drier era. Cities and huge populations located in deserts might become increasingly unsustainable, and perhaps even impossible. Agriculture located in deserts and dependent completely upon irrigation might also become increasingly unworkable if rivers dry up and aquifers fail.

3-4. In a compilation of thirty-two different sets of drought-sensitive tree-ring data, Gedalof et al. (see note 3-1) construct a picture of Columbia River flow and drought in The Dalles, Oregon. Among their observations: The period 1950–87 is "anomalous . . . for having no notable multiyear drought events." Multiyear drought events in the Pacific Northwest are overall generally much more common than they have been lately. There have been six multiyear droughts in the Northwest in the last 250 years, with the worst starting in 1840 and lasting twelve years. The second-worst was associated with the Dust Bowl period in the 1930s. This is among the reports that suggest that recent times have actually been unusually stable.

3-5. Where are we currently with respect to glacial cycles? Glacial cycles take about 100,000 years. The last several glacial cycles (indicated, as always, by proxy data) have featured a rapid rise from minimum temperatures to maximum temperatures that takes about 10,000 to 20,000 years. Then there is a slower erratic deterioration for about 80,000 years to minimum temperatures. We have just experienced the run-up to the warmest temperatures of the current interglacial period pretty much as expected by normal patterns. That is, proxy data are now where they have been when past interglacial periods have been at their warmest point and are due to begin the deterioration that leads to the next ice age. The last glacial maximum was about 20,000 years ago, which also suggests that what comes next is 80,000 years of global cooling. (That is, unless human activity overrides natural patterns.)

3-6. The evidence for a genetic bottleneck for humans is based upon genetic variability of human populations compared with those of apes and other animals. We are missing most of the expected variability. What variability we have is mostly between individuals rather than between populations, suggesting that it arose recently. The idea that the bottleneck happened about 72,000 years ago is based upon molecular clock evidence, which depends upon the rates of mutation of DNA. There are many who think that a major blowup of the volcano Toba (about 70,000 to 75,000 years ago) might have been responsible. It apparently caused massive climate change and made the ongoing ice age suddenly much worse. In this scenario, nearly all of humanity died; we descended from a surviving remnant that was possibly no more than 1,000 to 10,000 breeding pairs. It was a close call.

3-7. (Adventures . . .) I got the explanations for the strange weather patterns in maritime Oregon in 2005 from the weather column Climate Matters by Oregon State University climatologist George Taylor, particularly the column titled "2005: A year of drought and flooding." Climate Matters appears in the *Corvallis Gazette-Times* and other local and regional newspapers.

3-8. (The Little Ice Age . . .) For weather in the Little Ice Age and its effect on agriculture, and the agricultural revolution that occurred as an adjustment to it, I drew primarily on the books by Anderson, Fagan, Overton, Mann, and Stommel (see notes 3-1 and 3-11).

3-9. (Hopi . . .) Whiting, Alfred F. *Ethnobotany of the Hopi.* Flagstaff, AZ: Northern Arizona Society of Science and Art, 1939.

3-10. (Evaluating the Resilience and Use Potential of Your Land) Soil survey maps and information are online at http://soils.usda.gov/survey/.

3-11. Information and perspective on what America was like and how Indians did agriculture before European settlement came primarily from:

Anderson, Virginia DeJohn. *Creatures of Empire: How Domestic Animals Transformed Early America.* New York: Oxford University Press, 2004.

Botkin, Daniel B. *Our Natural History: Lessons of Lewis and Clark.* New York: Perigee, 1995.

Krech, Shepard, III. *The Ecological Indian: Myth and History.* New York: Norton, 1999.

Mann, Charles C. *1491: New Revelations of the Americas Before Columbus.* New York: Vintage, 2006.

Whiting, Alfred F. *Ethnobotany of the Hopi.* Flagstaff, AZ: Northern Arizona Society of Science and Art, 1939.

Wilson, Gilbert L. *Buffalo Bird Woman's Garden: Agriculture of the Hidatsa Indians.* St. Paul, MN: Minnesota Historical Society Press, 1987.

Chapter 4. Diet and Food Resilience

4-1. (Trading . . .) Juntunen, Judy Rycraft, May D. Dasch, and Ann Bennett Rogers. *The World of the Kalapuya: A Native People of Western Oregon.* Philomath, OR: Benton County Historical Society and Museum, 2005.

4-2. (Choosing . . . Calorie and Protein Staples) Calkins, Erica. *Hatchet, Hands & Hoe: Planting the Pioneer Spirit.* Caldwell, ID: The Caxton Printers Ltd., 1996.

4-3. The Teff Company. 1-888-822-2221. www.teffco .com.

4-4. Logsdon, Gene. *Small-Scale Grain Raising: An Organic Guide to Growing, Processing, and Using*

Nutritious Whole Grains for Home Gardeners and Local Farmers. 2nd ed. White River Junction, VT: Chelsea Green Publishing Co., 2009.

4-5. Sunroots, a.k.a. "sunchokes" or "Jerusalem artichokes," are easy to grow and are productive, and would seem to be a reasonable candidate for a carbohydrate staple. However, they aren't. The starch in sunroots is inulin. Humans don't digest inulin. Some major North American wild food plants have starches stored in the form of inulin. Camas was one. However, camas was baked for a day or more, dried, powdered, and made into cakes that were apparently as sweet as candy. (See note 4-1.) I suspect the long processing hydrolyzed the inulin into free sugar.

4-6. Kitinoja, Lisa, and Adel A. Kader. *Small-Scale Postharvest Handling Practices: A Manual for Horticultural Crops.* 3rd ed. Davis: Department of Pomology, University of California (Davis), 1995.

4-7. Mills that sell meal from heirloom or gourmet corns

Morgans Mills & Country Store, Old Route 17, Union, ME 04962. 207-785-4900. Morgans Mills sells cornmeal ground from 'Rhode Island Whitecap' corn, a classic true-flint corn.

Anson Mills. www.ansonmills.com. 1922-C Gervais Street, Columbia, SC 29201. 803-467-4122. Anson Mills is particularly noted for old-fashioned grits made from traditional southern heirloom corns.

4-8. Bob's Red Mill & Country Store. www.bobsred mill.com. 13521 SE Pheasant Court, Milwaukie, OR 97222. Whole Grain Store: 5000 SE International Way, Milwaukie, OR 97222. 503-607-6455. Mail-order: 800-349-2173.

4-9. Meadows Mills, Inc. www.meadowsmills.com. 1352 West D Street, P.O. Box 1288, North Wilkesboro, NC 28659. 800-626-2282; 336-838-2282.

4-10. (. . . Omega-3 Fatty Acids) "Omega" is the written form of the Greek symbol chemists use to indicate a double bond. For those familiar with the general structure of fatty acids, omega-3 fatty acids have the first double bond between the carbon atoms that are number 3 and 4 from the non-carboxylic-acid end. In omega-6 fatty acids the first double bond is between carbons 6 and 7.

4-11. For general nutrition and dietary advice I recommend:

Weil, Andrew. *Eating Well for Optimum Health: The Essential Guide to Bringing Health and Pleasure Back to Eating.* New York: Quill (HarperCollins), 2001.

Willett, Walter C. *Eat, Drink, and Be Healthy: The Harvard Medical School Guide to Healthy Eating.* New York: Free Press, 2001.

4-12. For additional information about omega-3 fatty acids see:

Robinson, Jo. *Pasture Perfect: The Far-Reaching Benefits of Choosing Meat, Eggs, and Dairy Products from Grass-Fed Animals.* Vashon Island, WA: Vashon Island Press, 2004.

Simopoulos, Artemis P., and Jo Robinson. *The Omega Diet: The Lifesaving Nutritional Program Based on the Diet of the Island of Crete.* New York: Harper Perennial, 1999.

Stoll, Andrew L. *The Omega-3 Connection: The Groundbreaking Antidepression Diet and Brain Program.* New York: Fireside (Simon & Schuster), 2001.

4-13. In choosing a cod liver oil, choose one that gives you an exact analysis of EPA and DHA, whose content is mostly EPA and DHA, that has a good balance of vitamins A and D, that is processed and packed so as to prevent oxidation (and packed under nitrogen), and that has been analyzed and found to be free of mercury contamination.

4-14. I strongly recommend all who are gluten intolerant join GIG, Gluten Intolerance Group of North America. It is a wonderful source of information, has a very useful publication, and reports early and often on relevant research.

4-15. (Preserving . . .) Here are some good books on food preservation and storage methods:

Bubel, Mike, and Nancy Bubel. *Root Cellaring: Natural Cold Storage of Fruits & Vegetables.* North Adams, MA: Storey Publishing, 1991. The definitive book on root cellaring, which also gives thorough coverage to in-garden and natural storage.

Excalibur/KBI, Inc. *Preserve It Naturally II: The Complete Guide To Food Dehydration.* Sacramento, CA: Excalibur/KBI, Inc., 1999. By the people who make Excalibur dehydrators, this is by far the best book I have seen on drying. It seems to be available only from the company.

The Gardeners & Farmers of Terre Vivante, Deborah Madison, and Eliot Coleman. *Keeping Food Fresh: Old World Techniques and Recipes.* White River Junction, VT: Chelsea Green Publishing Co., 1999.

Katz, Sandor, and Sally Fallon. *Wild Fermentation: The Flavor, Nutrition, and Craft of Live-Culture Foods.* White River Junction, VT: Chelsea Green Publishing Co., 2003.

Ziedrich, Linda. *The Joy of Pickling.* Boston: The Harvard Common Press, 1998.

4-16. Welby, Ellen M., and Brian McGregor. *Agricultural Export Transportation Handbook; Agriculture Handbook 700.* USDA, 2004 (revised). Available free on the Web.

4-17. (Hoarding and Saving Seeds) Ashworth, Suzanne. *Seed to Seed: Seed Saving Techniques for the Vegetable Gardener.* Decorah, IA: Seed Saver Publications, 1991.

Deppe, Carol. *Breed Your Own Vegetable Varieties: The Gardener's and Farmer's Guide to Plant Breeding and Seed Saving.* White River Junction, VT: Chelsea Green Publishing, 2000.

4-18. Woodford, Keith (Foreword by Thomas Cowan, M.D.) *Devil in the Milk: Illness, Health, and the Politics of A1 and A2 Milk.* White River Junction, VT: Chelsea Green Publishing Co., 2009.

4-19. Another reason Nate and I like the idea of water buffalo for milk, meat, and draft is the fact that they have huge feet. Here in maritime Oregon, cattle cannot usually be pastured in winter because their weight compresses the soggy land too much. Sheep are light enough so compaction isn't usually a problem. So sheep can be and usually are pastured year-round. Water buffalo with their disproportionately large feet might well create no more compaction problem than sheep. Water buffalo are also able to eat a bigger variety of forage plants than cattle, and also utilize low-grade feeds more efficiently. In addition, the bulls are apparently usually friendlier and gentler than most cattle bulls. Some water buffalo bulls (as well as steers and cows) are used for riding or draft. The meat is very similar to beef. A good cow can produce about 5 gallons of milk per day, with about 6 percent butterfat.

4-20. Green, Peter H. R., M.D., and Rory Jones. *Celiac Disease: A Hidden Epidemic.* Revised and updated edition. New York: HarperCollins (Morrow), 2006.

Chapter 5. Labor and Exercise

5-1. (Garden Beds . . .) Jeavons, John. *How to Grow More Vegetables (and Fruits, Nuts, Berries, Grains, and Other Crops) Than You Ever Thought Possible on Less Land Than You Can Imagine.* 7th ed. Berkeley, CA: Ten Speed Press, 2006.

5-2. (Weeds) Eliot Coleman designed Nate's favorite light weeding hoe, which Coleman calls the "collinear hoe," and we and others have started calling the

"Coleman hoe." Coleman's book is an excellent source of information on using hoes and other hand tools, including wheel hoes. *The New Organic Grower: A Master's Manual of Tools and Techniques for the Home and Market Gardener*. 2nd ed. White River Junction, VT: Chelsea Green Publishing Company, 1995.

5-3. (Mulch) Reich, Lee. *Weedless Gardening*. New York: Workman, 2001.

5-4. (Buying Tools) Red Pig Garden Tools and Blacksmith (formerly Denman and Company). (Bob and Rita Denman) 12040 SE Revenue Rd., Boring, OR 97009. 503-663-9494. The retail store is about thirty-five minutes from Portland, Oregon. However, it was in California back when I was buying my tools, and I always bought mail-order. This is the only source I know of for the furrowing plow. Only the small hand tools are listed on the Web site at www.redpigtools .com; however, there are many unique tools, including left-handed tools. To get long tools or custom tools, call and tell them what you want. Long tools have choices with respect to handle lengths, including lengths longer than those found on factory-made tools. I got my peasant hoe, furrowing plow, and diamond hoe from Red Pig Garden Tools.

5-5. Fedco, Johnny's Selected Seeds, and Peaceful Valley Farm Supply are mail-order seed companies with especially good selections of quality garden tools.

5-6. (Helpers) Wilson, Gilbert L. *Buffalo Bird Woman's Garden: Agriculture of the Hidatsa Indians*. St. Paul, MN: Minnesota Historical Society Press, 1987.

Chapter 6. Water and Watering

6-1. (Essential Water-Nature . . .) Lehman's Non-electric catalog. One Lehman Circle, P.O. Box 41, Kidron, OH, 44636. 877-438-5346. www.lehmans .com

6-2. Kourik, Robert. *Gray Water Use in the Landscape*. Santa Rosa, CA: Metamorphic Press, 1988.

6-3. (. . . Drip Irrigation) Kourik, Robert. *Drip Irrigation for Every Landscape and All Climates*. 2nd ed. Santa Rosa, CA: Metamorphic Press, 2009.

6-4. (Water Resilience and Vegetables) Solomon, Steve. *Water-Wise Vegetables*. Seattle, WA: Sasquatch Books, 1993. Much, but not all, of the water-related information was incorporated into *Gardening When It Counts*.
   Solomon, Steve. *Gardening When It Counts: Growing Food in Hard Times*. Gabriola Island, BC, Canada: New Society Publishers, 2005.

Chapter 7. Soil and Fertility

7-1. Solomon, Steve. *Growing Vegetables West of the Cascades*. 5th ed. Seattle, WA: Sasquatch Books, 2000.

7-2. King, F. H. *Farmers of Forty Centuries: Permanent Agriculture in China, Korea and Japan*. Emmaus, PA: Rodale Press (original copyright 1911). Traditional Asian farmers, unlike Europeans and Americans, were able to garden and grow crops on the same land for year after year and generation after generation without loss of productivity and during what was, by our standards, mostly hard times. Wasting absolutely no manure or humanure was a big part of the pattern. This book is a study of the methods of these experts at maintaining and scrounging fertility.

7-3. Jenkins, Joseph C. *The Humanure Handbook: A Guide to Composting Human Manure*. 3rd ed. (paperback) The first edition appeared in 1999. Self-published.

7-4. These days, I advise against using commercial blood meal or bone meal as fertilizer because of their potential as transmitters of mad cow disease.

Chapter 8. Potatoes

8-1. (. . . Nutrition . . .) For information on potatoes in the pre-famine Irish diet, see Bourne, P. M. Austin. "The Use of the Potato Crop in Pre-Famine Ireland." *Journal of the Statistical and Social Inquiry Society of Ireland*. Vol. 21 part 6 1967/1968. (Available free on the Internet.)

8-2. For nutrition information on potatoes and other foods—I got much of the raw data I used for the calculations from:

Watt, Bernice K., and Annabel L. Merrill. *Composition of Foods*. United States Department of Agriculture, Agriculture Handbook No. 8, 1963. I like this old version more than the modern updates because it has more information about the basic foods I use instead of the processed foods that I don't.

Woolfe, Jennifer A. *The Potato in the Human Diet*. Cambridge: Cambridge University Press, 1987. (Paperback edition, 2009.)

The caloric contents of various grain products such as breads and cereals I obtained by wandering around a grocery store and recording things off labels, then correcting to a serving size of 100 grams.

I calculated the protein amounts in 2,000-calorie diets of various kinds.

Information on potato protein absorption and quality came from de Romaña, Guillermo Lopez, E. David Mellits, and William C. MacLean, Jr. "Utilization of the Protein and Energy of White Potato by Human Infants." *Journal of Nutrition* 110 (1980): 1849–57. (Available free on the Internet.)

Excellent information on protein requirements of ordinary sedentary Americans (upon which the RDA is based) as well as other groups, including athletes and others who are physically active, the elderly, the ill, and others can be found in the work of Carmen Castanada Sceppa, M.D., Ph.D., which is described in Russell, Robert M., M.D., and Carmen Castanada Sceppa, M.D., Ph.D. "How Much Protein Do You Need?" (This free Internet article is easiest to find by googling "Carmen Castanada Sceppa.")

8-3. (. . . Glycoalkaloids . . .) Cantwell, Marita. "A Review of Important Facts on Potato Glycoalkaloids." I highly recommend this article to anyone who plans to sell potatoes. (It appeared originally in *Perishables Handling Newsletter* no. 87 (August 1996), p. 26.

The article can be found for free on the University of California–Davis Web site, http://postharvest.ucdavis.edu/.)

Lachman, J., K. Hamouz, M. Orsak, and V. Pivec. "Potato Glycoalkaloids and Their Significance in Plant Protection and Human Nutrition—Review." Czech University of Agriculture in Prague, Czech Republic, 2001. (Available free on the Internet.)

Childers, N.F., Ph.D., and M. S. Margoles, M.D. "An Apparent Relation of Nightshades (Solanaceae) to Arthritis." *Journal of Neurological and Orthopedic Medical Surgery* 12 (1993): 227–31. (Available free on the Internet.)

8-4. Feeding Potatoes to Livestock Snowdon, Murray. "Feeding Potatoes to Cattle." Brunswick, Canada Department of Agriculture and Aquaculture.

Weston, J. W. "Feeding Cull and Surplus Potatoes" (to livestock) Michigan Agricultural College Bulletin No. 25; Extension Series; December 1922. (Available free on the Internet.)

8-5. Sources for Potato Varieties Most general and regional mail-order seed companies carry certified potato seed. Fedco has an especially nice selection of potato varieties as well as good information about them. Two additional sources that sell primarily potatoes are the Potato Garden (Milk Ranch Specialty Potatoes), which has bought Ronniger's, and Wood Prairie Farm. Contact Tom Wagner directly about his varieties. (See appendix B.)

8-6. (Growing . . .) An excellent source for much more technical detail and information on growing potatoes is Western Potato Council's "Commercial Potato Production—Botany of the Potato Plant." 2003. (This is a free Internet adaptation of "Guide to Commercial Potato Production on the Canadian Prairies.")

8-7. Stiles, Shelly, and editors. "Hot Potatoes," *National Gardening* (July/August 1994). This article describes an experiment on hilling up with soil versus mulch. The *National Gardening* editors asked eight experienced test gardeners in different regions of the United States to each plant two rows of 'Katahdin' potatoes, one hilled with soil and one hilled with mulch. "The results were one-sided and surprising. From Massachusetts to California, on clay soil or sandy soil, in wet weather or dry, the potatoes hilled with soil outyielded the potatoes mulched with hay, straw or leaves by an average of one-third, and generally produced larger tubers."

8-8. Jeavons, John. *How to Grow More Vegetables (and Fruits, Nuts, Berries, Grains, and Other Crops) Than You Ever Thought Possible on Less Land Than You Can Imagine*, 7th ed. Berkeley, CA: Ten Speed Press, 2006.

8-9. (Storing . . .) Kitinoja, Lisa, and Adel A. Kader. *Small-Scale Postharvest Handling Practices: A Manual for Horticultural Crops*. 3rd ed. Davis: Department of Pomology, University of California–Davis, 1995. This book appears to be available for sale only from the University of California. It can be ordered from the Web site http://postharvest.ucdavis.edu. However, there is nothing more about potato storage in the book that I didn't incorporate into the "Storing Potatoes" section beyond the reprints of the potato storage structures, which weren't original with this publication. They are mostly from information by the International Potato Center (CIP) in a generally unavailable book, *Principles of Potato Storage* (Lima, Peru). The critical diagrams and information on potato storage in this book can be found on the Internet, however, by searching under the phrase "Principles of Potato Storage."

8-10. Bubel, Mike, and Nancy Bubel. *Root Cellaring: Natural Cold Storage of Fruits & Vegetables*. North Adams, MA: Storey Publishing, 1991.

8-11. (Saving . . . Seed . . .) I created this guide to saving your own potato seed by starting with about

eight hours of instruction from Tom Wagner, which forms the core of the section. Then I looked up and incorporated all relevant information I could find for producing certified potato seed, including that on training "roguers," the field hands responsible for identifying and eliminating diseased potato plants in fields of potatoes being grown for certified seed. Then I looked up specific potato diseases and made sure that my general guide would eliminate plants or tubers with those diseases (without requiring that you be able to recognize or identify any particular disease). The separate step of pooling potatoes from each plant and choosing the best plants is a step I added based upon first principles. It should add considerable power to the process of choosing the most disease-free seed. (This step isn't possible for those who harvest by machine.)

8-12. An especially useful source for learning to recognize potato diseases is Oregon State University Extension's "An Online Guide to Plant Disease Control" (http://plant-disease.ippc.orst.edu). The section on potato diseases gives an excellent description of disease symptoms and has lots of photos.

8-13. I believe the idea that blue potatoes are so different from white potatoes that they go best with different foods and need different recipes is original with me, as are all the recipes.

8-14. Seed Balls and True Seed I save seed balls with true seed in them whenever they appear on any of my potato plants. That way, if a super-mega-disaster wiped out all agriculture on Earth for years, wiping out all our supply of seed tubers, I could regenerate potato growing from true seed. True potato seed doesn't breed true. Each plant grown from a potato seed is different from all others, even others from the same seed ball, and represents the beginning of a new variety.

True potato seed will keep for many years at room temperature, and in a freezer, essentially indefinitely. Start true seed in pots and transplant, just as you would start seeds for their relative, the tomato. The potato plants started from seed will give just a few small tubers the first year, which are used as the seed tubers for the next year. The second year, you start getting decent yields of full-size spuds.

I encourage all gardeners to save any seed balls that appear in their potato patches. Seed balls do not occur on all varieties. And they depend a lot on weather conditions. We got lots of seed balls on 'Yukon Gold' last year, for example, and have never seen even a one on 'Yukon Gold' any other year. I just let the seed balls dry out with the seeds in them. I haven't yet grown out anything from seed balls.

Chapter 9. The Laying Flock

9-1. (Backyard Poultry) Holderread, Dave. *Storey's Guide to Raising Ducks*. 2nd ed. North Adams, MA: Storey Publishing, 2001. The definitive book on raising and managing ducks, including laying and rare breeds, many of which were imported, improved, and distributed in the United States by Dave Holderread himself. (Don't depend upon general poultry books for information on laying ducks. They are written by chicken raisers, most of whom have never kept ducks and know little or nothing about good breeds of laying ducks.)

9-2. Useful books on chicken raising include:

Damerow, Gail. *Storey's Guide to Raising Chickens*. North Adams, MA: Storey Publishing, 1995. A good general introduction.

Hastings, Milo M., and Robert Plamondon. *The Dollar Hen: The Classic Guide to American Free-Range Egg Farming*. *The Dollar Hen* was originally published in 1909 by Arkadia. This modern edition contains the text of the original with extensive and very useful commentaries by Robert Plamondon as to changes since 1909.

Lee, Andy, and Pat Foreman. *Day Range Poultry: Every Chicken Owner's Guide to Grazing Gardens and Improving Pastures*. Montpelier, VT: Good Earth Publications, 2002. This book has good

coverage, among other things, on electric poultry netting, by far the easiest way to keep poultry in and predators out of poultry yards and foraging areas.

Plamondon, Robert. *Success with Baby Chicks*. Blodgett, OR: Norton Creek Press, 2003.

Salatin, Joel. *Pastured Poultry Profits*. Swoope, VA: Polyface, 1996. Mostly about raising broiler chickens. You need a 1999 or later printing to get the appendix on free-range egg production.

9-3. If ducklings have access to swimming water within their first few days, their wax glands activate and they begin preening and waxing themselves a day or two later. With no swimming water the first few days, the wax glands fail to activate, then only activate after the ducks are about eight weeks old. Supervise the baby ducklings' swim. They are not waterproof and can drown.

9-4. Chickens of dual-purpose breeds are sometimes criticized as meat birds because they don't have the huge breasts of the Cornish cross hybrids. Actually, the genetic change that produces the big breasts also reduces the hindquarters. So if you like the dark meat, classically shaped dual-purpose and meat breeds are an advantage over the Cornish cross hybrids.

9-5. (Laying Duck Breeds . . .) The Holderread Khaki Campbell. For Khaki Campbells, get the Holderread line, not the older lines. Dave Holderread calls these the "Kortlang" or "Jansen Farm" or "English" line. Everyone else calls them the "Holderread" strain. Dave Holderread imported the Kortlang/Jensen bird into the United States and bred it for egg production via pedigreed matings for years. The Holderread strain is now widely available from many U.S. hatcheries. Holderread Campbells have flock averages of 320–340 eggs/bird during their first year of production, with individual birds laying for over 400 days without missing a day. No other breed of laying duck or chicken, including the fanciest, most productive commercial hybrids, even comes close.

Older Campbell lines are also readily available, have not been selected for production recently, and are likely to produce about 200–300 eggs/year. There are also other lines of Campbells that are dark or white. These don't lay as well as Khakis, but are good enough for many purposes.

9-6. The Kortlang/Jensen/English Khaki Campbell, Welsh Harlequin, Ancona, Saxony, Silver Appleyard, and Dutch Hookbill duck breeds were all originally imported, improved, and distributed by Dave Holderread, Holderread Waterfowl Farm & Preservation Center, P.O. Box 492, Corvallis, OR 97339. 541-929-5338. www.holderreadfarm.com.

Holderread's no longer sells Campbells or Anconas, however. The Holderread Campbells are now available from many sources. For sources for Anconas as well as additional information about them, see my Web site, www.caroldeppe.com.

9-7. All egg production records for various breeds are taken from Holderread. All poultry production records assume a controlled light regime. However, many people, myself included, don't bother with controlled lighting, and their birds lay well enough for their purposes without it.

9-8. Behavior of different breeds is from my own personal observations with my own flocks of different breeds.

9-9. Most egg cartons aren't big enough for Ancona duck eggs. The biggest cartons I have found are the Jumbo size produced by EggCartons.com (www.eggcartons.com). The jumbo size will take a dozen jumbo eggs or a mix of jumbos and super-jumbos, which is what Anconas produce.

9-10. Welsh Harlequins are by far the most people-oriented of the duck breeds I have kept. Most of the drakes especially take readily to being handled and like being lap ducks. If you have kids who will want to hold the ducks, consider Harlequins.

9-11. Campbells tend to lay soft-shelled eggs toward the end of their laying cycle. This may be because they tend to continue laying while molting. Other breeds generally stop laying when they molt.

9-12. Leaders. Anconas have female leaders, that is, it is a female who controls the movements of the flock when they are out foraging. The leader isn't always in front. There are sometimes front-runners who move out ahead once the leader has indicated when and where. But the female leader makes the decisions. She may or may not be the most dominant duck. Every cohort raised together is a subflock that has its own leader. (It retains its subgroup identity as long as it has its own drakes. It merges with another subflock if it loses its drakes.) Flock drakes follow the female leader, just as the other ducks do. Female-led flocks head directly for the best foraging area first thing in the morning when the foraging is best.

Welsh Harlequin females mostly just follow the drakes around. Drakes care more about mating than foraging. (Laying females have much higher nutritional needs.) So Harlequin drakes lead the flock to the bathing pond, where the females desperately denude the already denuded grass around the pond and look longingly at the better forage elsewhere where the female-led Anconas are foraging. In summer, by the time the Harlequin drakes are through bathing and mating and turn to foraging, the insects and slugs are mostly eaten by the Anconas or have hidden.

Campbell females have somewhat more leadership inclinations than Harlequins and somewhat less than Ancona females. They, too, however, usually spend the prime foraging time in or near the pond with the drakes instead of foraging most effectively.

In a mixed flock of Campbells and Anconas, the Campbell females happily accept the Ancona lady leaders and go forage with them instead of hanging with the drakes. (Campbell girls are usually front-runners. That is, they run out ahead of the leader as soon as they see where she is going.) So Campbells are more effective foragers when mixed with Anconas than when alone. Campbells are bolder than Anconas, and explore a new area faster, but also panic and stampede back frequently. Anconas are more wary about predators. They look a new area over cautiously and explore it carefully, making sure they know how to get back, and evaluating it carefully at every step. They are slower than Campbells to take over a new area, but they generally do it without any panics or stampedes along the way.

Ancona leaders may decide who gets to join or stay in a flock. I once saw a young overly aggressive big duck, Dovetail, temporarily ejected from the flock for bad behavior. Dovetail was actually the alpha duck at the time, with respect to dominance. She was aggressive by Ancona standards. Ancona dominance tends to be soft and subtle. Dovetail was throwing her weight around and acting rude. Grey Cape (co)leader ejected Dovetail from the flock. Every time Dovetail tried to fight back, Grey Cape was backed up by Lavender (co) leader. Dovetail was more powerful than either, but she couldn't fight Grey Cape very well with Lavender standing on her back attacking her head. Dovetail had to accept bottom-duck status for several days, and take guff from the least dominant ducks in the flock, all much smaller than she was, before Grey Cape forgave her and let her back. After her return to good graces, Dovetail never displayed dominance in an overt enough way for me to figure out where she stood. She did return to being a duck in good standing. A much politer, gentler duck in good standing.

When Grey Cape Leader died, Lavender Leader was really depressed. She didn't go for any of the special treats I offered. She barely ate. She didn't bathe. The other ducks kept asking Lavender to be the leader, but she refused. Lavender got her spirits back after a few months, but she never led again. I guess she figured it was time to retire. A couple of years after that, I saw a young subflock leader, Pigtail, asking Lavender to be *their* leader. (This is the only time I've ever seen ducks try to recruit a leader from outside their subflock. Apparently, Lavender's wisdom was universally recognizable.) But Lavender again refused, this time indicating that she thought Pigtail looked like the right duck for the job.

9-13. Mixed Duck Flocks Harlequins care about dominance more than other breeds, and are more aggressive than most during the period when they are establishing their hierarchy as ducklings. Harlequins can get themselves hated by other breeds in larger mixed flocks. With a handful of ducks, mixed breeds work OK. In larger flocks, Campbells and Anconas work well together, but use Campbell drakes. With a mixed flock, the drake or drakes should be the smaller breed to avoid damaging the legs of smaller females with the drake's weight when mating. Anconas and Harlequins don't work well together. The Harlequins end up subordinate to the larger Anconas, care about it a lot, and don't lay well or even at all. I advise keeping Harlequins in pure flocks. Campbells really like being raised with Anconas, who are gentle and tolerant toward the smaller ducklings. It is amazing how much guff an Ancona will take from a little Campbell. Because of the gentleness and the subtlety of Ancona dominance behavior, it takes most Campbells a couple of months to figure out that they aren't actually dominant to the Anconas. Bigger Ancona ducklings actually actively break up fights they consider too aggressive or over the top. Mixed flocks of Anconas and Campbells are calmer than pure Campbells but more nervous and skittish than pure Anconas, with a degree of nervousness reflecting the proportion of the two breeds. I think Campbells are better off in mixed Campbell-Ancona flocks, but Anconas are better off in pure Ancona flocks.

Heavy breeds need a restricted. feed regime to be kept productive. So combining heavy breeds with extreme-egg or dual-purpose types won't work if you use a free-choice feeding pattern. I had read this, but I had to confirm it for myself the hard way. When I kept Saxonies along with Anconas, Campbells, and Harlequins on a free-choice feed regime, the Saxonies got fat and quit laying by the end of their first season. Everyone else stayed nice and slender and laid well for years. Golden Cascades also got fat and quit laying when fed free-choice. All of the dual-purpose breeds except for Anconas may need a restricted feeding regime. (I haven't kept the other dual-purpose breeds and don't know.)

9-14. Raising and Feeding Ducklings Ducklings need much more niacin than chicks. I feed my ducklings the same unmedicated chicken starter chow or broiler chow I use for the adults. Then I add niacin to the drinking water for the first two weeks. I just get a bottle of 100 mg tabs of people-vitamin niacin from a pharmacy, then toss it into a cup of water to dissolve. (It takes a while. Get ordinary tabs, not time-release pills, which don't dissolve in water at all.) Then I add it to the duckling drinking water in the proportion of about 100 mg/gallon.

For ducklings, I use just the high-protein chow the first week. I wet the chow into a mud. Ducklings can't eat dry chow very well until they are several weeks old. I also give ducklings scrambled duck eggs, which they love. The second week, I add a container of cracked corn so the babies can start learning to mix and match. I crack the corn myself. Commercial cracked corn is often moldy and often is too coarse for ducklings. By the third week, the babies are mixing and matching chow and grain properly, and will eat greater proportions of corn as they get older. If ducklings are kept on just high-protein chow, they tend to develop leg and wing problems. They need to grow at a moderate rate, not as fast as possible. These days I raise my ducklings mostly on 'Sweet Meat' squash and potatoes as the high-carb food, as described in the text. Given good forage, I suspect I could raise ducklings completely on forage, duck eggs, squash, and potatoes. However, I haven't tried it.

See Holderread for information about brooding and housing ducklings.

For grit, I give ducklings coarse sand for their first week, and a choice of sand and #1 granite grit from about week two on. I introduce a flock of youngsters to the main flock at about five weeks of age, the determining factor being when the babies are big enough to eat and drink from the 2-gallon buckets I use with the adult flock. Young ducklings need to be kept separate from adults, even if they are being raised with a mother, as little ducklings are likely to get accidentally tromped by adults.

An advantage of using a starter or broiler chow as the commercial chow for the adults instead of laying chow is that I can feed babies as well as the adults with the same chow. (The calcium levels in laying chow will cripple chicks or ducklings.) Having two different kinds of grit helps when I merge a new teenage duckling flock with the main flock. The babies taste the oyster shell but then eschew it and stick with the granite grit, as they should.

I allow even five-day-old ducklings out to forage in a side yard adjacent to the duckling pen, but only with my supervision (unless they have a mother). Ducklings that age can walk right through most fencing. The biggest problem, though, is that jays and crows take an intense interest in the babies. They must be actively guarded every minute until about two or three weeks old.

Young ducklings are carnivores. They eat pretty much just critters. Good forage for babies means an area with lots of spiders, sow bugs, worms, and slugs. Duckling beaks aren't strong enough to pull off bits of vegetation until they are about two weeks old. So it is useless giving them greenery before then unless it is cut into very tiny bits. When they are two weeks old, ducklings relish greens such as kale. They can eat it best if it is left in whole big leaves, as a big leaf has enough weight to provide resistance when the ducklings tear off bits. I always sow white clover in the duckling yard. They like white clover. By the time the ducklings are three weeks old, they can be given free access to their forage area and allowed to come and go as they please (assuming you have allowed them to waterproof themselves, as I described).

Ducklings will turn into much friendlier ducks if you let them run out of food (briefly) and call them when you bring their food to them rather than rigging the amounts so they never run out. I call them using "Here ducks" every time I bring food. Don't quack at ducklings. That means "Danger! Predator!" You can say "wuk wuk," as a mother duck does when all is well. (She will also quack if somebody strays dangerously. That means "Attention! Danger! Come to me!") Best yet, peep. Play leader-duckling sister rather than mother. When I pen the ducklings, I make gentle scooping (herding) motions with my hands and say "Pen up ducks. Pen up. Pen up. Pen your fat feathered selves, please." It's useful to be able to call your ducks into the pen when it is pen-closing time. My ducks often come home in the evening but hang around the entrance of the pen until I call them.

Ducklings are afraid of anyone looming over or reaching down at them. Sit down at their level. To touch them, touch their chests and undersides, not their backs. I sit with the ducklings regularly and touch them all (from underneath) by running my hands through the entire baby flock (palms up). If you tap a halfway sleepy duckling on its breast and underneath, it will settle down on your hand almost in a trance. It appears to be a built-in response. I've seen mother ducks nudging babies like that in the nest.

Adult ducks don't like to be loomed over either. And don't stare at them if you are close to them. That's what predators do. If ducks need to pass you at close quarters, to get out of the pen, for example, the more cynical among them would prefer you to turn your back and fold your arms. Even the more trusting among the flock will become very suspicious and wary if you appear carrying any tool or weapon. Ducks don't get upset by your changing clothes or hats, however, as my geese used to.

Ducklings are flock animals. Never separate a duckling from the flock. If you want to pick one up, pick up at least two. If you pick up just one, it will give loud distress peeps, even with the flock just a foot away. Ducklings don't move around regularly as a flock the first few days. But they are learning. By about five days, they are a flock. It actually takes that long when they have a mother, too. And ducklings are more oriented toward their cohort flock than to their mother. Sometimes she has to come to them instead of the other way around. You can't herd ducklings initially, even with a staff. They don't move away from you or it. You can start herding ducklings when they are about a week old. I start herding them back to the pen after each supervised forage session saying, "Pen up ducks. Let's go. Let's go."

I waterproof my ducklings by giving them some warm bathing water within the first three days. I rig a piece of pond liner with boards on three sides and a shallow mound of sand underneath on one side so the babies can walk in and out. Then I fill the bath with hose water topped off with a kettle of hot water to create a warm bath. I watch the ducklings and drain the water after that first bath, as the ducklings float low and are waterlogged when they get out, and need to go under their brooder lamp immediately. They need supervision to avoid drowning or over-chilling. By two days later, their wax glands swell obviously, and the babies start waxing themselves furiously. After that, I put the pond back with ordinary hose water and leave it in the pen. (There is a brooder lamp and dry straw in a secluded corner they can get to at all times.) If a duckling doesn't have a chance to bathe in its first few days, the wax gland becomes dormant and doesn't activate until the bird is about eight weeks old. That is nearly full size (though not full weight). So in order to have ducklings that can grow up on forage, and forage in wet grass or cold rain, I let them waterproof themselves properly. The first two weeks, when they get supervised foraging only, I choose days or times with better weather. And I bring the ducklings back to their pen (with the brooder lamp in the corner) after each foraging session that first couple of weeks. At three weeks I just leave the pen open during the day and let the ducklings take responsibility for going off foraging and coming back when they need to.

(Chicks aren't waterproof and shouldn't be allowed out in cold, wet grass, and they are not nearly as hardy as ducklings. Most books on duck raising do not take full advantage of the natural extra hardiness of ducklings. They mostly just give slight adaptations of information appropriate for chicks. Hence this elaboration.)

Chapter 10. Squash and Pumpkins

10-1. References relevant to this chapter:

Ashworth, Suzanne. *Seed to Seed: Seed Saving and Growing Techniques for Vegetable Gardeners.* 2nd ed. Decorah, IA: Seed Savers Exchange, 2002. Every gardener and prospective seed saver should own a copy of this book.

Damerow, Gail. *The Perfect Pumpkin.* Pownal, VT: Storey Publishing, 1997. Especially useful with respect to pumpkin diseases and pests.

Deppe, Carol. *Breed Your Own Vegetable Varieties: The Gardener's and Farmer's Guide to Plant Breeding and Seed Saving.* White River Junction, VT: Chelsea Green Publishing, 2000.

Excalibur/KBI, Inc. *Preserve It Naturally II: The Complete Guide To Food Dehydration.* Sacramento, CA: Excalibur/KBI, Inc., 1999. www.excaliburdehydrator.com. Available only from the company.

Goldman, Amy. *The Compleat Squash: A Passionate Grower's Guide to Pumpkins, Squashes, and Gourds.* New York: Artisan (Workman), 2004. Glorious full-color pictures of hundreds of squash and pumpkin varieties with excellent and *reliable* information on culinary quality for every variety. The book to start with for the squash and pumpkin explorer and a must-have for any cucurbit enthusiast.

Wilson, Gilbert L. *Buffalo Bird Woman's Garden: The Agriculture of the Hidatsa Indians.* St. Paul, MN: Minnesota Historical Society Press, 1987.

10-2. (Seven Superb . . .) 'Sweet Meat–Oregon Homestead' was introduced to the seed trade by Nichols Garden Nursery and by Adaptive Seeds in 2008. Nate and I will be selling it through Fertile Valley Seeds starting in fall 2011.

10-3. (Fall Squash . . .) 'Sugar Loaf' and 'Honeyboat' were originally bred by Jim Baggett, vegetable breeder at Oregon State University. In the years after 'Sugar Loaf' was introduced, however, the commercial material deteriorated. The seed cavities became bigger and the flesh thinner and more irregular. The plants lost vigor. Sometimes they produced no good fruits for the year. The variety could no longer be direct-seeded; it was too wimpy. Meanwhile, my friend Mike Hessel had been keeping his own lines of 'Sugar Loaf'. Mike had been a graduate student working with Jim Baggett during the breeding of 'Sugar Loaf'. In subsequent years, while the commercial lines deteriorated, Mike was growing 'Sugar Loaf', eating 'Sugar Loaf', and keeping seed out of the best, most productive plants that gave fruits with the thickest flesh—that is, both preserving and continuing to improve the variety. The Hessel line of 'Sugar Loaf' was introduced by Nichols Garden Nursery in 2008 and is the line I recommend.

10-4. (A Modern Squash-Drying Rack) We measured the width and height of the stream of air that comes off one of my big, heavy-duty fans at about a 4-foot distance and based the dimensions of the rack partly upon that. Our rack is 6 feet tall because that is the tallest we can get through a door if we need to move the rack between outdoors and indoors while it is loaded with drying squash.

The two vertical sides are 6 feet tall. The two horizontal pieces of the frame are 40 inches long. This gives a frame that is just the right width for holding the 48-inch squash sticks and allowing just enough to project beyond the frame on each side for easy handling. The top 40-inch piece of wood is placed at the very top so that it can serve as a support for a cover if the rack needs to be covered. We put the cross pieces between the uprights. The uprights and the top piece are drilled for a heavy screw that bolts the uprights and top horizontal together. The lower horizontal is placed in a position that makes it easy for me to move the rack by grabbing the top horizontal with one hand and the bottom horizontal with the other. For my size and armspan, positioning the bottom horizontal about 16 inches from the bottom of the frame is about right. (I'm 5'9" tall.) We positioned the braces above the bottom horizontal instead of below it to better support the weight of a fully loaded frame when it is lifted using the bottom horizontal.

Finally, we ran a series of nails spaced at 2-inch intervals down each of the two vertical sides, starting 6 inches from the top and ending 22 inches from the bottom. Spacing the nails this way gives us a lot of versatility. When squash sticks are loaded with fat squash that make big rounds, we need more space between sticks than when they are loaded with thinner squash that give smaller rounds. Also, less space is needed between sticks as the squash dry. Our squash rack is used slightly slanted, supported either by being leaned against something or by a forked stick braced against the top horizontal.

10-5. "Isolation distance" refers to how far apart we need to separate two different varieties of the same species in order to ensure that they won't cross. For squash species, which are pollinated by bees of various kinds, the distance is usually given as a half mile. Bees get around. That is, if we wanted to grow a single pepo variety without having to hand-pollinate, we would need to be half a mile away from neighbors growing any different pepo varieties. And likewise for the other squash species. (And for everything else that's bee-pollinated.) However, there are lots of tricks we can use that can let us get away with lots less distance, and various methods for cheating. In addition, it also depends upon our situation and purposes. If we are selling seed, we need to be more stringent than if we are just saving seed for ourselves and have some good seed tucked away in the freezer anyway if we gamble

and lose one year. In my book on plant breeding and seed saving, I have a table that gives basic breeding characteristics, including isolation distances, for eight-hundred plants, as well as an entire chapter on isolation distances that's full of tricks and methods for evaluating or cheating at isolation distances in different kinds of situations.

10-6. If you are seed-saving culinary pepos, I advise not planting pepo-species gourds, even if hand-pollinating, just to be on the safe side. Crosses with gourds have ruined many a line of pepos, introducing firey chemicals that burn the mouth or throat or that cause medically serious allergic reactions.

10-7. When hand-pollinating a variety that is relatively uniform, I usually use pollen from a plant different from that of the female flower so as to increase the total number of parent plants represented in the next generation. However, if the variety is variable, I often self-pollinate; that is, use pollen from the same parent as the female flower. With lots of variability, it can get improbable to have both the male and female parents turn out to be superior. Often just finding superior individuals is as good as we can do. When I have self-pollinations I consider each fruit a separate line, then cross the lines in subsequent years.

10-8. The standard seed-saving rule of thumb is to save seeds from 20 plants if the species is an inbreeder, and from 100 or more if it is an outbreeder. Having separate male and female flowers is an outbreeding tactic plants use to encourage fertilization from other plants rather than self-fertilization. So squash have the anatomy of outbreeders. However, squash do not have other genetic characteristics of outbreeders, such as an incompatibility system or inbreeding depression. Just the size of the plants and the fact that they have multiple vines and no incompatibility system means that quite a lot of selfing (self-fertilization) happens naturally. I think that while squash have a basic outbreeding anatomy, they have been secondarily selected to be quite competent at reproducing by inbreeding. Hence I take twenty plants as the base number.

10-9. Inbreeding Depression, Genetic Bottlenecking We are usually told to save seed from twenty or more plants to prevent inbreeding depression or genetic bottlenecking. However, squash and pumpkins are not very subject to inbreeding depression. It is possible for highly inbred varieties to be quite vigorous. And generally, most varieties have been thoroughly bottlenecked by several generations of inbreeding as part of the breeding process involved in getting high-quality fruits, which depends upon combinations of many genes that are mostly recessives. Generally, any variety of squash or pumpkin that is vigorous and productive has actually been selected in part for the ability to be vigorous and productive in a pretty inbred condition.

Chapter 11. Beans

11-1. References relevant to this chapter:

Ashworth, Suzanne. *Seed to Seed: Seed Saving and Growing Techniques for Vegetable Gardeners*, 2nd ed. Decorah, IA: Seed Savers Exchange, 2002.

Deppe, Carol. *Breed Your Own Vegetable Varieties: The Gardener's and Farmer's Guide to Plant Breeding and Seed Saving.* White River Junction, VT: Chelsea Green Publishing, 2000.

11-2. Peace Seeds offers 'Withner White Cornfield Bean'. Nate and I plan to offer 'Withner White' through Fertile Valley Seeds. Southern Exposure Seed Exchange and Baker Creek seed lists include many heirloom pole and cornfield beans (but not 'Withner').

11-3. 'Black Jet' is sold by Johnny's Selected Seeds. It's earlier than most soybeans and makes a delicious dry bean. Peace Seeds offers many soybean varieties.

11-4. Peace Seeds and Seeds of Change sell 'Iant's Yellow' fava bean.

11-5. Nate and I are expecting to introduce 'Hannan Popbean' and 'Fast Lady Northern Southern Pea' in fall 2010 through Fertile Valley Seeds.

11-6. Native Seeds/SEARCH offers many varieties of teparies, but not 'Black Mitla'. Peace Seeds, Seeds of Change, and Fedco all offer 'Black Mitla' tepary.

Chapter 12. Corn

12-1. Dent Corn Sources Sand Hill has a nice selection of traditional Corn Belt dents and other corns. Southern Exposure has a good selection of traditional southeastern dents and other corns. Seeds of Change and Redwood City Seeds have many corns, including a number of traditional open-pollinated dents.

12-2. Members of the Seed Savers Exchange maintain hundreds of corn varieties that are not available commercially.

12-3. Sources of Cornmeal to Eat These mills sell by mail-order and sell cornmeal of named traditional varieties:

Paul's Grains. ('Reid's Yellow Dent') 2475-B 340th St., Laurel, IA 50141. 641-476-3373. www.paulsgrains.com

Morgan's Mills. ('Rhode Island Whitecap') 168 Payson Rd., Union, ME 04862. 800-373-2756.

Anson Mills. (southern dent cornmeal and grits) www.ansonmills.com

12-4. Flint Corns, Sources of Seeds 'Longfellow' is available from Baker Creek. 'Abenaki' (a.k.a. 'Roy's Calais', a.k.a. 'Abenaki Calais') is available from High Mowing Seeds and from Fedco. I hope to introduce one or two of the Cascade series in December of 2010 and the other(s) in the year or two thereafter through my fledgling seed company, Fertile Valley Seeds. 'Narragansett' and 'Rhode Island Whitecap' aren't readily available at the moment. I hope to reintroduce them soon. One can get whole seed of 'Rhode Island Whitecap' from Morgan's Mill by calling and making arrangements. However, the last time I did that, in

2003, the seed was not nearly as pure in flint type as it had been. Fortunately, I have lots of seed sequestered from years earlier.

12-5. Johnnycakes. Johnnycakes start off as a mush boiled a mere few seconds by dropping flint cornmeal into boiling water. The mush is then fried. Here's how I make mine: First, I mill the corn. White flint is my favorite for johnnycakes because it is the thick crust that is special, and the thick crust made by white flints is especially delicious. So I use 'Rhode Island Whitecap', 'Cascade Creamcap', or the cream ears from 'Narragansett'.

Johnnycake meal should have some texture. The Whispermill grinds too fine. So I use my Corona mill. I run the grain through three times total, first making polenta meal in two passes as described in the polenta section. Then I make a third pass grinding the grain as fine as I can with a Corona mill. The meal ends up with bits up to about 1 mm long, no more.

I use 1 cup of meal, 1½ cups water, 2 Tbs. butter (or other oil or fat), and ⅛ tsp. salt. I start heating the skillet or griddle to medium-high, or 400°F, before making the mush so it will be ready as soon as the mush is ready. I put the water, butter, and salt in a pot and bring it to a boil. Then I add and whisk in the meal. I put the pot back on the burner briefly (a few seconds). It spurts and threatens to lob thick wads of mush at me. Before it actually does so, I remove the pot from the heat and give the contents a last whisk. The mush should be thick enough to pour out into ½-inch-thick patties. I grease the pan or griddle with butter just before adding the mush. Then I pour the mush out onto the pan or griddle into patties about 3 inches across.

Next comes patience. It takes about 8 to 10 minutes on the first side to develop a solid thick brown crust. I then turn the cakes and flatten them down further so that the wet mush in the middle runs out around the edges. (I lift each cake with a spatula, rebutter the spot under it with a chunk of butter on a fork, then turn the cake.) Then I cook until the second side is thoroughly brown. One wants to end up with two thick brown crusts with just a little cooked mush in between. I eat johnnycakes with butter and maple syrup.

12-6. Additional Real Corn (and Other Gluten-Free) Recipes Check www.caroldeppe.com.

12-7. Buckwheat Skillet Bread Use Carol's Universal Skillet Bread recipe, but use only ¼ of the total flour in the pre-batter step, and increase the water to 4½ cups. The batter stays batterlike just long enough to mix the dry ingredients and wet ingredients, then becomes a lump of dough. Scrape the dough into the hot skillet and proceed as for corn skillet bread. This bread, though made from pure buckwheat flour, is surprisingly mild in flavor and is quite delicious.

For **Teff Skillet Bread**. Use ¼ of the flour in the pre-batter, and use 4 cups of water.

12-8. Flour Corns, Sources of Seeds 'Parching Magenta' and 'Parching Red Supai' are offered by Seeds of Change. 'Parching Lavender Mandan' (a.k.a. 'Mandan Clay Red') and 'Tuscarora' are offered by Seed Dreams. 'Hopi Chinmark', 'Hopi Pink', and many other southwestern flour and other corns are offered by Native Seeds/SEARCH. 'Aztec Red' and many other corns are offered by Redwood City Seeds. Sand Hill has a huge selection of traditional flint, flour, and dent corns. I plan to introduce 'Magic Manna' through Fertile Valley Seeds in December 2010 or in 2011.

12-9. (Growing . . .) Lehman's Non-electric Catalog. 877-438-5346. www.Lehmans.com. One Lehman Circle, P.O. Box 270, Kidron, OH 44636.

Seed Companies and Sources

Here is a list of the seed companies mentioned in this book along with a few others. This list is limited largely to those with major collections of potatoes or open-pollinated corn, beans, or squash, or those that are based in the Northwest. Many small innovative or regional seed companies are one- or two-person operations that are more public services than profit-making centers. Many are Web site only or mail-order only and have no ability to deal with phone calls. Where no phone is listed, this usually means that there is no one around to answer phones and they aren't set up for ordering via phone. Where I have referred to a particular person in this book and that person is associated with a seed company, I list the person's name in parentheses after the seed-company name.

Adaptive Seeds—The Seeds of the Seed Ambassadors Project. www.adaptiveseeds.com. Seed Ambassadors Project, 25079 Brush Creek Road, Sweet Home OR 97386.

Baker Creek Heirloom Seeds. www.rareseeds .com. 417-924-8917. 2278 Baker Creek Road, Mansfield, MO 65704.

Bountiful Gardens. www.bountifulgardens.org. 707-459-6410. 18001 Shafer Ranch Road, Willits, CA 95490.

Burpee. www.burpee.com. 800-333-5808. 300 Park Avenue, Warminster, PA 18974.

Deppe, Carol. www.caroldeppe.com. Information about my further activities, research, and projects in various fields (plant breeding, resilience gardening, gluten-free cooking and recipes, free-range laying ducks, Taoist philosophy).

541-745-7002. (To talk about plant breeding or resilience gardening or ducks. I'm most likely to be available by phone, 2 p.m.–5 p.m. Pacific.) 7263 NW Valley View Drive, Corvallis, OR 97330. For seed orders see Fertile Valley Seeds.

Fedco Seeds. www.fedcoseeds.com. 207-873-7333. P.O. Box 520, Waterville, ME 04903.

Fertile Valley Seeds (Carol Deppe and Nate France). www.fertilevalleyseeds.com. 7263 NW Valley View Drive, Corvallis, OR 97330. Web site only.

High Mowing Organic Seeds (Tom Stearns). www.highmowingseeds.com. 802-472-6174. 76 Quarry Road, Wolcott, VT 05680.

Holderread Waterfowl Hatchery and Preservation Center (Dave and Millie Holderread). www.holderreadfarm.com. 541-929-5338. P.O. Box 492, Corvallis, OR 97339.

Johnny's Selected Seeds (Rob Johnston). www .johnnyseeds.com. 877-564-6697. 955 Benton Avenue, Winslow, ME 04901.

Native Seeds/SEARCH. www.nativeseeds.org. 520-622-5561. 3061 N. Campbell Avenue, Tucson, AZ 85719.

Nichols Garden Nursery (Rose Marie Nichols McGee and Keane McGee). www.nichols gardennursery.com. 800-422-3985. 1190 Old Salem Road Northeast, Albany, OR 97321-4580.

Peace Seedlings (Dylana Kapuler and Mario DiBenedetto). www.peaceseedlings.cn. 2385 SE Thompson Street, Corvallis, OR 97333.

Peace Seeds (Alan Kapuler). www.peaceseeds .com. 2385 SE Thompson Street, Corvallis, OR 97333. Web site only. (See also Peace Seedlings, the next generation.)

Peaceful Valley Farm Supply, Inc. www.grow organic.com. 888-784-1722. P.O. Box 2209, Grass Valley, CA 95945.

Pinetree Garden Seeds. www.superseeds.com. 207-926-3400. P.O. Box 300, New Gloucester, ME 04260.

Potato Garden (Milk Ranch Specialty Potatoes; bought Ronniger's). www.potatogarden.com 800-314-1955. 12101 2135 Road, Austin, CO 81410.

Redwood City Seed Company (Craig Dremann). www.ecoseeds.com. 650-325-7333. P.O. Box 361, Redwood City, CA 94064.

Renee's Garden Seeds. www.reneesgarden.com. 888-880-7228. 6060A Graham Hill Road, Felton, CA 95018. Online catalog only.

Salt Spring Seeds. www.saltspringseeds.com. Box 444, Ganges P.O., Salt Spring Island, BC, V8K 2W1, Canada.

Sand Hill Preservation Center—Heirloom Seeds & Poultry. www.sandhillpreservation.com. 563-246-2299. 1878 230th Street, Calamus, IA 52729.

Seed Ambassadors Project. www.seedambassadors .org. The Seed Ambassadors Project, 25079 Brush Creek Road, Sweet Home OR 97386.

Seed Dreams (Tessa Gowan and Shane Murphy). gowantoseed@yahoo.com. 360-385-4308. P.O. Box 106, Port Townsend, WA 98368.

Seed Savers Exchange. www.seedsavers.org. 563-382-5990. 3094 North Winn Road, Decorah, IA 52101.

Seeds of Change. www.seedsofchange.com. 888-762-7333. P.O. Box 15700, Santa Fe, NM 87592.

Southern Exposure Seed Exchange. www.south ernexposure.com. 540-894-9480. P.O. Box 460, Mineral, VA 23117.

Synergy Seeds. www.synergyseeds.com. 530-469- 3319. P.O. Box 415, Willow Creek, CA 95573.

Territorial Seed Company. www.territorialseed .com. 541-942-9547. P.O. Box 158, Cottage Grove, OR 97424-0061.

Victory Seed Company. www.victoryseeds.com. 503-829-3126. P.O. Box 192, Molalla, OR 97038.

Wagner, Tom. 8407 18th Avenue West, 7-203, Everett, WA 98204.

West Coast Seeds. www.westcoastseeds.com. 888-804-8820. 3925 64th Street, RR#1, Delta, British Columbia, Canada V4K 3N2.

Wild Garden Seeds (Frank Morton). www.wild gardenseed.com. 541-929-4068. P.O. Box 1509, Philomath, OR 97370.

Wood Prairie Farm (certified potato seed). www .woodprairie.com. 800-829-9765. 49 Kinney Road, Bridgewater, ME 04735.

Index

Note: *ci* page references can be found in the Color Insert

ABOUT THE AUTHOR

Keane McGee / Nichols Garden Nursery

Oregon plant breeder Carol Deppe specializes in developing public-domain crops for organic growing conditions, sustainable agriculture, and human survival. She is author of *Breed Your Own Vegetable Varieties: The Gardener's and Farmer's Guide to Plant Breeding and Seed Saving* (Chelsea Green, 2000) and *Tao Te Ching: A Window to the Tao through the Words of Lao Tzu*. Deppe, who has been experimenting with crops and gardening in Corvallis, Oregon since 1979, has a BS in zoology from the University of Florida and a PhD in biology from Harvard University. Please visit Carol's Web site at www.caroldeppe.com.